Content and Justification

Content and Justification

Philosophical Papers

PAUL A. BOGHOSSIAN

CLARENDON PRESS · OXFORD

OXFORD

UNIVERSITY PRESS

Great Clarendon Street, Oxford OX2 6DP

Oxford University Press is a department of the University of Oxford.
It furthers the University's objective of excellence in research, scholarship,
and education by publishing worldwide in

Oxford New York

Auckland Cape Town Dar es Salaam Hong Kong Karachi
Kuala Lumpur Madrid Melbourne Mexico City Nairobi
New Delhi Shanghai Taipei Toronto

With offices in

Argentina Austria Brazil Chile Czech Republic France Greece
Guatemala Hungary Italy Japan Poland Portugal Singapore
South Korea Switzerland Thailand Turkey Ukraine Vietnam

Oxford is a registered trade mark of Oxford University Press
in the UK and in certain other countries

Published in the United States
by Oxford University Press Inc., New York

British Library Cataloguing in Publication Data

Data available

Library of Congress Cataloging in Publication Data

Data available

Typeset by Laserwords Private Limited, Chennai, India
Printed in Great Britain
on acid-free paper by
CPI Antony Rowe, Chippenham, Wiltshire

ISBN 978–0–19–929210–3 (Hbk)
ISBN 978–0–19–929216–5 (Pbk)

10 9 8 7 6 5 4 3 2 1

For Tamsin

Contents

Preface   ix
Acknowledgements   xi

Introduction   1

PART I. THE NATURE OF CONTENT

1. The Rule-Following Considerations   9
2. The Status of Content   51
3. Naturalizing Content   71
4. Is Meaning Normative?   95
5. Epistemic Rules   109
   Suggestions for Further Reading   135

PART II. CONTENT AND SELF-KNOWLEDGE

6. Content and Self-Knowledge   139
7. The Transparency of Mental Content   159
8. What the Externalist Can Know A Priori   177
   Suggestions for Further Reading   189

PART III. CONTENT AND THE A PRIORI

9. Analyticity Reconsidered   195
10. Epistemic Analyticity: A Defense   225
11. How are Objective Epistemic Reasons Possible?   235
12. Blind Reasoning   267
    Suggestions for Further Reading   289

PART IV. COLOR: CONCEPTS AND PROPERTIES

13. Colour as a Secondary Quality (with J. David Velleman)   293
14. Physicalist Theories of Color (with J. David Velleman)   315
    Suggestions for Further Reading   345

Bibliography   347
Index   355

Preface

Over the past twenty years or so, my research interests have focused mainly on a cluster of inter-related questions concerning the notion of mental content. (1) What is mental content and can it be understood in wholly naturalistic terms? (2) How, if at all, can we know the contents of our thoughts, especially if those contents are individuated externalistically? (3) What, if anything, can we know on the basis of our knowledge of content alone?

This volume collects together some of the principal papers I have written on these questions. Among the central claims that are argued for are the following. (A) That we cannot make sense of irrealist conceptions of mental content. (B) That mental content cannot be understood in wholly naturalistic terms. (C) That there really is a problem accounting for our privileged knowledge of our own mental contents, especially if those contents are individuated externalistically. (D) That our only hope for explaining the possibility of a priori justified beliefs is through deployment of the notion of a proposition that is justifiably accepted just by virtue of being understood; but that this style of explanation need have nothing to do with the notion, discredited by Quine, of a factually vacuous proposition.

Along the way, a number of other topics are treated: the normativity of content; the intelligibility of eliminativism about the mental; belief and meaning holism; Kripke's puzzle about belief; relativism and objectivity.

In addition to the papers on these foundational topics about content and its relation to the a priori, I have also included a pair of essays that I co-authored with David Velleman on the nature of color properties and color concepts. These papers are less unrelated to the others than may appear at first: in their own way, they also illustrate the connections between content and the a priori. They do this not by showing how content might explain our knowledge of the a priori, of course, but rather by showing how what we know a priori about something (in this case, the colors) can constrain acceptable accounts of the relevant (color) concepts and properties.

I have resisted making substantive changes to the papers. Published papers have a life of their own and it would be confusing to republish them with significant alterations. I have allowed myself to make some small stylistic changes here and there; I cleaned up the garbled use of quotation marks and corner quotes in one paper ("The Rule-Following Considerations") and I deleted several pages from another ("Epistemic Analyticity") because they overlapped too much in content with "Blind Reasoning." I have also added some footnotes that refer the reader to other papers in the volume in which a particular point under discussion is treated in greater detail. In addition, I have included at the end of each of the sections a list of the critical discussions of the papers in that section that I am aware of. In the introduction to the volume, I have tried to indicate where a later paper reflects a change of mind on a particularly central point.

Over the years I have benefited from the wisdom and advice of a large number of philosophers, all of whom, I hope, are acknowledged in connection with the individual papers printed below. Special mention should be made of three teachers at Princeton who were particularly influential on my philosophical development. Richard Rorty awoke me from my dogmatic realist slumber and showed me how difficult it was to explain how objective truth and justification were possible. Saul Kripke inspired in many ways, in part by the intensity of his philosophical engagement and in part by the brilliance of his insights into the topics that interested me. Paul Benacerraf supervised, with his usual wisdom and clarity, my dissertation on meaning and rule following, out of which grew most of the papers of Part I.

Over the course of writing these papers, I was fortunate to have been associated with three superb philosophy departments—those at Princeton, Michigan and NYU. Each of them, in its own way, provided an invigorating intellectual context in which to pursue these studies and I am grateful to all three places for that stimulation and support.

Finally, I want to express my thanks to Peter Momtchiloff for suggesting this volume and shepherding it through, and to Shamik Dasgupta for his efficient, gracious and insightful help in preparing it.

Acknowledgements

Chapter 1—The Rule-Following Considerations—first appeared in *Mind* 1989, volume 98, pp. 507–49.

Chapter 2—The Status of Content—first appeared in *The Philosophical Review* 1990, volume 99, pp. 157–84.

Chapter 3—Naturalizing Content—first appeared in *Meaning in Mind: Essays on the Work of Jerry Fodor*, edited by Barry Loewer, 1991, pp. 65–86. Oxford: Basil Blackwell.

Chapter 4—Is Meaning Normative?—first appeared in *Philosophy–Science–Scientific Philosophy: Fifth International Congress of the Society for Analytical Philosophy*, edited by C. Nimtz and A. Beckermann, 2005, pp. 205–18.

Chapter 5—Epistemic Rules—is forthcoming in *Journal of Philosophy*, 2008.

Chapter 6—Content and Self-Knowledge—first appeared in *Philosophical Topics* 1989, volume 17, pp. 5–26.

Chapter 7—The Transparency of Mental Content—first appeared in *Philosophical Perspectives* 1994, volume 8, pp. 33–50.

Chapter 8—What the Externalist Can Know A Priori—first appeared in *Proceedings of the Aristotelian Society* 1997, volume 97, pp. 161–75. Reprinted by courtesy of the Editor of the Aristotelian Society: ©1997.

Chapter 9—Analyticity Reconsidered—first appeared in *Noûs* 1996, volume 30, pp. 360–91.

Chapter 10—Epistemic Analyticity: A Defense—first appeared in *Grazer Philosophische Studien* 2003, volume 66, pp. 15–35.

Chapter 11—How are Objective Epistemic Reasons Possible?—first appeared in *Philosophical Studies* 2001, volume 106, pp. 1–40.

Chapter 12—Blind Reasoning—first appeared in *Proceedings of the Aristotelian Society, Suppl. Vol.*, 2003, volume 77, pp. 225–48.

Chapter 13—Colour as a Secondary Quality—first appeared in *Mind* 1989, volume 98, pp. 81–103.

Chapter 14—Physicalist Theories of Color—first appeared in *Philosophical Review* 1991, volume 100, pp. 67–106.

Introduction

PART I: THE NATURE OF CONTENT

It is appropriate that Part I should open with "The Rule-Following Considerations" since that essay contains, in condensed form, a statement of most of the central claims that are expanded upon by the other papers in that section.

RFC was the result of an invitation by the journal *Mind* to write a "State of the Art" article on the flood of literature that was being produced in the 1980s in response to Saul Kripke's brilliant *Wittgenstein on Rules and Private Language*. It contains almost no Wittgenstein exegesis but a great deal on the relevance of Kripke's arguments to a raft of foundational issues in the philosophies of mind and language. Ironically, it also contains almost nothing about *rule following per se*. The reasons why are hinted at in RFC but emerge most clearly in the essay that closes Part I ("Epistemic Rules"), an essay that was written shortly before the present volume went to press.

Kripke writes as though his primary topic is rule following, but with special attention being paid to that all-important *sub-species* of rule following, meaning. A skeptical paradox about rule following is then to be used to justify a paradox about meaning, the resolution of which is a startling and dubious non-factualism about meaning.

But, as I explain more fully in the later essay, Kripke is operating with a personal-level notion of rule following, according to which when a person S follows a rule R, S's acceptance of R both explains and rationalizes S's behavior. In that sense of rule following, however, it cannot be true that all meaning is the result of rule following—in particular, it cannot be true that mental meaning is. Any paradox about meaning, however, can succeed only if it threatens both linguistic and mental meaning simultaneously. Hence, either Kripke's argument doesn't work or there is an alternative way of developing the paradox, one that doesn't rely on the claim that all meaning is engendered by rule following.

My tack in RFC was the latter—to sideline the topic of rules and to concentrate on meaning directly, most especially on mental content. Viewed in that light, Kripke's discussion provided a springboard for two important claims. First, that, *pace* Kripke's Wittgenstein, no irrealist view of meaning facts can be coherently sustained. Second, that meaning facts cannot be reduced to purely naturalistic facts. The first claim is presented in a highly compressed form in RFC but significantly expanded upon in Chapter 2, "The Status of Content." The second is extensively discussed in RFC and extended to informational theories of content facts in Chapter 3, "Naturalizing Content," with special reference to Jerry Fodor's stimulating experiments with that style of naturalistic theory.

I wrote "Epistemic Rules" when it finally occurred to me what Wittgenstein's discussion would look like if one took seriously the claim that it was about *rules* rather than about meaning or content. If the arguments of ER are correct, then there is indeed a paradox about rule following. Unlike Kripke's paradox, however, it cannot be resolved by helping ourselves to even the most generous form of anti-reductionism about meaning possible. The argument for this is developed in ER.

One of Kripke's most striking claims was that meaning facts could not be naturalized because meaning is a *normative* notion. Kripke didn't make it very clear what he meant by that. In RFC, I interpreted the claim in a bland way to mean that any meaningful expression has *conditions of correct use* — for example, that any predicate has satisfaction conditions. That much is uncontroversial and was all that was needed for the anti-reductionist argument I was pursuing in that paper. However, I went along with Kripke's rhetoric in calling this 'normativity about meaning.' In Chapter 4, "Is Meaning Normative?" I discuss the matter much more explicitly and show that there is no directly interesting sense in which meaning is a normative notion, though there may be an indirect sense in which it is, through its role in elucidating the normative notion of belief. The issue of normativity is also revisited in ER, where I argue that, while meaning may not be normative, there is an attenuated sense in which a personal-level notion of rule following is: when a person follows rule R, his acceptance of R *rationalizes* his behavior.

For all the attention they have received, in my view both Wittgenstein's discussion and Kripke's exposition of it remain underappreciated, to the detriment of current work in the philosophy of mind. That is not to say, by any means, that a proper engagement with those arguments would result in a moral that is recognizably "Wittgensteinian." On the contrary, on my view what emerges from such an engagement is a conception of meaning that is anything but: realist, anti-reductionist and in no obvious way hostile to the idea of a private language. Nevertheless, it seems to me that both Kripke's and Wittgenstein's texts contain considerable insights and it is a pity that they have come to be relatively neglected.

PART II: CONTENT AND SELF-KNOWLEDGE

All three of the essays in Part II are primarily concerned with the difficulty of explaining how we are able to have the sort of privileged knowledge of the contents of our own mental states that we credit ourselves with—especially if those contents are individuated externalistically, as much contemporary thinking would have it.

The first paper, "Content and Self-Knowledge," does more than develop an argument for incompatibilism between privileged self-knowledge and externalism. In its first section, it outlines a general framework for talking about knowledge of our own contents and shows why, given relatively weak internalist assumptions about justification, knowledge of our own contents could not be *inferential*. That implies that our knowledge must either be based on introspection or based on nothing.

In its remaining two sections, the paper explores difficulties with each of those models. Those difficulties are exposed by the consideration of "slow-switching" scenarios, first introduced by Tyler Burge in defense of a compatibilist view. In such scenarios, a subject is unwittingly switched between two externally distinct environments, each time staying long enough to acquire the concepts that, according to externalism, are characteristic of the environmentg in question. The discussion of slow-switching has given rise to a large literature, much of which is cited in the section on "Further Readings."

"What the Externalist Can Know A Priori" pursues a different strategy for arguing against compatibilism, a strategy that is related to but distinct from the one described by Michael McKinsey in his much discussed 1991 (I was not aware of McKinsey's effort when I first began to develop my own).[1] It argues that, if compatibilism were true, we would be able to know certain propositions a priori that we could only know a posteriori.

Finally, "The Transparency of Mental Content," looks not at privileged knowledge of the contents of individual thoughts but at our ability to know facts about the sameness and difference of the contents of distinct thought tokens. Beginning with Frege, the assumption that the contents of our thoughts are transparent to us in this sense has played a fundamental role in our thinking about content and in its relation to the notion of rationality.[2] I argue for two claims. First, that transparency is irredeemably compromised by externalist views of content; and, second, that we have been offered no satisfactory view of what the notion of content would look like—or what it would be good for—if we abandoned transparency.

Although I have often wanted to return to the topic of self-knowledge, I have not done so since writing these papers over ten years ago. I remain convinced, however, that we are very far from understanding this issue and that much important work remains to be done.

PART III: CONTENT AND THE A PRIORI

In Part III, I turn from knowledge *of* content to knowledge *on the basis of* content.

---

[1] See McKinsey 1991.
[2] See Frege 1966.

Quine taught many philosophers to be suspicious of the idea of a priori justification—justification for believing something that is independent of empirical
evidence. For my part, though, I have never seen how to do without this idea.
Furthermore, it has always seemed to me that if there is to be a non-mystifying
explanation of a priori justification, it has to be based on the idea that a thinker's
understanding of a sentence or a proposition can be sufficient, all by itself, for
his being justified in accepting that sentence or proposition. The papers in Part III
begin the elaborate program of developing such a meaning-based account of a
priori justification.

Of course, the idea is hardly a new one. Previous incarnations of it, though,
suffered, in my view, from two major deficiencies. First, it was thought that
if the mere understanding of a sentence S was to be sufficient for a thinker's
being justified in accepting S, S had to be "factually vacuous": its truth had
to be dependant on its meaning alone and not in any way on the facts. And
the trouble was that Quine seemed right to claim that there could be no such
thing as a factually vacuous sentence; at a minimum, he seemed right to claim
that the classic examples of analytic sentences—e.g., claims such as "Bachelors
are unmarried men," and "Squares have four equal sides"—were not "factually
vacuous."

Second, no one had bothered to explain how a thinker's mere understanding
of a sentence *could* suffice for his being justified in accepting it. What, exactly,
were the principles that connected a descriptive fact about meaning with a normative fact about justification? It is the burden of the papers in this section to
begin the complicated task of making good on those deficiencies.

The first and most important task was to detach the idea of *epistemic analyticity*—*justification* on the basis of meaning alone—from the idea of *metaphysical analyticity*—*truth* on the basis of meaning alone—and to show that
the former idea could survive without any help from the latter.

But how could the mere understanding of a sentence's meaning ever suffice
for a thinker's being justified in believing it to be true, especially if the sentence
is not taken to be factually vacuous? "Analyticity Reconsidered" begins by
rescuing two semantical notions from Quine's attacks, notions that are crucial
to meaning-based explanations of the a priori. The first is the idea of a sentence
that is transformable into a logical truth by the substitution of synonyms for
synonyms—what I dubbed "Frege-analyticity." And the second is the idea of a
sentence that serves as an implicit definer for one of its ingredient terms—what
I called the notion of "Carnap-analyticity." As against Quine, I argued that,
given some fairly austere assumptions, both notions must be in good standing.

What I wasn't so clear about, when I wrote "Analyticity Reconsidered," is
how to use these semantical notions to provide a satisfactory explanation of
the a priori. In particular, I didn't appreciate a distinction between two sorts of
case. First, one in which a thinker's *knowledge* of the relevant semantical facts
provides the basis for his knowledge of a given sentence's truth, by way of an
inference from the former to the latter. Second, one in which the explanation

could not proceed in that way, but in which it would have to be the semantical facts *themselves*, as opposed to a thinker's knowledge of them, that provide the requisite justification. We may call the former model *inferential* and the latter *constitutive*. The distinction between these models is discussed in Chapter 10, "Epistemic Analyticity".

In papers subsequent to "Analyticity Reconsidered," I try to be much more careful about this distinction. In "How are Objective Epistemic Reasons Possible?" I distinguish sharply between justifying our *belief* that a given deductive rule of inference (for example, Modus Ponens) is valid, versus our priori justification for *inferring* according to that rule. I argue that if there is to be any justification for the former, it would have to be inferential in nature. And I try to explain why, even if that inference turned out to be rule-circular, employing the very rule that it was attempting to justify, it could still constitute a genuine justification.

By contrast, our justification for *inferring* according to Modus Ponens cannot consist in any sort of inference; rather, the fact that that rule is constitutive of our possession of *if* must somehow, by itself, provide our justification for inferring according to that rule. The question is how it could do that.

In "Objective Reasons," I followed Christopher Peacocke in assuming that meaning-constituting rules would have to be truth-preserving; and I used that claim to explain how a meaning-constituting rule could provide a priori justification for inferences. However, that explanation later came to me to seem unsatisfactory, for two reasons. First, it seemed to presuppose a reliabilist view of justification, a view I reject. Second, and more importantly, it seemed to me to me to assume an overly stringent conception of concepts. Concepts seem relatively easy to come by; in particular, there seem to be possible concepts—such as Dummett's pejorative concept *boche*—whose meaning-constituting rules would not be truth-preserving.

In "Blind Reasoning," I offer an alternative picture of the relation between meaning and justification, in terms of the distinction between defective and non-defective concepts. I consider this neo-rationalist program to be in its very earliest stages. We are very far from knowing whether there are any satisfactory meaning-based explanations of the a priori and, if there are, exactly how they are to be formulated and how far they can be made to extend.

PART IV: COLOR: CONCEPTS AND PROPERTIES

The final two papers in this collection concern the nature of color properties. According to the main realist accounts of the colors, colors are either dispositions on the parts of objects to affect us in certain ways or physical properties of a certain sort to be uncovered by color science. David Velleman (with whom I had the pleasure to co-author these papers) and I argue against both of these realist accounts. The dispositional suggestion is discussed at length in the earlier paper, "Colour as a Secondary Quality," and the physicalist suggestion, while mentioned briefly in the first, is given a proper treatment in the second, "Physicalist Theories of Color."

In contrast to these accounts, we urge, but do not fully defend, that the colors are monadic, non-dispositional, non-relational, essentially qualitative properties. Since we think that it follows from this characterization that no external object is actually colored, we also defend the viability of an error theory of color discourse in the earlier paper. And in the course of defending that error theory, we incautiously give the impression that, while the colors may not be instantiated by external objects, they *are* instantiated by our mental states and "projected" onto external objects.

Both of these further claims are optional from the standpoint of the main aims of the papers. It may be that, even if an error theory is correct, the colors are not instantiated by anything, let alone by mental states.[3] And it may be that, even if the colors are what we say they are, an error theory is not correct, that external objects are able to instantiate the colors as we characterize them. Our claims about the nature of color properties are arrived at on the basis of a consideration of the nature of color concepts. What we know about the colors a priori and what we know about the nature of color experience is used to constrain the correct account of the content of color concepts. And that account in turn is used to constrain the correct account of the nature of color properties. The arguments as a whole illustrate the complex interplay that there is between meaning, reference and a priori knowledge.

---

[3] See Pautz, forthcoming, for such a theory.

PART I
The Nature of Content

1 *The Rule-Following Considerations*[1]

INTRODUCTION

1. Recent years have witnessed a great resurgence of interest in the writings of the later Wittgenstein, especially with those passages—roughly, *Philosophical Investigations* ##138–242 and *Remarks on the Foundations of Mathematics*, section VI—that are concerned with the topic of rules. Much of the credit for all this excitement, unparalleled since the heyday of Wittgenstein scholarship in the early 1960s, must go to Saul Kripke's *Wittgenstein on Rules and Private Language*.[2] It is easy to explain why.

To begin with, the dialectic Kripke uncovered from Wittgenstein's discussion is enormously exciting on its own terms. On Kripke's reading, the passages on rule-following are concerned with some of the weightiest questions in the theory of meaning, questions—involving the reality, reducibility, and privacy of meaning—that occupy centre-stage in contemporary philosophy. Furthermore, Kripke represented Wittgenstein as defending a set of unified and extremely provocative claims concerning these questions. And, finally, he argued for these claims with power and clarity. The ensuing flood of articles and books on the subject of rule-following was both predictable and warranted.

The present paper is the result of an invitation to survey this literature. It could have been about exegetical matters, on what the recent discussions have had to teach us about the historical Wittgenstein's philosophical views. In the event, however, it is almost entirely concerned with a retrospective assessment of the *philosophical* contributions. Limitations of space dictated that a choice be made; and the philosophical assessment seemed the more fruitful thing to do.[3] Despite a lot of discussion, there is room for an improved understanding of the precise nature of Kripke's arguments, of their ultimate cogency, and of their relation to the wider discussion of meaning in contemporary philosophy of mind and language. Pulling on the thread that is Kripke's argument leads

---

[1] This paper appeared in *Mind* 1989 as the fifth of their commissioned State of the Art Series.
[2] Kripke 1982.
[3] The main reason is that I have actually come to despair of a satisfactory interpretation of Wittgenstein's views. I try to say why in my 1988.

quite naturally to a discussion of many of the most significant issues occupying philosophers today; in that lies the main impetus behind the present essay.

I proceed as follows. In Parts I and II, I lay out the essentials of Kripke's argument. In subsequent parts, I offer an extended critique of the dialectic it presents, considered on its own terms and independently of exegetical concerns. A discussion of the critical literature will be woven in as appropriate. The moral will not be recognizably Wittgensteinian: I shall argue that, *pace* Kripke's intent, the conception of meaning that emerges is a realist, non-reductionist, and judgement-independent conception, one which, moreover, sustains no obvious animus against private language.

I. KRIPKE ON MEANING AND THE SCEPTICAL PROBLEM

The Sceptical Problem

2. As Kripke sees it, the burden of the rule-following considerations is that it cannot literally be true of any symbol that it expresses some particular concept or meaning. This is the now-famous 'sceptical conclusion' he attributes to Wittgenstein:

[T]here is no fact about me that distinguishes between my meaning a definite function by '+' ... and my meaning nothing at all.[4]

How is such a radical thesis to be supported? Kripke argues, in effect, by elimination: all the available facts potentially relevant to fixing the meaning of a symbol in a given speaker's repertoire—facts about how the speaker has actually used the expression, facts about how he is disposed to use it, and facts about his qualitative mental history—are canvassed, and found wanting. Adequate reflection on what it is for an expression to possess a meaning would betray, so Kripke invites us to believe, that that fact could not be constituted by any of *those*.

The claim is, of course, indisputable in connection with facts about actual use and qualitative phenomena; it is a familiar and well-assimilated lesson of, precisely, Wittgenstein's *Investigations*, that neither of those species of fact could, either in isolation or in combination, capture what it is for a symbol to possess a meaning. Much more important and controversial, however, is Kripke's rejection of a *dispositional* account of meaning facts. Why are facts about how a speaker is disposed to use an expression held to be insufficient to determine its meaning?

Kripke develops two sorts of consideration. First, the idea of meaning something by a word is an idea with an infinitary character—if I mean *plus* by '+', then there are literally no end of truths about how I ought to apply the term,

---

[4] Kripke 1982, p. 21.

namely to just the members of this set of triples and not to others, if I am to use it in accord with its meaning. This is not merely an artefact of the arithmetical example; it holds for any concept. If I mean *horse* by 'horse', then there are literally no end of truths about how it would be correct for me to apply the term—to horses on Alpha Centauri, to horses in Imperial Armenia, and so on, but not to cows or cats wherever they may be—if I am to use it in accord with its meaning. But, Kripke argues, the totality of my dispositions is finite, being the dispositions of a finite being that exists for a finite time. And so, facts about dispositions cannot capture what it is for me to mean addition by '+'.

The second objection to a dispositional theory stems from the so-called 'normativity' of meaning. This objection is somewhat harder to state, but a rough formulation will do for now. The point is that, if I mean something by an expression, then the potential infinity of truths that are generated as a result are *normative* truths: they are truths about how I *ought* to apply the expression, if I am to apply it in accord with its meaning, not truths about how I *will* apply it. My meaning something by an expression, it appears, does not guarantee that I *will apply* it correctly; it guarantees only that there will be a fact of the matter about whether my use of it is correct. Now, this observation may be converted into a condition of adequacy on theories of meaning: any proposed candidate for being the property in virtue of which an expression has meaning must be such as to ground the normativity of meaning—it ought to be possible to read off from any alleged meaning-constituting property of a word, what is the correct use of that word. And this is a requirement, Kripke maintains, that a dispositional theory cannot pass: one cannot read off a speaker's disposition to use an expression in a certain way what is the *correct* use of that expression, for to be disposed to use an expression in a certain way implies at most that one will, not that one should.

The Contents of Thought

3. But what about thoughts, intentions, and other content-bearing mental states? How do they figure in the sceptical argument? More specifically: is the sceptical thesis directed against them as well, or is it confined solely to *linguistic* representation?

It is hard to see how a convincing meaning scepticism could be confined purely to the linguistic domain, given the intimate relation between thought and language. Philosophers divide, of course, on the precise nature of this relation and, in particular, on the question of priority: Do the semantic properties of language derive from the representational properties of thought, or is it the other way round? Whatever the correct answer, however, there would appear to be no plausible way to promote a *language-specific* meaning scepticism. On the former (Gricean) picture, one cannot threaten linguistic meaning without threatening thought content, since it is from thought that linguistic meaning is held to derive; and on the latter (Sellarsian) picture, one cannot threaten linguistic meaning without *thereby* threatening thought content, since it is from linguistic meaning that thought content is held to derive. Either way, content and meaning must stand or fall together.[5]

If a sceptical thesis about linguistic meaning is to have any prospect of succeeding, then, it must also threaten the possibility of mental meaning (or content). Of course, on a Sellarsian view, that result is automatic, given a demonstration that nothing *non-mental* fixes linguistic meaning. But on a Gricean view matters are not so simple. Since the Gricean holds that linguistic items acquire their meaning from the *antecedently* fixed content of mental states, an argument to the effect that nothing non-mental fixes linguistic meaning would leave the Gricean unmoved; he needs to be given a *separate* argument against the possibility of mental content. Does Kripke see this need and does he show how it is to be met?

Colin McGinn has argued that the answer to both questions is 'no':

My third point ... points up a real lacuna in Kripke's presentation of his paradox. The point is that it is necessary for Kripke to apply his paradox at the level of *concepts*; that is, he has to argue that the notion of possessing a determinate concept is likewise devoid of factual foundation. ... It cannot be said, however, that Kripke explains how this need is to be met, how this extension of the paradox to the level of concepts is to be carried out; and brief reflection shows that the exercise is by no means trivial.[6]

I think McGinn is wrong on both counts; it will be worthwhile to see why.

In fact, the suggestion that some appropriately general thought or intention constitutes the sought after meaning-determining fact comes up early in Kripke's presentation, *before* the dispositional account of meaning is considered and found wanting:

This set of directions, I may suppose, I explicitly gave myself at some earlier time. It is engraved on my mind as on a slate. It is incompatible with the hypothesis that I meant quus. It is this set of directions, not the finite list of particular additions that I performed in the past, that justifies and determines my present response.[7]

And his response to it seems clear (p. 16 ff). The idea is that thoughts that someone may have had concerning how he is prepared to use a certain expression will help determine a meaning for that expression only if their correct interpretation is presupposed. But this is equivalent to assuming, Kripke suggests, that the sceptical challenge has been met with respect to the *expressions*

---

[5] In the United States, it is the Gricean view, that linguistic expressions acquire their semantic properties by virtue of being used with certain intentions, beliefs, and desires, that is most influential; whereas in Britain it appears to be the Sellarsian (Wittgensteinian?) view that thinking is a form of internalized speaking—speech *in foro interno*, as Sellars likes to put it—that tends to predominate.

For the Gricean view see Grice 1957 and related papers. See also Schiffer 1972. For the Sellarsian view see his 1963. For a debate on the priority question see Chisholm and Sellars 1972.

[6] McGinn 1984, pp. 144–6.

[7] Kripke 1982, pp. 15–16.

that figure in those thoughts. But how was *their* meaning fixed? Not by facts about their actual or counterfactual history of use, (if the argument against a dispositional account of meaning is to be believed); and not by facts concerning associated experiential episodes. Hence—on the assumption that no other sort of fact is relevant to the fixation of meaning—by nothing.

The strategy seems clear; but is it not problematic? The trouble is that it seems to depend on the assumption that thought contents are the properties of syntactically identifiable bearers—properties, that is, of expressions belonging to a 'language of thought'. And although there may be much to recommend this view, still, does Kripke really wish to rest the sceptical conclusion on so contestable a premisses?

Fortunately for the sceptical strategy, we will see below that, although a contestable premiss about thought is involved, it is nothing so rich as a language of thought hypothesis. But we will be in a position to appreciate this properly only after we have examined McGinn's claim that, even granted a linguistic model of thinking, it is still impossible to run a Kripke-style sceptical argument against thought.

The Normativity of Meaning

4. McGinn writes:

The issue of normativeness, the crucial issue for Kripke, has no clear content in application to the language of thought: what does it mean to ask whether my current employment of a word in my language of thought (i.e. the exercise of a particular concept) is *correct* in the light of my earlier employment of that word? What kind of linguistic mistake is envisaged here? ... There is just no analogue here for the idea of linguistic incorrectness (as opposed to the *falsity* of a thought): linguistic incorrectness (of the kind we are concerned with) is using the same word with a different meaning from that originally intended (and doing so in ignorance of the change), but we cannot in this way make sense of employing a concept with a different content from that originally intended—it would just be a *different concept*.[8]

The idea of mental content cannot be threatened by Kripke, McGinn argues, because the principal requirement by which putative reconstructions of that notion are to be dispatched—the normativity requirement—has no cogent application to the language of thought. The claim calls for a somewhat more searching articulation of the normativity thesis than we have attempted so far. In what does the normativity of meaning consist?

McGinn offers the following characterization:

The notion of normativeness Kripke wants captured is a transtemporal notion. ... We have an account of this normativeness when we have two things: (a) an account of

---

[8] McGinn 1984, p. 147.

what it is to mean something at a given time and (b) an account of what it is to mean the *same* thing at different times—since (Kripkean) normativeness is a matter of meaning now what one meant earlier.[9]

So, the later use of the expression is 'correct', according to McGinn, if it then expresses the same meaning as it did earlier; 'incorrect' if, without intending to introduce a change of meaning by explicit stipulation, it expresses a different meaning. It is in such facts as this that the normativity of meaning is said to consist.

Supposing this were the right understanding of normativity, how would it affect mental content scepticism? McGinn says that the problem is that we cannot make sense of employing a concept with a different content from that originally intended—it would just be a different concept. But although that is certainly true, it is also irrelevant: what we need to make sense of is not employing a *concept* with a different content from that originally intended, but employing an *expression in the language of thought* with a different content from that originally intended, which is a rather different matter.

As it happens, however, it is an idea that is equally problematic. The difficulty is that we do not have the sort of access to the expressions of our language of thought that an attribution to us of semantic intentions in respect of them would appear to presuppose. You cannot intend that some expression have a certain meaning unless you are able to refer to that expression independently of its semantic properties. But we have no such independent access to the expressions of our language of thought; we do not, for instance, know what they look like. So we cannot have semantic intentions in respect of them and, hence, cannot make sense of using them correctly or incorrectly in the sense defined by McGinn.

If McGinn's understanding of normativity were the correct one, then, it would indeed be difficult to see how it could operate at the level of thought (though not quite for the reasons he gives). It ought to be clear, however, that the 'normativity' requirement defined by McGinn has nothing much to do with the concept of meaning *per se* and is not the requirement that Kripke is operating with.

We may appreciate this point by observing that the requirement defined by McGinn could hardly act as a substantive constraint on theories of meaning, even where these are theories solely of *linguistic* meaning. *Any* theory of meaning that provided an account of what speakers mean by their expressions at arbitrary times—however crazy that theory may otherwise be—would satisfy McGinn's constraint. In particular, the main theory alleged by Kripke to founder on the normativity requirement, would easily pass it on McGinn's reading: since there are perfectly determinate facts about what dispositions are associated with a given expression at a given time—or, rather, since it is no part of Kripke's intent to deny that there are—it is always possible to ask whether an expression

---

[9] McGinn 1984, p. 174.

has the same or a different meaning on a dispositional theory, thus satisfying McGinn's requirement. How to explain, then, Kripke's claim that a dispositional theory founders precisely on the normativity requirement?

5. The answer is that the normativity requirement is not the thesis McGinn outlines. What is it then?

Suppose the expression 'green' means *green*. It follows immediately that the expression 'green' applies *correctly* only to *these* things (the green ones) and not to *those* (the non-greens). The fact that the expression means something implies, that is, a whole set of *normative* truths about my behaviour with that expression: namely, that my use of it is correct in application to certain objects and not in application to others. This is not, as McGinn would have it, a relation between meaning something by an expression at one time and meaning something by it at some later time; it is rather, a relation between meaning something by it at some time and its *use at that time*.

The normativity of meaning turns out to be, in other words, simply a new name for the familiar fact that, regardless of whether one thinks of meaning in truth-theoretic or assertion-theoretic terms, meaningful expressions possess conditions of *correct use*. (On the one construal, correctness consists in *true* use, on the other, in *warranted* use.) Kripke's insight was to realize that this observation may be converted into a condition of adequacy on theories of the determination of meaning: any proposed candidate for the property in virtue of which an expression has meaning, must be such as to ground the 'normativity' of meaning—it ought to be possible to read off from any alleged meaning con-stituting property of a word, what is the correct use of that word. It is easy to see how, on this understanding of the requirement in question, a dispositional theory might appear to fail it: for, it would seem, one cannot read off a dispos-ition to use a word in a certain way what is the correct use of that word, for to be disposed to use a word in a certain way implies at most that one *will*, not that one *should* (one can have dispositions to use words *incorrectly*).[10, 11]

6. With this clarification of the normativity thesis in place we are finally in a position to settle the question: can Kripke develop the same sort of meaning-sceptical argument against a language of thought as he develops against public language? And the answer is: clearly, yes. For: what fixes the meaning of expres-sions in the language of thought? Not other thoughts, on pain of vicious regress. Not facts about the actual tokening of such expressions or facts about associated qualitative episodes, for familiar reasons. And not dispositional facts about the tokening of such expressions, for, since meaningful expressions of mentalese

---

[10] As we shall see below, however, the question whether dispositional accounts of meaning really do succumb to the normativity objection is much more complicated than this. I am not here trying to assess the objection, but merely to state it.

[11] A more detailed discussion of the sense in which meaning might be said to be normative can be found in my 2005a (this volume, Chapter 4).

possess conditions of correct use in precisely the same sense as public language expressions do, because correctness cannot be reconstructed dispositionally. So, nothing fixes their meaning.

Indeed, we are also now in a position to see, as promised, that nothing so rich as a language of thought hypothesis is strictly needed. A language of thought model is composed out of two theses: (*a*) that thinking the thought that *p* involves tokening an item—a representation—that means that *p*; and (*b*) that the representation whose tokening is so involved possesses a combinatorial syntactic and semantic structure. In other words, according to a language of thought hypothesis, thought contents are the semantic properties of syntactically and semantically *structured bearers*. But it should be quite clear that nothing in the sceptical argument depends on the assumption of *structure*: even if the representation were to possess no internal syntax, we could still ask, in proper Kripkean fashion, what its correctness conditions are and in virtue of what they are determined.

It would appear, however, that the sceptical argument's strategy does presuppose that content properties have *some* sort of bearer (even if not necessarily a structured one). For, otherwise, there will be no natural way to formulate a dispositional theory of thought content, and no natural way to bring the normativity requirement to bear against it. There has to be *something*—a state, event, or particular, it need not matter which—whose disposition to get tokened under certain circumstances constitutes, on a dispositional theory, its possession of a certain content. And although this commitment is, I suppose, strictly speaking contestable, it is also very natural and plausible. After all, contents do not figure in a mental life except as subtended by a particular *mode*—belief, desire, judgement, wish—and, hence, are naturally understood as the properties of the states or events that instantiate those modes.

And so we see that the sceptical argument must, can, and does (in intent, anyway) include mental content within the scope of the scepticism it aims to promote.[12]

The Constitutive Nature of the Sceptical Problem

7. Having a meaning is essentially a matter of possessing a correctness condition. And the sceptical challenge is to explain how anything could possess *that*.

Notice, by the way, that I have stated the sceptical problem about meaning without once mentioning Kripke's notorious sceptic. That character, as everyone knows, proceeds by inviting his interlocutor to defend a claim about what he previously meant by the expression '+'. The interlocutor innocently assumes himself to have meant addition; but the sceptic challenges him to prove that the

---

[12] Since nothing will hang on it, and since it will ease exposition, I shall henceforth write as if a language of thought hypothesis were true.

concept in question was not in fact *quaddition*, where quaddition is just like addition, except for a singularity at a point not previously encountered in the interlocutor's arithmetical practice.

It may seem, then, that the sceptical problem I have described could not be Kripke's. For Kripke's problem appears to be essentially *epistemological* in character—it concerns a speaker's ability to defend a particular meaning ascription; whereas the problem I have outlined is *constitutive*, not epistemological—its topic is the *possibility* of meaning, not our knowledge of it.

In fact, however, the two problems are the same; Kripke merely chooses to present the constitutive problem in an epistemological guise. Epistemological scepticism about a given class of judgements is the view that our actual cognitive capacities are incapable of delivering justified opinions concerning judgements in that class. Kripke's sceptic is not after a thesis of that sort. This is evident from the fact that his interlocutor, in being challenged to justify his claim that he meant addition by '+', is permitted *complete and omniscient* access to all the facts about his previous behavioural, mental, and physical history; he is not restricted to the sort of knowledge that an ordinary creature, equipped with ordinary cognitive powers, would be expected to possess.[13] Kripke's sceptical scenario is, thus, completely unsuited to promoting an epistemological scepticism. What it *is* suited for is the promotion of a constitutive scepticism. For if his sceptic is able to show that, even with the benefit of access to all the relevant facts, his interlocutor is still unable to justify any particular claim about what he meant, that would leave us no choice but to conclude that there are no facts about meaning.[14]

Pace many of Kripke's readers, then, the problem is not—not even in part—epistemological scepticism about meaning.[15] But, of course, one may agree that the problem is constitutive in character, and yet believe it to have an epistemological dimension. According to Crispin Wright, for example, Kripke is not interested in the mere possibility of correctness conditions; he is interested in the possibility of correctness conditions that may be, at least in one's own case, *known non-inferentially*.[16] The problem is essentially constitutive in character; but acceptable answers to it are to be subject to an epistemic constraint.

---

[13] McGinn's failure to note this leads him to wonder how the constitutive and epistemological aspects of Kripke's discussion are related, 'for the epistemological claim is clearly distinct from the metaphysical claim' (McGinn 1984, p. 149).

[14] This point is made very nicely by Crispin Wright in his 1984b, pp. 761–2. Wright, however, discerns another sort of epistemological dimension to the sceptical problem. I will discuss that below.

[15] For example, McGinn 1984, pp. 140–50; Baker and Hacker 1984, pp. 409–10. Neil Tennant has complained that Kripke's sceptic does not ultimately supply a convincing bent-rule reinterpretation of his interlocutor's words. See his 1989. Tennant may well be right about this. But here again, I think, the perception that this affects the force of the sceptical problem about meaning is a result of taking the dialogic setting too seriously. The constitutive problem about meaning—how could there so much as be a correctness condition—can be stated quite forcefully without the actual provision of a convincing global reinterpretation of a person's words.

[16] See Wright 1984b, pp. 772–5.

I do not wish to argue about this at length. It does seem to me that, once we have corrected for the distortions induced by the dialogic setting, there ought not to be any residual temptation to think that epistemological considerations are playing a critical role in Kripke's argument. In any case, whatever intention Kripke may have had, the considerations he adduces on behalf of the sceptical conclusion appear to owe nothing to epistemological constraints and can be stated without their help.[17] That, anyway, is how I shall present them.

The 'Rule-Following' Considerations?

8. It would not be inappropriate to wonder at this point what all this has to do with the topic of *rule-following*? Where, precisely, is the connection between the concepts of meaning and content, on the one hand, and the concept of following a rule, on the other, forged? I shall argue that, in an important sense, the answer is 'nowhere', and hence that 'the rule-following considerations' is, strictly speaking, a misnomer for the discussion on offer.[18]

Many writers seem to assume that the connection is straightforward; they may be represented as reasoning as follows. Expressions come to have correctness conditions as a result of people following rules in respect of them; hence, exploring the possibility of correctness is tantamount to exploring the possibility of rule-following.

But, at least on the ordinary understanding of the concept of following a rule, it cannot be true of *all* expressions—in particular, it cannot be true of *mental* expressions—that they come to have correctness conditions as a result of people following rules in respect of them. The point is that the ordinary concept of following a rule—as opposed to that of merely conforming to one—is the concept of an *intentional* act: it involves the intentional attempt to bring one's behaviour in line with the dictates of some grasped rule. Crispin Wright has decribed this intuitive conception very clearly:

Correctly applying a rule to a new case will, it is natural to think, typically involve a double success: it is necessary both to apprehend relevant features of the presented situation and to know what, in the light of those apprehended features, will fit or fail to fit the rule. Correctly castling in the course of a game of chess, for instance, will depend both on apprehension of the configuration of chessmen at the time of the move, and on a knowledge of whether that configuration (and the previous course of the game) permits castling at that point.[19]

As such, however, the ordinary concept of following a rule is the concept of an act among whose causal antecedents lie contentful mental states; consequently, it is a concept that *presupposes* the idea of a correctness condition, not one that

---

[17] With one relatively minor exception to be noted below.
[18] For a more detailed discussion, see my 2005a (this volume, Chapter 4).
[19] Wright 1989, p. 255.

can, in full generality, help explain it. Since it makes essential play with the idea of a propositional attitude, which in turn makes essential play with the idea of content, rule-following in this sense presupposes that *mental expressions* have conditions of correct application. On pain of regress, then, it cannot be true that mental expressions themselves acquire meaning as a result of anyone following rules in respect of them.

What Kripke's discussion is concerned with is the possibility of correctness; so long as we keep that clearly in mind, talk of 'rule-following' is harmless. Simon Blackburn has captured this perspective very well:

> I intend no particular theoretical implications by talking of rules here. The topic is that there is such a thing as the correct and incorrect application of a term, and to say that there is such a thing is no more than to say that there is truth and falsity. I shall talk indifferently of there being correctness and incorrectness, of words being rule-governed, and of their obeying principles of application. Whatever this is, it is the fact that distinguishes the production of a term from mere noise, and turns utterance into assertion—into the making of judgment.[20]

II. THE SCEPTICAL SOLUTION

A Non-Factualist Conception of Meaning

9. Having established to his satisfaction that no word could have the property of expressing a certain meaning, Kripke turns to asking how this conclusion is to be accommodated. The question is urgent, in his view, because the conclusion threatens to be not merely shocking but paradoxical. The trouble is that we would ordinarily take a remark to the effect that there could not be any such thing as the fact that I mean something by the '+' sign, to entail that there is nothing I could mean by the use of that sign. Applied quite generally, across all signs and all people, the claim becomes the seemingly paradoxical and self-refuting thesis that no one could mean anything by their use of linguistic expressions.

A scepticism about meaning facts would appear to be, then, prima facie anyway, an unstable position. Sustaining it requires showing that what it asserts does not ultimately lapse into a form of pragmatic incoherence. What is called for, in other words, is a rehabilitation of our ordinary practice of attributing content to our thoughts and utterances, which nevertheless conserves the sceptical thesis that there are no facts for such attributions to answer to. That is what the 'sceptical solution' is designed to do. It is alleged to have the following startling consequence: the idea of a language whose meanings are constituted solely out

---

[20] Blackburn 1984b, pp. 281–2. My only disagreement with this passage concerns its identification of correctness conditions with truth conditions. Truth conditions are simply one species of a correctness condition; proof conditions or justification conditions supply further instances.

of an individual's speaker's properties, considered 'completely in isolation from any wider community to which he may belong', is incoherent.[21]

The sceptical solution has two parts that are usefully distinguished. The first consists in the suggestion that we replace the notion of truth conditions, in our intuitive picture of sentence meaning, by that of *assertibility* conditions. The second consists in a *description* of the assertibility conditions for meaning-attributing sentences, in the course of which it is argued that it is essential to such sentences that their assertibility conditions advert to the actions or dispositions of a community.

The adjustment recommended in the first part is supposed to help because

> if we suppose that facts or truth conditions are of the essence of meaningful assertion, it will follow from the skeptical conclusion that assertions that anyone ever means anything are meaningless. On the other hand, if we apply to these assertions the tests suggested ... no such conclusion follows. All that is needed to legitimize assertions that someone means something is that there be roughly specifiable circumstances under which they are legitimately assertible, and that the game of asserting them has a role in our lives. No supposition that 'facts correspond' to those assertions is needed.[22]

The proposed account is, in effect, a *global* non-factualism: sentence significance is construed quite generally in assertion-theoretic terms and no invidious distinction is drawn between the sort of significance possessed by meaning-attributing sentences and that possessed by sentences of other types.

The Argument Against Solitary Language

10. The argument against 'solitary language' emerges, according to Kripke, from the observation that, so long as a speaker is considered in isolation we can assign no assertibility conditions to judgements to the effect that he has misapplied a symbol in his repertoire:

> [I]f we confine ourselves to looking at one person alone, this is as far as we can go. ... There are no circumstances under which we can say that, even if he inclines to say '125', he should have said '5', or *vice-versa*. ... Under what circumstances can he be wrong? No one else by looking at his mind or behavior alone can say something like, 'He is wrong if he does not accord with his own intention'; the whole point of the skeptical argument was that there are no facts about him in virtue of which he accords with his intentions or not.[23]

---

[21] Following Goldfarb 1985, we may call this the concept of a 'solitary language'. Goldfarb goes on to say that the idea of a solitary language is more general than that of a Wittgensteinian 'private language', for the latter essentially involves the idea of *necessary unintelligibility* to another. It is hard to assess this, because it is hard to know how to interpret 'necessary unintelligibility'. Surely it cannot mean: a language to whose predicates no two people *could* attach the same descriptive conditions. And it is not clear what it is to mean, if not that. For useful discussion see Wright 1986.

[22] Kripke 1982, pp. 77–8.

[23] Ibid., p. 88.

The possibility of error, however, is essential to our ordinary concept of meaning, and can only be accommodated if we widen our gaze and take into consideration the interaction between our imagined rule-follower and a linguistic community. Were we to do so, Kripke continues, we could introduce assertibility conditions for judgements about error in terms of the agreement, or lack of it, between a given speaker's propensities in the use of a term and the community's. Since, however, this would appear to be the *only* way to give substance to the correlative notions of error and correctness, no one considered wholly in isolation from other speakers could be said to mean anything. And so a solitary language is impossible.

Let us turn now to an assessment of the various central aspects of Kripke's argument.

III. ASSESSMENT OF THE ARGUMENT AGAINST SOLITARY LANGUAGE

Constitutive Accounts and Solitary Language

11. Kripke is very clear about the limited, wholly descriptive nature of the sceptical solution, at least in his 'official' explications of the view:

We have to see under what circumstances attributions of meaning are made and what role these attributions play in our lives. Following Wittgenstein's exhortation not to think but to look, we will not reason *a priori* about the role such statements *ought* to play; rather we will find out what circumstances *actually* license such assertions and what role this license *actually* plays. It is important to realize that we are *not* looking for necessary and sufficient conditions (truth conditions) for following a rule, or an analysis of what such rule-following 'consists in'. Indeed such conditions would constitute a 'straight' solution to the skeptical problem, and have been rejected.[24]

It is important to see that the counselled modesty—we will not reason a priori about the role such statements ought to play—is compulsory. The assertibility conditions may not be understood to provide the content (or truth conditions) of the meaning-attributing sentences, on pain of falling prey to the accepted sceptical considerations (That is why the solution on offer has to be *sceptical*: it has already been conceded that nothing could cogently amount to the fact that a meaning sentence reports). It would appear to follow from this, however, that the sceptical solution can do no more than record the conditions under which speakers in fact consider the attribution of a certain concept warranted and the endorsement of a particular response appropriate. The Wittgensteinian exhortation 'not to think but to look' is not merely (as it may be) good advice; the modesty it counsels is enforced by the fact that truth conditions for these sentences has been jettisoned. For how, in the absence of a conception of the truth conditions of meaning attributing sentences, could the project of providing

---

[24] Ibid., pp. 86–7.

an account of their assertion conditions aspire to anything more than descriptive adequacy? Were we equipped with an account of their truth conditions, of course, we might be able to reason a priori about what their assertion conditions *ought* to be and, hence, potentially, to revise the conditions for assertion *actually* accepted for them. But without the benefit of such an account there is no scope for a more ambitious project: a descriptively adequate account of the *actual* assertion conditions for such sentences is the most one may cogently aim for.

If this is correct, however, we ought to be puzzled about how the sceptical solution is going to deliver a conclusion against solitary language of the requisite modal force: namely, that there *could not* be such a language. For even if it were true that our *actual* assertibility conditions for meaning-attributing sentences advert to the dispositions of a community, the most that would license saying is that *our* language is not solitary. And this would be a lot less than the result we were promised: namely, that any *possible* language has to be communal.

Communal Assertibility Conditions?

12. Putting this worry to one side, let us ask whether it is in fact true that, if we accept the sceptical conclusion, we cannot introduce substantive assertibility conditions for meaning-attributions that do not advert to the dispositions of a community of speakers? It appears, on the contrary, that not only can we introduce such conditions, but have actually done so.[25] Consider the following:

(A) It is warranted to assert of Jones that he means addition by '+', provided he has responded with the *sum* in reply to most arithmetical queries posed thus far.

As a description of our practice, (A) is, of course, quite rough: room has to be made for the importance of systematic deviations, the greater importance attaching to simple cases, and many other such factors. But all these refinements may be safely ignored for the purpose of raising the following critical question: what in the sceptical conclusion rules out attributions of form (A)? It had better rule them out, of course, if the argument against solitary language is to be sustained, for (A) adverts to no one other than the individual. But as Goldfarb points out, there appears to be nothing in the sceptical conclusion that will rule it out.[26] It can hardly be objected that the interpretation of 'sum' is being presupposed in the statement of the condition, for the sceptical solution is not meant to be a *straight* solution to the problem about meaning; as Kripke himself says, in fending off a similar imagined objection to his own account of the assertibility conditions:

What Wittgenstein is doing is describing the utility in our lives of a certain practise. Necessarily he must give this description in our own language. As in the case of

---

[25] This sort of rejoinder is canvassed both in Goldfarb 1985, and in McGinn 1984.
[26] Goldfarb 1985.

any such use of our language, a participant in another form of life might apply various terms in the description (such as 'agreement') in a non-standard 'quus-like' way. ... This cannot be an objection to Wittgenstein's solution unless he is to be prohibited from any use of language at all.[27]

Nor is there any problem in the assumption that it is a genuinely factual matter what any two numbers sum to; as Kripke himself repeatedly emphasizes, the sceptical argument does not threaten the existence of *mathematical* facts. But how, then, is (A) to be ruled out, and the argument against solitary language preserved?

13. Could it perhaps be argued that (A) is permissible though *parasitic* on the communal assertibility conditions Kripke outlines? As a matter of fact, just the opposite seems true.[28]

Kripke's communitarian account of meaning-attributions runs as follows:

Smith will judge Jones to mean addition by 'plus' only if he judges that Jones's answers to particular addition problems agree with those he is inclined to give. ... If Jones consistently fails to give responses in agreement ... with Smith's, Smith will judge that he does not mean addition by 'plus'. Even if Jones did mean it in the past, the present deviation will justify Smith in judging that he has lapsed.[29]

According to this account, then, I will judge that Jones means addition by 'plus' only if Jones uses 'plus' enough times in the same way I am inclined to use it. As a rough description of our practice, and many important refinements aside, this seems acceptable enough. One of the refinements that is called for, however, exposes the fact that Kripke's communitarian conditions are parasitic on the solitary conditions, and not the other way round.

It would be absurd for me, under conditions where I had good reason to believe that I had become prone to making arithmetical mistakes—perhaps owing to intoxication or senility or whatever—to insist on agreement with me as a precondition for crediting Jones with mastery of the concept of addition. And this would appear to show that, at a minimum, Kripke's communitarian account must be modified to read:

(B) It is warranted to assert of Jones that he means addition by '+', provided he agrees with my responses to arithmetical queries, *under conditions where I have been a reliable computer of sums.*

But this modification would seem immediately to reveal that the reference to 'my own responses' is idle, and that the basic assertion condition I accept is just (A):

It is warranted to assert of Jones that he means addition by '+', provided he has responded with the *sum* in reply to most arithmetical queries posed thus far.

[27] Kripke 1982, p. 146.
[28] This is argued in McGinn 1984, pp. 185–7, from which this point is derived.
[29] Kripke 1982, p. 91.

It would appear, in other words, that the acceptability of the communitarian conditions is strongly parasitic on the acceptability of the solitary ones, and not the other way around.

In sum: both because it is difficult (impossible?) to generate constitutive results out of non-constitutive accounts, and because our actual assertibility conditions for meaning ascriptions appear not to be communitarian, I conclude that the sceptical solution does not yield a convincing argument against solitary language.

IV. IRREALIST CONCEPTIONS OF MEANING

14. The argument against solitary language was supposed to flow from the adjusted understanding of sentence significance forced by the sceptical conclusion. The sceptical conclusion has it that it cannot literally be true of any symbol that it expresses a particular meaning: there is no appropriate fact for a meaning-attributing sentence to report. The sceptical solution's recommendation is that we blunt the force of this result by refusing to think of sentence significance in terms of possession of truth conditions, or a capacity to state facts. We should think of it, rather, in terms of possession of assertibility conditions. But is this solution forced? Are there not, perhaps, other ways of accommodating the sceptical conclusion?

The solution on offer is bound to strike one as an overreaction, at least at first blush, in two possible respects. First, in that it opts for a form of *non-factualism*, as opposed to an *error* theory; and second, in that the recommended non-factualism is *global*, rather than restricted solely to the region of discourse—meaning talk—that is directly affected by the sceptical result it seeks to accommodate.

Semantically speaking, the most conservative reaction to the news that nothing has the property of being a witch is not to adopt a non-factualist conception of witch talk, it is to offer an *error* conception of such talk. An error conception of a given region of discourse conserves the region's semantical appearances—predicates are still understood to express properties, declarative sentences to possess truth conditions; the ontological discovery is taken to exhibit—merely—the *systematic* falsity of the region's (positive, atomic) sentences.[30]

Could not the moral of the sceptical argument be understood to consist in an error conception of meaning discourse? It could not, for an error conception of such discourse, in contrast with error conceptions of other regions, is of doubtful coherence. The view in question would consist in the claim that all meaning-attributions are false:

---

[30] See Mackie 1977 for such a conception of moral discourse.

(1) For any S, p: $\ulcorner$'S' means that $p\urcorner$ is false.

But the disquotational properties of the truth predicate guarantee that (1) entails

(2) For any S: S has no meaning.

(1) implies, that is, that no sentence whatever possesses a meaning. Since, however, a sentence cannot be *false* unless it is meaningful to begin with, this in turn
implies that (1) cannot be true: for what (1) says is that some sentences—namely
meaning-attributing sentences—are false.[31]

So it appears that Kripke was right to avoid an error conception of meaning
discourse. But does his *non-factualist* conception fare any better?

15. The canonical formulation of a non-factualist view—and the one that Kripke
himself favours—has it that some targeted declarative sentence is not genuinely truth-conditional. A non-factualism about meaning consists, that is, in the
view that

(3) For any S, p: $\ulcorner$'S' means that $p\urcorner$ is not truth-conditional.

As I noted above, however, the projectivism recommended by the sceptical
solution is intended to apply globally: it is not confined solely to meaning-
attributing sentences. Thus,

(4) For any S: S is not truth conditional.

Why does Kripke adopt so extreme a view? Why does he not suggest merely
that we abandon a truth-conditional model for *semantic* discourse, while preserving it, as seems natural, for at least *some* regions of the rest of language?
Kripke does not say. But it may be that he glimpsed that the global character
of the projectivism is in fact *forced* in the present case.[32] For consider a non-
factualism solely about meaning—the view that, since there is no such property
as a word's meaning something, and hence no such fact, no meaning-attributing
sentence can be truth-conditional. Since the truth condition of any sentence S
is (in part, anyway) a function of its meaning, a non-factualism about meaning will enjoin a non-factualism about truth conditions: what truth condition S
possesses could hardly be a factual matter if that in virtue of which it has a
particular truth condition is not itself a factual matter. And so we have it that
(3) entails:

(5) For all S, p: $\ulcorner$'S' has the truth condition that $p\urcorner$ is not truth-conditional.

---

[31] An error conception of meaning has been advocated by Churchland 1981. This argument is
elaborated and defended in my 1990 (this volume, Chapter 2).
[32] Somewhat different arguments are given for this both in Wright 1984b, pp. 769–70, and in
Part I of my 1986.

However, since, courtesy of the disquotational properties of the truth predicate, all instances of the form

" '*S*' has the truth-condition that *p*" is true if and only if *S* has the truth condition that *p*

are true, and since (5) has it that no instance of the form

'*S*' has the truth condition that *p*

is true, it follows that

(4) For any *S*: *S* is not truth-conditional

just as predicted.

It is, then, a fascinating consequence of a non-factualism about meaning, that it entails a *global* non-factualism; in this respect, if no other, a non-factualism about meaning distinguishes itself from a similar thesis about *any* other subject matter. Crispin Wright has suggested that it also renders it irremediably problematic:

it is doubtful that it is coherent to suppose that projectivist views could be applied quite globally. For, however exactly the distinction be drawn between fact-stating and non-fact-stating discourse, the projectivist will presumably want it to come by way of a *discovery* that certain statements fail to qualify for the former class; a statement of the conclusion of the skeptical argument, for instance, is not *itself* to be projective.[33]

It is hard not to sympathize with Wright's suggestion that there must be something unstable about a projectivist thesis that is itself within the scope of the projectivism it recommends. But it is also not entirely clear to me in what the instability consists. To be sure, a global projectivism would have to admit that it is no more than *assertible* that no sentence possesses a truth condition. But what is wrong with that? If there is an instability here, it is not a transparent one.

16. In fact, however, I do believe that a non-factualism about meaning is unstable, but not because of its global character. Rather, the reasons have to do with the clash between what you have to suppose about truth in order to frame a non-factualist thesis about anything, and what you have to suppose about truth as a result of accepting a non-factualism about meaning. I have developed the argument for this in some detail elsewhere;[34] here I have space only to sketch its outlines.

Consider a non-factualist thesis about, say, the good:

(7) All sentences of the form $\ulcorner x$ is good$\urcorner$ are not truth-conditional.

---

[33] Wright 1984b, p. 770.
[34] In my 1990 (this volume, Chapter 2).

The point that needs to be kept in focus is that the sentence of which truth conditions are being denied is a significant *declarative* sentence. For this fact immediately implies that the concept of truth in terms of which the non-factualist thesis is framed cannot be the *deflationary* concept that A. J. Ayer succinctly described as follows:

... to say that p is true is simply a way of asserting p. ... The traditional conception of truth as a 'real quality' or a 'real relation' is due, like most philosophical mistakes, to a failure to analyze sentences correctly. ... There are sentences in which the word 'truth' seems to stand for something real ... [but] our analysis has shown that the word 'truth' does not stand for anything.[35]

If the concept of truth were, as Ayer claims in this passage, merely the concept of a device for semantic ascent, and not the concept of some genuine property—some 'real relation'—that a sentence (or thought) may enjoy, then non-factualism is nowhere a coherent option. For on a deflationary understanding of truth, a sentence will be truth-conditional provided only that it is apt for semantic ascent; and it will be apt for semantic ascent provided only that it is a significant, declarative sentence. But it is constitutive of a non-factualist thesis precisely that it denies, of some targeted, significant, declarative sentence, that it is truth-conditional. It follows, therefore, that a non-factualism about any subject matter presupposes a conception of truth richer than the deflationary: it is committed to holding that the predicate 'true' stands for some sort of language-independent property, eligibility for which will not be certified purely by the fact that a sentence is declarative and significant. Otherwise, there will be no understanding its claim that a significant sentence, declarative in form, fails to possess truth conditions.

So we have it that any non-factualist thesis presupposes that truth is, as I shall henceforth put it, *robust*. But, now, notice that judgements about whether an object possesses a robust property could hardly fail to be factual. If *P* is some genuinely robust property, then it is hard to see how there could fail to be a fact of the matter about whether an object has *P*. It does not matter if *P* is subjective or otherwise dependent upon our responses. So long as it is a genuine, language-independent property, judgements about it will have to be factual, will have to be possessed of robust truth conditions. In particular, if *truth* is a robust property, then judgements about a sentence's truth value must themselves be factual. But we saw earlier—see (5) above—that a non-factualist thesis about meaning implies that judgements about a sentence's truth cannot be factual: whether a certain sentence is true cannot be a factual matter if its meaning is not. And this exposes the contradiction we have been stalking: a non-factualism about meaning implies both that truth is robust and that it is not.

[35] Ayer 1952, p. 89.

17. It is hard to do justice to the issues involved within the confines of the present essay.[36] I do hope, however, that the preceding discussion has succeeded in sowing some doubts about the cogency of irrealist conceptions of meaning—whether in the form of a non-factualism about meaning, as in the sceptical solution, or an error theory, as suggested, for instance, by Churchland.

The uncompromising strength of the claim is bound to arouse suspicion. Irrealist conceptions of other domains may not be particularly appealing or plausible, but they are not incoherent. Why should matters stand differently with meaning discourse?

The source of the asymmetry is actually not that hard to track down. It consists in the fact that error and non-factualist theories about *any* subject matter presuppose certain claims about truth and truth-conditions, that an error or non-factualist conception directed precisely at our talk of meaning itself ends up denying. Not surprisingly the ensuing result is unstable.

Thus, an error thesis about any subject matter presupposes that the target sentences are truth-conditional. But an error thesis directed precisely at our talk about meaning entails the denial of that presupposition. Thus, also, a non-factualism about any subject matter presupposes a robust conception of truth. But a non-factualism directed precisely at our talk about meaning entails the denial of that presupposition.

If these considerations are correct, then, they would show that the sceptical conclusion cannot be sustained: there appears to be no stable way of accommodating the claim that there are no truths about meaning. Something must be wrong, therefore, with the argument that appeared to lead us to it. What could it be?

V. REDUCTIVE ACCOUNTS OF MEANING

18. The sceptical argument has been faulted on a number of grounds, the most important being:

> That its arguments against dispositional accounts of meaning do not work.
> That it neglects to consider all the available naturalistic facts.
> That its conclusion depends on an unargued reductionism.

The first two objections issue from a naturalistic perspective: they claim that the sceptical argument fails to establish its thesis, even granted a restriction to *naturalistic* facts and properties. The final objection concedes the failure of naturalism, but charges that the sceptical argument is powerless against an appropriately anti-reductionist construal of meaning. In this part I shall examine the naturalistic objections, and in the next the anti-reductionist suggestion.

---

[36] Again, for a more detailed treatment see my 1990 (this volume, Chapter 2).

I should say at the outset, however, that I see no merit to objections of the second kind and will not discuss them in any detail here. All the suggestions that I have seen to the effect that Kripke ignores various viable reduction bases for meaning facts seem to me to rest on misunderstanding. Colin McGinn, for example, claims that Kripke neglects to consider the possibility that possession of a concept might consist in possession of a certain sort of capacity. Capacities, McGinn explains, are distinct from dispositions and are better suited to meet the normativity constraint.[37] This rests on the misunderstanding of normativity outlined above. Warren Goldfarb charges that Kripke neglects to consider causal/informational accounts of the determination of meaning.[38] This derives from a failure to see that, in all essential respects, a causal theory of meaning is simply one species of a dispositional theory of meaning, an account that is, of course, extensively discussed by Kripke. It is unfortunate that this connection is obscured in Kripke's discussion. Because Kripke illustrates the sceptical problem through the use of an *arithmetical* example, he tends, understandably, to focus on *conceptual role* versions of a dispositional account of meaning, rather than on causal/informational versions. This has given rise to the impression that his discussion of dispositionalism does not cover causal theories. But the impression is misleading. For the root form of a causal/informational theory may be given by the following basic formula:

O means (property) *P* by predicate *S* iff (it is a counterfactual supporting generalization that) *O* is disposed to apply *S* to *P*.

Dispositions and Meaning: Finitude

19. The single most important strand in the sceptical argument consists in the considerations against dispositional theories of meaning. It would be hard to exaggerate the importance of such theories for contemporary philosophy of mind and semantics: as I have just indicated, the most influential contemporary theories of content-determination — 'informational' theories and 'conceptual-role' theories — are both forms of a dispositional account.[39] In my discussion I shall tend to concentrate, for the sake of concreteness, on informational theories of the content of *mental* symbols; but the issues that arise are general and apply to any dispositional theory whatever.

The root form of an information-style dispositional theory is this:

My mental symbol 'horse' expresses whatever property I am disposed to apply it to.

---

[37] See McGinn 1984, pp. 168–74.

[38] See Goldfarb, 1985, n. 13.

[39] For informational theories see Dretske 1981, Stampe 1977, and Fodor 1987. For conceptual role theories see Field 1977 and Block 1986.

Kripke's first objection amounts, in effect, to suggesting that there will always be a serious *indeterminacy in what my dispositions are*, thus rendering dispositional properties an inappropriate reduction base for meaning properties. For, Kripke argues, if it is indeed the property *horse* that I am disposed to apply the term to, then I should be disposed to apply it to *all* horses, including horses so far away and so far in the past that it would be nonsense to suppose I could ever get into causal contact with them. Otherwise, what is to say that my disposition is not a disposition to apply the term to the property *nearby horse*, or some such? But no one can have a disposition to call all horses 'horse', for no one can have a disposition with respect to inaccessible objects.

The argument does not convince. Of course, the *counterfactual*

If I were now to go to Alpha Centauri, I would call the horses there 'horse',

is false. If I were now to go to Alpha Centauri, I probably would not be in any position to call anything by any name, for I would probably die before I got there. But that by itself need not pose an insuperable obstacle to ascribing the disposition to me. *All* dispositional properties are such that their exercise—the holding of the relevant counterfactual truth—is contingent on the absence of interfering conditions, or equivalently, on the presence of ideal conditions. And it certainly seems conceivable that a suitable idealization of my biological properties will render the counterfactual about my behaviour on Alpha Centauri true. Kripke considers such a response and complains:

But how can we have any confidence in this? How in the world can I tell what would happen if my brain were stuffed with extra brain matter? ... Surely such speculation should be left to science fiction writers and futurologists.[40]

If the point is supposed to be, however, that one can have no reason for accepting a generalization defined over ideal conditions unless one knows exactly which counterfactuals would be true if the ideal conditions obtained, then, as Jerry Fodor has pointed out, it seems completely unacceptable.[41] For example, no one can claim to know all of what would be true if molecules and containers actually satisfied the conditions over which the ideal gas laws are defined; but that does not prevent us from claiming to know that, if there were ideal gases, their volume would vary inversely with the pressure on them. Similarly, no one can claim to know all of what would be true if I were so modified as to survive a trip to Alpha Centauri; but that need not prevent us from claiming to know that, if I were to survive such a trip, I would call the horses there 'horse'.[42]

Still, it is one thing to dispel an objection to a thesis, it is another to prove the thesis true. And we are certainly in no position now to show that we do

---

[40] Kripke 1982, p. 27.
[41] See Fodor 1990.
[42] For a related criticism of Kripke on this score see Blackburn 1984b.

have infinitary dispositions. The trouble is that *not every* true counterfactual of the form:

If conditions were ideal, then, if *C*, *S* would do *A*

can be used to attribute to *S* the disposition to do *A* in *C*. For example, one can hardly credit a tortoise with the ability to overtake a hare, by pointing out that if conditions were ideal for the tortoise—if, for example, it were much bigger and faster—then it would overtake it. Obviously, only certain idealizations are permissible; and also obviously, we do not now know which idealizations those are. The set of permissible counterfactuals is constrained by criteria of which we currently lack a systematic account. In the absence of such an account, we cannot be completely confident that ascriptions of infinitary dispositions are acceptable, because we cannot be completely confident that the idealized counterfactuals needed to support such ascriptions are licit. But I think it is fair to say that the burden of proof here lies squarely on Kripke's shoulders: it is up to him to show that the relevant idealizations would be of the impermissible variety. And this he has not done.

Dispositions and Meaning: Normativity

20. Few aspects of Kripke's argument have been more widely misunderstood than his discussion of the 'normativity' of meaning and his associated criticism of dispositional theories. This is unsurprising given the difficulty and delicacy of the issues involved. In what sense is meaning a normative notion? Kripke writes:

Suppose I do mean addition by '+'. What is the relation of this supposition to the question how I will respond to the problem '68 + 57'? The dispositionalist gives a *descriptive* account of this relation: if '+' meant addition, then I will answer '125'. But this is not the right account of the relation, which is normative, not descriptive. The point is not that, if I meant addition by '+', I will answer '125', but that, if I intend to accord with my past meaning of '+', I should answer '125'. Computational error, finiteness of my capacity, and other disturbing factors may lead me not to be disposed to respond as I should, but if so, I have not acted in accordance with my intentions. The relation of meaning and intention to future action is *normative*, not *descriptive*.[43]

The fact that I mean something by an expression, Kripke says, implies truths about how I *ought* to use that expression, truths about how it would be *correct* for me to use it. This much, of course, is incontestable. The fact that 'horse' means *horse* implies that 'horse' is correctly applied to all and only horses: the notion of the extension of an expression just is the notion of what it is correct to apply the expression to. It is also true that to say that a given expression has

---

[43] Kripke 1982, p. 37.

a given extension is not to make any sort of *simple* descriptive remark about it. In particular, of course, it is not to say that, as a matter of fact, the expression *will* be applied only to those things which are in its extension. Kripke seems to think, however, that these observations by themselves ought to be enough to show that no dispositional theory of meaning can work. And here matters are not so straightforward.

Let us begin with the very crude dispositional theory mentioned above: 'horse' means whatever property I am disposed to apply it to. This is a hopeless theory, of course, but the reasons are instructive. There are two of them, and they are closely related. The first difficulty is that the theory is bound to get the extension of 'horse' wrong. Suppose I mean *horse* by it. Then, presumably, I have a disposition to call horses 'horse'. But it will also be true that there are certain circumstances—sufficiently dark nights—and certain cows—sufficiently horsey looking ones—such that, I am disposed, under those circumstances, to call those cows 'horse' too. Intuitively, this is a disposition to make a mistake, that is, to apply the expression to something not in its extension. But our crude dispositional theory, given that it identifies *the property I mean by an expression* with *the property I am disposed to apply the expression to*, lacks the resources by which to effect the requisite distinction between correct and incorrect dispositions. If what I mean by an expression is identified with whatever I am disposed to apply the expression to, then everything I am disposed to apply the expression to is, *ipso facto*, in the extension of that expression. But this leads to the unacceptable conclusion that 'horse' does not express the property *horse* but rather the disjunctive property *horse or cow*.

There is a related conceptual difficulty. Any theory which, like the crude dispositional theory currently under consideration, simply equates how it would be correct for me to use a certain expression with how I am disposed to use it, would have ruled out, as a matter of definition, the very possibility of error. And as Wittgenstein was fond of remarking, if the idea of correctness is to make sense at all, then it cannot be that whatever seems right to me is (by definition) right.

One would have thought these points too crucial to miss; but it is surprising how little they are appreciated. In a recent, comprehensive treatment of conceptual role theories, Ned Block has written

of a choice that must be made by [conceptual role semantics] theorists, one that has had no discussion (as far as I know): namely, should conceptual role be understood in ideal or normative terms, or should it be tied to what people actually do? ... I prefer not to comment on this matter ... because I'm not sure what to say ...[44]

This ought to seem odd. If conceptual role is supposed to determine meaning, then there can be no question, on pain of falling prey to Kripke's objection, of identifying an expression's conceptual role with a subject's actual dispositions with respect to that expression.

---

[44] Block 1986, p. 631.

21. The objections from normativity show, then, that no dispositional theory that assumes the simple form of identifying *the property I mean by 'horse'* with *the property I am disposed to call 'horse'*, can hope to succeed. But what if a dispositional theory did not assume this simple form? What if, instead of identifying what I mean by 'horse' with the *entire* range of my dispositions in respect of 'horse', it identified it only with certain select dispositions. Provided the theory specified a principle of selection that picked out only the extension-tracking dispositions; and provided also that it specified that principle in terms that did not presuppose the notion of meaning or extension, would it not then be true that the objections from normativity had been disarmed?

Let us try to put matters a little more precisely. If a dispositional theory is to have any prospect of succeeding, it must select from among the dispositions I have for 'horse', those dispositions which are *meaning-determining*. In other words, it must characterize, in non-intentional and non-semantic terms, a property M such that: possession of M is necessary and sufficient for being a disposition to apply an expression in accord with its correctness conditions.[45] Given such a property, however, could we not then safely equate meaning something by an expression with: *the set of dispositions with respect to that expression that possess M*? For, since dispositions with that property will be guaranteed to be dispositions to apply the expression correctly, both of the objections from normativity canvassed so far would appear to have been met. There will be no fear that the equation will issue in false verdicts about what the expression means. And, since it is only M-dispositions that are guaranteed to be correct, it will no longer follow that *whatever* seems right is right: those dispositions not possessing M will not be dispositions to apply the expression to what it means and will be free, therefore, to constitute dispositions to apply the expression falsely.

At this point two questions arise. First, is there really such a property M? And, second, supposing there were, is there really no more to capturing the normativity of meaning than specifying such a property?

Now, Kripke is clearly sceptical about the existence of an appropriate M-property. I will consider that question below. But more than this, Kripke seems to think that even if there were a suitably selected disposition that captured the extension of an expression accurately, that disposition could still not be identified with the fact of meaning, because it still remains true that the concept of a disposition is descriptive whereas the concept of meaning is not. In other words, according to Kripke, even if there were a dispositional predicate that logically covaried with a meaning predicate, the one fact could still not be

[45] It is occasionally suggested that it would be enough if possession of M were *sufficient* for the disposition's correctness. But that is not right. If only sufficiency were required we would not know, simply by virtue of a definition of M, the expression's meaning. For although we would know what properties were definitely part of the expression's meaning we would not know if we had them all. And so we would not have even a sufficient condition for the expression's possessing a given meaning.

identified with the other, for they are facts of distinct sorts. A number of writers have been inclined to follow him in this. Simon Blackburn, for instance, has written:

I share Kripke's view that whatever dispositions we succeed in identifying they could at most give us standards for selection of a function which we mean. They couldn't provide us with an account of what it is to be faithful to a previous rule. It is just that, unlike Kripke, I do not think dispositions are inadequate to the task of providing standards. Indeed, I think they must be.[46]

Blackburn here is explicitly envisaging the successful, substantive specification of dispositions that mirror the extensions of expressions correctly. But he cites the normative character of facts about meaning as grounds for denying a dispositional *reduction*. But what precisely has been left over, once the extensions have been specified correctly?

One might have a thought like this. A proper reduction of the meaning of an expression would not merely specify its extension correctly, it would also reveal that what it is specifying is an *extension* — namely, a *correctness* condition. And this is what a dispositional theory cannot do. There might be dispositions that logically covary with the extensions of expressions; so that one could read off the dispositions in question the expressions' correctness conditions. But the dispositional fact does not amount to the meaning fact, because it never follows from the mere attribution of any disposition, however selectively specified, that there are facts concerning *correct* use; whereas this does follow from the attribution of an extension. To be told that 'horse' means *horse* implies that a speaker ought to be motivated to apply the expression only to horses; whereas to be told, for instance, that there are certain select circumstances under which a speaker is disposed to apply the expression only to horses, seems to carry no such implication.[47]

It is not clear that this is in general true. Perhaps the *M*-dispositions are those dispositions that a person would have when his cognitive mechanisms are in a certain state; and perhaps it can be non-question-beggingly certified that that state corresponds to a state of the *proper* functioning of those mechanisms. If so, it is conceivable that that would amount to a non-circular specification of how the person would *ideally* respond, as compared with how he actually responds; and, hence, that it would suffice for capturing the normative force of an ascription of meaning.

There is clearly no way to settle the matter in advance of the consideration of particular dispositional proposals. What we are in a position to do, however, is state conditions on an adequate dispositional theory. First, any such theory must specify, without presupposing any semantic or intentional materials, property *M*.

---

[46] Blackburn 1984b, pp. 289–91. Similar concessions are made by Wright 1984b, pp. 771–2; and by McDowell 1984, p. 329.

[47] For more discussion on this topic, see my 2005a (this volume, Chapter 4).

This would ensure the theory's extensional correctness. Second, it must show how possession of an M-disposition could amount to something that deserves to be called a *correctness* condition, something we would be inherently motivated to satisfy. This would ensure the intensional equivalence of the two properties in question, thus paving the way for an outright reduction of meaning to dispositions.

What property might M be? There are, in effect, two sorts of proposal: one, long associated with Wittgenstein himself, seeks to specify M by exploiting the notion of a community; the other, of more recent provenance, attempts to define M in terms of the notion of an optimality condition. I shall begin with the communitarian account.

The Communitarian Account

22. The idea that correctness consists in agreement with one's fellows has a distinguished history in the study of Wittgenstein. Even before the current concern with a 'rule-following problem', many commentators—whether rightly or wrongly—identified communitarianism as a central thesis of the later writings. As a response to the problem about meaning, it found its most sustained treatment in Wright's *Wittgenstein on the Foundations of Mathematics*.[48] Which of the many dispositions a speaker may have with respect to a given expression determine its meaning? Or, equivalently, which of the many dispositions a speaker may have with respect to an expression are dispositions to use it correctly? Wright's communitarian account furnishes the following answer:

... it is a community of assent which supplies the essential background against which alone it makes sense to think of individuals' responses as correct or incorrect. ... None of us can unilaterally make sense of correct employment of language save by reference to the authority of communal assent on the matter; and for the community itself there is no authority, so no standard to meet.[49]

It is important to understand that, according to the proposal on offer, the correct application of a term is determined by the *totality* of the community's *actual* dispositions in respect of that term. The theory does not attempt, in specifying the communal dispositions that are to serve as the constitutive arbiters of correctness, to select from among the community's actual dispositions a privileged subset. There is a reason for this. Communitarianism is a response to the perceived inability to define a distinction, at the level of the individual, between correct and incorrect dispositions. The suggestion that correctness consists in agreement with the dispositions of one's community is designed to meet this need. The proposal will not serve its purpose, however, if the problem at the level of

---

[48] Wright 1980. (His more recent writings suggest that Wright no longer holds this view.) See also Peacocke 1981.

[49] Ibid., pp. 219–20.

the individual is now merely to be replayed at the level of the community. A communitarian does not want it to be a *further* question whether a given actual communal disposition is itself correct. The proposal must be understood, therefore, as offering the following characterization of M: M is the *property of agreeing with the actual dispositions of the community*.

How does the proposal fare with respect to the outlined adequacy conditions on dispositional theories?

Consider first the 'intensional' requirement, that possession of the favoured M-property appear intuitively to resemble possession of a correctness condition. Does *communal consensus* command the sort of response characteristic of truth?

A number of critics have complained against communitarianism that communal consensus is simply not the same property as truth, that there is no incoherence in the suggestion that all the members of a linguistic community have gone collectively, but non-collusively, off-track in the application of a given predicate.[50] This is, of course, undeniable. But the communitarian is not best read as offering an *analysis* of the ordinary notion of truth, but a *displacement* of it. His thought is that the emaciated notion of truth yielded by communitarianism is the best we can hope to expect in light of the rule-following considerations. The crucial question, then, is not whether communitarianism captures our ordinary notion of truth, for it quite clearly does not; it is, rather, whether communitarianism offers *any* concept deserving of that name.

This is a large question on which I do not propose to spend a lot of time.[51] Although there are subtle questions about how much of logic will be recoverable from such a view, and whether it can be suitably non-reductively articulated (can 'non-collusive agreement' be defined without the use of intentional materials?), I am prepared to grant, for the sake of argument, that the proposal does not fare all that badly in connection with the 'intensional' requirement. Non-collusive communal agreement on a judgement does usually provide one with some sort of reason for embracing the judgement (even if, unlike truth, not with a decisive one); it thus mimics to some degree the sort of response that is essential to truth. Where communitarianism fails, it seems to me, is not so much here as with the extensional requirement.

Consider the term 'horse'. What dispositions do I have in respect of this expression? To be sure, I have a disposition to apply it to horses. But I also have a disposition, on sufficiently dark nights, to apply it to deceptively horsey looking cows. Intuitively, the facts are clear. 'Horse' means *horse* and my disposition to apply it to cows on dark nights is mistaken. The problem is to come up with a theory that delivers this result systematically and in purely dispositional terms. The communitarian's idea is that the correct dispositions are constitutively those which agree with the community's. What, then, are the community's dispositions likely to be?

[50] See Blackburn 1984b.
[51] For a more extensive discussion see my 1986; see also Blackburn 1984a, pp. 82ff.

The community, I submit, however exactly specified, is bound to exhibit precisely the same duality of dispositions that I do: it too will be disposed to call both horses and deceptively horsey looking cows on dark nights 'horse'. After all, if *I* can be taken in by a deceptively horsey looking cow on a dark night, what is to prevent 17,000 people just like me from being taken in by the same, admittedly effective, impostor? The point is that many of the mistakes we make are *systematic*: they arise because of the presence of features—bad lighting, effective disguises, and so forth—that have a generalizable and predictable effect on creatures with similar cognitive endowments. (This is presumably what makes 'magicians' possible.) But, then, any of my dispositions that are in this sense systematically mistaken, are bound to be duplicated at the level of the community. The communitarian, however, cannot call them *mistakes*, for they are the community's dispositions. He must insist, then, firm conviction to the contrary notwithstanding, that 'horse' means not *horse* but, rather, *horse or cow*.

The problem, of course, is general. There are countless possible impostors under countless possible conditions; and there is nothing special about the term 'horse'. The upshot would appear to be that, according to communitarianism, none of our predicates have the extensions we take them to have, but mean something wildly disjunctive instead. Which is to say that communitarianism is bound to issue in false verdicts about the meanings of most expressions, thus failing the first requirement on an adequate dispositional theory.

It seems to me that we have no option but to reject a pure communitarianism. If we are to have any prospect of identifying the extensions of our expressions correctly, it will simply not do to identify truth with communal consensus. Even from among the *community's* dispositions, we have to select those which may be considered meaning-determining, if we are to have a plausible theory of meaning. Which is to say that we are still lacking what communitarianism was supposed to provide: the specification of a property *M* such that, possession of *M* by a disposition is necessary and sufficient for that disposition's correctness.

Of course, once we have abandoned communitarianism, we lack any motive for defining *M* over *communal* dispositions; nothing—at least nothing obvious—tells against defining *M* directly over an *individual's* dispositions. Which is precisely the way the voluminous literature on this topic approaches the problem and to a discussion of which I now propose to turn.

Optimal Dispositions

23. The literature supplies what is, in effect, a set of variations on a basic theme: *M* is the property of: being a disposition to apply (an expression) *in a certain type of situation*.[52] The idea behind such proposals is that there is a certain

---

[52] There is one exception to this generalization: Fodor 1990 has it that *S*'s meaning-determining dispositions are those that serve as an 'asymmetric dependence base' for *S*'s other dispositions.

set of circumstances—call them 'optimality conditions'—under which subjects are, for one or another reason, incapable of mistaken judgements; hence, we may equate what they mean by a given (mental) expression with, the properties they are disposed to apply the expression to, under optimal conditions. Different proposals provide different characterizations of the conditions that are supposed to be optimal in this sense. Fred Dretske, for example, holds that optimal conditions are the conditions under which the meaning of the expression was first acquired. A number of other writers subscribe to some form or other of a *teleological* proposal: optimality conditions are those conditions—defined by evolutionary biology—under which our cognitive mechanisms are functioning just as they are supposed to.[53]

Now, Kripke is very short with such possible elaborations of a dispositional theory. He briefly considers the suggestion that we attempt to define idealized dispositions and says that 'a little experimentation will reveal the futility of such an effort'.[54] But, surely, this underestimates the complexity of the problems involved and fails to do justice to the influence that such proposals currently exert. What Kripke needs, if his rejection of dispositional accounts is to succeed, but does not really provide, is a set of principled considerations against the existence of non-semantically, non-intentionally specifiable optimality conditions. What I would like to do in the remainder of this section is to begin to sketch an argument for that conclusion. Several specific problems for specific versions of an optimality theory have received discussion in the literature.[55] Here, however, I want to attempt an argument with a more general sweep: I want to argue that we have reason to believe that there could not be naturalistically specifiable conditions under which a subject will be disposed to apply an expression only to what it means; and, hence, that no attempt at specifying such conditions can hope to succeed.[56]

24. It will be worthwhile to lay the problem out with some care. Consider Neil and a particular expression, say, 'horse', in Neil's mental repertoire. And suppose that Neil is disposed to token that expression 'in the belief mode' both in respect of horses and in respect of deceptively horsey looking cows on dark nights. Let it be clear, furthermore, that 'horse' for Neil means *horse*, and that on those occasions when he applies 'horse' to cows, this amounts to his *mistaking* a cow for a horse. Now, the thought behind an optimality version of a dispositional theory is that there is a set of naturalistically specifiable conditions under which

---

In my 1991 (this volume, Chapter 3) I argue that this theory is subject to the same difficulties as confront standard optimality versions.

[53] For theories of this form see Papineau 1987 and Fodor 1984. I shy away from saying whether Millikan 1987 presents a theory of this form.

[54] Kripke 1982, p. 32.

[55] Against Dretske see Fodor 1984; against teleological theories see my 1986 and Fodor 1990.

[56] This amounts to saying that such theories cannot meet the extensional requirement; so I shall not even consider whether they meet the intensional one.

Neil cannot make mistakes in the identification of presented items.[57] Under those conditions, then, he would believe that there is a horse in front of him only if there is one. But that in turn implies that, under those conditions, 'horse' will get tokened (in the belief mode) only in respect of the property it expresses. So, to figure out what any expression means: look at the properties Neil is disposed to apply the expression to, when conditions are in this sense optimal. The end result is a dispositional reconstruction of meaning facts: for Neil to mean horse by 'horse' is for Neil to be disposed to call only horses 'horse', when conditions are optimal. Clearly, two conditions must be satisfied: (i) the specified conditions must really be such as to preclude the possibility of error—otherwise, it will be false that under those conditions 'horse' will get applied only to what it means; (ii) the conditions must be specified purely naturalistically, without the use of any semantic or intentional materials—otherwise, the theory will have assumed the very properties it was supposed to provide a reconstruction of.

What I propose to argue is that it is impossible to satisfy both of these conditions simultaneously.[58]

Optimal Dispositions and Objective Contents

25. The dispositionalist is after a non-semantically, non-intentionally specifiable set of conditions O, which will be such as to yield true, a priori *optimality equations* of the form:

(8) For any subject S and concept R: $O \to (S$ judges $Rx \to Rx)$.

Could there be such a set of conditions?

Notice, to begin with, that where R is the concept of an *objective* property, we ought not to expect optimality equations for R, even if O were not required to meet the rather stiff constraints imposed by a reductive dispositionalism—namely, specification in non-semantic and non-intentional terms. For, intuitively, the very idea of a wholly objective property (or object or relation) is the idea of a property (object, relation) whose nature is independent of any given person's abilities or judgements: for such a property, in other words, there is no necessary function from a given person's abilities and judgements to truths about that property.[59] The contrast is with a class of contents for which there does exist a range of circumstances such that, appropriate subjects are necessarily authoritative about those contents under those circumstances. Philosophers disagree, of course, about what contents fall where, but it is typical to think of judgements about shape as wholly objective and of judgements about pain

---

[57] This restriction to perceptually fixed beliefs stems partly from a desire to simplify exposition and partly from a desire to consider such theories at their strongest.

[58] I argue for this in more detail in my 1991 (this volume, Chapter 3).

[59] See, for example, Burge 1986, p. 125, for a similar formulation of the concept of an objective property.

as representing an extreme example of the contrasting class. Let us call this a distinction between *accessible* versus *inaccessible* contents.[60]

We are now in a position to see, however, that a dispositional theory of meaning, by virtue of being committed to the existence of optimality equations for every concept, is committed thereby to treating every concept as if it were accessible. It is thus committed to obliterating the distinction between accessible and inaccessible contents.

Of course, this objection will not impress anyone reluctant to countenance wholly objective, inaccessible contents in the first place. I turn, therefore, to arguing against the dispositional theory on neutral ground: for any concept, subjective or objective, it is impossible to satisfy dispositionalism's basic requirement: the specification of a set of conditions *O, in non-semantic, and non-intentional terms*, such that, under *O*, subjects are immune from error about judgements involving that concept.

Optimal Dispositions and Belief Holism

26. The basic difficulty derives from the holistic character of the processes which fix belief. The point is that, under normal circumstances, belief fixation is typically mediated by background theory—what contents a thinker is prepared to judge will depend upon what other contents he is prepared to judge. And this dependence is, again typically, arbitrarily robust: just about any stimulus can cause just about any belief, given a suitably mediating set of background assumptions. Thus, Neil may come to believe *Lo, a magpie*, as a result of seeing a currawong, because of his further belief that that is just what magpies look like; or because of his belief that the only birds in the immediate vicinity are magpies; or because of his belief that whatever the Pope says goes and his belief that the Pope says that this presented currawong is a magpie. And so on. The thought that something is a magpie can get triggered by a currawong in any of an indefinite number of ways, corresponding to the potentially indefinite number of background beliefs which could mediate the transition. Now, how does all this bear on the prospects for a dispositional theory of meaning?

A dispositional theorist has to specify, without use of semantic or intentional materials, a situation in which a thinker will be disposed to think, *Lo, a magpie* only in respect of magpies. But the observation that beliefs are fixed holistically implies that a thinker will be disposed to think *Lo, a magpie* in respect of an indefinite number of *non-magpies*, provided only that the appropriate background beliefs are present. Specifying an optimality condition for 'magpie',

---

[60] It is important to appreciate that this is an *epistemological* distinction, not a constitutive one. It does not follow from the fact that a content is accessible, that it is therefore constituted by our best judgements about it. (I take it no one is tempted to conclude from the fact that we are authoritative about our pains, that pains are *constituted* by the judgements we make about them. We shall have occasion to discuss constitutive claims of this sort later on in the paper.)

therefore, will involve, at a minimum, specifying a situation characterized by the absence of *all* the beliefs which could potentially mediate the transition from non-magpies to *magpie* beliefs. Since, however, there looks to be a potential infinity of such mediating background clusters of belief, a non-semantically, non-intentionally specified optimality situation is a non-semantically, non-intentionally specified situation in which it is guaranteed that none of this potential infinity of background clusters of belief is present. But how is such a situation to be specified? What is needed is precisely what a dispositional theory was supposed to provide: namely, a set of naturalistic necessary and sufficient conditions for being a belief with a certain content. But, of course, if we had *that* we would already have a reductive theory of meaning—we would not need a dispositional theory! Which is to say that, if there is to be any sort of reductive story about meaning at all, it cannot take the form of a dispositional theory.

VI. ANTI-REDUCTIONIST CONCEPTIONS OF MEANING

An Argument from Queerness?

27. If these considerations are correct, there would appear to be plenty of reason to doubt the reducibility of content properties to naturalistic properties. But Kripke's sceptic does not merely draw an anti-reductionist conclusion; he concludes, far more radically, that there simply could not *be* any content properties. Suppose we grant the anti-reductionism; what justifies the content *scepticism*? Not, of course, the anti-reductionism by itself. At a minimum one of two further things is needed. Either an independent argument to the effect that only naturalistic properties are real. Or, failing that, a frontal assault on the irreducible property in question, showing that it is, in Mackie's phrase, somehow inherently 'queer'.

The single greatest weakness in Kripke's sceptical argument is that he fails to bring off either requirement. He does not even try to defend a reductionist principle about the intentional; and his brief attempt at a 'queerness' argument is half-hearted and unconvincing:

Perhaps we may try to recoup, by arguing that meaning addition by 'plus' is a state even more sui generis than we have argued before. Perhaps it is simply a primitive state, not to be assimilated to sensations or headaches or any 'qualitative' states, nor to be assimilated to dispositions, but a state of a unique kind of its own.

Such a move may in a sense be irrefutable, and if it is taken in an appropriate way Wittgenstein may even accept it. But it seems desperate: it leaves the nature of this postulated primitive state—the primitive state of 'meaning addition by "plus"'—completely mysterious. It is not supposed to be an introspectible state, yet we supposedly are aware of it with some fair degree of certainty whenever it occurs. For how else can each of us be confident that he does, at present, mean addition by 'plus'? Even more important is the logical difficulty implicit in Wittgenstein's sceptical argument. I think that Wittgenstein argues, not merely as we have said hitherto, that introspection shows that the alleged 'qualitative' state of understanding is a chimera, but also that it is logically impossible (or at least that there is a considerable logical difficulty) for there to be a state of 'meaning addition by "plus"' at all.

Such a state would have to be a finite object, contained in our finite minds. It does not consist in my explicitly thinking of each case of the addition table. ... Can we conceive of a finite state which *could* not be interpreted in a quus-like way? How could that be?[61]

There are several problems with this passage. In the first place, it misconstrues the appropriate anti-reductionist suggestion. I take it that it really is not plausible that there are 'primitive states' of meaning *public language* expressions in certain ways, one state per expression. The process by which the inscriptions and vocables of a public language acquire meaning is a manifestly complex process—involving an enormous array of appropriate propositional attitudes—the outlines of which may arguably be found in the writings of Paul Grice and others.[62] A plausible anti-reductionism about meaning would not wish to deny that there is an interesting story to be told about the relation between *linguistic content and mental content*; what it maintains, rather, is that there is no interesting reduction *of mental content properties* to *physical/functional properties*. According to anti-reductionism, in other words, at some appropriate level mental content properties must simply be taken for granted, without prospect of identification with properties otherwise described.

Does Kripke manage to create a difficulty for *this* suggestion? The passage contains a couple of considerations that may be so construed.

The first charge is that we would have no idea how to explain our ability to know our thoughts, if we endorsed a non-reductionist conception of their content. Now, no one who has contemplated the problem of self-knowledge can fail to be impressed by its difficulty.[63] But I think that we would be forgiven if, before we allowed this to drive us to a dubiously coherent irrealism about content, we required something on the order of a *proof* that no satisfactory epistemology was ultimately to be had.

Kripke, however, provides no such proof. He merely notes that the non-phenomenal character of contentful states precludes an introspective account of their epistemology. And this is problematic for two reasons. First, because there may be non-introspective accounts of self-knowledge.[64] And second, because it does not obviously follow from the fact that a mental state lacks an individuative phenomenology, that it is not introspectible.[65]

[61] Kripke 1982, pp. 51–2.

[62] See the papers cited under n. 5 above.

[63] For discussion of some of the difficulties see my 1989a (this volume, Chapter 6).

[64] See, for example, Burge 1988 and Davidson 1987.

[65] It is interesting to note, incidentally, that one of the more striking examples of the introspective discernment of a non-qualitative mental feature is provided by, of all things, an experiential phenomenon. I have in mind the phenomenon, much discussed by Wittgenstein himself, of seeing-as.

Kripke's second objection to the anti-reductionist suggestion is that it is utterly mysterious how there could be a finite state, realized in a finite mind, that nevertheless contains information about the correct applicability of a sign in literally no end of distinct situations. But, again, this amounts merely to insisting that we find the idea of a contentful state problematic, without adducing any independent reason why we should. We *know* that mental states with general contents are states with infinitary normative characters; it is precisely with that observation that the entire discussion began. What Kripke needs, if he is to pull off an argument from queerness, is some substantive argument, distinct from his anti-reductionist considerations, why we should not countenance such states. But this he does not provide.

None of this should be understood as suggesting that an anti-reductionism about content is unproblematic, for it is far from it. There are, for example, familiar, and serious, difficulties reconciling an anti-reductionism about content properties with a satisfying conception of their causal efficacy.[66] But in the context of Kripke's dialectic, the anti-reductionist suggestion emerges as a stable response to the sceptical conclusion, one that is seemingly untouched by all the considerations adduced in the latter's favour.

McDowell on Privacy and Community

28. If we endorse a non-reductionist conception of meaning, does that mean that the rule-following considerations disturb nothing in our ordinary conception of that notion? A number of writers who have found an anti-reductionist suggestion attractive have certainly not thought so; they have discerned in those considerations important lessons for the correct understanding of the possibility of meaning, while rejecting substantive reductive answers to the constitutive question: in virtue of what do expressions possess meaning?

John McDowell, for example, has written that:

By Wittgenstein's lights, it is a mistake to think we can dig down to a level at which we no longer have application for normative notions (like 'following according to the rule').[67]

We have to resist the temptation, according to McDowell's Wittgenstein, to form a picture of 'bedrock' — 'of how things are at the deepest level at which we may sensibly contemplate the place of [meaning] in the world' — which does not already employ the idea of the correct (or incorrect) use of an expression.

We see the duck–rabbit now as a duck, now as a rabbit; we see the Necker cube now with one face forward, now with another. And we know immediately precisely how we are seeing these objects as, when we see them now in one way, now in the other. But this change of 'aspect', although manifestly introspectible, is nevertheless not a change in something qualitative, for the qualitative character of the visual experience remains the same even as the aspect changes.

[66] See below.

[67] McDowell 1984, p. 341.

Oddly, however, McDowell does not take this to commit him to a *quietism* about meaning, a position from which no substantive results about the conditions for the possibility of meaning can be gleaned. On the contrary, he claims that it is the discernible moral of the rule-following considerations that correctness, and hence meaning, can exist only in the context of a *communal practice*, thus precluding the possibility of a private language. He writes:

Wittgenstein warns us not to try to dig below 'bedrock'. But it is difficult, in reading him, to avoid acquiring a sense of what, as it were, lies down there: a web of facts about behavior and 'inner' episodes, describable without using the notion of meaning. One is likely to be struck by the sheer contingency of the resemblances between individuals on which, in this vision, the possibility of meaning seems to depend. ...[68]

And:

It is true that a certain disorderliness below 'bedrock' would undermine the applicability of the notion of rule-following. So the underlying contingencies bear an intimate relation to the notion of rule-following. ...[69]

This is, of course, McDowell's characterization of the familiar Wittgensteinian claim that a certain measure of agreement in communal responses is a precondition for meaning. But how is such a thesis to be motivated? How, in light of the rejection of substantive answers to the constitutive question, is it to be argued for? The claim that communal practice is necessary for meaning is a *surprising* claim; mere reflection on the concept of meaning does not reveal it. And what, short of a substantive constitutive account, could conceivably ground it?

Consider the contrast with the communitarian view considered above. That view engages the constitutive question, offers a substantive answer to it, and generates, thereby, a straightforward argument for the necessity of a communal practice: since correctness is said to *consist* in conformity with one's fellows, correctness, and with it meaning, are possible only where there are others with whom one may conform. But McDowell, rightly in my view, rejects the suggestion that correct application might be analysed in terms of communal dispositions. Indeed, as I have already noted, he rejects the very demand for a substantive account of correctness: norms are part of the 'bedrock', beneath which we must not dig. But if we are simply to be allowed to take the idea of correctness for granted, unreduced and without any prospect of reconstruction in terms of, say, actual and counterfactual truths about communal use, how is the necessity of an 'orderly communal' practice to be defended? From what does the demand for orderliness flow? And from what the demand for community? McDowell's paper contains no helpful answers.[70]

---

[68] McDowell 1984, p. 348.

[69] Ibid., p. 349.

[70] Though see his remarks—which I am afraid I do not understand—on a 'linguistic community [that] is conceived as bound together, not by a match in mere externals (facts accessible to just anyone), but by a meeting of minds'. McDowell's problems here echo, I think, Wittgenstein's

Wright on the judgement-dependence of meaning

29. Crispin Wright has written about the anti-reductionist conception that:

[t]his somewhat flat-footed response to Kripke's Sceptic may seem to provide a good example of 'loss of problems.' ... In fact, though, and on the contrary, I think the real problem posed by the Sceptical Argument is acute, and *is* one of Wittgenstein's fundamental concerns. But the problem is not that of *answering* the Argument. The problem is that of seeing how and why the correct answer given can *be* correct.[71]

Wright's intriguing suggestion is that there are important constitutive results to be gleaned from the epistemological question we shelved some pages back: namely, how, if content properties are simply to be taken for granted, without prospect of reconstruction either in experiential or dispositional terms, can they be known? As we saw, Kripke attempted to use this question to embarrass his anti-reductionist opponent. Wright, however, has a more constructive project in mind. Pressing the epistemological question will reveal, so he claims, that facts about content are essentially 'judgement-dependent'.

What does it mean for a class of facts to be judgement-dependent? Wright's explanation is framed in terms of a failure to pass the 'order-of-determination test':

The order-of-determination test concerns the relation between *best* judgements— judgements made in what are, with respect to their particular subject matter, *cognitively ideal* conditions of both judger and circumstance—and truth. ... Truth, for judgements which pass the test, is a standard constituted independently of any considerations concerning cognitive pedigree. For judgements which fail the test, by contrast, there is no distance between being true and being best; truth, for such judgements, is constitutively what we judge to be true when we operate under cognitively ideal conditions.[72]

We may explain the contrast Wright has in mind here by recurring to the idea of an accessible content (see above). An accessible content is one about which subjects are necessarily authoritative under cognitively optimal circumstances. Now, a question may be raised about the correct explanation for this authority: is it that, under those optimal circumstances, subjects are exceptionally well-equipped to *track* the relevant, independently constituted facts? Or is it, rather, that judgements under those circumstances simply *constitute* the facts in question? A fact is judgement-independent if the former, judgement-dependent if the latter.

---

own. The main difficulty confronting a would-be interpreter of Wittgenstein is how to reconcile his rejection of substantive constitutive accounts—especially of meaning, see Wittgenstein 1967: 'The mistake is to say that there is anything that meaning something consists'—with the obvious constitutive and transcendental pretensions of the rule-following considerations. It is fashionable to soft-pedal the rejection of constitutive questions, representing it as displaying a mere 'distrust' on Wittgenstein's part. But this ignores the fact that the rejection of analyses and necessary and sufficient conditions is tied to extremely important first-order theses about meaning, including, most centrally, the family-resemblance view of concepts.

[71] Wright 1989, p. 237.
[72] Ibid., p. 246.

The contrast, then, is between facts which are constituted independently of our judgements, however optimal, and facts which are constituted precisely by the judgements we would form under cognitively ideal circumstances. And the claim is that facts about content have to be construed on the latter model. *Pace* Kripke, the target of the rule-following considerations is not the reality of content facts, but, rather, a judgement-independent (or *Platonist*, if you think these come to the same thing) conception of their *constitution*. Best judgements constitutively determine the truth-value of sentences ascribing content to mental states; they do not *track* independently constituted states of affairs which confer truth or falsity upon them.

Wright argues for this 'judgement-dependent' conception of content by attacking the epistemologies available on the alternative model. Drawing extensively on Wittgenstein's actual text, Wright reconstructs an interesting set of considerations against both *introspective* and *inferential* conceptions of self-knowledge, thus, presumably, exhausting the epistemologies available to his opponent. So long as facts about our mental states are construed as independent of, and, hence, as tracked by our self-regarding judgements, we can have no satisfactory explanation of our ability to know them. On the assumption, then, that Kripke's unstable content irrealism is to be avoided at all costs, that leaves the judgement-dependent conception as the only contender. So goes Wright's argument.

Wright's discussion raises a number of interesting and difficult questions. Is it really true that Wittgenstein's discussion destroys all 'cognitive accomplishment' theories of self-knowledge? Supposing it does, does this inevitably drive us to a judgement-dependent conception of content? Are there not other conceptions that would equally accommodate the rejection of a tracking epistemology? Unfortunately, none of these questions can be adequately addressed within the confines of the present paper. Here I have to settle for raising a question about whether a judgement-dependent conception of *content* could *ever* be the cogent moral of any argument.

30. The suggestion is that we must not construe facts concerning mental content as genuine objects of cognition, and that this is to be accomplished by regarding them as constituted by truths concerning our best judgements about mental content. Well, what does this amount to? For illustrative purposes, Wright offers the case of colour. What would have to be true, if facts about colour are to judgement-dependent? We would need, first and foremost, to secure the *accessibility* of colour facts, and so a biconditional of the following form:

if C: S would judge x to be blue $\leftarrow x$ blue.

But not just any biconditional of this form will serve to secure the accessibility of colour. For example, unless restrictions are placed on the permissible specifications of *C, every* property will turn out to be accessible; just let *C* be: conditions under which *S* is infallible about colour. So, it must be further required that *C* be specified in substantial terms, avoiding a 'whatever-it-takes' formulation.

Now, what would it take to ground not merely the accessibility of colour, facts, but their *judgement-dependence*? What is needed, as Wright points out, is that

the question whether the C-conditions, so substantially specified, are satisfied in a particular case is logically independent of any truths concerning the details of the extension of colour concepts.[73]

This seems right. For unless the specification of the *C*-conditions, or, indeed, of anything else on the left-hand side, is precluded from presupposing facts about the colours of objects, it will remain entirely open whether subjects' judgements, formed under the relevant *C*-conditions, really did determine facts about colour. For satisfaction of the conditions described on the left-hand side would always presuppose some antecedently fixed constitution of colour facts, thus undermining the claim that it is precisely truths about best judgement that fix those facts.

No doubt, other requirements are in order as well.[74] But it is, I trust, already clear that there is a serious difficulty seeing how facts about mental content could conceivably satisfy the stated requirements on judgement-dependence. For it is inconceivable, given what *judgement-dependence* amounts to, that the biconditionals in the case of mental content should satisfy the requirement that their left-hand sides be free of any assumptions about mental content. For, at a minimum, the *content of the judgements* said to fix the facts about mental content have to be presupposed. And that means that any such biconditional will always presuppose a constitution of mental content quite independent of constitution by best judgement.

In a way, an intuitive difficulty should have been clear from the start. A 'judgement-dependent' conception of a given fact is, by definition, a conception of that fact according to which it is *constituted* by our *judgements*. The idea is clearly appropriate in connection with facts about the *chic* or the *fashionable*; familiar, though less clearly appropriate, in connection with facts about colour or sound; and, it would appear, impossible as a conception of facts about mental content. For it cannot in general be true that facts about content are constituted by our judgements about content: facts about content, constituted independently of the judgements, are presupposed by the model itself.

---

[73] Wright 1989, pp. 247–8.

[74] For a very illuminating discussion of the conditions that would have to be met, see Wright 1989, pp. 246–54.

Conclusion: Robust Realism—Problems and Prospects

31. Let *robust realism* designate the view that judgements about meaning are factual, irreducible, and judgement-independent. Then the moral of this paper—if it has one—is that the major alternatives to robust realism are beset by very serious difficulties.

Irrealism—the view, advocated by Kripke's Wittgenstein, that judgements about meaning are non-factual—appears not even to be a coherent option. (An error-theoretic variant, as promoted, for example, by Paul Churchland, seems no better.)

Reductionist versions of realism appear to be false. The proposal that judgements about meaning concern communal dispositions is unsatisfactory not merely because, implausibly, it precludes the possibility of communal error, but because it appears bound to misconstrue the meaning of every expression in the language. The rather more promising (and rather more popular) proposal, that judgements about meaning concern a certain sort of *idealized* disposition, also appears to confront serious difficulties: it is hard to see how the idealizations are to be specified in a non-question-begging way.

And, finally, a *judgement-dependent* conception of meaning seems not to be a stable option, because the very idea of constitution by best judgement appears to presuppose a judgement-*independent* conception of meaning.

It is sometimes said that an anti-reductionist conception is too facile a response to the problem about meaning. It is hard not to sympathize with this sentiment. But if the considerations canvassed against the alternatives are correct, and if it is true that the 'rule-following' considerations leave an anti-reductionist conception untouched, it is hard, ultimately, also to agree with it. Meaning properties appear to be neither eliminable, nor reducible. Perhaps it is time that we learned to live with that fact.

I do not pretend that this will be easy. Robust realism harbours some unanswered questions, the solutions to which appear not to be trivial. There are three main difficulties. First: what sort of room is left for *theorizing* about meaning, if reductionist programs are eschewed? Second: how are we to reconcile an anti-reductionism about meaning properties with a satisfying conception of their causal or explanatory efficacy? And, finally: how are we to explain our (first-person) knowledge of them?

I cannot, of course, hope to address any of these questions adequately here. A few brief remarks will have to suffice.

To begin with the last question first, I cannot see that an anti-reductionist conception of content has a *special* problem about self-knowledge. As far as I am concerned, no one has a satisfactory explanation of our ability to know our own thoughts.[75] But I do not see that the anti-reductionist need feel any special embarrassment about this. If anything, it seems to me, the prospects are better

---

[75] See my 1989a (this volume, Chapter 6).

for him than for his opponent. A reductionist would have it that meanings are fixed by certain kinds of dispositional fact, the sort of fact that could hardly be known observationally. It would appear to follow that the reductionist is committed, if he is to have a substantial epistemology of self-knowledge, to an inferential conception—a conception that may be, as I have argued elsewhere, worse than implausible.[76] The anti-reductionist labours under no comparable burden.

As for the charge that there would be nothing left for a theory of meaning to be, if reductionism is eschewed, it seems to me simply false. Let me here mention just a few of the questions that survive the rejection of reductionist programmes. For one thing, as I have stressed, a non-reductionism about meaning is best understood as a thesis about *mental* meaning, not about linguistic meaning. So anti-reductionism, as I understand it, is not only consistent with, but positively invites, a theory about the relation between thought and language. How do public language symbols come to acquire meaning and what role does thought play in that process? Secondly, anti-reductionism in my sense is consistent with wanting a general account of the principles by which we interpret other people. The important work of Quine, Davidson, Lewis, Grandy, and others on the theory of radical interpretation neither needs, nor is best understood in terms of, reductionist aspirations. Its proper goal is the articulation of the principles we evidently successfully employ in interpreting the speech and minds of others. And, finally, an anti-reductionism about mental content is perfectly consistent both with substantive theories of the nature of the propositional *attitudes*—that is, of what makes a given mental state a *belief*, as opposed to a wish or a desire; and with the claim that the grasping of certain mental contents depends on the grasping of others, and so with theories of the *compositional structure* of mental content.

There is hardly any fear, then, that we shall run out of things to do, if we forego reductionist programmes in the theory of mental content.

Finally, though, there is the question of mental causation: how are we to reconcile an anti-reductionism about content properties with a satisfying conception of their causal efficacy? It is a view long associated with Wittgenstein himself, of course, that propositional attitude explanations are not causal explanations. But, whether or not the view was Wittgenstein's, it has justifiably few adherents today. As Davidson showed, if propositional attitude explanations are to rationalize behaviour at all, then they must do so by causing it.[77] But propositional attitudes rationalize partly by virtue of their content—it is partly because Neil's belief is *that there is wine in his glass*, that he reaches for it; so, propositional attitude explanations commit us to holding that content properties have a genuine causal role in the explanation of intentional action. But, now, how is an anti-reductionist about content properties to accord them a genuine causal

[76] Again see my 1989a.
[77] See Davidson 1980a.

role without committing himself, implausibly, to the essential incompleteness of physics?

This is, I believe, the single greatest difficulty for an anti-reductionist conception of content. It may be that it will eventually prove its undoing. But the subject is relatively unexplored, and much interesting work remains to be done.[78, 79]

[78] For some recent papers see LePore and Loewer 1987, and Fodor 1989.

[79] I am grateful to many people for helpful discussion of the issues covered in this paper, including Barry Allen, John Burgess, Jerry Fodor, Mark Johnston, Saul Kripke, Barry Loewer, Richard Rorty, Larry Sklar, Neil Tennant, Nick White, Crispin Wright, Steve Yablo, and participants in various seminars at the University of Michigan. Special thanks are due to Paul Benacerraf, Jennifer Church, and David Velleman.

2 *The Status of Content*

INTRODUCTION

An irrealist conception of a given region of discourse is the view that no real properties answer to the central predicates of the region in question. Any such conception emerges, invariably, as the result of the interaction of two forces. An account of the meaning of the central predicates, along with a conception of the sorts of property the world may contain, conspire to show that, if the predicates of the region are taken to express properties, their extensions would have to be deemed uniformly empty. The question then becomes whether the predicates are best understood as expressing properties, and hence as founded on error, or whether they ought to be understood along non-factualist lines.[1]

Historically, irrealist models were developed primarily in connection with evaluative discourse, although as physicalism has flourished and as reductionist programs have failed, their application has been extended to many other domains. Indeed, it is one of the more influential suggestions in contemporary philosophy of mind that they apply even to ordinary belief/desire psychology. A correct understanding of the semantics and metaphysics of content-based psychology leaves us, so the proponents of the influential suggestion claim, with no option but to embrace an irrealist conception of that region of discourse.[2]

The influential suggestion has not gone unchallenged. Many philosophers have dissented from it—some by disputing the assumed metaphysics, others by rejecting the assumed account of psychological concepts—with inconclusive results.[3] In this paper I wish to argue that, at least as things now stand, one or another of these dissidents must be right, for the irrealist conclusion itself is demonstrably unacceptable: at least as traditionally formulated, an irrealism about content is not merely implausible, it is incoherent. The present paper is

---

[1] In reserving the label "irrealism" for the positions outlined I mean to be making a stipulative claim, not a controversial one. Although it seems to me that the label has traditionally been used chiefly to denominate error and non-factualist theories, it remains true that "realism" and "irrealism" are terms of art which may be, and have been, used in a variety of ways.

[2] See, for example, Churchland 1984 and Dennett 1971.

[3] For criticisms of the first sort see Searle 1983; for the other see Fodor 1987.

intended as a challenge, to those who wish to propound such an irrealism, to formulate their view in a way that is not subject to the difficulties it raises.

The basic arguments are fairly straightforward. They require mostly some clear thinking about what irrealist conceptions involve in general; what they involve as applied to content discourse in particular; and what sorts of consideration fuel content skepticism in the first place. Their combined destructive impact, however, is far-reaching and has not been adequately appreciated.

The paper proceeds as follows. Part I explores the two different ways in which one might seek to make sense of the claim that no property answers to a given predicate. Part II outlines and clarifies what such irrealist conceptions look like when applied to contentful psychological idiom. Part III argues that these standard irrealist conceptions are unstable when applied to content discourse. Part IV attempts a redefinition that evades the outlined difficulties. Part V then argues (i) that even if this redefined position were stable, it could not accommodate the standard *motivations* for content irrealism; and (ii) that there is every good reason to doubt its own stability.

I. IRREALIST CONCEPTIONS

Consider a fragment of discourse F, possessing a set of characteristic predicates and a set of declarative sentences involving those predicates. And suppose you come to have a worry of the following form: nothing possesses (or, perhaps, could possess) the sorts of property denoted by the characteristic predicates of F (if the predicates of F denote any sort of property at all). You become convinced, in other words, that if the predicates of F did express properties, their extensions would be uniformly empty: nothing in the world possesses the sorts of property that are the only candidates for being named by such predicates.

A conviction of this sort has traditionally given rise to one of two possible conceptions of F, answering, respectively, to the assumption that the predicates of F express properties and to the assumption that they don't.

The first option leads to an *error* conception of F. An error theorist about a given fragment of discourse takes that fragment's semantical appearances at face value: predicates denote properties and (hence) declarative sentences express genuine predicative judgments, equipped with truth conditions. However, the error theorist continues, because nothing actually exemplifies the properties so denoted, all the fragment's (atomic) declarative sentences are systematically *false*. Most of us are error theorists about witch talk, for example, in something like this sense: we recognize that "is a witch" denotes a property that nothing really has. John Mackie has defended such a view of moral discourse.[4]

An error thesis about some fragment may give rise to one of two recommendations. It can lead to the "eliminativist" suggestion that the systematic falsity

---

[4] Mackie 1977.

of F's sentences constitutes sufficient grounds for its (eventual) elimination and replacement. Or, alternatively, it could result in an "instrumentalism" about F: in the view that, the falsity of its sentences notwithstanding, the continued use of F serves an instrumental purpose that will not easily be discharged in some other way.

An error conception is the milder of the two possible reactions to our original ontological worry. A more radical reaction would be *non-factualism*. According to this view, although F's declarative sentences appear to express genuine predicative judgments, that appearance is wholly illusory. In actual fact, a non-factualist alleges, F's predicates do not denote properties; nor, as a result, do its declarative sentences express genuine predicative judgments, equipped with truth conditions: seeing as such sentences would be making no claim about the world, so nothing about the world could render them true or false.

A non-factualist conception of F may itself come in one of two versions, depending on whether the attributed reference failure is thought of as "intended." For, on the one hand, a predicate may fail to refer to a property even though it *aspires* so to refer; and, on the other, it may fail to refer to a property because it is no part of its semantic function so to refer. Naturally, the first verdict would lead to the recommendation that F be eliminated; whereas the second would merely prompt an alternative account of what the declarative sentences of F are designed to accomplish. How, if not as providing a vehicle for a statement of fact, should the semantic function of F's sentences be understood? Perhaps as providing a vehicle for the expression of certain sorts of attitude. Such an "expressivist" view, applied to moral discourse, was presented with characteristic brio by A. J. Ayer:

The presence of an ethical symbol in a proposition adds nothing to its factual content. Thus if I say to someone, 'You acted wrongly in stealing that money', I am not stating anything more than if I had said, 'You stole that money'. In adding that this action is wrong I am not making any further statement about it. I am simply evincing my moral disapproval of it. It is as if I had said 'You stole that money', in a peculiar tone of horror, or written it with the addition of some special exclamation marks.[5]

Conceptions similar in spirit have been proposed for a wide variety of regions of assertoric discourse, including the aesthetic, the causal, and the counterfactual.

---

[5] Ayer 1952, p. 107.

It is important to note that it is not essential to an expressivist conception of a given sentence that utterances of that sentence express only *non-cognitive* states of mind. (This is why I have chosen not to call the generic view "non-cognitivism," but rather "non-factualism.") It is open to such a non-factualist to hold, in other words, that utterances of the sentence in question express, for instance, *beliefs*, provided that the content of those beliefs may not be understood to provide the content of the sentence.

Hume, for example, is plausibly read as holding that an utterance of a sentence of the form "a caused b" expresses a belief to the effect that a certain sort of regularity has obtained in the past and will persist in the future. What makes Hume nonetheless a non-factualist about causal discourse is his denial that facts about regularity *analyze* facts about causation. It still remains true, consequently, that the presence of a causal symbol in a sentence adds nothing to its factual content.

What all non-factualist conceptions have in common—what in effect is constitutive of such a conception of a declarative sentence of the form "x is P"—is

(1) The claim that the predicate "P" does not denote a property[6]

and (hence)

(2) The claim that the overall (atomic) declarative sentence in which it appears does not express a truth condition.

Now, the first point I wish to underscore is that there is a perspective within the foundations of semantics—specifically, a conception of truth and of truth conditions—from which any such non-factualist view is bound to appear unintelligible. Curiously, it is again in Ayer that we find an incisive statement of the perspective in question:

[T]here is no problem of truth as it is ordinarily conceived. The traditional conception of truth as a 'real quality' or a 'real relation' is due, like most philosophical mistakes, to a failure to analyze sentences correctly. There are sentences ... in which the word 'truth' seems to stand for something real ... [but] our analysis has shown that the word 'truth' does not stand for anything.[7]

The conception of truth Ayer is giving voice to here has come to be known as a "deflationary" or "disappearance" view of truth. It is characterized by the claim that there is no such thing as the property of truth, a property that sentences or thoughts may enjoy, and that would be named by the words "true" or "truth." By way of probing such a view, let us ask how it understands the significance of "truth attributions"—of sentences of the form "x is true." There are, in effect, two options. On the one hand, a deflationist may attempt a general account of truth attributions that explains in what their semantic function consists, if it is not to consist in that of attributing a property; or, on the other, he may reject the very idea of such a general account, recommending in its place the much more modest task of specifying truth-in-a-particular-language—"truth-in-L." In a word, the options are "performative" theories, on the one hand, and "disquotational" theories, on the other.

Performative theories, originally proposed by William James,[8] and later by Peter Strawson,[9] are in effect analogues of expressivist conceptions of ethical statements. Acts of calling something true (compare acts of calling something good) are assimilated to acts of expressing praise for something, rather than to acts of describing that thing as possessing some specific property. As Rorty has

---

[6] I shall talk mostly of predicates "denoting" or "referring to" properties, but nothing much depends on this particular choice of semantic terminology. Talk of predicates "expressing" properties or "standing for" them may be substituted without affecting the argument.

[7] Ayer 1952, p. 89.

[8] See James 1978. For defense of the attribution see Brandom 1988.

[9] Strawson 1964.

succinctly put it, the proposal is that "true" is simply a compliment we pay sentences we are prepared to assert.[10]

Disquotational theories, by contrast, forego any attempt at a general account of truth attributions. According to them, the basic deflationary thought that truth is not a real property is correctly elaborated not by an alternative account of what truth in general consists in, but by the rejection of any such account. To the extent that we can talk about a theory of truth at all, this is to consist in no more than a recursive definition of truth-in-L. What sort of notion is that of truth-in-a-language? It is, in Quine's apt phrase, the idea of a device for semantic ascent—a device for talking about snow or whiteness, by talking about sentences that are about snow or whiteness. To be sure, such a device has a use: it provides a handy way of affirming or rejecting an infinite lot of facts; but it is, for all that, in principle, dispensable.[11]

My concern just now is not with a deflationary conception of truth as such;[12] it is, rather, with the *tension* between such a conception and a non-factualist thesis about a given region of assertoric discourse.[13]

To bring the tension into focus, let us ask what conditions a sentence must satisfy if, on a deflationary construal of truth, it is so much as to be a candidate for truth. What, in other words, certifies a sentence as truth-conditional, on a deflationary construal of truth?

Two minimal requirements suggest themselves: first, the sentence must be significant, and second, it must be declarative in form. Unpacking somewhat, the requirements are that the sentence possess a role within the language: its use must be appropriately disciplined by norms of correct utterance; and that it possess an appropriate syntax: it must admit of coherent embedding within negation, the conditional, and other connectives, and within contexts of propositional attitude.[14]

The status of these two requirements, as individually necessary conditions for candidacy for deflationary truth, is certified by the deflationary conception itself

---

[10] See Rorty 1986, p. 334. Needless to say, there are significant differences among the theories united under the "performative" label; but they do not matter for present purposes.

[11] See Quine 1986, pp. 11–12. See also Field 1986.

[12] I will, however, be concerned with this question towards the end of the paper. For a sympathetic discussion of deflationary construals of truth talk see Brandom 1988. Brandom sees deflationism as receiving its finest elaboration to date in a version of the "prosentential" theory of truth proposed in Grover, Camp and Belnap 1975. He writes in conclusion

[that] the pragmatists' strategy has been vindicated at least this far: It is possible to account for truth talk without invoking a property of truth that such talk must be understood as answering to (p. 90).

[13] Since one elaboration of a deflationary construal—the pragmatists'—is an expressivist conception of truth talk, this is tantamount to saying that an expressivist conception of truth talk is inconsistent with an expressivist conception of any other fragment. Many people have noticed the tension between deflationism and non-factualism. For some recent examples see McGinn 1984, p. 71, and Blackburn 1984b, pp. 281–302.

[14] Crispin Wright has suggested that these two requirements collapse into each other because "the operation of such [normative] constraint has no expression except in such syntactic conditioning of a region of discourse." See his 1993. It would be fine by me if this were so.

(which is just as it should be). Thus, it is required by the claim that "true" is a device for semantic ascent, that the sentence to which "true" is predicated be both meaningful and declarative. Since, on such a view, the overall effect of asserting that a sentence is true is just to assert the sentence itself, the requirements on truth predication must include whatever requirements attend candidacy for assertion itself; and, clearly, a sentence must be both meaningful and assertoric in form if it is to be a candidate for assertion. Similarly, a sentence must satisfy both these minimal conditions if it is to be a candidate for "performative" truth, for they are both required by the claim that "true" is a compliment we pay sentences we are prepared to assert.

The tension between a deflationary understanding of truth and a non-factualist thesis stems from the fact that these requirements would seem also to be *jointly sufficient* for truth conditionality, on a deflationary understanding of truth. For if they are jointly sufficient, then there is *no more* to a sentence's being truth-conditional—genuinely apt for (deflationary) truth and falsity—than its being a significant sentence possessing the appropriate syntactic potentialities. But it is constitutive of non-factualism precisely that it denies, of some targeted significant, declarative sentence that it is truth-conditional. On a deflationary conception of what it is to possess truth conditions, there would be, simply, no space for such a possibility.

But why must the conditions be thought of as jointly sufficient? Isn't there room for the suggestion that *more* is required for truth conditionality, consistent with subscription to a deflationism about truth? Isn't it imaginable, that is, that someone might require that a given region of discourse meet certain further conditions—reducibility to the vocabulary of basic science, for example—if it is to be genuinely truth-conditional, and yet remain a deflationist about truth?

It is hard to make sense of the suggestion. The difficulty lies in seeing how any such further requirement would be motivated. Any proposed requirement on candidacy for truth must be grounded in the preferred account of the nature of truth. On a deflationary account of truth, there is no substantive property—truth—that sentences or thoughts may enjoy; on such a view, on the contrary, all truth talk consists either in the evincing of a certain sort of praise (with the pragmatists) or in the deployment of semantic ascent (with the disquotationalists). Both of these articulations of deflationism require the two conditions outlined. But how could they conceivably require more? Any meaningful, declarative sentence would be (at a minimum) a *candidate* for assertion; it would be, thereby, a candidate for the compliment we pay sentences we are prepared to assert, or, as the alternative would have it, a candidate for semantic ascent. Any such sentence would count, therefore, as truth-conditional in a deflationary sense.[15]

---

[15] Compare this with a robust conception—say, a coherence theory—of truth. On such a theory, truth is construed as a particular sort of coherence between meaningful sentences. Here it is easy to imagine that candidacy for truth might require more than the two conditions outlined. Suppose, for example, that on the favored notion of coherence, coherence between regions

It would appear to be a point to which Ayer must have paid inadequate attention. A non-factualism about any subject matter presupposes a conception of truth richer than the deflationary: it is committed to holding that the predicate "true" stands for some sort of real, language-independent property, eligibility for which will not be certified solely by the fact that a sentence is declarative and significant. Otherwise, there will be no understanding its claim that a significant sentence, declarative in form, fails to possess truth conditions.[16]

It will be important to the argument later on to observe that we could have approached this very conclusion from a somewhat different direction: by beginning with the non-factualist's denial that the predicate in "x is P" refers to a property, rather than with his denial that the sentence as a whole possesses factual content.

Corresponding to the distinction between deflationary and robust conceptions of truth, there is a distinction between deflationary and robust conceptions of reference. A deflationary understanding of "refers" would be this: a term refers to a property provided it has the syntax of a predicate and possesses a role in the language. What is denied is that the expression "refers to a property" expresses some sort of objective relation that may obtain between predicates and language-independent properties, a relation of the sort that causal theories of predicate reference may be understood to be attempting to elucidate.[17] And, again, it is clear that a non-factualist is committed to a conception of predicate reference richer than the deflationary. For what a non-factualist wishes precisely to say is that some expressions—like "wrong" or "cause" or "beautiful" or "funny"—which have the syntax of predicates and which possess perfectly well-defined roles within the language, nevertheless fail to refer to any real property. This claim is intelligible only against the background of a robust conception of reference.

Since, however, it is a platitude that "x is P" is true if and only if the object denoted by "x" has the property expressed by "P," a non-factualist's denial that a particular predicate refers to a property is by itself sufficient to anchor his commitment to a robust conception of truth. For if the predicate in "x is P"

with highly disparate vocabularies is not an intelligible possibility. On such a view, a sentence would have to satisfy a reductionist requirement before it even made sense to ask whether it was true.

[16] Whether truth is robust or deflationary constitutes the biggest decision a theorist of truth must make. But decide he must. It is an assumption of the present paper that the concept of truth is *univocal* as between these two conceptions, that a concurrent commitment to *both* a robust and a deflationary concept of truth would be merely to pun on the word "truth." We should not confuse the fact that it is now an open question whether truth is robust or deflationary for the claim that it can be both. There is no discernible plausibility in the suggestion that the concept of a correspondence between language and world and the concept of a language-bound operator of semantic ascent might both be versions of the same idea.

[17] For deflationary conceptions of reference see Brandom 1984, Schiffer 1987, and Rorty 1982. For causal theories of predicate reference see, for example, Dretske 1981 and Fodor 1987.

might fail to refer to a property, then the overall declarative sentence of which it's a part might fail to possess a truth condition. However, declarative sentences cannot fail to possess truth conditions except against the background of a robust conception of truth. Hence, a commitment to a robust conception of reference would appear to entrain a commitment to a robust conception of truth, just as expected.

Our discussion of error theories can afford to be much briefer. An error thesis about the sentence "x is P" is simply the view that, because nothing has the property avowedly denoted by "P,"

(3) "x is P" is always false.

It is easy to see that an error theory, in contrast with a non-factualist thesis, is not locked into any particular understanding of the central semantic notions. Because an error theory does not rely upon a distinction between apparently referential and genuinely referential devices, or apparently truth-conditional and genuinely truth-conditional sentences, it is intelligible on both robust and deflationary understandings of reference and truth.

What any error theory *is* committed to, however, is simply this: that there *actually* are some sentences that possess truth conditions (on whatever understanding of that notion is favored). The commitment is evident: an error thesis presupposes that the targeted declarative sentences possess truth conditions, otherwise it couldn't call them "false."

To sum up this general discussion of irrealist conceptions: I have argued that a non-factualist model of a given region of discourse presupposes robust conceptions of truth and reference; and that an error theory of that region presupposes that its sentences are truth-conditional, on whatever construal of truth is favored.

What I am going to argue is that an application of these models to content discourse itself runs afoul of their respective presuppositions.[18]

II. THE STATUS OF CONTENT DISCOURSE

Irrealist construals of content-based psychology have been formulated in both error-theoretic and non-factualist versions; and the error alternative, at least, in both eliminative and instrumentalist guises.

---

[18] It is sometimes suggested that there is a *third* sort of irrealist conception of a given property, one according to which truths about a property are constituted by the judgments that we would make about it under specified circumstances. Some versions of a dispositional analysis of color assume this form. I don't consider such a view in this paper because it does not seem to me to be an irrealist view in the proper sense of the term. After all, on such a view it is neither true that the property is not instantiated nor that it is non-existent. All that follows is that the property in question is *judgment-dependent*; and I don't see why there couldn't be perfectly objective truths about judgment-dependent properties. For discussion of a judgment-dependent conception of content see my 1989b (this volume, Chapter 1).

Thus, Paul Churchland has defended the thesis that

> our common sense psychological framework is a false and radically misleading conception of the causes of human behavior and cognitive activity. On this view, folk psychology is not just an incomplete representation of our inner states; it is an outright misrepresentation of our internal states and activities. Consequently, we cannot expect a truly adequate neuroscientific account of our lives to provide theoretical categories that match up nicely with the categories of our common sense framework. Accordingly, we must expect that the older framework will simply be eliminated, rather than reduced, by a matured neuroscience.[19]

And Daniel Dennett and Kripke's Wittgenstein have endorsed a conception of psychological discourse that seems best understood along non-factualist lines.

According to Dennett, the "attribution" of beliefs and desires to something consists in nothing over and above the adoption of a certain sort of (predictive) "stance" toward it; it ought not to be understood as an attempt to describe properties of that thing, an attempt that would misfire if the relevant properties were not to obtain. A system counts as having beliefs and desires if it is an intentional system; and it counts as an intentional system if it can be successfully predicted from the intentional stance.

> We do quite successfully treat these [chess-playing] computers as intentional systems, and we do this quite independently of any considerations about what substance they are composed of, their origin, their position or lack of position in the community of moral agents, their consciousness or self-consciousness. ... The decision to adopt the [intentional] strategy is pragmatic, and is not intrinsically right or wrong.[20]

And Kripke has interpreted Wittgenstein as holding that statements involving the notion of meaning or content have no truth conditions, but only conditions of warranted or justified use.

> All that is needed to legitimize assertions that someone means something is that there be roughly specified circumstances under which they are legitimately assertable, and that the game of asserting them has a role in our lives. No supposition that 'facts correspond' to those assertions is needed.[21]

It is important to emphasize that these conceptions of content-based psychological discourse have been presented as conforming fully to the paradigm examples of irrealism about other domains. The motivations for psychological irrealisms

---

[19] Churchland 1984, p. 43. See also his 1981, p. 67.

[20] Dennett 1978, p. 7. Dennett has written further on the subject of intentional attributions: see the papers collected in his 1987. I have to confess, however, to not fully understanding in what direction the view has evolved. The exegetical issues don't matter all that much, I take it, so long as non-factualisms and error theories exhaust the available irrealist options.

[21] Kripke 1982, pp. 77–8. See also Stich 1983: "What this suggests is that *there is no such thing as the property of believing that p*. The predicate 'is a belief that p' does not express or correspond to a property" (pp. 225–6).

See also Schiffer 1987, pp. 144–5; and Quine's conception of propositional attitude discourse as a "dramatic idiom," in his 1960.

conform to the traditional model: the worry is that nothing in the world answers to our talk of belief and desire. And the irrealist reactions have been formulated in traditional ways: as recommending either that we view content attributions as false, or that we view them as not fact stating.

In Parts III–V, I shall turn to a discussion of the cogency of such conceptions. But first I want to clear up a couple of questions about how precisely they are to be understood.

The first question comes up as follows. Irrealists about content tend to restrict their thesis to our ordinary talk of the *psychological*; missing, usually, is any suggestion that we should also regard it as the correct conception of the idioms we employ in characterizing linguistic behavior.[22] Indeed, not only is such a suggestion typically missing, it is occasionally explicitly denied. (This comes up particularly sharply in some of Churchland's writings, where he goes so far as to call for the creation of a new theory of meaning for natural languages, one that would be consistent with the falsity of ordinary psychological discourse.)[23]

The suggestion that we treat the notions of linguistic and mental meaning differentially is surprising, however, given the very close affinity between them. Could an irrealism about mental content really be made to cohabit with a realism about linguistic meaning?

One argument for the conclusion that it cannot has been given by Lynne Rudder Baker. She has argued that the claim that public-language expressions derive their content from the content properties of mental states is platitudinous and non-optional:

[L]anguage can be meaningful only if it is possible that someone mean something. This is a platitude, not a theory. It is clearly incumbent upon anyone who wants to deny the platitude to show that there can be meaningful language even if no one has meant anything, even if no one has ever intended anything.[24]

Unfortunately, the argument doesn't convince. Of course, we may grant Baker that there are platitudes connecting our talk of linguistic meaning with our talk of contentful mental states; so that it is, let us suppose, always permissible to move from "S means something in O's mouth," to "O intends something by the use of S." But such platitudes, by themselves, can do nothing to secure Baker's claim; for they cannot, by themselves, constrain how they are to be understood. In particular, they cannot ensure that the sentence "O intends something by the use of S" has to be understood realistically, as describing a genuine mental fact from which the meaning of S is derived, rather than being understood as a mere notational variant for the sentence—"S means something in O's mouth"—to which it is, by assumption, platitudinously connected. And so, for all that the platitudes show, it remains wide open that the meaning of S is determined by

---

[22] This is not true of Kripke's Wittgenstein.

[23] See 1981, p. 89.

[24] Baker 1988, p. 14.

non-mental factors, by facts about "use," for example. None of this, of course, amounts to an endorsement of non-mental theories of linguistic meaning. It amounts simply to the insistence that the question of the truth of such theories is not settled by the availability of platitudes connecting linguistic and mental concepts.

The real difficulty with the suggestion that one may sustain differential attitudes toward mental and linguistic content stems from the fact that the *best* arguments for the claim that nothing mental possesses content would count as *equally* good arguments for the claim that nothing linguistic does. For these arguments have nothing much to do with the items being *mental* and everything to do with their being *contentful*: they are considerations, of a wholly general character, against the existence of items individuated by content. If successful, then, they should tend to undermine the idea of linguistic content just as much as they threaten its mental counterpart.[25] The considerations in question are classifiable into four kinds: arguments from the indeterminacy of content, arguments from the holistic character of content, arguments from the irreducibility of content and arguments from the "queerness" of content.

It is a famous claim of Quine's that for any mental state or linguistic expression, a pair of content ascriptions can always be devised which would be such that, although they could not both be true, no rational considerations could decide between them. He took this to show that ascriptions of meaning were not a genuinely factual matter.[26] Considerations of the second kind, due to Stephen Stich, attempt to show that attributions of contentful states are governed by holistic and context-sensitive criteria, and that this feature militates against the existence of content properties.[27] A third kind of content-skeptical

---

[25] Not all the content-skeptical considerations that have ever been put forward have this general character; but the ones that don't, tend, in my view, to be toothless. Paul Churchland, for example, seems to find it quite compelling to argue from the fact that ordinary psychology does not provide adequate accounts of such things as "the nature and dynamics of mental illness, the faculty of creative imagination ... the nature and psychological functions of sleep ... the common ability to catch an outfield fly ball on the run" (Churchland 1981, p. 73) to the conclusion that there are no beliefs and desires. This argument is psychology-specific in the sense that the reasons it provides for skepticism about contentful psychological items do not generalize to a similar skepticism about contentful linguistic items. Unfortunately, the argument is a poor one. First, because it is never a good idea to do what the argument in effect does: viz., legislate a priori the phenomena that a theory should encompass within its explanatory purview. (I owe this observation to Jerry Fodor.) And, second, because although ordinary psychology may not itself harbor detailed views about the phenomena Churchland mentions, empirical theories employing concepts deriving from folk psychology promise to offer rich and elaborate accounts of them. Contemporary cognitive psychology, for example, is replete with theories about visual perception, memory, and learning that employ constructs recognizably similar to the ordinary concepts of belief, desire and judgment (see here Woodward and Horgan 1985). To argue, then, from the fact that ordinary psychology has no theory of sleep or perception, to the conclusion that there are no beliefs or desires, would seem to be like arguing from the fact that ordinary common-sense physics has no adequate theory of motion, to the conclusion that there are no such properties as mass or length.

[26] See Quine 1960.

[27] See Stich 1983.

argument, common to many philosophers, proceeds from the presumed failure of naturalistic reductions of content: content properties are not genuine properties because they are not reducible to the only properties that are.[28] And, finally, arguments from "queerness"—advocated recently by Kripke's Wittgenstein—claim that the content properties envisaged by common sense could not be real, because *no* real property could have the sorts of feature that common sense considers constitutive of content.[29]

I have no interest at the moment in the soundness of these arguments. My only concern is to point out that, if effective at all, they should be as effective against linguistic content as they are against mental content. This is evident from the fact that the arguments construct their skeptical case by exploiting features of content properties, but without exploiting any facts about the putative *bearers* of those properties. Thus, they would apply to anything said to possess content, whether it was mental or not.

I have been arguing that one ought not to be an irrealist about mental content attributions, unless one is prepared to be an irrealist about all content attributions. But what notion of content is in question, exactly?

It is a question of considerable contemporary controversy whether the ordinary notion of content may be understood to consist simply in the idea of a truth condition, or whether it has to be conceived as consisting in something more fine-grained. Fregean opacity phenomena pull, of course, in the latter, more ambitious, direction; but it remains unclear whether those phenomena are decisive or whether they can be handled in a way that conserves the more modest, truth-conditional construal.[30] What is not controversial, however, is that the essential *core* of the ordinary notion of content does consist simply in the idea of a truth condition; so that even if, for whatever reason, we had to forego something more fine-grained, that would still count as a significant commitment to the ordinary notion. And, for all we now know, truth conditions may be all the ordinary notion calls for in any event.

What this suggests is that a skepticism about content, if it is to be *interesting*, must be directed primarily at the idea of a truth condition and not at any more ambitious construal of the ordinary notion. Otherwise, it will be easy to deflect the skepticism by settling for the modest construal, a course of action that may be forced upon us in any case by considerations *internal* to the theory of content. Fortunately for contemporary content skeptics, it seems clear that the standard arguments for content skepticism (reviewed above) do not exploit the complexities that opacity phenomena induce: they would apply even on a

---

[28] Schiffer 1987, pp. 146–56.

[29] Kripke has in mind the infinitary and normative character of the ordinary notion of content; see his 1982. For further discussion see my 1989b (this volume, Chapter 1). The use of the term "queerness" for arguments of this kind derives from Mackie 1977.

[30] There is a very large literature on this subject. For a recent attempt to get by with the more modest construal, see Fodor 1987.

modest, truth-conditional construal of content.[31] For the remainder of this paper, therefore, I will assume that contents just are truth conditions.

III. IRREALIST CONCEPTIONS OF CONTENT

A summary may be useful at this stage. An examination of the standard recipes for constructing irrealist conceptions revealed that *non-factualist* theories presuppose robust conceptions of truth and reference; and that error theories presuppose that the target sentences possess truth conditions (on either a robust or a deflationary construal of truth). I have also argued that one ought not to be an irrealist about psychological content without being an irrealist about all content attributions; and that the relevant notion of content may be assumed to consist simply in the idea of a truth condition. We are finally in a position to assess the cogency of irrealist construals of content.

Consider first an error conception. As the preceding discussion has argued, this amounts finally to the claim that

(4) All sentences of the form "S has truth condition p" are false,

where S is to be understood as ranging over sentences in the language of thought, or neural structures, as well as over public-language sentences. But, now, (4) would seem to have the immediate consequence that *no sentence* has a truth condition. For whatever one's conception of "true"—whether robust or deflationary—a sentence of the form "S has truth condition p" will be true if and only if S really does have truth condition p; this is, of course, nothing but a reflection of the truth predicate's disquotational properties, properties it possesses on any conception of truth. And so, since "S has truth condition p" is true if and only if S has truth condition p, then, since *all* sentences of that form are held to be *false*, for no S and for no p does S have truth condition p. Now, however, a problem would seem immediate. For (4) implies, that is, that no sentence whatever has a truth condition. But what (4) *says* is that all truth condition-attributing sentences are false. And these sentences cannot be false unless they have truth conditions to begin with. Hence, (4) implies both that truth condition-attributing sentences have truth conditions and that they don't have them. This is a contradiction.

What about a non-factualist conception of content? Applying the standard recipe for constructing such conceptions—namely, (1) and (2)—to this case, we

---

[31] The only argument that may seem to be at risk is Stich's argument from holism, but I think this appearance illusory. The *criteria* for ascriptions of *referential* content seem to me to be just as holistic as the criteria for ascription of meaning—by manipulating the background beliefs, one can raise just as much of a worry about whether Mrs. T. is referring to McKinley, as one can about whether she is expressing the concept of assassination. Even if this were false, of course, the problem would be Stich's, not mine.

see that a non-factualism about content comes to the view that content predicates do not express properties and (hence) that content-attributing sentences are not genuinely truth-conditional. That is, the view consists in the pair of claims:

(5) The predicate "has truth condition p" does not refer to a property,

and

(6) "S has truth condition p" is not truth-conditional.

Notice, however, that (5) entails

(7) "true" does not refer to a property.

For the truth value of a sentence is fully determined by its truth condition and the relevant worldly facts. There is no way, then, that a sentence's possessing a truth value could be a thoroughly factual matter ("true" does express a property) if there is non-factuality in one of its determinants ("has truth condition p" does not express a property). A non-factualism about content amounts, therefore, to (6) and (7).[32]

But now here too a contradiction seems apparent. For we saw in Part I that the idea of a significant declarative sentence failing to possess truth conditions is an idea that *presupposes* that "true" does refer to a property: it presupposes a robust, as opposed to deflationary, conception of truth. It follows, therefore, that a non-factualism about content is seen to consist in a pair of claims, one of which presupposes the negation of the other. For (6) is the denial that a declarative sentence possesses truth conditions, which presupposes that truth is robust; whereas (7) is the denial that truth is robust.

Now, this seems an extremely curious result, doesn't it?—no irrealist conception of content, modelled on standard formulations of irrealist theses about other subject matters, yields a coherent view. How can this be? Irrealist conceptions of other domains—of ethics, for example, or of mathematics—may not be particularly appealing or plausible; but they're not incoherent. Why should matters stand differently with content discourse?

The source of the asymmetry is not hard to find. It derives from the fact that error and non-factualist theories about *any* subject matter presuppose certain claims about truth and truth conditions, which an error or non-factualist conception directed precisely at truth ends up denying. Not surprisingly, the ensuing result is unstable.

Thus, an error thesis about any subject matter presupposes, by its very nature, that the target sentences are truth-conditional. But an error thesis directed precisely at our talk of truth conditions themselves entails the denial of that presupposition. Thus, also, a non-factualism about any subject matter presupposes a robust conception of truth and reference. But a non-factualism directed precisely at truth entails the denial of that presupposition.

---

[32] I am indebted here to Crispin Wright.

The conclusion, it seems to me, is inescapable: if there is a genuine issue about the status of content discourse, it cannot be formulated in accordance with our standard irrealist models.

IV. A REFORMULATED CONTENT IRREALISM

The question arises whether there is some other, more salutary, way of formulating an irrealism about content and truth.

Well, one set of views we may simply set aside: *no* version of an *error* conception of content can be made to yield anything satisfactory. So long as there is no hope of confining a skepticism about content purely to the psychological domain, an error thesis about content will yield a contradiction. But it might seem that the non-factualist conception could be modified to yield something more promising.

A standard non-factualist conception, applied to content discourse consists, as we saw, of the following pair of claims:

(7) The predicate "true" does not refer to a property

and

(6) "S has truth condition p" is not truth-conditional.

The difficulty was that (6) presupposes that (7) is false, so they cannot both be true.

Given, however, that the difficulties for this position appear to stem solely from the *joint* assertion of (6) and (7), it is natural to wonder whether an acceptable content irrealism might not be formulable with the aid of only *one* of these propositions. After all, the non-factualist position currently under consideration was generated by a fairly mechanical application of standard non-factualist recipes. It remains conceivable, therefore, that there exists some non-standard way of expressing an irrealism about content properties, one that will not fall prey to the difficulties uncovered above.

One unpromising strategy would be to give up (7) in favor of (6). The idea here is that an irrealism about content could be secured by asserting—with (6)—that truth condition-attributing sentences are non-factual (non-truth-conditional), without having to say—with (7)—that truth is not robust, that the predicate "true" does not name a genuine property. But the position is unstable, for familiar reasons. The trouble is that since truth condition-attributing sentences are declarative, denying of them—with (6)—that they are truth-conditional presupposes that truth is robust, that "true" does name a genuine property. But if "true" does name a genuine property, how could sentences which attribute such properties be—as (6) claims—non-factual, not capable of genuine truth and falsehood?

The opposite strategy of giving up (6) but retaining (7) seems much more promising. For a deflationism about truth—the thesis expressed by (7)—would appear to be an impeccably content irrealist position. And although now it will be impossible for the content irrealist to say, given the loss of (6), that truth condition-attributing sentences are non-truth-conditional, it should also be clear that there is no longer any *need* to say that. He can happily admit that such sentences are fact-stating and even that they are occasionally true. For with the denial that "true" refers to a robust semantical property, the admission is innocuous: it is perfectly consistent with his irrealism about the central semantic concepts. The proposal that recommends itself would appear to be, then, that content irrealism be reformulated so as to consist *solely* in (7)—in the denial that the predicate "true" expresses a property.

The remainder of this paper will be devoted to an examination of this proposal. I shall first question whether it can accommodate the sorts of *motivation* that have traditionally fueled content irrealism. Then I shall question whether it manages to evade the sorts of problem that beset the earlier formulations.

V. DEFLATIONARY CONCEPTIONS OF TRUTH AND CONTENT IRREALISM

Most proponents of content irrealism came to that view by way of the conviction that neuroscience, or something else similarly physically basic, will ultimately provide the true story about the etiology of human behavior and cognitive activity, and that ordinary content-based psychology will not, for one reason or another, reduce to that story. In short, irrealists about content tend to be realists about physics, and, indeed, the former because the latter.

But there is a serious difficulty seeing how this original motivation for content irrealism can be conserved, on the adjusted understanding of what the view consists in. For how is a realist/irrealist contrast between physics and semantics to be formulated, if content irrealism is expressed as a deflationism about truth?

The arguments against error theories of content bar the irrealist from saying that content-ascribing sentences differ from the sentences of physics in that the former, but not the latter, are systematically false. And the adjusted formulation of content irrealism bars him from saying that the difference consists in their differential capacities for stating facts. For if an irrealism about content is simply a deflationism about truth, then, as the discussion of Part I showed, such a view will entail that all declarative sentences, regardless of subject matter, must be treated on a par: there can be no interesting distinction between sentences that are genuinely in the business of stating facts and those that aren't.

But how now to express the conviction that inspired the whole program in the first place: namely, that there is something specifically suspect about *content*?

If content irrealism is formulated as a deflationism about truth, no latitude is left for expressing invidious distinctions between content discourse and physics. In particular, the suggestion championed by Churchland, that content irrealism might lead to the *elimination* of content discourse, can no longer be coherently motivated, for the basis on which an invidious distinction between our talk of content and our talk about any other subject matter was to be constructed, no longer exists. Content irrealism itself guarantees that.

The difficulties encountered here—in the attempt to preserve a special place for physics while avoiding the pitfalls of the sorts of standard irrealist construals of content lately discussed—are nicely illustrated by Stephen Schiffer's recent book *Remnants of Meaning*.[33] Schiffer there argues for an irrealism about content characterized by the following pair of theses: *Ontological Physicalism*, which holds that there are no extra-linguistic, irreducibly psychological entities of any ontological category; and *Sentential Dualism*, which holds that there are true, but irreducible, belief-ascribing sentences.

The attractions of the view are unmistakable: it promises to satisfy simultaneously the conviction that there are no non-physical properties, and the conviction that psychological descriptions play an indispensable role in our self-conception, and all this without relying on an implausible reductionism.[34] But can it be brought off? One way to appreciate its difficulties is as follows.

Ontological Physicalism is the view that there are no extra-linguistic psychological properties. But let us ask this: are there any extra-linguistic *physical* properties according to Schiffer? If he says "yes," then Sentential Dualism—the view that there are *true* belief-ascribing sentences—will have been exposed as a sham. For if there are extra-linguistic physical properties for the sentences of physics to answer to, but no extra-linguistic psychological properties for the sentences of psychology to answer to, then it isn't true, in the strict and literal sense, that there are *true* sentences of psychology, and the overall view is indistinguishable from the sorts of standard irrealism about content that we recently found so problematic.

On the other hand, if Schiffer denies the existence of properties altogether, then the view can hardly be described as a combination of Ontological *Physicalism* and Sentential Dualism: it would be more appropriate to describe it as a combination of Ontological *Nihilism* and Sentential Dualism. Or, if we prefer, and on the assumption that we can now provide a deflationary construal of "ontology," we may describe it as a combination of *Ontological Dualism* and *Sentential Dualism*. Either way, we would have been unable to preserve a special and privileged place for *physics* to occupy relative to the rest of discourse.[35]

---

[33] Schiffer 1987.

[34] This sort of view was probably first proposed by Donald Davidson; see his 1980b.

[35] It ought to be recorded that Schiffer himself takes this latter course, preferring to say that there are no properties of any kind (see pp. 146–56). He does not explain how, in light of this, he feels entitled to call himself an "ontological physicalist."

An irrealism about content can only be a deflationism about truth. And this is a significantly different view from what we had been led to expect. But is it at least stable in this guise?

The suggestion that it isn't is likely to meet with some resistance. Deflationary conceptions of truth, although of relatively recent provenance, have had many distinguished proponents, including many of the Vienna positivists, some of the American pragmatists, Ayer, Quine, Rorty, and others. And although one may be inclined to believe that these philosophers are wrong about truth, it seems hard to believe that their view is not even a coherent option.

Be that as it may, it is actually *implicit* in the foregoing discussion that a deflationism about truth is an inherently unstable position.

A deflationary conception of truth is the view that there really is no such property, that talk about truth and truth conditions must be understood in some way other than as talk about genuine, language-independent properties that sentences or thoughts may enjoy. It is typically expressed, as Ayer and others have expressed it, like this:

(7) The predicate "true" does not refer to a property.

But there is a serious problem seeing how any such view could itself be true. The point to bear in mind, from the discussion in Part I, is that the denial that a given predicate refers to, or expresses, a property, only makes sense on a *robust* construal of *predicate reference*; on a deflationary construal, there is, simply, no space for denying, of a significant, predicative expression, that it expresses a property.

But, then, if this is correct, the denial—expressed in (7)—that the truth predicate refers to a property, must itself be understood as framed in terms of a robust notion of reference. Otherwise, it would amount to the *false* claim that a significant, predicative expression—in this case "true"—fails of deflationary reference. But this result, in conjunction with the platitude connecting reference and truth noted above—namely, that "x is P" is true if and only if the object denoted by "x" has the property expressed by "P"—implies that (7) presupposes that truth is robust. So the denial that truth is robust attempted in (7) can succeed only if it fails.

It is natural to wonder whether the difficulty can be got around like this: first, deny that predicate reference is a robust notion; and then define a deflationary notion of truth in terms of this deflationary notion of reference. Notice that in so doing there is no longer any need to use the offending sentence (7); for granted the deflationism about reference, the concession that "true" does refer to a property would be innocuous: it would be perfectly consistent with a deflationism about the central semantic notions.

The trouble is that an offending sentence is bound to crop up somewhere. For what, after all, is a deflationary conception of reference? Presumably, it is the view that

(8) The expression "refers to a property" does not itself refer to a property.

And here, it would seem, the same problem simply recurs. For, again, if the notion of "refers to a property" that is used in (8) is a deflationary notion, then (8) amounts to the *false* claim that a significant, predicative expression—in this case, "refers to a property"—fails of deflationary reference. It must, therefore, be understood as expressing a robust conception of reference. On the terms of this understanding, however, what it says is false, too. So yet again the attempt to state a deflationism about the central semantic notions results in incoherence.

VI. CONCLUDING REMARKS

By way of closing, I would like to recapitulate the principal conclusions and to indicate, however briefly, where we require more understanding than we currently possess.

The history of philosophy has furnished us with two ways of thinking about a region of discourse, once we have become convinced that nothing in the world answers to its characteristic predicates—an error theory and a non-factualist theory. Both these models are constructed with the aid of certain theses about the concepts of truth, truth conditions and reference. Thus, error theories about a given region presuppose that the target sentences possess truth conditions; and non-factualist theories presuppose robust conceptions of truth and reference.

Recently, the suggestion that one or another of these models might apply also to ordinary, content-based psychology has become increasingly influential. The suggestion, however, rightly understood, is tantamount to the proposal that we construe semantic discourse as a whole along irrealist lines. And this proposal is of dubious coherence; for any irrealist conception presupposes certain claims about truth and truth conditions, which an irrealism precisely about truth entails the denial of. Perhaps the right way to express an irrealism about content is through *deflationism*? But this won't help, for a deflationism about truth and reference is just a version of a non-factualist thesis about semantic concepts, and is subject to the same sorts of difficulty.

If these considerations are correct, the upshot is that we have not been shown how to make sense of the question: do any properties answer to our talk about truth, truth conditions and reference? On the face of it, this is a surprising result; for it seems that we should be able to wonder whether anything answers to our semantic discourse, much as we have profitably wondered whether anything answers to our evaluative discourse. But if the argument of the present paper is correct, the whole enterprise of asking such questions is itself based on a realist understanding of semantic discourse; the suggestion, then, that irrealism might turn out to be the correct model for semantic discourse itself is a suggestion that we cannot coherently entertain.

What recourse might a content irrealist have in the face of these arguments? Two main possibilities suggest themselves. He may seek to deny that it follows inexorably from a deflationary conception of reference, that every significant predicative expression expresses a property. Or, he may attempt to deny that the nature of his worries about content discourse is best expressed in terms of our standard irrealist models.

The first option strikes me as extremely unpromising. I simply cannot see how, if we refuse to think of truth and reference as substantive properties, we can motivate stronger-than-minimal requirements on eligibility for truth and reference. It seems to me—as it has seemed to most deflationists—almost *definitional* of a deflationary conception, that eligibility should in this way be trivial.[36]

What of the second suggestion? The contrast between realism and irrealism has traditionally served as the contrast of choice between cognitively reputable and cognitively disreputable discourse. It ought to be noted, however, that some philosophers have recently begun to explore the possibility that a cognitively interesting contrast may be drawn in non-truth-theoretic terms.[37] It is too early to say whether this project will succeed, or, for that matter, whether it would ultimately be of use in the present context, if it did. But, in light of the difficulties confronting a truth-theoretic formulation of content irrealism, it seems an avenue well worth exploring.

I am inclined to believe, however, that the correct moral of the considerations on offer here is just what it appears to be: that we really cannot make sense of the suggestion that our thoughts and utterances do not possess robust truth conditions. Much as Descartes's *cogito* argument may be understood to have shown that I cannot make sense of the suggestion that I do not exist, by showing that the claim that I do exist is a presupposition of the most refined attempt to deny that I do; so the present argument should be understood as showing that we cannot make sense of the claim that our thoughts and utterances do not possess robust truth conditions by showing that the claim that they do possess robust truth conditions is a presupposition of the most refined attempt to deny that they do. In either case, whether the argument ultimately succeeds depends upon whether an alternative formulation of the disputed thesis can be found, one which does not carry the self-defeating presupposition.[38]

---

[36] See for example Schiffer 1987, pp. 146–56.

[37] See Wright 1993.

[38] For helpful comments I am grateful to Anne Bezuidenhout, Rudiger Bittner, Jennifer Church, Jerry Fodor, David Hills, Jaegwon Kim, Frank Jackson, Mark Johnston, Barry Loewer, Philip Pettit, Stephen Schiffer, Lawrence Sklar, Sigrun Svavarsdottir, Neil Tennant, David Velleman, Crispin Wright and Stephen Yablo; and to audiences at The University of Wisconsin, Madison, McGill University, Monash University, and the Australian National University.

3 *Naturalizing Content*

INTRODUCTION

The conviction that intentional realism requires intentional reductionism has the philosophy of mind in its grip. Thus, Jerry Fodor:

I suppose that sooner or later the physicists will complete the catalogue they've been compiling of the ultimate and irreducible properties of things. When they do, the likes of *spin, charm,* and *charge* will perhaps appear on their list. But *aboutness* surely won't; intentionality simply doesn't go that deep. It's hard to see, in face of this consideration, how one can be a Realist about intentionality without also being, to some extent or other, a Reductionist. If the semantic and the intentional are real properties of things, it must be in virtue of their identity with (or maybe their supervenience on?) properties that are themselves *neither* intentional *nor* semantic. If aboutness is real, it must be really something else.[1]

It is worth noting—if only because it so seldom is nowadays—that this rationale for the naturalistic conviction begs a question that doesn't obviously deserve to be begged. Why, indeed, must we think that no property can be real unless it is identical with, or supervenient upon, the properties that appear in the catalogues provided by physics? There is, I think, no *obvious* answer.

For one thing, *identity* of intentional properties with physical properties would appear to be out of the question. Not only does nothing seem to be identical to anything else, but there are several, to all appearances decisive, reasons why the intentional in particular is not identical to the physical in particular. If the naturalistic conviction is to have any face plausibility whatever, then, it must be formulated as a supervenience claim. And what the naturalist needs is an argument why, in general, it is a condition on a property's being real that it supervene on the properties recognized by physics. There are, to be sure, specific local areas in which some sort of supervenience thesis seems correct. For example, mere reflection on the *concept* of a moral property reveals that moral properties weakly supervene on non-moral properties: someone isn't so much as competent with moral concepts, if he treats non-evaluatively equivalent cases

---

[1] Fodor 1987, p. 97.

differentially from a moral point of view.[2] But this sort of deliverance—which, it is worth emphasizing, is in any case only of a *weak* supervenience thesis—does not appear to be forthcoming in general. It is simply not true that mere reflection on the concept of an arbitrary property discloses that property's supervenience—however weak—on the physical. In particular mere reflection on the concept of an intentional property doesn't.

If any of this is right, we are owed an explanation why we ought to believe in the supervenience thesis.[3] Let us pretend, however, and for the sake of argument, that we have been given one. Now, Fodor seems to believe that his commitment to the supervenience thesis requires him to provide

a *naturalized* theory of meaning; a theory that articulates, in non-semantic and non-intentional terms, sufficient conditions for one bit of the world to *be about* (to express, represent, or be true of) another bit.[4]

It will prove useful to pause a while here to reflect on the connection: how, precisely, does commitment to the supervenience thesis imply a commitment to a naturalized theory of meaning in Fodor's sense?

The answer is that a naturalized theory of meaning is needed—as I should like to put it—to render the supervenience thesis intelligible. In its absence, a supervenience thesis linking the intentional and the physical must be regarded as hopelessly mysterious and cannot be accepted. I shall explain.

A set of properties A supervenes on another set B just in case no two things can differ in their A-properties without differing in their B-properties. It follows that if A supervenes on B, then for every property P in the supervenience set A, there exists a property Q in the subvenient set B, which is a sufficient condition for it.[5] The relation of supervenience implies, in other words, that there are necessary connections between the properties that it relates. In particular, if intentional properties supervene on physical properties, then every intentional property has a physical property that necessitates it.

Now, we may appreciate the role of a naturalized theory of meaning by observing that, in the absence of further comment, a relation of supervenience between sets of distinct and highly disparate properties is puzzling. How could there be a set of necessary connections between such properties as being a certain configuration of molecules and believing that *Lully was a better composer than Purcell*, given the admittedly highly divergent characters of the properties involved? We are entitled to be mystified.

---

[2] A set of properties A *weakly* supervenes on a set B, if no two objects in a given world could differ in their A-properties without differing in their B-properties. On the other hand, a set of properties A *strongly* supervenes on set B, if no two objects drawn from any two worlds could differ in their A-properties without differing in their B-properties.

[3] I think, actually, that considerations based upon the problem of mental causation may provide such an explanation; but here is not the place to go into why. For useful discussion see Yablo 1992a and McLaughlin 1989.

[4] Fodor 1987, p. 98.

[5] See Kim 1984.

It is the point of a naturalized theory of meaning to help remove this mystification. By supplying a property that is both *incontestably physicalistic* and *recognizably sufficient for the instantiation of an intentional property*, a naturalized theory of meaning seeks to render intelligible the existence of necessary connections between the physical and the intentional and, thereby, the existence of a supervenience relation between them. It attempts to purchase a right to believe in the supervenience thesis.

So, a naturalized theory of meaning is what you need, if the naturalistic conviction has you in its grip. In this paper, however, I want to argue that, the naturalistic conviction notwithstanding, a naturalized theory of meaning is precisely what you are not likely to get. Not, at any rate, if what you mean by a naturalized theory of meaning is an information-theoretic semantics.[6]

INFORMATIONAL THEORIES OF MEANING AND TYPE 1 SITUATIONS

The Basic Formula

Let's assume, for ease of exposition, that we think in a 'language of thought': having the concept *cow* involves having a mental symbol—"cow" as it may be—which means *cow*. Now, an informational theory of meaning is the idea that the meaning of such a mental symbol is determined by the information it carries. The root idea—and the basis for all further refinements—is supplied by the following *basic formula*:

> S-events (e.g. the tokenings of symbols) express the property P, if (it's a law that) Ps cause S-events.[7]

[6] Which is not, perhaps, as big an "if" as it may at first appear. For I am inclined to believe that if there is to be a naturalized theory of meaning at all, it is likely to be a causal theory: i.e., it is likely to attempt to reconstruct the relation between a predicate and the property it expresses in terms of the *causal* relations between that predicate and that property. (What *other* sort of possible naturalistic relation between a predicate and a property looks even remotely semantically relevant?) Furthermore, any such theory is likely to be framed, not just in terms of the *actual*, but in terms of the *counterfactual*, causal relations that may obtain between a predicate and a property. In contrast with the case of the reference of proper names—where actual causal history seems paramount—it seems wrong to ignore counterfactuals in determining the meaning of predicates. But a causal theory of meaning couched in terms of truths about a symbol's counterfactual causal history is precisely what an information-theoretic semantics is all about.

[7] For theories based on this basic formula see Dretske 1981, Stampe 1977, Stalnaker 1984, and Fodor 1987 and 1990. It is with this latter piece that the present paper is most concerned.

In the interests of presenting the strongest possible version of a causal theory, I am going to suppress many qualms and follow Fodor in two important respects. First, I am going to allow that we can talk about genuine (obviously *ceteris paribus*) laws here—despite the fact that what's in question are such "laws" as that presidents cause "president" tokens and that sopranos cause "soprano" tokens. And, second, I will allow that "it's bedrock that the world contains properties and their nomic relations" (Fodor 1990, p. 93), so that it counts as a perfectly objective matter what properties are causally responsible for what effects. Notice by the way, that it can be a law that Ps

The prospects for such a theory depend entirely on whether this basic formula can be converted, via the imposition of appropriate non-semantic and non-intentional constraints, into a plausible theory of meaning.

Why does the basic formula need to be modified at all? Consider some mental symbol S and suppose it means *horse*. Now we all make mistakes: we are all prone, when conditions are sufficiently unfavorable, to misidentifying items that we are presented with. So it can happen that, when presented with a deceptively horsey looking cow, I misclassify it as a horse: I believe *falsely* of some cow that it is a horse. But that is just to say that, on a given occasion, it is the property of being a cow that is nomically sufficient to cause a tokening of a symbol which means *horse*.

The basic formula, however, can make no sense of this. For according to it, a symbol expresses whatever property is nomically sufficient to cause its tokening; it follows, therefore, that since tokenings of S are also being caused by cows, S cannot simply mean *horse*, but must mean *cow or horse*. In other words, what intuitively seemed to be a case of a non-disjunctive symbol being applied falsely to something not in its extension, the basic formula would have us describe as a case of a disjunctive symbol being applied correctly to something in its extension.

In general, then, since applying a symbol falsely involves applying it to something not in its extension and since, according to the basic formula, every property that can cause the tokening of a symbol is, *ipso facto*, in the extension of that symbol, the basic formula can make no sense of error.

Errors, however, aren't the only way in which a symbol might get caused by something that isn't in its extension. The thought that cows are mammals might get caused by the thought that platypi aren't; this would be a non-erroneous tokening of the expression "cow" yet, nevertheless, not a tokening of the expression that is caused by the property it expresses. Here again, and for much the same reason as before, the basic formula yields the wrong result: it has "cow" meaning *cow or platypus-thought*, whereas "cow" means *cow* and no more.

In sum: because under ordinary circumstances it is possible for a symbol to be caused by something that it does not express—either through error or through its occurrence in a sequence of non-labelling thoughts—the basic formula appears bound to deliver the wrong verdicts about the meaning of practically every expression in the language. Following tradition, we may call this the *disjunction problem*.[8]

It is a condition of adequacy on a causal theory of meaning that it solve this problem. Solving it requires selecting, from among all the laws that govern the

cause S-events, even if there are no Ps: all that's required is that Ps would cause S-events, if there were any.

[8] Causal theories of meaning face, I believe, another serious problem, that of accounting for the *normative* character of the notion of meaning. For a discussion of this point see my 1989b (this volume, Chapter 1).

tokening of a symbol S, that law which is *meaning-determining*: a property M, specifiable without the use of semantic or intentional materials, must be defined so that: possession of M by a nomic cause of a tokening of S is necessary and sufficient for that cause to be in the extension of S.[9]

Those causes of S not possessing M would then not count as in the extension of S and would be free, therefore, to cause tokenings of S that are false.

Meaning-Determining Causal Laws and Type 1 Situations

Suppose that both P and Q are nomic causes of tokenings of S. And suppose that S means P. The causal theorist must somehow select the P → S law as the one that fixes S's meaning. He must specify a property M that is possessed only by the P → S relation. How is this trick to be turned? As Fodor notes, the standard attempts to turn it exhibit a common feature: they attempt to select the P → S law by defining a *situation* in which only Ps can cause tokenings of S. In other words, their common strategy is to attempt to define a situation in which only the referent of a symbol can cause its tokening; they then proceed to identify the fact that the symbol expresses a given property with the fact that it is that property that is solely responsible for causing tokenings of the symbol under that sort of situation. Let us call a situation in which nothing but the referent of a symbol can cause its tokening, a situation of type 1; and let us call theories that specify meaning in terms of such situations, type 1 theories.

Teleological Type 1 Theories

The literature contains a number of proposals concerning the identity of situations of type 1, of which the most influential is the *teleological* proposal. The idea here is that there is a set of Normal conditions, specified by evolutionary biology—hence, one presumes, naturalistically—under which our cognitive mechanisms are functioning just as they are supposed to. The teleological proposal is that we equate type 1 situations—situations under which nothing but the referent of a symbol can cause its tokening—with Normal conditions so specified.

Its prima facie appeal notwithstanding, the teleological proposal suffers from a number of severe problems, some of which are outlined very effectively by

---

[9] Strictly speaking, of course, it is instances of a property, rather than the property itself, that are said to be in extensions. To avoid prolixity, however, I shall continue to talk of properties as being in extensions; it is hardly likely to cause confusion.

It is sometimes suggested that it would be enough if possession of M were *sufficient* for being in the extension of S. But that is not right. If only sufficiency were required, we would not know S's meaning simply as a result of a definition of M. For although we would know what properties were definitely in the extension of S, we would not know if we had them all. Thus, a definition of M would not even constitute a sufficient condition for a symbol possessing a given meaning, which is the very least required from a (naturalistic) theory meaning.

Fodor.[10] First, it rests on an incredible conception of evolutionary selection assuming, for instance, that cognitive mechanisms are never selected for the purpose of hiding, rather than tracking, the truth. Second, it does not really solve the disjunction problem because facts about teleological function go soft at precisely the point at which the disjunction problem arises. And, finally, the root idea upon which the teleological proposal depends—the assumption that "when things go right" S will be tokened only in application to its referent—seems simply wrong. As Fodor observes, a glaring counterexample is provided by the humdrum phenomenon of one thought causing another. In the course of musing about horses I might be led to muse about cows. This would be a case of a horse-thought causing a cow-thought, hence, not a case of a cow-thought being caused by its referent. But also, surely, not a case where anything has gone wrong from a teleological point of view. The point is that, even if evolutionary biology could help define a set of conditions which abstract from sources of *error*, it is hardly likely to help define a set of conditions which abstract from *thinking*. It is hardly likely, therefore, to deliver what a type 1 theory of meaning needs: a non-intentionally, non-semantically specified situation in which only the referent of a symbol can cause its tokening.

Fodor's Theory: Assymmetric Dependence

Now, all this is, I think, pretty much decisive against teleological versions of type 1 theories. In fact, however, Fodor disapproves not merely of *teleological* versions of type 1 theories, but of *any* type 1 causal theory of meaning. He says:

what's *really* wrong with teleological theories of content … is the idea that [in a certain kind of circumstance] the tokens of a symbol can have only one kind of cause—viz. the kind of cause that fixes meaning. … But surely this underestimates … the *robustness* of meaning: In actual fact, "cow" tokens get caused in *all sorts* of ways, and they all mean *cow* for all of that … If there's really going to be a causal theory of content, there has to be some way of picking out *semantically relevant* causal relations from all the other kinds of causal relations that the tokens of a symbol enter into. *And we'd better not do this by implicitly denying robustness—e.g. by idealizing to contexts of etiological homogeneity.*[11]

And he commends his own view (to which we will come below) for having

the desirable property of not assuming that there are such things as Type one situations; in particular, it doesn't assume that there are circumstances—nomologically possible and naturalistically and otherwise nonquestion beggingly specifyable—in which it's semantically necessary that only cows cause "cows."[12]

---

[10] Fodor 1990, ch. 3.
[11] Ibid., pp. 90–1; final emphasis mine.
[12] Ibid., p. 91.

Well, how are we to naturalistically specify a symbol's meaning-determining causal relations without "assuming that there are such things as type 1 situations." The crux of Fodor's proposal is neatly summed up in the following passage:

Cows cause "cow" tokens, and (let's suppose) cats cause "cow" tokens. But "cow" means *cow* and not *cat* or *cow or cat* because *there being cat-caused "cow" tokens depends on there being cow-caused "cow" tokens, but not the other way around.* "Cow" means *cow* because, as I shall henceforth put it, noncow-caused "cow" tokens are *assymmetrically dependent upon* cow-caused "cow" tokens.[13]

How, precisely, is this to be understood? It's not, I'm afraid, all that easy to say.

The trouble stems, on the one hand, from Fodor's insistence that the theory is best understood directly in terms of the nomic concepts in which it's couched; and, on the other, from the conspicuous absence of any account of those concepts. Fodor bemoans counterfactual analyses of law and possible worlds analyses of counterfactuals, castigating them as exemplifying the "sort of reductive move that is always blowing up in philosophers' faces." It is hard, in view of the less than spectacular achievements of the analytic enterprise, not to sympathize with this. But the fact remains that we need *some* handle on how the theory is to be understood and those accounts, warts and all, are the best we've got at the present time. Having acknowledged Fodor's reservations, then, I propose henceforth to ignore them. I shall expound his theory in terms of the language of counterfactuals and possibilia of which he disapproves. In proceeding in this fashion, I am emboldened by the fact that, although I may be flouting Fodor's ideology, I am not flouting his actual practice:

Having gotten all that off my chest, I shall join the crowd and talk counterfactuals from time to time, faute de mieux. And since it's widely supposed that talk about counterfactuals itself translates into talk about possibilia, I shall sometimes equate "there is a nomic dependence between the property of being a *Y* and the property of being a cause of *X*s" with "*Y*s cause *X*s in all (nearby? see below) nomologically possible worlds."[14]

What, then, is the proposed sufficient condition for S's meaning P? A first counterfactual approximation would have it that S means P if it satisfies the following condition. If P ceases being capable of causing S tokens, then every other cause of S is rendered similarly impotent; but not the other way around: any non-P could cease being capable of causing S tokens without this affecting P's ability to do so.

It may strike you, right off the bat, that this suggestion couldn't be right because it would have us thinking not about, say, cows but about their proximal projections. For it's presumably true that no cow would cause a "cow" token

---

[13] Ibid., p. 91.
[14] Ibid., p. 95.

except as it produces some proximal projection. And it's plausible, moreover, that such proximal stimuli would be sufficient to cause "cow" tokens even if they weren't produced by cows. If all this is true, then it would appear that the cow-prompted "cow" tokens are asymmetrically dependent on the disjunction of proximal cow projections, and hence, on the terms of the theory on offer, that "cow" means not *cow* but that inner disjunction instead.

Fodor, however, won't admit any of this and for reasons to which we shall have occasion to return:

It might still be said, however, that the dependence of cow thoughts on distal cows is asymmetrically dependent on their dependence on *disjunctions* of proximal cow projections; distal cows wouldn't evoke COW tokens but that they project proximal whiffs or glimpses or snaps or crackles or. ... well, or what? Since, after all, cow spotting can be mediated by theory to any extent you like, the barest whiff or glimpse of cow can do the job for an observer who is suitably attuned ... To the extent that this is so, just about *any* proximal display might mediate the relation between cows and cow-thoughts for some cow-thinker on some or other cow-spotting occasion ... So barring appeals to *open* disjunctions, it seems likely that there is just no way to specify an array of proximal stimulations upon which the dependence of cow-thoughts on cows is asymmetrically dependent.[15]

The bruited objection is no good, Fodor says, because it ignores the holistic and open-ended character of belief fixation. Since just about any theory can mediate the fixation of beliefs about cows, just about any proximal stimulation can cause a "cow" token; and open disjunctions of properties are not eligible to serve as the referents of our primitive expressions.

Now, there is room for doubting the effectiveness of this rejoinder, but I propose for the time being to accept it. The effect is to restrict the referents of our predicates to their *distal* causes; and so, on Fodor's view, S means P, if P is the distal cause of S tokens on which all the other distal causes of S tokens depend. Henceforth, let it be so understood.

Another prima facie difficulty with the theory will help specify it further. So far we have it "cow" has cows in its extension but not cats, because if the cow → "cow" connection were to break, then so would the cat → "cow" connection, but not vice versa. Put in the language of possibilia, this seems best interpreted as suggesting that "cow" has cows in its extension and not cats, provided that, although there are worlds in which *cow* can cause a "cow" token but *cat* can't, there are no worlds in which *cat* can cause a "cow" token, but *cow* can't.

This, however, can't be precisely what's meant. The point is, of course, that even by the theory's own lights, there have to be *some* worlds in which the property of being a cat can cause "cow" tokens even if the property of being a cow can't, for there presumably are some worlds in which "cow" means

---

[15] Fodor 1990, pp. 109–10.

cat. A more accurate statement of the theory, then, would have it that what's required

is *not* that cows cause "cow"s in *every* nomologically possible world where *X*s cause "cow"s. Rather, what's required is just that there be worlds where cows cause "cow"s and noncows don't; and that they be nearer to our world than any world in which some noncows cause "cow"s and no cows do.[16]

Asymmetric Dependence and Type 1 Situations

A really plausible theory of content, Fodor says, would not be a type 1 theory: it would not commit itself to the existence of naturalistically specifiable circumstances in which a symbol can get caused only by its referent. As we shall see later on, there is much to be said in favor of this claim.

The trouble is, however, that in all essential respects Fodor's own theory would appear to be a type 1 theory and, hence, itself vulnerable to the attendant problems. Let me explain.

A traditional type 1 theory has it that S means P because, in a favored naturalistically specified circumstance C, only P can cause S tokens. In such theories, then, the meaning of a symbol is specified directly in terms of *the causes that tokenings of that symbol may have in a certain type of situation*. Now, admittedly, Fodor's theory does not look like that. On his view, the meaning-determining cause is picked out not in terms of its relation to certain kinds of situation, but in terms of its relation to the symbol's other causes: that cause on which the other causes of the symbol asymmetrically depend, is the symbol's meaning. I propose to argue, however, that on the most favorable understanding of the theory on offer, if symbol S possesses asymmetric dependence base P, then there exists a world in which *only* P can serve as a cause of tokenings of S. I propose to argue, in other words, that even Fodor's theory is a type 1 theory, because even asymmetric dependence implies the existence of type 1 situations for symbols.

Suppose that among S's causes are properties P and Q. Now, clearly, a distribution of nearby worlds according to which there are some worlds in which S has only P as a cause, but no worlds in which it has only some non-Ps as a cause, would be *sufficient* to ground P's status as S's asymmetric dependence base; the question is whether such a distribution is *necessary*. Well, what *other* distribution of worlds would also ground the fact in question? The only remotely plausible suggestion is that a distribution of nearby worlds which contains worlds in which both P and Q can cause S tokens, and worlds in which both P and R can, but no world in which only P can and no world in which only non-Ps can, would equally suffice to certify P's status as S's asymmetric dependence base.

---

[16] Fodor 1990, p. 113.

And even *it* doesn't work. For there is nothing to distinguish the envisaged distribution from one in which the real asymmetric dependence base for S's causal relations is not P but, rather,

$$(P \& R)v(P \& Q).$$

Without a world in which only Ps can cause S, the most we would be entitled to claim is that it seems impossible to break any particular non-P causal relation without enforcing at least one of the others (in combination with P). And this falls far short of saying that it is precisely the P → S connection that cannot be broken without breaking all the others.

Now, it might be objected that we are not *guaranteed* that (P & R)v(P & Q) will be a candidate asymmetric dependence base for S whenever P is. That is true, but irrelevant. It is true because there is, in general, no guarantee that whenever P → S is a law and R → S is a law that (P & R)v(P & Q) → S will be a law also. It is irrelevant because the point at issue requires only that there be at least *one* case in which (P & R)v(P & Q) → is a law and, hence, (P & R)v(P & Q) a candidate asymmetric dependence base for S. Since Fodor's theory says that it is a *sufficient* condition of S's meaning X that X be S's asymmetric dependence base, any case in which S has both P and (P & R)v(P & Q) as candidate asymmetric dependence bases will be a case in which his theory yields either the wrong result or an indeterminiate one. Hence, any such case would constitute a straightforward counterexample to his theory. So, as I have said, all that's required is that there be at least one case in which (P & R)v(P & Q) → S is a law whenever P → S is and R → S is; and it seems pretty obvious that there will be plenty of such cases.

To be sure to have eliminated this entire class of counterexamples, then, Fodor's theory must be read as follows: S means whatever properties are possible causes of S tokens in the closest world with the smallest subset of S-token causes in the actual world. Or, in the case of an expression with a *single* property P as referent, S means P if P is the sole cause of S tokens in the closest single-cause world. Or, to put this yet another way: Fodor's theory is a type 1 theory where the type 1 situation for S is specified as being: the closest world in which S can get tokened by only one sort of cause.

Now, Fodor has admitted that asymmetric dependence implies a commitment to the existence of circumstances in which a symbol can get caused only by its referent. But he has denied that this commits him to the sorts of situation envisaged by traditional type 1 theories.

...real type 1 theories say that situations in which only Xs cause Ss are nomologically possible. Whereas my theory says only that the dependence of Ss on Xs is nomically dependent on their dependence on Xs. If you spell this out in terms of possible worlds, then what you get is that worlds in which Xs cause Ss but nonXs don't, are closer, ceteris paribus, than worlds in which nonXs cause Ss but Xs don't. But, notice, ALL THE WORLDS THAT FIGURE IN THIS RELATION ARE, BY ASSUMPTION, NOMOLOGICALLY IMPOSSIBLE. In particular, even the nearest of these worlds breaks the connection between nonXs and Ss, and that connection is, by assumption lawlike. ... So, the difference between my story and a true type 1 story is that true type 1 stories hold that type 1 situations are nomologically possible; and my story doesn't.[17]

I must admit to being somewhat confused by this response, but for reasons that will detain us too long to look into. So I wish simply to grant the point: traditional type 1 situations are conceived as nomologically possible, whereas Fodor's type 1 situations aren't.[18] This particular difference won't matter to anything that's to follow.

For what follows is a set of objections to theories that are based on the existence of type 1 situations, regardless of their nomological status. I shall argue for two main claims. First, that there couldn't be naturalistically specifiable circumstances under which nothing but the referent of a symbol can cause its tokening. And, second, that even if there were such conditions, we could never be in a position to *certify* that there were. I'll end by returning to Fodor's theory and showing explicitly that it does not provide a convincing naturalistic sufficient condition for meaning.

COULD THERE BE NATURALISTIC CONDITIONS OF TYPE 1?

Causal Theories and Verificationism

I propose to begin by arguing that any attempt at specifying a type 1 situation for a symbol S, however refined, is bound to fail: *any* specified situation will contain possible causes of S tokens not in the extension of S.

The reason is painfully obvious: any situation in which X is a possible cause of my S-tokens is also a situation in which any other property Y, indistinguishable from X in all physically possible circumstances accessible to me, is *also* a possible cause of my S-tokens. Since there are no physically possible circumstances accessible to me in which X and Y can be told apart, any circumstance in which X can cause my S tokens is also a circumstance in which Y can. It follows, therefore, that on a type 1 theory, if S has X in its extension, then it also has all these other "X-equivalent" properties equally in its extension. But is this plausible? Is it really true that my having a symbol that means X but not Y depends on my being able to tell Xs and Ys apart? After all, it surely doesn't follow from the fact that Xs and Ys can only be told apart in worlds that are too far for *me* to get to, that being X and being Y are the same property.

---

[17] This is cited from Fodor's reply to a talk I gave on asymmetric dependence at the Eastern Division of the APA in Washington D.C. in December 1988. I shall refer to this reply henceforth as "D.C. Notes." The passage is from p. 9.

[18] Of course, both types of situation are *physically* possible—that is, possible relative to the laws of physics, even if not possible relative to the laws of psychology—which is all that will matter to the discussion that follows.

But, then if the difference between being X and being Y is real, then so too, presumably, is the difference between being X and being (X or Y). And if this difference is real, then why shouldn't we be able to think in ways that respect that difference?[19]

Natural Kind Terms

It will prove useful to present a concrete case of an expression that has X in its extension, but not all its X-equivalent cousins.

I have chosen to focus on natural kind expressions. The choice is particularly apt, for three reasons. First, because natural kind terms are of incontestable importance. Second, because there is the fairly widespread conviction that recent philosophy of language has made significant progress in understanding their *intuitive semantics*. One of the many difficulties that bedevil discussion of the naturalization of semantic properties is the absence, in a significant range of cases, of an intuitively correct semantics to naturalize: we simply don't know what extensions to assign to various expressions under various counterfactual circumstances, and, hence, don't know whether particular naturalistic proposals capture those extensions correctly. Through the recent work of Kripke and Putnam, however, we have in hand the rough contours of a convincing and widely accepted description of the semantic functioning of natural kind expressions; and so a meaningful test becomes possible. Finally, and perhaps most importantly; because causal theorists themselves invariably illustrate their theories with the use of natural kind expressions. It is widely supposed by the proponents of such theories, that causal theories are at their strongest in application to natural kind expressions. It is easy to explain why. The point is that it is part of the moral of the Kripke/Putnam story about natural kind expressions, that they have an intuitively *externalist*, indeed *causal*, semantics: according to such views, it is true independently of any attachment to informational theories of meaning, that causal relations play an important part in fixing the reference of natural kind expressions. So what better candidate for naturalization via a causal theory than a natural kind expression?

In fact, I wish to argue, just the opposite is true; the semantics of such terms, properly understood, resist naturalization by a causal theory.

We need to start off with an account of their intuitive semantics. What, in rough outline, is the Kripke/Putnam account of the reference of such terms as "water," "cow," or "gold"? The essentials are neatly summarized in the following passage from Kripke. A natural kind concept, says Kripke, is the concept of

that kind of thing, where the kind can be identified by paradigmatic instances. It is not something picked out by any qualitative dictionary definition ... [20] The same

---

[19] Cf. Fodor 1990, p. 119.
[20] Kripke 1972, p. 122.

observations hold for such a general term as 'gold.' If we imagine a hypothetical (admittedly somewhat artificial) baptism of the substance, we must imagine it picked out as by some such 'definition' as, 'Gold is the substance instantiated by the items over there, or at any rate, by almost all of them' ... terms for natural kinds (e.g., animal, vegetable, and chemical kinds) get their reference fixed in this way; the substance is defined as the kind instantiated by (almost all of) a given sample.[21]

According to this plausible proposal, then, a natural kind expression S functions *as if* it had been introduced via a reference-fixing description of the following form: S names the naturally delineated kind exemplified by all, or most, of certain local exemplars.[22] Several aspects deserve comment.

First, there is the commitment that the expression name a naturally occurring kind, hence that some sort of basic naturally explanatory property unite all the things that are correctly said to fall in its extension.[23]

Which kind? The kind exemplified by all, or better *most*, of certain local samples. Not simply "all," for we need to allow for impurities in the local samples. "Gold" refers to the substance with atomic number 89, even though not *everything* in the local samples has that atomic number: some of the samples are iron pyrites.

Finally, what if there is no dominant natural kind in the local samples? If investigation uncovers that there is no single hidden structure uniting the local samples, but that there are two (or so) well-defined such structures, then there appears to be a temptation to say that the expression has both of those structures in its extension. Thus, "jade," for example, applies to two minerals, jadeite and nephrite, which are chemically quite different. But if it turns out that nothing but a messy motley of basic properties unites the local samples, then the correct conclusion would appear to be that the term fails to refer: there simply is no naturally delineated kind for the term to refer to.

Does an information-theoretic semantics correctly capture these intuitive results? I shall argue that it does not, and could not.

---

[21] Kripke 1972, pp. 135–6.

[22] I stress the "as if." What we are after here is a description of the intuitive semantics of natural kind expressions, not a theory of the facts in virtue of which they come to have those semantics. What we need to know is what the intuitively correct assignments would be under a variety of counterfactual circumstances, so that we can assess theories that purport to capture those assignments; we don't also need to commit ourselves to a conception of the mechanisms by which they come to have those assignments. I emphasize this because causal theories are restricted to primitive symbols, which for our purposes means "syntactically primitive symbols that are not introduced by definitions." And so, I wish to emphasize that accepting the Kripke/Putnam account of the functioning of natural kind expressions does not imply that these expressions had to have been introduced by definitions. (As Kripke himself notes, the idea of such introductory baptisms is in any case artificial.)

[23] What counts as a basic explanatory property? That's a good question to which I have no decisive answer. Information-theoretic semantics is in any event committed to hyperrealism about which properties are suitable for entering into nomic relations; it is enough for our purposes if we say that the basic explanatory properties will be some proper subset of these.

Causal Theories and Natural Kind Terms

Consider "water." "Water" functions so as to name all and only the stuff bearing the same-liquid relation to all, or most, of such-and-so local samples. As it happens, that stuff is H_2O; so "water" refers to H_2O. It has all and only H_2O molecules in its extension. It does not have such possible substances as XYZ in its extension because XYZ is not of the same kind as H_2O, even though an ordinary speaker exposed to XYZ would call it "water."

Now, XYZ does not provide a straightforward counterexample to a type 1 informational theory of meaning, because it is part of the standard story about XYZ that there are physically accessible circumstances under which XYZ is distinguishable from H_2O. So there presumably are worlds where you would call H_2O "water" but not XYZ—namely, in those worlds where you could tell them apart.

But consider a substance—ABC—which is just like XYZ in being kind-distinct from H_2O, but yet which is distinguishable from H_2O only in circumstances that are physically inaccessible to humans. Let's suppose that this is because ABC would exhibit its distinctive characteristics only in gravitational fields of such intensity—characteristic of the interior of black holes—that nothing as complex as a human body could survive in them long enough to perform even the fleetest measurement; we needn't be too fussy about the physical details. ABC exists in abundance on Pluto, and hence is a potential, even if not actual, cause of "water" tokens.

Is such a substance coherently imaginable? Well, is there anything in physics that precludes the possibility of kind-distinct molecules that behave in precisely the same ways *in all circumstances physically accessible to human beings?* I know of no theorem of physics that precludes this. Which is not, if you think about it, all that surprising. For, remember, what's at issue is not the possibility of kind-distinct molecules that behave in exactly the same way in *all* physically possible worlds, but only the possibility of kind-distinct molecules that behave in exactly the same ways in all the physically possible worlds *that we can get to*, which is a rather different matter. And so physics couldn't preclude the possibility of such substances, because physics doesn't taxonomize molecules with reference to our biological and medical limitations. So far as I can tell, then, there is absolutely no reason to believe that two molecules *couldn't* differ in respect of the sorts of property that make for a difference in kind, if they are distinguishable only in situations that are inaccessible to human beings.

Yet standard intuition would have it, I submit, that ABC is no more in the extension of "water" than XYZ is. "Water" is, as we have said, a natural kind term; it either denotes the non-disjunctive property exemplified by most paradigm local samples, or it denotes nothing. This kind, as it happens, is H_2O, not XYZ or ABC. Yet pure informational theories cannot respect this result. Since such theories equate what a term means with what could cause their tokening under a certain sort of physically accessible circumstance, and since there is no physically accessible circumstance under which H_2O could but ABC couldn't cause a tokening of "water," pure informational theories have to conclude—contrary to intuition—that both H_2O and ABC are in the extension of "water."

The problem, of course, is general. Provided only that it is consistent with the laws of physics that there could have been substances, kind-distinct from the ones that are actual, but which would manifest their distinctive features only in circumstances that are inaccessible to humans, it will follow, on a pure informational theory, that all our 'natural kind terms' have wildly disjunctive extensions, and hence are not really natural kind terms after all. And I would be very surprised if it weren't consistent with physics that there could be such substances.[24]

The Actual History Condition

Now, as I have already indicated, Fodor has expressed considerable sympathy with this sort of worry. Indeed, he has gone so far as to propose a modification to his own pure informational theory in an attempt to meet it.[25]

[Pure informational] theories distinguish between concepts only if their tokenings are controlled by different laws. Hence only if different counterfactuals are true of their tokenings. Hence only if there are (possible) circumstances in which one concept

---

[24] In the interests of keeping matters as simple as possible, I have described the case directly in terms of molecules; but it is probably more intuitive to do it first at the level of elementary particles and then work up to the molecular level.

Thus, consider "T." "T" is a name for a certain kind of elementary particle characterized by a particular array of fundamental features—charge, mass, baryon number, charm, what-have-you. It has been frequently observed and its fundamental features have been accurately recorded. It is often the cause of "T" tokens. Now, suppose that there is a physically possible particle T* that, although possessing some fundamental features distinct from T—and, hence, although constituting a different kind of particle than T, according to the basic principles of elementary particle taxonomy—nevertheless would behave just like T in all circumstances accessible to humans, or to appropriate idealizations thereof.

Now, standard intuition would have it, I submit, that T* is not in the extension of "T." "T" is a term in a basic science; it is intended to denote a natural kind: the kind defined by the non-disjunctive property exemplified by paradigm local samples. This kind, as it happens, is T. T* is not of the same kind as T. That much can be incontrovertibly clear: simply let T and T* possess different values for the basic parameters in terms of which physics taxonomizes elementary particles. So T* cannot count as within the extension of "T" and, hence, the use of "T" in application to T* is false.

If there can be kind-distinct *particles* that are indistinguishable, it seems overwhelmingly plausible that there could be kind-distinct *molecules* that are indistinguishable. Not to say that this is an automatic inference. But what with molecules being individuated partly in terms of the atoms that constitute them, and what with atoms being individuated partly in terms of the particles that constitute them, it would be very surprising, to say the least, if it were simply inconsistent with physics that there should be kind-distinct molecules between which no humanly possible experiment could distinguish.

[25] I first expressed this objection in the APA paper. The modification found its way into later drafts of Fodor 1990.

would be caused to be tokened and the other would not ... That is how you get from informational semantics to verificationism ... Correspondingly, the way you avoid the verificationism is: You relax the demand that semantic relations be construed solely by reference to subjunctive conditionals; you let the actual histories of tokenings count too.[26]

Fodor's idea is to block the objectionable verificationist consequences of a pure informational theory by adding an 'actual history' condition: it is now to be required not merely that it be a law that Xs cause S-tokenings, if S is to mean X; it is further required that some S-tokenings *actually* be caused by Xs. And this would appear to rule out the sort of case we have just been contemplating: since it is true by assumption that ABC is only a *potential* cause of "water" tokens, it couldn't actually have caused any tokenings of "water," and, hence, doesn't satisfy the actual history condition. It is, therefore, ineligible to be in the extension of "water," just as intuition requires. So everything would appear to be OK.

Unfortunately, matters are not quite so simple. For one thing, the actual history condition is purchased at a terrible cost. For another, it doesn't ultimately help with the problem about verificationism. And, finally, even if we ignored the issue about verificationism, it still doesn't yield the right meaning ascriptions. All that, in any case, is what I propose to argue next.

It is one of the virtues of a pure informational theory that it can treat "unicorn" in just the way it treats every other syntactically primitive symbol. Since, according to such theories, all that semantic relations care about are nomic connections between properties, and since there can be nomic connections between uninstantiated properties, such theories would appear well-poised to explain—or at least not precluded from explaining—how it is possible for us to represent unicorns, even though there are actually no unicorns. And this seems highly desirable because, on the face of it anyway, there would appear to be no deep connection between being a primitive concept and being instantiated; there seems no reason to believe that every concept that has an empty extension in the *actual* world will turn out to be *complex*.

The actual history condition, however, incurs that implausible commitment. Since it requires that an instance of some property actually have caused a tokening of a symbol that has it in its extension, it must hold that all uninstantiated concepts are, appearances to the contrary notwithstanding, complex. But just what is the (non-question-begging) argument which shows that you couldn't get a primitive concept that was uninstantiated?

The second difficulty with the actual history condition is that it doesn't really help with the problem about verificationism.

Partly for heuristic reasons, I stipulated that ABC was to be found only on Pluto, and not on Earth. But this is, I think, completely inessential to the point it

[26] Fodor 1990, p. 120.

is meant to illustrate. The basic intuition behind the anti-verificationist objection, to repeat, is that there is no reason whatever—intuitive or otherwise—to believe that having a word S that means X but not Y depends on being able, in principle, to tell Xs apart from Ys. If the difference between being X and being (X or Y) is real, why shouldn't we be able to think in ways that respect that difference? But there is absolutely nothing in this intuition which depends on Y's being *remote*. The intuition persists even on the supposition that both of the substances in question are involved in the actual causal history of S-tokenings. Fodor says:

The mixed theory is itself just a *soupçon* verificationist, but only in a way that might surely be considered untendentious. We used to have to say that "X"'s meaning X requires the nomological possibility of distinguishing X from any property that *would* cause "X"s *if it were instantiated* ... Now all we require is that it be nomologically possible to distinguish X from any property that is *actually* instantiated in the causal history of "X"s.[27]

But I don't see that this is any less tendentious than the verificationism entrained by the original pure version. To be sure, the present proposal cuts down on the number of properties that must be distinguishable, if they are to be ineligible to count as in the extension of the term in question. But the end result is no more plausible: the theory continues to deliver verdicts that are at odds with the intuitive semantics of natural kind terms.

We may illustrate this by describing a situation in which ABC is instanced locally. Trace quantities of it, let us suppose, exist in our lakes and rivers and in the atmosphere. It is sometimes, even if rarely, the cause of "water" tokenings. It remains, as before, however, indistinguishable from H_2O in any circumstance accessible to humans. Thus, there is no possible circumstance under which H_2O can cause "water" tokens and ABC can't.

Standard intuition would have it, I submit, that ABC is still not in the extension of "water." ABC remains a different *kind* of stuff from H_2O; and the intuitive semantics of "water" is such that, if it denotes anything at all, it denotes the kind exemplified by most of the paradigmatic local samples. ABC, however, is not exemplified by most of the local samples; by stipulation, it exists only in trace quantities. It stands to water like iron pyrites stand to gold: it is an impurity. Hence, it does not count as within the extension of "water."

Still, this is a judgment that the mixed theory cannot respect. ABC is an occasional cause of "water" tokens, so it satisfies the actual history condition. Since it is not physically distinguishable from H_2O, there is no physically possible circumstance in which H_2O can and ABC can't cause tokenings of "water." So, contrary to intuition, it counts as in the extension of "water."

In sum: an informational theory of meaning is necessarily verificationist and the implausibility of this verificationism can be vividly illustrated through

---

[27] Fodor 1990, p. 122.

the consideration of expressions—like natural kind terms—which intuitively possess non-disjunctive extensions but which are assigned wildly disjunctive extensions by such theories.[28]

COULD YOU RECOGNIZE NATURALISTIC CONDITIONS OF TYPE 1?

I have been arguing that it won't prove possible to naturalistically specify a situation of type 1 because, even if you could naturalistically specify a situation in which all *verifiable* sources of error had been removed, you couldn't, in the nature of things, specify a situation in which all *unverifiable* sources of error had been removed. But since unverifiability doesn't correctness make, the most refined attempt at a naturalistic specification of a type 1 situation is bound to fail.

I now want to argue that, even if, *per impossible*, there were naturalistic situations of type 1, we could never be in a position to recognize that there were. If, by a stroke of vastly implausible luck, we were to stumble onto a specification of such a condition, we could never be entitled to conclude that we had. If this is true, then there can be no point in attempting to develop such theories.

Type 1 Conditions and Belief Holism

The single most impressive reason for being skeptical about the existence of situations in which only the referent of a symbol can cause its tokening has to do with what we may call the *holistic character of belief fixation*.[29] I shall explain.

Under normal circumstances, belief fixation is mediated by background theory—what contents a thinker is prepared to judge depends upon what other

---

[28] That's one side of the coin; the other side is that such theories would assign disjunctive extensions to expressions even when the correct result is that they have *no* extensions, because they fail to refer.

Thus, it would appear to follow from the account of natural kind expressions that we have been working with, that if there were no natural kind uniting the local paradigm samples used to fix the referent of S—if, for example, the only thing the chosen exemplars had in common was a messy motley of basic properties—that S would fail to refer. But informational theories cannot respect this result.

Again, the easiest way to see this is by emphasizing the verificationism entrained by such theories. Just imagine that the samples used to fix the extension of "water" contain a myriad distinct but indistinguishable substances. Then, all those substances will be in the extension of the term "water," even though the intuitive result is that none should be. (A myriad of kind-distinct but humanly indistinguishable water-like substances may seem far-fetched; but that's no objection to its use in the present context.)

[29] A version of this argument was first given in my 1986. I also give a related argument in my 1989b (this volume, Chapter 1).

contents he is prepared to judge.[30] And this dependence is again typically, arbitrarily robust: just about any stimulus can cause just about any belief, given a suitably mediating set of background assumptions.

So, for example, suppose you think, in response to some stimulus or other, "Lo, a magpie." Need there really be a magpie in respect of which this is thought? Of course not. It could be that you saw a currawong, but believing there to be no currawongs in Australia, and believing this to be Australia, you concluded it was a magpie. Or perhaps you heard a currawong call and you believe that that is just what magpies sound like. Or then, again, perhaps you believe that whatever the Pope says goes and the Pope says that this presented currawong is a magpie. Or … . The point is that magpie beliefs can be mediated by theory to any extent you care to imagine. The thought that something is a magpie can get triggered by a currawong in any of an *indefinite* number of ways, corresponding to the potentially indefinite number of background beliefs which could mediate the transition.

We have had occasion to remark on this doctrine before and to note its importance for Fodor's purposes. The point surfaces, as we saw, in the course of showing that it doesn't follow from the asymmetric dependence story about meaning that the intentional content of "cow" is not *cow*, but rather some disjunction of proximal cow projections. Just about any cow-projection can cause a cow-thought, Fodor argues, since just about any theory can mediate the fixation of beliefs about cows. That is why cow-projections are not eligible to serve as the referents of our expressions. But by the same token, just about any *non-cow* can cause a cow-thought too, if just about any theory can mediate the fixation of beliefs about cows. Indeed, it follows, and is in any case independently plausible, that just about any property can cause just about *any* thought, given a suitable set of background assumptions.

But now we are in a position to see why the existence of naturalistically specifiable situations of type 1 should appear so wild. A type 1 situation is, by definition, a situation in which, if the concept *magpie* gets tokened, then it's nomologically necessary that that tokening was caused by a magpie. Specifying a situation of type 1 naturalistically will involve, therefore, specifying a situation, in non-semantic and non-intentional terms, in which one can think "Lo, a magpie" only in application to magpies.

But the point about the holistic character of belief fixation suggests that *anything* can cause the thought "Lo, a magpie" in just about *any* type of situation provided only that the appropriate background beliefs are present. And, as I have argued, these background beliefs could be just about anything. Consequently, specifying a situation in which no non-magpie can cause the thought "Lo, a magpie" involves, at a minimum, specifying a situation that ensures the absence of

---

[30] Note that this is *psychological* holism, not the controversial doctrine of semantic holism. Fodor, for example, rejects the latter; but, as we have seen, it is very important for his purposes that he accept the former.

all the beliefs which could potentially mediate the transition from non-magpies to magpies. Since, however, there looks to be a potential infinity of such mediating background clusters of belief, a non-semantically specified situation of type 1 would consist in the specification of a situation in which it has somehow been non-semantically guaranteed that none of this potential infinity of background clusters of belief is present. And it appears utterly incredible that there should be such a specification.

The impact of this observation on various *particular* proposals is transparent. For example, the observation that type 1 conditions must exclude a potentially indefinite array of frustrating background beliefs provides us with one more way of saying what is wrong with a teleological causal theory: it is simply not plausible to suppose that our cognitive mechanisms' functioning as they are supposed to is sufficient to ensure the absence of any untoward background theory. Hence, it is not plausible to claim, as a teleological theory does, that when they are so functioning, it will prove impossible to think "Lo, a magpie," except in application to magpies. But does the observation provide us with a more general reason for doubting the feasibility of a type 1 style causal theory of meaning? I think it does.

Suppose you come up with a naturalistic specification of some situation C, which you conjecture to be a type 1 condition: under C, nothing but the referents of symbols can cause their tokenings. Could you show that your conjecture was in fact true? I want to argue that you could never non-question-beggingly certify that C is a condition of the required kind, even if it is one.

The worry that needs allaying is that the specified condition is consistent with the presence of background beliefs which would frustrate the covariation between symbol tokenings and their referents—magpie beliefs and magpies, as it may be. Putting this worry to rest requires showing that the situation's being C is enough to ensure the truth of the following open conjunction:

$$(*) \qquad \sim\text{Bel}_1 \ \& \sim\text{Bel}_2 \ \& \sim\text{Bel}_3 \ \& \ldots$$

where the Bel_i stand for the various clusters of background beliefs which could potentially frustrate the connection between being a magpie and the tokening of an expression which refers to it. Well, could C ever be recognized as sufficient for the truth of $(*)$?

Recognizing that a particular naturalistic condition ensures the absence of a set of beliefs, requires possession of naturalistic *necessary* conditions for those beliefs; we need to be able to tell that nothing in the naturalistic condition in question adds up to one of the beliefs in question. Now, we may, for present purposes, assume that we possess naturalistic necessary conditions for something's being a *belief*. But possession of naturalistic necessary conditions for being the *belief that p* requires possession of naturalistic necessary conditions for something's *meaning p*.

Now, suppose that the envisaged C condition is in fact a type 1 condition for *magpie*. Under the terms of this assumption, there would be naturalistic *sufficient* conditions for meaning: type 1 causal theories of meaning, remember, are advertised as providing no more than sufficient conditions for meaning. However, what's needed to certify that C is a type 1 condition for *magpie* is a certification that it is sufficient for the truth of (*); and what's needed to certify that it is sufficient for the truth of (*) is a set of naturalistic *necessary* conditions for meaning. So, we can't certify that C is a type 1 condition for *magpie*, even on the assumption that it is one. So, we can't certify that it is one.

Suppose, however, that the causal theorist sheds his modesty and promotes his theory as providing both necessary and sufficient conditions for meaning. As before, we have a specification of C, but now it is a clause in a *necessary and sufficient* condition for S meaning M. Could we now certify that C is a type 1 condition for *magpie*, on the assumption that it is one?

Well, on the assumption that it is one, there would be a set of necessary and sufficient conditions for an expression's expressing a certain property. Unfortunately, even so, we would still not be in a position to certify that C is a type 1 condition. The trouble is that proposition (*) is not finitely stateable: there is no finite way to state what beliefs the causal theorist must exclude before he may be assured of the desired concomitance of magpie beliefs and magpies. Literally any belief can frustrate the desired connection. So, there is no way to certify that C is sufficient for the truth of (*), even granted a set of naturalistic necessary and sufficient conditions for meaning. So, there is no way to certify that C is a type 1 condition for *magpie*.

If these considerations are correct, then there can be no point in constructing type 1 naturalistic theories of meaning. Even if, *per impossibile*, we were somehow to stumble onto such a theory, we could never convince ourselves that we had. For perfectly general reasons, we could never non-question-beggingly certify that a particular naturalistic condition was in fact a type 1 situation.

ASYMMETRIC DEPENDENCE REVISITED

If any of this is true, then Fodor's asymmetric dependence proposal could not constitute a convincing naturalistic sufficient condition for meaning. For as we have seen, Fodor's theory is a type 1 theory in disguise: to say that P is an asymmetric dependence base for S is simply to say that P is the sole cause of S tokens in the closest world where S has a single cause. And so, since it is the burden of the preceding considerations that there can be no convincing naturalistic specification of a type 1 situation, either Fodor's criterion yields the wrong meaning ascriptions, or it is not naturalistic in character.

Nevertheless, since arguments at this level of generality can seem disengaged from their targets, and since it may in any event prove independently edifying, I now propose to run through the relevant dialectic with explicit reference to the details of Fodor's particular proposal. I propose to show directly, in other words, that Fodor's asymmetric dependence condition for S's meaning P is either not naturalistic, or not sufficient for S's meaning P.

Let's go back to H_2O and XYZ. As before, "water" is undoubtedly a natural kind term, so it has H_2O in its extension but not XYZ; and, as before, it is true by stipulation that both H_2O and XYZ are nomically sufficient to cause tokenings of "water." What makes it true, according to Fodor, that "water" means H_2O and not XYZ, is that the closest world in which "water" tokens can get caused by one and not the other of these properties, is a world in which it is H_2O that can do the causing, and not XYZ.

But *closer* with respect to what? Clearly, everything depends on whether the relevant similarity relation can be specified non-question-beggingly—without the benefit of sidelong looks at the meanings of the expressions in question. What the success of Fodor's theory depends on, in other words, is that when nearness of worlds is judged from a purely non-semantic and non-intentional—for our purposes, therefore, from a purely physical—point of view, the H_2O-only world always turns out to be closer than the XYZ-only world. Will this be true?

Now, Fodor thinks that the results are bound to turn out as desired because:

... to get to a world where we can [infallibily] tell XYZ from H_2O, you have to either change us (provide us with instruments of observation we don't now have, for example) or change H_2O/XYZ (make their molecular structure visible to the naked eye, for example) or do both. But now, having gotten to such a world, if you want to also make it the case that our "water" tokens track XYZ rather than H_2O (or XYZ and H_2O) you would also have to change something about us which corresponds to the disposition which, I take it, everybody agrees underlies our use of "water" in THIS world, viz., our disposition to use "water" only of things that bear the same kind relation to our local samples.

So you'd have to change more things to get to a world where XYZ is distinguishable from H_2O and our use of "water" tracks XYZ than you would to get to a world where XYZ is distinguishable from H_2O and our use of "water" tracks H_2O ... of course, this extra thing that you'd have to change IS an intention to use "water" as a kind term; and that intention may or may not be a physical state (depending on whether physicalism is true of our intentions).[31]

To get from our world to an XYZ-only world, argues Fodor, you have to make H_2O infallibly distinguishable from XYZ *and* you have to change whatever intentional facts ground the fact that in this world "water" means H_2O; whereas, to get to an H_2O-only world, you have only to make XYZ infallibly distinguishable from H_2O. Hence, any XYZ-only world is bound to be further than any H_2O-only world.

To begin to get a sense of what's wrong with this argument we may start with the observation that the purely physical changes involved need not be on a par. From a purely physical standpoint, it may be much easier to get to a world

[31] D.C. Notes, p. 10.

where you will apply "water" only to XYZ, if you want to, than to get to a world where you will apply "water" only to H_2O, if you want to. This ought to be obvious. To bring it about that H_2O never gets confused for XYZ (or anything else for that matter), you only have to bring it about that H_2O has some unique distinguishing and infallibly detectable property; you don't also have to bring it about that XYZ is never confused for anything else. Vice versa for bringing it about that XYZ is never confused for H_2O. But bringing it about that some substance has some unique infallibly detectable property is a function not only of our detecting capacities but of the substance's chemistry as well. And so, it seems inevitable that it will be easier to render some substances infallibly detectable than others.

Imagine, in fact, that the chemistry of XYZ is such that, by the merest altera- tion of some tissue in our nostrils, we are able to *smell* its presence wherever it may be. In a world with the contemplated nasal alteration, XYZ is uniquely and infallibly detectable by the foul scent it gives off. In that world, then, there is no problem ensuring that "water" gets applied only to XYZ (if that's what you want to do): all you have to do is ensure that it gets applied only to substances that give off the distinctive scent. It doesn't follow, of course, that this foul-smelling world is equally optimal for the infallible detection of H_2O—H_2O need give off no distinctive scent of its own in this world, and may remain confusable with substances other than XYZ. Nor does it follow that it will be *equally* easy to get to a world in which H_2O is in like manner infallibly detectable: H_2O's chemistry may not allow for that. Getting to a world in which you apply "water" only to H_2O, if you want to, may involve making many more changes in us and our surroundings than it took getting to the foul-smelling XYZ world.

Suppose in fact that that's precisely the way things are. To get, then, from our world—in which "water" means H_2O—to a world in which "water" gets applied only to H_2O, you have to make a big physical change; to get to a world in which it gets applied only to XYZ, you have to make a small physical change and a small intentional change. Now: which world is closer to ours?

Well, if the distance measure were specified as follows, the answer would be clear: all physical changes are on a par, and every intentional change counts for as much as every physical change. But, of course, this specification would be entirely question-begging in the present context. It is not allowed to specify the similarity relation in intentional terms. And yet, on the other hand, I don't see that any other specification will yield anything like the desired results.

Fodor says:

... of course, this extra thing that you'd have to change IS an intention to use "water" as a kind term; and that intention may or may not be a physical state (depending on whether physicalism is true of our intentions). But you don't ... have to MENTION its being an intention to say what I just did say ... viz., that you have to change more things to get to worlds where H_2O is distinguishable from XYZ AND our "water" tokens track XYZ ... than you have to change to get to a world where H_2O

is distinguishable from XYZ and our "water" tokens track just H_2O. So it doesn't look to me as though the required notion of distance is question-begging.[32]

This argument depends on the claim that getting to a world in which H_2O is infallibly detectable involves exactly as much (or as little) as getting to a world in which XYZ is. Thus, the detecting changes drop out, leaving the intentional change to settle the matter. But as I have just argued, there is absolutely no reason to believe this.

If we correct for the false assumption, it is perfectly plain, I think, that there will be no non-question-begging way of getting the H_2O-only world to come out closer than the XYZ-only world. Judged from a purely physical standpoint, the XYZ-only world may well come out closer. And no other standpoint is acceptable in the present context. Hence, Fodor's theory is either false, or it's not naturalistic.[33]

---

[32] D.C. Notes.

[33] I want to express a special debt of gratitude to Jerry Fodor for sharing and discussing his work with me over several years. For much helpful discussion I am also grateful to Jennifer Church, Allan Gibbard, Jaegwon Kim, Barry Loewer, Stephen Schiffer, Larry Sklar, David Velleman and Steve Yablo.

4 *Is Meaning Normative?*[1]

INTRODUCTION

The claim that meaning is a normative notion has become very influential in recent philosophy: in the work of many philosophers it plays a pivotal role.[2] Although one can trace the idea of the normativity of meaning at least as far back as Kant, much of the credit for its recent influence must go to Saul Kripke who made the thesis a centerpiece of his much-admired treatment of Wittgenstein's discussion of rule-following and private language.

Kripke, as you may recall, attributes to Wittgenstein the exciting and potentially paradoxical thesis that there can be no facts to the effect that people mean things by their words. To establish this startling claim, he proceeds by elimination: all the facts that are potentially relevant to fixing the meaning of an expression are examined and rejected.[3]

Among the most promising candidates for being the facts in virtue of which I mean, for example, addition by '+' are facts concerning my dispositions to use that symbol in a certain way. Although this may not appear obvious at first sight, in fact the two leading naturalistic theories for the fixation of content—informational semantics and inferential role semantics—are both versions of a dispositional theory in the relevant sense.

Against this popular idea about naturalizing meaning, Kripke deploys a number of considerations: that our dispositions are finite; that one cannot read off our dispositions what we mean because our dispositions may include dispositions to make errors; and so forth. However, even if it were possible to overcome these objections, Kripke argues, one could still not identify meaning facts with dispositional facts because at bottom the relation between meaning and future use is *normative*, whereas the dispositionalist construes it descriptively.

In a moment, we shall look at how this observation is supposed to work in some detail. But the important point to note is that, if the alleged normativity of meaning is to be used in this anti-naturalist way, to knock out proposed

---

[1] This paper overlaps with, and tries to improve upon, the discussion of this issue in my 2003c.
[2] See McDowell 1984, Wright 1984b, Blackburn 1984b, and Gibbard 2003b.
[3] I discuss Kripke's line of reasoning in more detail in my 1989b (this volume, Chapter 1).

theories of meaning, it must be established intuitively and pre-theoretically, as something that every theory of meaning would have to respect, and not on the basis of assumptions about the nature of meaning that a naturalist could regard as optional.

In what, sense, then, is meaning intuitively normative and how does that help defeat naturalist conceptions of it?

KRIPKE ON THE NORMATIVITY OF MEANING

For expository purposes, I will work with the simple version of the dispositional theory that Kripke operates with, for nothing essential will depend on the simplification. As Kripke tells it, then, the dispositionalist attempts to explain what it is for me to mean addition by '+' by saying that it consists in my being disposed to respond to the question

$$x + y = ?$$

with a number that is the *sum* of x and y, as opposed to my being disposed to respond with a number that is their *quum* (where the quum of $x + y$ is their sum if x, y < 57, and is 5 otherwise).

There are, of course, serious problems in getting a dispositionalist account to work, even putting aside issues about normativity. The main difficulty is to get a dispositional theory to be extensionally adequate so that it yields the correct verdicts about what people mean by their expressions. And the main problem here is to naturalistically specify a set of optimality conditions which will be such that, under those conditions a thinker will be disposed to apply an expression to something if and only if that item is in its extension.[4]

According to Kripke, though, we needn't bother trying to see if we can ever find such a set of optimality conditions because there is a problem of principle in seeking to reduce meaning facts to facts about dispositions. Kripke writes:

Suppose I do mean addition by '+'. What is the relation of that supposition to the question of how I will respond to the problem '68 + 57'? The dispositionalist gives a descriptive account of this relation: if '+' meant addition, then I will answer '125'. But this is not the proper account of the relation, which is normative, not descriptive. The point is not that, if I meant addition by '+' I will answer '125', but that I *should* answer '125'. ... The relation of meaning and intention to future action is normative and not descriptive.[5]

Notice that Kripke's formulations—both of problem and of solution—tend to be in terms of the notion of *linguistic meaning* rather than in terms of *mental content*, although his argumentative strategy makes it clear that he holds that both

---

[4] This problem is discussed at some length in my 1989b and my 1991 (this volume, Chapters 1 and 3 respectively).

[5] Kripke 1982, p. 37.

notions are normative. In fact, it is important for present purposes to distinguish between them. I will begin with the thesis as applied to linguistic meaning.

Is it really true that, if I mean addition by '+', then, if am asked what the sum of 58 and 67 is, I *should* answer '125'? What if I feel like lying or misleading my audience? Is it still true then that I should answer '125'? If I want to mislead, it looks as though I should not say '125' but rather some other number.

Of course, we can say that, if you mean addition by '+' and have a desire to tell the truth, then, if you are asked what the sum of those two numbers is, you should say '125.' But that is mere hypothetical normativity, and that is uninteresting: every fact is normative in that sense. (Compare: if it's raining, and you don't want to get wet, you should take your umbrella.)

If there is to be an interesting thesis of the normativity of meaning, we ought to be able to derive a should or an ought from the mere attribution of meaning to someone and without having to rely on any auxiliary desires that that person may or may not have. But can we do that?

Does it follow from the mere fact that I mean addition by '+' that I should not lie or mislead? There may be, for all I know, a *moral* prohibition against lying or misleading; but are there such prohibitions flowing from the nature of meaning itself? I suppose there have been philosophers who have held complicated views to the effect that the very possibility of meaning requires that lies and deception not be very common.

But, first, it is not at all clear that these philosophers are right. And, second, and as I emphasized at the beginning, what we are after is some intuitive thesis to the effect that meaning is normative, not something that would lie at the end of some complicated 'transcendental' argument. What, however, is the intuitive normative truth that falls directly out of the attribution of meaning, so that such normativity can then be used as a constraint on theories of meaning?

One thought that might seem to be in the right neighborhood is this:

> If I mean addition by '+' then, although I may not be disposed to say '125', in response to the question $68 + 57 =$?, it is *correct* for me to say '125'.

The trouble is that it is not clear that, at least as it is being used here, "correct" expresses a normative notion, for it may just mean "true." Of course, if I mean addition by '+' then I will only have said something *true* if I say '125.' But there is no obvious sense in which truth is a normative notion.

In my own earlier work on what are referred to as the "rule-following considerations," I underestimated the force of this point. In that paper, I wrote:

Suppose the expression 'green' means *green*. It follows immediately that the expression 'green' applies *correctly* only to these things (the green ones) and not to those (the non-greens). ... The normativity of meaning turns out to be, in other words, simply a new name for the familiar fact that ... meaningful expressions possess conditions of *correct use*. Kripke's insight was to realize that this observation may be converted into a condition of adequacy on theories of the determination of meaning: any proposed candidate for the property in virtue of which an expression has meaning, must be such as to ground the 'normativity' of meaning ... it ought to be possible to read off from any alleged meaning-constituting property of a word what is the correct use of that word.[6]

As I now see it, there is nothing wrong with the substance of this passage: there *is* a problem capturing an expression's satisfaction conditions in dispositional terms. But it is misleading at best to use the label "the normativity of meaning" in connection with this problem since, as I remarked above, there is nothing obviously normative about the notion of a truth condition or a satisfaction condition. (Putting the word 'normativity' in shudder quotes, as I did, helps, but in retrospect, more skepticism about its use was probably in order.)

Well, what conditions must an expression satisfy if it is to express a genuinely normative notion? This is, of course, a difficult question, but a first stab might well look like this:

> An expression E expresses a normative notion only if it is *constitutive* of our *understanding* of E that its application implies an *ought* or a *may*.

Later on, I will come back to what we should take "constitutive" and "ought" to mean in this context. But however liberal we may be with these notions, it seems to me, we have been shown no clear reason to think that "true" is a normative notion (I shall come back to this).

Consider, however, the corresponding observation in the case of *content and belief* rather than in that of *meaning and assertion*:

> If it is addition that I am thinking in terms of, rather than quaddition, then although I may not be disposed to believe that $68 + 57 = 125$, because I have, we may suppose, a tendency to make certain kinds of arithmetical error, still it is only *correct for me to believe* that $68 + 57 = 125$.

In this case, it looks as though there may be a real chance that the notion of correctness in question doesn't just mean "true" but expresses something genuinely normative, something that would ground an *ought*. ... although I may not be disposed to believe that $68 + 57 = 125$, still that is what I *ought* to believe, given that I mean addition by '+'. This formulation does not offend in the way in which the claim about linguistic meaning did.

Or consider the following claims:

> If you mean *negation* by 'not', then you ought not to accept both 'p' and 'not-p.'

> If you mean *if* by 'if' then if you accept 'It is raining', and you accept 'If it is raining, then the streets are wet,' then you ought to accept 'The streets are wet.'

> Each of these claims seems plausible and yet neither of them seems to depend for its truth on any auxiliary desire by the thinker.

---

[6] Boghossian 1989b, p. 513 (Chapter 1, this volume).

Not so fast, you might think: don't these oughts depend on your wanting to believe the truth, so that they are at best hypothetical imperatives, just like the imperatives in the case of linguistic meaning and assertion?

I think that there is a good basis for saying that the answer to this question is 'No,' that the aim of truth is built into the nature of belief in the way that it is not built into the nature of assertion. If that's right, then we don't need to invoke any auxiliary desires in order to explain why these ought statements come out true. At least if we are looking at belief and mental content, then, rather than at assertion and linguistic meaning, there seems to be a chance that the thesis of the normativity of meaning might actually be true.

GIBBARD'S OBJECTIONS

Allan Gibbard has objected to the idea that we can ground the normativity of content in this way, through content's link to what it is correct to believe. Let us switch to an empirical example. Concerning Mallory's last day on Everest we can say:

(0) It is correct to believe that Mallory reached the summit iff Mallory did reach the summit.

Now, suppose we understand "correct" in a normative sense, so that it is taken to imply an ought. Then (0) would appear to yield:

(1) One ought to believe that Mallory reached the summit iff Mallory did reach the summit.

Now Gibbard raises two objections.

First, the sense of ought involved in (1) is clearly (what is known as) an "objective" ought, an ought that kicks in in light of what is true rather than in light of the evidence currently available to one. To appreciate this distinction, suppose you have a choice of two flights, one operated by British Airways and the other by Lufthansa, leaving at more or less the same time, from the same airport, the British Airways flight costing significantly less than the Lufthansa flight. Naturally, you opt for the British Airways flight, seeing no reason to prefer the Lufthansa flight. Unfortunately, the BA flight ends up being canceled because of a late-breaking labor strike and you are stranded. You think: I should have taken the Lufthansa flight. There is a sense in which that thought is true—in an "objective" sense, in light of what has turned out to be true. Subjectively speaking, in terms of the evidence available to you at the time of decision, it wasn't true that you should take the Lufthansa flight: by hypothesis, the evidence available to you favored the BA flight.

Similarly in the case of our belief about Mallory, perhaps Mallory was a clever illusionist who only made it seem as though he had scaled the summit of Everest. Then, in a subjective sense, I ought to believe that he scaled the summit even if he didn't. So the sense of "ought" in which (1) is guaranteed to be true must be an "objective" sense and not a subjective one.

Now, Gibbard continues, if we nevertheless insist that this objective ought is genuinely normative, then we will have to say that all facts are normative; and that would clearly be absurd.

For suppose that this objective ought is both genuinely normative and genuinely constitutive of our thought that Mallory reached the summit. Well, if it is genuinely constitutive, then (1) gives, as Gibbard puts it, an "analytic equivalence": Meaning facts alone enable us to see that the biconditional in (1) is true. And if the implicated ought is genuinely normative, then, given the analytic equivalence, the right-hand side, that Mallory reached the summit, describes a normative fact as well. But, surely, that Mallory reached the summit, is a non-normative claim if anything is.

I think there are a number of ways of resisting Gibbard's argument here, the most direct one being this. It is not true, I think, that the relation between a thought's correctness conditions and the corresponding ought claims is biconditional in form. (1) may be broken up into two conditional statements:

(2) One ought (objectively) to believe that Mallory reached the summit, only if Mallory reached the summit.

And

(3) If Mallory reached the summit, then one ought (objectively) to believe that he did.

Putting them in their general form:

(4) For any p: One ought to believe that p only if p.
(5) For any p: If p, then one ought to believe that p.

It's clear, I think, that these two claims are not on a par. The first, I think, may be taken to be the correct expression of the norm for belief—that one ought to believe only what's true (more on this below). But no one thinks that it's a norm on belief that one believe *everything* that's true. How could it be, given the metaphysical impossibility of believing everything that's true?

I'm inclined to hold, therefore, that one can infer p from 'One ought to believe that p,' but not 'One ought to believe that p' from p. This by itself disarms the fear that a correctness-based normativity thesis will lead to a normative explosion.

OBJECTIVE AND SUBJECTIVE NORMS

But even if that is so, isn't there still something irredeemably fishy about this "objective" sense of ought: something that one ought to believe just because it's true rather than because it's compelled by the evidence available to one. It can objectively be the case that one ought to believe p, even though, subjectively, one might well be required by the evidence at one's disposal to believe not p. I think it is relatively easy to defend the importance of the idea of objective oughts.

The main problem with the norm encoded in (4) is that it is not a norm that is directly followable. One may well have to follow *other* norms as a means towards obeying it. But the mere fact that (4) is a norm whose satisfaction isn't transparent doesn't mean that it isn't important, or that it's not a real norm.

We are often in the position of attempting to comply with some non-transparent norms by following other more transparent ones. Traders on the stock markets are attempting to comply with the rule: Buy low, sell high. But there is no direct way to recognize when a stock's price is low relative to the price for which one will be able to sell it. So traders follow certain other rules as a means of attempting to comply with the non-transparent rule that truly captures the aim of their trading activity. Some will use rules based on technical indicators, others will use rules based on fundamentals. These are rules that may be followed directly, by doing what the rules call for when their input conditions are recognized to obtain. However, we would give a seriously misleading account of their activity if we left out the fact that the following of these rules isn't an end in itself but only a means of complying with the non-transparent rule of buying low and selling high.

Just so, I think, with the "objective" norm that one ought to believe only what's true. Once again, this is not a rule that can be followed directly, but that can only be followed by following certain other rules, the so-called norms of rational belief. For example: that we ought to believe that which is supported by the evidence and not believe that which has no support; that we ought not to believe p if some alternative proposition incompatible with p has a higher degree of support; that we ought to believe p only if its degree of support is high enough, given the sort of proposition that it is. And so on.

But, just as before, our story would be incomplete if we left out the fact that our following of these rules is a means of following the norm that we ought to believe only what is true. All of these epistemic norms are grounded in the objective norm of truth. It is that ought that supplies their rationale, even if it has proven extremely difficult to say—in the theory of knowledge—exactly how.

It is this objective norm that captures the idea that it is constitutive of belief to aim at the truth, and so that something goes wrong if a belief is false. That, in my view, is what makes belief the state that it is.

NORMATIVITY OF CONTENT VS. NORMATIVITY OF BELIEF

Early on in the paper, I said that there was a difference between the normativity thesis as it applies to mental content and as it applies to linguistic meaning. We are in a better position now to say what that difference is and why it holds.

To put the matter concisely, the linguistic version of the normativity thesis, in contrast with its mentalistic version, has no plausibility whatever; and the reason is that it is not a norm on assertion that it should aim at the truth, in the way in which it is a norm on belief that it do so. Thus, the only imperatives that flow from attributions of linguistic meaning are hypothetical imperatives.

Kripke says: If I mean addition by '+' then it doesn't follow that I *will* say that '68 + 57 = 125', but only that I *ought* to say that it does. But it seems to me that neither claim follows. In particular, the ought claim doesn't follow because, even though I mean addition by '+' and know therefore that it would only be correct to say that '68 + 57 = 125', I might still not choose to say it because I might deliberately not choose to say what I know to be correct. Deciding knowingly to assert what is false is not to undermine the very possibility of assertion.

By contrast, no desire or decision is needed for it to be true that I ought to believe that 68 + 57 = 125. Indeed, the very fact that the imperative here is not hypothetical is, as I've just been arguing, a defining feature of belief. It is what makes it the state that it is.

The difficult question in this vicinity, I think, is not about the truth of the claim that attributions of the form *Wolfgang believes that p* are constitutively normative, nor is it about its importance; rather, it is about its *source*: Does the fact that such attributions are normative reveal something about our notion of *content*, or does it reveal something, rather, about our notion of *belief*? Do we have here a thesis of the normativity of content, or a thesis of the normativity of belief?

We have said that belief attributions are normative because it's a condition on understanding them that one understand that one ought to believe that p only if p. If we look at things this way, then it does seem as if what's responsible for the normativity is the concept of belief and not that of content. After all, contents can figure in *other* attitudes about some of which there aren't norms. If it's *content* as such that's normative, why aren't there norms governing these other attitudes? If it's genuinely constitutive of content that it be normative, shouldn't it carry this normativity with it wherever it goes?

Take a concrete example. Suppose I say of Ebenezer that he *wants* that Howard Dean be the next President. In making this attribution, am I in any way speaking oughts?

There are views, of course, according to which there are facts about what is objectively desirable. On such views, one could say that desires are correct only in so far as they line up with those objective facts. If such a species of evaluative realism were true, that would ground oughts about desires. But the source of these oughts would lie squarely in the evaluative realism, whereas what I'm asking is whether there are oughts about desires in virtue of the mere fact that they are contentful states. To be sure, Ebenezer's desire has conditions of satisfaction—it will be satisfied if and only if Dean is the next president. But, in and of itself, this doesn't translate either into a correctness fact or into an ought of any kind. Of course, Ebenezer may have this particular desire because he believes it to be a way of securing the satisfaction of another of his desires, and so his desire may be said to be correct to the extent that his belief is true. But that would be entirely a matter of the correctness of the underlying belief; it wouldn't introduce a sense in which the desire itself may be subject to normative evaluation.

It's not clear to me, then, that there are norms on desire merely qua contentful state. The matter is perhaps even clearer in the case of pure thinking, the pure entertaining of a proposition. Suppose I say that Ebenezer is merely entertaining the thought that Dean will be the next president. He doesn't believe it, he doesn't desire it—he's merely thinking about it, turning it over in his mind. In attributing this content to him, am I in any way attributing oughts? It seems not. As far as entertainings are concerned, you can do what you want with them.

Doesn't all this imply that the notion of thought content is not normative as such, that the answer to the question that constitutes the title of this paper is 'No?'

I think that it does, *unless* the following is true: that we understand the role that contents play in propositional attitudes generally only *through* our understanding of their role in belief. If our grasp of the notion of content were somehow to depend in a privileged and asymmetric way on our grasp of the concept of belief, then our only route to the notion of a contentful state would be through our grasp of a constitutively normative notion, and—although we would have arrived at this result in a way not envisioned by its proponents, still—that would be enough to substantiate the claim that content itself is normative, in spirit if not in letter.

Let me review the dialectic up to this point. I have said that a judgment type is normative just in case it's constitutive of our understanding of judgments of that type that they imply oughts. I have also argued that attributions of belief are normative judgments in this sense. If, then, we could be said to understand content only through our understanding of belief, then the notion of content would turn out to be a constitutively normative notion. We would understand content only through belief, and belief only through normative notions. This may not be quite what Kripke, Sellars and others had in mind, but it would still count as an interesting thesis. If, however, it is not true that content depends on belief, that content may be understood through its role in other non-normative attitudes, such as desire or the pure entertaining of a proposition, then we would not have a thesis of the normativity of content but only the rather different thesis of the normativity of belief.

IS BELIEF SPECIAL?

Now, I take it that the concept of a proposition, or content, just is the concept of whatever it is that is the object of the attitudes. And, of course, the notion of content could, in principle, be introduced in connection with the notion of, say, desire: prima facie, at least, it doesn't seem to have a *privileged* connection to belief. So our question isn't so much whether the notion of content *can* be understood in connection with attitudinal concepts other than that of belief, but whether any non-belief based understanding would covertly presuppose an understanding of its role in belief. In other words, is belief, in some appropriate sense, conceptually primary?

Let us ask this question not in full generality, but in connection with the notions of desire and belief, extending the question to the other attitudes only later. Is there any asymmetry in our understanding of belief and desire? Do we understand the one notion through understanding the other? Or are they on a par, either both depending, or neither depending, on the other?

A functionalist about the concepts of the attitudes would, of course, deny that there is any asymmetry. He would view the two concepts as graspable only jointly. However, just as I earlier didn't want to assume a controversial theory of how content is determined, so I don't now want to assume a controversial theory of the concepts of the propositional attitudes. To whatever extent it is possible, I want to ask about our understanding of the attitude concepts in a pre-theoretic and intuitive manner.

Let us begin, then, with the following question: Could someone have the concept of belief without having the concept of desire? Prima facie, this would appear to be so: it does seem possible for someone to have the idea of *accepting a content as true* without having any idea of what it would be to *desire a content to be true*.

One way in which this conceptual appearance could be falsified is if it turned out that I couldn't coherently think of someone as believing something without also thinking of them as desiring something, if it were conceptually impossible to think of someone as a believer without also thinking of them as a desirer. But this doesn't seem impossible. At least at the intuitive level, there appears to be no difficulty in thinking of someone as a pure believer: that is, as a creature who only has views about how things are, but no conception of how she would want them to be.

Let us now ask the converse question: Could someone have the concept of desire, but not yet the concept of belief? Could someone understand the idea of wanting the world to be a certain way, but have no idea at all of what it would be to take it to be a certain way, to accept its being a certain way?

This does seem bizarre. Don't I have to think of someone as having some beliefs about how things are, in order to coherently think of them as having wants about how things should be? Where the desires in question are conceived of as perceptually mediated *de re* desires, the purported possibility does seem incoherent. It's hard to understand how someone could be said to want that perceptually presented apple without (in some appropriate sense) believing that there is an apple there.

What about *de dicto* desires? Could I think of a person as wanting that all sorts of propositions be true without thinking of it as having any beliefs whatever? It's hard to imagine. The reason is that we think that someone can want p at some time t only if he either believes it to be not p at t, or if he is unsure whether it is p at t. You cannot want p at a given time, if at that time you already believe that p has occurred. You can be glad at t that p has occurred, if you already believe that p has occurred; but you cannot want it to occur. If I now want it to snow, that can only be because I currently believe it not to be snowing.

If that's so, then understanding desire involves understanding the idea of wanting things to be different than they are actually believed to be, and so presupposes the concept of belief.

These considerations are admittedly sketchy. But they suffice, I think, to make a plausible prima facie case for an asymmetry in our grasp of belief and desire: grasp of the concept of desire seems to asymmetrically depend on our grasp of the concept of belief in just the way that, I have argued, the normativity of content thesis requires. (If this is right, then we would have here a significant objection to the functionalist analysis of the concepts of belief and desire, for those analyses treat grasp of these concepts as symmetric: either you grasp both or you grasp neither).

A full treatment would require conducting similar investigations into the relations between all the other non-normative attitudes with reference to which the notion of content can be understood and seeing whether for each of them it is true that an understanding of that attitude depends asymmetrically on an understanding of belief. Until such an investigation is carried out, one which I think has an interest quite apart from the focus of our present concerns, the question whether content is normative will have to remain unresolved.

Just looking at the matter in a cursory way, it's impressive, I think, how many concepts of the propositional attitudes depend asymmetrically on the concept of belief: for example, all of the following seem to me to conceptually presuppose the belief that Bush won the election:

Being glad that Bush won
depressed that he won
sad that he won
angry that he won
conflicted about the fact that he won

In fact, the only sort of attitude concept that doesn't seem to presuppose that of belief is that of the mere entertaining of a proposition. What isn't clear to me, however, is whether this appearance isn't after all illusory. For is it clear that the peculiar notion of entertaining a proposition is not just a negative notion, the notion of

Thinking about a proposition without taking up any doxastic or conative attitude towards it.

NATURALISTIC THEORIES OF CONTENT

However this more extensive investigation may ultimately turn out, what is clear, ironically enough, is that the philosopher with perhaps the most reason to believe the asymmetric dependency thesis, and hence the normativity thesis, is the *naturalist* about mental content. For the most promising ideas that I know of concerning how to understand content naturalistically come in either one of two forms: either through an informational semantics or, especially in the important case of the logical constants, through an inferential role semantics. Both of these sorts of account, however, have to understand the fixation of content through its role in the fixation of *belief*.

To see why, reflect on how such theories propose to naturalize content. Let us begin with the case of an informational role semantics and, to ease exposition, let us assume that propositional attitudes are relations to mental representations, say, though this is not essential, to sentences in a language of thought. For example, let us take the state of desiring that p to be, or to be realized by, the state of desiring a sentence S of mentalese that means that p. Informational semantics theories attempt to specify naturalistically what it is for a mentalese sentence S to mean that p. If you look at how these theories attempt to achieve this, you will see that they inevitably go through the notion of belief, or at least through its computational counterpart. All such theories attempt to understand what it is for an arbitrary mentalese sentence S to mean that p by specifying the conditions under which S would be placed in the belief box (to use Stephen Schiffer's useful metaphor):

> S means that p iff under optimal conditions O, S would be placed in the belief box iff p.

In other words, these theories depend on the idea that there is a set of conditions under which one will believe something when and only when it's true. As such, they seek to understand the notion of content through its role in the fixation of belief. Not only is this the way things are typically done; it's very hard to see how they are to be done otherwise: for no attitudinal state other than belief has anything like the hope of covarying naturalistically with the conditions under which its content is realized.

To put the point abstractly, the idea would be to come up with the specification of a set of conditions C and a propositional attitude PA, such that, for all the atomic propositions in an organism's repertoire, the following holds true:

$$C: PA(p) \leftrightarrow p.$$

That there should be such a set of conditions for belief is already incredible enough.[7] But it doesn't have any chance, it seems to me, where the propositional

---

[7] For discussion see my 1989b and 1991 (this volume, Chapters 1 and 3 respectively).

attitude in question is anything other than belief. For example, and in part for reasons reviewed earlier, there is no chance that there is a set of conditions under which one will desire something only if that content is already realized.

All of this is even more true in the case of an inferential role semantics, as its name already implies. In the case of an inferential role semantics, the idea is that S's meaning is fixed by the set of beliefs that lead one to accept it and by the set of beliefs to which accepting it gives rise.

Interestingly enough, then, the philosopher with the most reason to believe in the primacy of belief and, hence, given the way I have set things up, in the normativity of content is, ironically enough, the naturalist about content. But if this is the only way in which the normativity of content can turn out to be true, it shows what an uninteresting thesis it is, especially in the context of the dispute with the naturalist. For on this setup, the naturalist will only have reason to believe in the normativity of content if his naturalistic theories of content fixation are true. But that means that there is no longer any way in which to use the putative normativity of content to argue that those naturalistic theories are not true.

I don't want to leave you with the misleading impression that I have suddenly become a naturalist about content. I have not. For reasons that I have given elsewhere, I still don't see how to pull off the trick of specifying a naturalistically adequate set of optimality conditions that will allow naturalistic theories to specify the meanings of expressions correctly. But this is not because content attributions are constitutively normative but because intentional facts seem not to be reducible to naturalistic facts.

5 *Epistemic Rules*

INTRODUCTION

According to a very natural picture of rational belief, we aim to believe only what is true. However, as Bernard Williams used to say, the world doesn't just inscribe itself onto our minds. Rather, we have to try to figure out what is true from the evidence available to us. To do this, we rely on a set of epistemic *rules* that tell us in some general way what it would be most *rational* to believe under various epistemic circumstances. We *reason* about what to believe; and we do so by relying on a set of rules.[1]

Although there is some controversy about exactly how these rules are to be formulated, we take ourselves to know roughly what they are. For example, we have a rule linking visual appearances to beliefs:

> (Observation) If it visually seems to you that p, then you are prima facie rationally permitted to believe that p.

We have some sort of *inductive* rule linking beliefs about the observed to beliefs about the unobserved, an example of which might be:

> (Induction) For appropriate F's and G's, if you have observed n (for some sufficiently large n) F's and they have all been G's, then you are prima facie rationally permitted to believe that all F's are G's.

We also have *deductive* rules, such as:

> (Modus Ponens): If you are rationally permitted to believe both that p and that 'If p, then q', then, you are prima facie rationally permitted to believe that q.[2]

These rules, and others like them, constitute what me may call our *epistemic system*. They represent our conception of how it would be most rational for a thinker to form beliefs under different epistemic circumstances.

---

[1] We could put everything in terms of partial belief, but that won't matter for our purposes.

[2] Of course, this is not quite the rule that is labeled Modus Ponens in logic textbooks. It is actually quite mysterious what the logic textbook rule is supposed to be, but I can't go into that here.

Let us call this the *rule-following picture of rational belief*. It is a very familiar picture and has tempted many. As I shall try to explain later, its roots run very deep.[3] Because we accept this picture, we take seriously a number of questions that it seems to entrain.

For example, we recognize that, in addition to the rules that we actually use, there are other rules, different from and incompatible with ours, which we might have used instead. And this seems to raise the question: Are our rules the right ones? Are they the ones that deliver genuinely justified belief?

These questions in turn raise a more fundamental one: In what sense could there be a fact of the matter as to what the right epistemic rules are? And if there is such a fact of the matter, how do we find out what it is? And what, in any case, entitles us to operate with the rules that we actually operate with?

None of these familiar and compelling questions would make much sense in the absence of the rule-following picture of rational belief. Each of them presupposes that we rely on rules in forming rational beliefs.

I find the rule-following picture, along with the questions that it entrains, as natural and as compelling as the next person. However, I have also come to worry about its ultimate intelligibility, a worry that I find myself unable to lay to rest. In this paper, I aim to explain the considerations that give rise to this worry.

I have been talking about the rule-governed picture of rational belief. But rational belief is hardly the only domain in which rule-following has been thought to play a prominent role. The sort of generalist picture I have been sketching for epistemology has of course always loomed large in ethics. We find it very natural to think that, in our moral judgments, we are guided by a set of general *moral* principles that tell us what we have most reason to do under various practical conditions.

Recent writers have complained about this generalist picture in ethics. They say that moral reasons are too *holistic* for there to be general principles that can tell us what it would be morally correct to do under varying practical conditions.[4] That is not the sort of problem I have in mind for the generalist picture of rational belief. Rather, I will develop two other types of difficulty.

The first concerns how to understand the notion of a "rule" as it is used in the rule-following picture. What exactly is it that we are being said to follow, when we are said to follow epistemic rules?

The second difficulty concerns what it is to *follow* a rule regardless of how exactly a rule is construed. My worry here is closely related to the famous discussion of following a rule that was inaugurated by Wittgenstein and brilliantly expounded by Saul Kripke.[5]

---

[3] For explicit endorsements of the view, see, among many others, Pollock and Cruz 1999, chapter 5; Peacocke 2004; Wedgwood 2002; Field 2000.

[4] See, for example, Dancy 2006.

[5] See Wittgenstein 1953 and Kripke 1982.

Like Kripke, I think that there really is a skeptical problem about rule-following that can be derived from Wittgenstein's discussion. But my problem is not Kripke's. Unlike Kripke's problem, my problem arises in an especially virulent form for *epistemic rules,* as opposed to rules of other kinds. And it cannot be solved, as Kripke's problem can, by our helping ourselves to various forms of anti-reductionist conceptions of meaning or content.

All of this is what I propose to explain in what follows.

I. WHAT DO WE FOLLOW: IMPERATIVES OR NORMATIVE PROPOSITIONS?

Imperatives vs. Norms

We talk interchangeably about epistemic *rules* and about epistemic *norms.* Are these the same sorts of thing or are there important differences between them? This is an area in which our language is sloppy and we are not often very explicit about what we mean.

Take the word "rule." By and large, when Kripke talks about "rules" he is talking about general imperatival contents of the form:

If C, do A!

where 'C' names a type of situation and 'A' a type of action. On this construal, rules are general contents that *prescribe* certain types of behavior under certain kinds of condition.

However, not everything that we call a rule in ordinary language conforms to this characterization. For example, we talk about the "rules of chess." One of these rules is:

(Castle) If the configuration is C, you *may* castle.

This does not look like an imperative. Unlike an imperative, it seems truth-evaluable. It looks more like something we should call a *normative proposition* or norm, for short. It is a norm of *permission.* In addition to the permissive norms, of course, there are norms of *requirement*:

(First Move) At the beginning of the game, White *must* make the first move.

Arguments for the Propositional Construal

We need, then, to recognize a distinction between two different kinds of content—the imperatival and the propositional; and we need to clarify whether, in talking about epistemic rules, we are talking about contents of the one type or the other.

When I gave a rough characterization of these rules above, I gave them a normative propositional formulation. There are at least three considerations that favor this construal.

To begin with, epistemic justification is a normative notion. We would expect, therefore, that the contents that encode our conception of it would be normative contents. However, imperatives are not normative in any way. They are merely commands or instructions.[6] If such commands or instructions do play a role in our epistemic systems, it is natural to think of them as having a derivative status—a status derived from the more fundamental normative propositions that encode our conception of epistemic justification.

The second reason for favoring a propositional construal has to do with our need to distinguish between different kinds of action-guiding or belief-guiding rules. Thus, there are epistemic rules, prudential rules, aesthetic rules, moral rules and so forth. It is easy to distinguish among these types of rule in propositional terms, by building their identity into their propositional content. Thus, an epistemic rule would be a normative proposition of the following kind:

If C, then S is epistemically permitted to believe that p.

A prudential rule, on the other hand, would involve the concept of a prudential permission; and so forth.

By contrast, it is hard to see how to get this differentiation on an imperatival picture. The trouble is that all imperatives are alike—they all assume the form

If C, do A!

And so the mere content of an imperative is incapable of telling us whether it's an epistemic, prudential or moral imperative.[7]

A third reason for favoring a propositional construal of epistemic rules has to do with the need to capture not only requirements but permissions as well. The trouble, however, is that there looks to be a real difficulty capturing a norm of *permission* in imperatival terms.

The difficulty, in a nutshell, is this: An imperative, by definition, tells you to do something, if a certain condition is satisfied. However, a norm of permission doesn't call on you to do anything; it just says that, if a certain condition were satisfied, then performing some particular action would be alright.

Thus, obviously, the norm of permission (Castle) cannot be expressed in terms of the imperative

If configuration is C, Castle!

---

[6] A point emphasized to me by Derek Parfit.

[7] One idea about how to remedy this would be to look at a thinker's *grounds* for accepting any given imperative—the idea being to try to distinguish between an epistemic imperative and a prudential one not in terms of their overt content but in terms of the characteristic grounds on which they are accepted. But this is a difficult program to execute because it depends on the not obviously correct idea that, corresponding to each type of norm, there exists an individuating type of ground on which a thinker accepts it.

because that would suggest that whenever the configuration is C one must castle, whereas the norm merely permits castling and does not require it. Could we perhaps express (Castle) as:

Castle!, only if C.

But this seems to want to embed an imperative in the antecedent of a conditional:

If Castle!, then C

and I don't know what that means.

Gideon Rosen has suggested another strategy for the imperativalist—using complex imperatives with disjunctive consequents.[8] Thus, he suggests that the imperative that corresponds to an epistemic norm of permission of the form:

(4) If for some e, f(e, h), then it is rationally permissible to believe h (on the basis of e)

would be something more like this:

(5) If for some e, f(e, h), then either believe h (on the basis of e), or suspend judgment about h.

Now, I take it that "suspending judgment" about h isn't simply: not believing h. If it were, then the imperative at (5) would amount to saying:

If e, then either believe h or don't believe h!

which doesn't say much of anything. Suspending judgment, then, requires something active—considering whether h and then rejecting taking a view on the matter.

If that's right, though, (5) now seems to call for you to do things that go well beyond what (4) says. According to (4), if a certain kind of evidence is available, then, *if* you believed h on its basis, that belief would be justified. (4) does not say that you should believe h; it doesn't say that you should consider whether h; it doesn't say that you should *do* anything.

In other words, (5) is most naturally seen not as the imperatival counterpart of the norm of permission formulated in (4) but as the imperatival counterpart of the norm of *requirement* formulated in

(6) If for some e, f(e, h), then you are required either to belief h (on the basis of e) or to suspend judgment on h.

Would we do better with something more along the lines of (7) rather than (5)?

(7) If for some e, f(e, h), then either believe h (on the basis of e) or don't do anything (on the basis of e)!

---

[8] See Rosen 2007.

But this doesn't seem right, either. Even without going into the details of what it might mean for someone to "not do something on the basis of e", I hope it's clear that, whatever exactly it means, if, in response to e, I scratched my nose on the basis of e, I wouldn't have done anything that is in violation of the norm of permission issued by (4).

There are, no doubt, many other proposals that could be considered, but I hope it is clear that there really is a problem capturing a norm of permission in imperatival terms. An imperative, however disjunctive its consequent, will require you to do something, or to refrain from doing something; but a norm of permission doesn't say anything about anyone's doing anything, or refraining from doing anything. It just says that, under the appropriate conditions, *if* one were to do something, doing that thing would be alright.[9]

Arguments for the Imperatival Construal

These, then, are some of the considerations that push one in favor of a propositional view of rules. On the other hand, there is the following argument that pushes one in the opposite direction.

Recall that the picture we are working with says that it is necessary and sufficient for a belief to be rational that it be held in accordance with the correct epistemic rules. In other words, we are working with:

(RuleRatBel) S's belief that p is rationally permitted if and only if S arrived at the belief that p by following the correct rule N.

Now, suppose we take N to be an epistemic normative proposition of the form:

(EpNorm) If C, then S is rationally permitted to believe that p.

Now, EpNorm—the norm we are said to be following—says that it is sufficient for my being rationally permitted to believe that p that condition C obtains.

However, the rule-following picture of rational belief (RuleRatBel) implies that it is not sufficient for my being rationally permitted to believe that p that C obtains—in addition, *I need to have followed the rule EpNorm.*

If we put these two facts together, we get the following peculiar result: The only way to implement the rule-following picture of rational belief, with the rules construed as normative propositions, is to accept that the normative propositions that we are required to follow, in order to acquire rational belief, must be *false* epistemic propositions! To have rationally permitted beliefs a thinker is required to follow *false* epistemic normative propositions.

---

[9] There are a number of other proposals that we could consider, but I can't go into them here. Probably the most promising is the one employed by Allan Gibbard: think of accepting a rule of permission as consisting in the *rejection* of a rule of requirement. So accepting the permissibility of castling under C would consist in rejecting the rule: If C, don't castle! But we are now owed an account of what it is to reject an imperative. See Gibbard 2003a.

And that is surely very odd. How could it be that, in order to arrive at genuinely rationally permitted beliefs, I must be armed with, and guided by, a set of false epistemic propositions about the conditions under which a belief would be genuinely epistemically justified?

It is important to note two points. First, the problem here is structural. Whatever proposition we replace (EpNorm) with, we will face some version or other of this false rules problem, because the rule-following picture will always insist on imposing a *further* necessary condition on rational belief beyond that recognized by the proposition that is said to constitute an epistemic rule—namely, the condition that that rule be followed.[10]

Second, this problem of false rules would *not* arise on the imperatival picture of epistemic rules, on which the rules are of the form:

If C, believe that p!

Since, on this conception, the rules themselves don't make any claims, they can hardly *conflict* with the claims being made by the rule-following picture of rational belief (RuleRatBel) about the conditions necessary for rational belief.

That constitutes a significant argument in favor of an imperatival construal of epistemic rules. The trouble is that, on such a construal, we would face all the other problems outlined above.

This, then, is the first difficulty I wanted to raise for the rule-following picture of rational belief: it is very unclear what satisfactory answer we can give to the question: What sort of content can a rule be such that following it is necessary for a belief to be rational?[11]

II. HOW CAN WE FOLLOW RULES?

The Intuitive Notion

Let us assume, though, for the purposes of argument, that we have a satisfactory solution to this problem. Let us now turn to asking how it is possible for someone to *follow* a rule. For the purpose of posing this question it won't much matter whether we construe rules in imperatival or propositional terms.

---

[10] It might be thought that some self-referential device might meet this problem. Perhaps we should think of the epistemic rules as consisting in propositions of the following form:

(EpNorm*) If C, then if S were to believe that p on the basis of this very norm, he would be rationally permitted to believe that p.

This suggestion is worth exploring, although, for obvious reasons, I am always leery of self-referential devices and am not sure I understand them.

[11] Limitations of space prevent me from considering various ways of responding to this difficulty for the propositional construal. For further discussion, see my *Rules and Intentionality in Nature* (forthcoming).

Before proceeding we should clarify what we mean to be asking about. What intuitive phenomenon is at issue when we talk about someone *following* a rule?

In answering this question, we should distinguish between a *personal-level* notion of rule-following and a *sub-personal* notion. We should not assume, at the outset, that our talk of a person's following a rule comes to exactly the same thing as our talk of, say, his brain's following a rule, or of his calculator's computing a function. We should also recognize that, prima facie, anyway, it is the personal-level notion that is involved in the generalist, rule-following picture of rational belief with which we are concerned. *I* reason about what to believe, not a part of my brain.

I propose, therefore, to start with attempting to understand the personal-level notion, returning to the sub-personal notion later. My view will be that there is a core concept that is common to both notions, but that the personal-level notion is richer in a particular respect that I shall describe below. Once we have a handle on the personal-level notion it will be easy to indicate the weakening that gets us the sub-personal notion.

A propos of the personal-level notion, we certainly know this much: to say that S is following rule R is not the same as saying that S's behavior happens to *conform* to R. Conforming to R is neither necessary nor sufficient for following R.

It is not necessary because S may be following R even while he fails to conform to it. This can happen in one of two ways. Say that R is the instruction 'If C, do A!' S may fail to recognize that he is in circumstance C, and so fail to do A; yet it may still be true that S is following R. Or, he may correctly recognize that he is in conditions C, but, as a result of a performance error, fail to do A, even though he tries.

Conformity to R is not sufficient for S's following R because for any behavior that S displays, there will be a rule—indeed, infinitely many rules—to which his behavior will conform. Yet it would be absurd to say that S is following all the rules to which his behavior conforms.

There is another possible gloss on our notion that we need to warn against. There is a persistent tendency in the literature to suggest that the claim that S is following rule R means something roughly like: R may correctly be used to *evaluate* S's behavior. Crispin Wright, for example, often introduces the topic of rule following with something like the following remark:

The principal philosophical issues to do with rule-following impinge on every normatively constrained area of human thought and activity: on every institution where there is right and wrong opinion, correct and incorrect practice.[12]

---

[12] Wright 2003, p. 1.

The suggestion seems to be that rule-following and normative constraint come to much the same thing. Or, if not quite that, that rule following on S's part is necessary for S's behavior to be subject to normative assessment.

But this seems wrong. Intuitively, and without the help of controversial assumptions, it looks as though there are many thoughts that S can have, and many activities that he can engage in, that are subject to assessment in terms of rule R even if there is no intuitive sense in which they involve S's following rule R.

Consider Nora playing roulette. She has a "hunch" that the next number will be '36' and she goes with it: she bets all her money on it. We need not suppose that, in going with her hunch, she was following any rule—perhaps this was just a one-time event. Still, it looks as though we can normatively criticize her belief as *irrational* since it was based on no good evidence.

Or consider Peter who has just tossed the UNICEF envelope in the trash without opening it. Once more, we need not suppose that Peter has a standing policy of tossing out charity envelopes without opening them and considering their merits. However, even if no rule was involved it can still be true that Peter's behavior was subject to normative assessment, that there are norms covering his behavior.

In both of these cases, then, norms or rules *apply* to some thought or behavior even though there is no intuitive sense in which the agent in question was attempting to observe those norms or follow those rules himself.

Of course, some philosophers—like Kripke's Wittgenstein—think that wherever there is *intentional content* there must be rule-following, since meaning itself is a matter of following rules. But that is not a suitably pre-theoretic fact about rule-following; and what we are after at the moment is just some intuitive characterization of the phenomenon. We will come back to the question whether meaning is a matter of following rules.

When we say that S is following a rule R in doing A, we mean neither that S conforms to R nor simply that R may be used to assess S's behavior, ruling it correct if he conforms and incorrect if he doesn't. What, then, do we mean?

Let us take a clear case. Suppose I receive an email and that I answer it immediately. When would we say that this behavior was a case of following the:

> (Email Rule) Answer any email that calls for an answer immediately upon receipt!

as opposed to just being something that I happened to do that was in conformity with that rule?

Clearly, the answer is that it would be correct to say that I was following the Email Rule in replying to the email, rather than just coincidentally conforming to it, when it is *because* of some appropriate relation that I bear to the Email Rule that I reply immediately.

I shall refer to this relation as S's *acceptance* or *internalization* of the rule, though, clearly, it will be very important to understand this as neutrally as possible for now.[13]

Equally clearly, the because here is not any old causal relation: if a malicious scientist (or an enterprising colleague) had programmed my brain to answer any email upon receipt (in some zombie-like way) because *he* accepted the rule that I should answer any email upon receipt, that would not count as *my* following the Email Rule. (It might count as my brain following the rule.) Rather, for me to be following the rule, the 'because' must be that of rational action explanation: I follow the Email Rule when my acceptance of that rule serves as my *reason* for replying immediately, when that rule *rationalizes* my behavior.

However exactly the notion of acceptance or internalization is understood, what is important is that, in any given case of rule-following, we have something with the following structure: a state that can play the role of rule acceptance; and some non-deviant casual chain leading from that state to a piece of behavior that would allow us to say that the accepted rule explains and rationalizes the behavior.

Occasionally, I will also describe the matter in terms of the language of commitment. In rule-following there is, on the one hand, a *commitment*, on the part of the thinker to uphold a certain pattern in his thought or behavior; and, on the other, some behavior that expresses that commitment, that is explained and rationalized by it.

It will be up to the reader to discern whether I have loaded these notions in a way that is illicit. For the moment, let me just note that this characterization coincides well with the way Kripke seems to be thinking about the phenomenon of rule-following. As he says a propos of following the rule for addition:

I learned—and internalized instructions for—a *rule*, which determines how addition is to be continued ... This set of directions, I may suppose, I explicitly gave myself at some earlier time ... It is this set of directions ... that justifies and determines my present response.[14]

I think it was a mistake on Kripke's part to use the word "justify" in this passage rather than the word "rationalize." In talking about rule-following, it is important to bear in mind that we might be following *bad* rules. The problem of rule-following arises no less for Affirming the Consequent or Gambler's Fallacy than it does for Modus Ponens. If I am following Gambler's Fallacy, my betting the house on black after a long string of reds at the roulette wheel wouldn't be *justified* but it would be *rationalized* by the rule that I am following. Given that

---

[13] "Internalization" is Kripke's preferred word, as we see below; it is probably more neutral than "acceptance."

[14] Kripke 1982, p. 16.

I am committed to the fallacious rule, it makes sense that I would bet the house on black.

We may summarize our characterization of personal-level rule-following by the following four theses:

(Acceptance) If S is following rule R ('If C, do A'), then S has somehow accepted R.

(Correctness) If S is following rule R, then S acts correctly relative to his acceptance if it is the case that C and he does A; incorrectly otherwise.

(Explanation) If S is following rule R by doing A, then S's acceptance of R *explains* S's doing A.

(Rationalization) If S is following rule R by doing A, then S's acceptance of R rationalizes S's doing A.

Against the backdrop of this characterization of the personal-level notion, we can see the sub-personal notion of following a rule as involving the first three elements but not the fourth. If I say of a calculator that it is adding, then I am saying that its 'internalization' of the rule for addition explains why it gives the answers that it gives. But I am obviously not saying that the addition rule *rationalizes* the calculator's answers. The calculator doesn't act for reasons, much less general ones.

Following Epistemic Rules

If we apply this analysis to the rule following picture of rational belief with which we began, we arrive at the view that our internalization of general epistemic rules—like Modus Ponens and Induction—explain and rationalize why we form the beliefs that we form. And that seems intuitively correct.

As in the case of our linguistic and conceptual abilities, our ability to form rational beliefs is *productive*: on the basis of finite learning, we are able to form rational beliefs under a potential infinity of novel circumstances. The only plausible explanation for this is that we have, somehow, internalized a rule that tells us, in some general way, what it would be rational to believe under varying epistemic circumstances.

Furthermore, we form beliefs for reasons. As Kripke likes to say, when we form the belief that $68 + 57 = 125$, that does not feel like a stab in the dark, a result that is spat out by some sub-personal mechanism that we find ourselves giving and which, to our surprise, turns out be reliable.

Rather, the processes by which we fix beliefs are personal-level processes, processes of which we are, in some appropriate sense, aware. In that appropriate sense, we know why, on any given occasion, we are inclined to believe what we believe, what our grounds are.

Combining these two natural thoughts gives us the personal-level rule-following picture of rational belief. And a very natural picture it is. The picture is perhaps most obviously at work in the case of deductive reasoning; but it applies equally to inductive reasoning, arithmetical reasoning and moral reasoning. Let us take a somewhat closer look at the deductive case.

Suppose someone asks me to accept that

Mitochondria are mitochondria.

Even if I knew very little about what mitochondria are, I would be very confident that I should accept this proposition. What could be the reason for my confidence if not that I have accepted the general principle:

Accept any proposition of the form *All F's are F's.*

Or consider the inference:

If x is a Malament-Hogarth space-time, then it has no Cauchy surface. x is a Malament-Hogarth space-time.

Therefore,

x doesn't have a Cauchy surface.

Once again, I may know very little about the ingredient concepts. But I can be very confident that, if I were justified in believing the premises, I would be justified in believing the conclusion. Once more, the only plausible explanation is that I have internalized (or accepted) a general Modus Ponens rule.

Acceptance and Intention

Let us turn now to asking why there is supposed to be a problem about rule-following. Why, in particular, does Kripke's Wittgenstein maintain that it is not possible for us to follow rules?

Kripke's problem is focused on *Acceptance*. He is struck by the fact that the patterns to which we are said to be able to commit ourselves are *infinitary* patterns. Thus, we claim to follow the rule of inference Modus Ponens:

(Modus Ponens): If you are rationally permitted to believe both that p and that 'If p, then q', then, you are prima facie rationally permitted to believe that q.

MP, however, is defined over an infinite number of possible propositions. How is it possible, Kripke asks, for a thinker to commit himself to uphold this potentially infinitary pattern? Kripke despairs of answering this challenge head-on.

As we all know, Kripke's argument proceeds by elimination. There look to be only two serious candidates for constituting the state of rule acceptance: either it consists in some *intentional state* of a thinker, or it consists in his *dispositions*, very broadly understood, to use that symbol in certain ways. And he finds fault with both options.

Let's go along for now with the rejection of the dispositional suggestion. Still, what could possibly be wrong with invoking some intentional notion, as Crispin Wright has done? As Wright puts it:

... so far from finding any mystery in the matter, we habitually assign just these characteristics [the characteristics constitutive of the acceptance of a rule] to the ordinary notion of *intention* ... intentions may be general, and so may possess, in the intuitively relevant sense, potentially infinite content.[15]

Let us call this the *Intention View* of rule acceptance.[16]

The Intention View is itself just a special version of a more general class of views according to which rule acceptance consists in some *intentional state* or other, even if it is not identified specifically with an intention. Call this more general view the Intentional View of rule acceptance.

I will focus my discussion on the Intention View but most everything I say will apply equally to the less committal Intentional View.

Some Problems for the Intention View

Why not just accept the Intention View? What, if anything, is wrong with this flat-footed response to the rule-following challenge?

The problem with the Intention View cannot be that there are no cases that are accurately described by it, for there clearly are. If I now adopt a policy of always answering any email that I receive immediately upon receipt and if, on some future occasion, I answer an email immediately upon receipt precisely because it is my policy to do so, then all this would be very well captured by the Intention View.

The question can only be whether, on the one hand, the Intention View is a sufficiently *fundamental* account, and, on the other, whether it is a sufficiently *general* account of rule-following, so that all relevant cases can be said to fall under it.

A reductive Naturalist would have reason to think of it as insufficiently fundamental. Such a Naturalist would insist that intentional states be shown to be naturalistically reducible before they may legitimately be appealed to in solving the rule acceptance problem. However, it is none too clear how such a reduction of the intentional to the naturalistic is to be pulled off (and Kripke's own discussion may be seen to provide a battery of arguments against its feasibility—more on this below).

Second, and even if we were to put reductive Naturalism to one side, there look to be two severe difficulties with taking the Intention View to be a sufficiently *general* account: not everything that we would intuitively count as rule-following looks like a case if acting on an intention.

[15] Wright 2003, p. 125–6
[16] See also Pettit 2002, p. 27: "The notion of following a rule, as it is conceived here, involves an important element over and beyond that of conforming to a rule. The conformity must be intentional, being something that is achieved at least in part, on the basis of belief and desire. To follow a rule is to conform to it, but the act of conforming, or at least the act of trying to conform—if that is distinct—must be intentional. It must be explicable, in the appropriate way, by the agent's beliefs and desires."

One problem is posed by the fact that we typically think of ourselves as having quite good—indeed, especially privileged—access to our own intentions: we know without empirical investigation what they are. Yet, although we are able to give some rough indication of what our epistemic rules are, there continues to be some controversy about their precise formulation (are we dogmatists or conservatives about perception, for example?).[17] If they were the contents of intentions of ours, wouldn't we expect to know what they are with a much higher degree of precision and clarity than we seem capable of?

A second type of consideration against the generality of the Intention View is provided by an assumption that is crucial to Kripke's thinking about rule-following. Kripke sets up the rule-following problem by asking what determines whether I am using the '+' sign according to the rule of addition as opposed to the rule for quaddition, where quaddition is a function just like addition, except that it diverges from it for numbers larger than we are able to compute. He considers saying that what determines that rule-following fact is some general intention I formed to use the symbol according to the one rule rather than the other:

What was the rule? Well, say, to take it in its most primitive form: suppose we wish to add x and y. Take a huge bunch of marbles. First count out x marbles in one heap. Then count out y marbles in another. Put the two heaps together and count out the number of marbles in the union thus formed. The result is x + y. This set of directions, I may suppose, I explicitly gave myself at some earlier time. It is engraved on my mind as on a slate. It is incompatible with the hypothesis that I meant quus. It is this set of directions, not the finite list of particular additions I performed in the past that justifies and determines my present response.

Kripke continues:

Despite the initial plausibility of this objection, the sceptic's response is all too obvious: True, if 'count' as I used the word in the past, referred to the act of counting (and my other words are correctly interpreted in the standard way) then 'plus' must have stood for addition. But I applied 'count' like 'plus' to only finitely many past cases. Thus the sceptic can question my present interpretation of my past usage of 'count' as he did with 'plus.'[18]

How should we understand this passage? On one way of reading it, Kripke would be assuming that the contents of mental states are derived from the contents of public language linguistic expressions. But if that's the assumption, it is vulnerable: most philosophers think that the relation between mind and language is in fact the other way round, that linguistic meaning derives from mental content.

On another way of reading it, Kripke would be assuming not some controversial view of the relation between thought and language, but rather that thoughts

---

[17] For the distinction between dogmatists and conservatives about perception, see Pryor 2000.
[18] Kripke 1982, p. 16.

themselves involve the tokenings of expressions (of mentalese) and that those expressions, too, get their meaning by our following rules in respect of them.

I think this latter assumption is clearly what Kripke had in mind. Let's call it Kripke's *Meaning Assumption* and let's go along with it for now.

Now, it should be obvious that combining the Meaning Assumption with the Intention View will lead rather quickly to the conclusion that rule-following, and with it mental content, are metaphysically impossible. For given the two assumptions, we would be able to reason as follows. In order to follow rules, we would antecedently have to have intentions. To have intentions, the expressions of our language of thought would have to have meaning. For those expressions to have meaning, we would have to use them according to rules. For us to use them according to rules, we would antecedently have to have intentions. And so on, ad infinitum. If we combine the Meaning Assumption with the Intention View, neither mental content nor rule-following would be able to get off the ground and rather obviously so.

Since Kripke regards the Meaning Assumption as non-optional, he rejects the Intention View. The problem then becomes to find a way in which someone could be said to have committed himself to a certain pattern of use for a symbol without this being the result of his forming an *intention* (or other intentional state) to uphold that pattern.

And that is why so much attention is focused on the dispositional view.

Some Solutions to these Problems for the Intention View

If the second of the three objections to the Intention View that we have outlined, the one based on the relative opacity of our rules, is correct, then there must be a species of rule-acceptance that is non-intentional. And, if either the first or the third of our three considerations is correct—that is either the one based on reductive Naturalism or the one based on the Meaning Assumption, then not only must there be a species of rule-acceptance that is non-intentional, *all* rule-acceptance must at bottom *be* non-intentional, because even *intentional* forms of rule-acceptance will presuppose the *non-intentional* kind.

Now, since we know that it's going to be extremely difficult to pull off a non-intentional, dispositional account of rule-acceptance, we should ask whether there is any way around these considerations. How strong are they? Can they be answered?

To the first objection, one might respond by saying that reductive Naturalism is not obviously correct and so can hardly be used to constrain the acceptability of an otherwise intuitively compelling account of rule-following. After all, it continues to prove difficult to account for other important phenomena, such as consciousness, within a reductive naturalistic setting.

To the second objection one could try responding by appealing to the notion of a *tacit* intention, an intention to do something that is not explicitly articulated in someone's consciousness but which he could be said to have implicitly or tacitly. The idea would be that the mental states by which rules are accepted or internalized are tacit intentions, rather than the sorts of explicit intention with which we are familiar in ordinary action.

Specifying such a notion in a satisfactory way has defied many serious attempts. But it is not clearly hopeless. And if we could explain what it is for someone to have an intention to do something in a way that is not explicitly articulated in some conscious state of his, that might then be used to explain why we don't have the sort of super sharp access to our rules as we do to our ordinary intentions.

However, even if the foregoing responses were accepted, I hope it is clear that we would still be stuck with a huge problem for the Intention View, if Kripke's Meaning Assumption were left in place.

The problem, of course, is that even unreduced, tacit intentions are contentful states. As a result, it would still not be possible to combine the Intention View with the Meaning Assumption. But can the Meaning Assumption be plausibly rejected?

Let's distinguish between the question whether *public language* expressions get their meaning through rule-following and the question whether the *expressions of the language of thought* do.

Is the Meaning Assumption correct at least when it comes to the words of public language? Is it right to say that the words of English, for example, get their meaning as a result of our following rules in respect of them?

Well, a word is just an inscription, a mark on paper. Something has got to be done to it by its user for it to get a meaning. That much is clear. It is also clear that meaningful words have conditions of *correct application*. Thus, the word 'tiger' is correctly applied only to tigers and the word 'red' only to red things.

But it doesn't follow from these obvious truths that the way the word 'tiger' comes to mean what it does for a given speaker S—that the way it comes to have the correctness conditions that it has in S's idiolect—is by S committing himself to using it according to the rule: Apply the word 'tiger' only to tigers![19]

For meaning to be a matter of rule-following in the sense presupposed by the Meaning Assumption, it must be true not only that words *have* satisfaction conditions, but that they *get* their satisfaction conditions by their users committing themselves to using them according to certain patterns.

Still, it does look as though one can make a strong case for the Meaning Assumption as applied to public language expressions.[20] When I apply the

[19] Jerry Fodor may have been the first to appreciate this clearly; see his 1990, pp. 135–6. I don't believe that any of the main arguments of my 1989b (this volume, Chapter 1) are affected by paying greater heed to this distinction, although I am sure I wasn't as clear about it in that paper as I should have been.

[20] I have gone back and forth about the plausibility of the Meaning Assumption as applied to public language expressions. In my NYU seminar of Spring 2006, I defended it, but in an earlier version of this paper I retreated to saying that it was not settled. I thank Christopher Peacocke for rightly insisting to me that it met my characterization of person-level rule-following.

word 'tiger' to a newly encountered animal, it is very natural to think that my application of the word is guided and rationalized by my understanding of its meaning, an understanding that is rule-like in its generality.

What about the expressions of our language of thought? Is it similarly compelling to say that that they get their meaning by our following rules in respect of them?

Here things may look quite different, especially if we emphasize that we are dealing with a personal-level of rule-following according to which it is a person who follows a rule and not just his brain.

At a personal level it appears to make very little sense to say that we follow rules in respect of our mental expressions, expressions to which the ordinary person has no access and which, for all that such a person knows, may not even exist.

Kripke is clearly working with a person-level notion of rule-following. That is why he can confidently claim that when someone is following a rule that rule *justifies* (or as I would prefer to say, rationalizes) his behavior. But it can hardly be true that all meaning is a matter of rule-following in this sense. In particular, it can hardly be true that the expressions of mentalese get their meaning by our following rules in respect of them in this sense.

It looks, then, as though, at least as far as personal-level rule-following is concerned, we are free to reject Kripke's Meaning Assumption, at least as it applies to mental expressions. And with that observation we seem to have answered the third of the three objections we had posed for the Intention View.[21]

If we reject the Meaning Assumption, we give up on the claim that mental expressions get their meaning by our following rules in respect of them. How, then, do they get their meaning?

Kripke's discussion may be seen as containing a battery of arguments against *reductive* accounts of mental content facts, accounts such as those provided by dispositional or functionalist or informational theories. And I am inclined to think that these arguments, along with others that may be found in the literature, are very persuasive.[22]

Even if we concede all this, however, that still appears to leave anti-reductionist conceptions of mental content untouched. Kripke tries to undermine such conceptions of content as well, of course; but, as I have argued at length elsewhere, those arguments seem to me to be answerable.[23]

If we were to adopt such an anti-reductionist conception of mental content, wouldn't that mean that we would now be free to adopt the Intention View of rule following?

---

[21] For all that we have said, of course, it remains possible that we need to think of mental meaning as generated by sub-personal rule-following and that this will cause problems of its own. I shall come back to this question towards the end of the paper.

[22] For discussion and references, see my 1989b (this volume, Chapter 1). More on this below.

[23] See my 1989b (this volume, Chapter 1).

The Real Problem for the Intention View

Not quite. For what I now want to argue is that even if *all* of these responses were to pan out, that still wouldn't suffice to salvage the Intention View. The Intention View suffers from a further and seemingly fatal flaw. It concerns not, as Kripke alleges, the Acceptance aspect of rule-following, but rather, the aspects that I earlier labeled Explanation and Rationalization.

To see what this problem is, let us waive Naturalism; let us ignore the examples of putatively non-intentional forms of rule-acceptance; let us reject the Meaning Assumption. And let us simply help ourselves to an anti-reductionist view of mental content.

Once such contentful thoughts are available, they can be used to frame intentions—and so, it would seem, to account for our acceptance of rules. If something like this picture could be sustained, wouldn't that imply that there is nothing left of the rule-following problem?

In a passage whose import I believe many commentators have missed, Wittgenstein seems to indicate that the answer to this question is 'No'—even if we could simply help ourselves to the full use of intentional contents, there would still be a problem about how rule-following is possible.

The passage I have in mind is at *Philosophical Investigations* 219. In it Wittgenstein considers the temptation to say that when we commit ourselves to some rule, that rule determines how we are to act in indefinitely many future cases:

"All the steps are really already taken," means: I no longer have any choice. The rule once stamped with a particular meaning, traces the lines along which it is to be followed through the whole of space.

If we were reading this with Kripke's eyes, what would we expect Wittgenstein to say? Something along the following lines (with absolutely no aspiration to capturing Wittgenstein's literary style):

And how did you get to stamp the rule with a particular meaning so that it traces the lines along which it is to be followed through the whole of space? To do that you would need to be able to think, to frame intentions. But that assumes that we have figured out how we manage to follow rules in respect of mental expressions. And that is something that we have not yet done.

But what Wittgenstein says in reply is rather this:

But if something of this sort really were the case, how would it help?

Even if we were to grant that we could somehow imbue the rule with a meaning that would determine how it applies in indefinitely many cases in the future, Wittgenstein seems to be saying, it would still not help us understand how rule-following is possible.

How mystifying this must seem from a Kripkean point of view. How would it help? How could it not help? We wanted an answer to the question: By virtue of what is it true that I use the '+' sign according to the rule for addition and not some other rule? According to the picture currently under consideration, one of our options is to say that it is by virtue of the fact that I use the '+' sign with the intention that its use conform to the rule for addition, and where it is understood that the availability of such intentions is not itself a function of our following rules in respect of them. Under the terms of the picture in place, what would be left over?

How should we understand what Wittgenstein is saying here? It is, of course, always hard to be confident of any particular interpretation of this philosopher's cryptic remarks; but here is a suggestion that seems of independent philosophical interest.

Let us revert to our email example. Suppose I have adopted the rule: Answer any email (that calls for an answer) immediately upon receipt. And let us construe my adoption of this rule as involving an explicit intention on my part to conform to the instruction:

> Intention: For all x, if x is an email and you have just received x, answer it immediately!

Now, how should we imagine my following this rule? How should we imagine its guiding, or explaining, the conduct that constitutes my following it?

To act on this intention, it would seem, I am going to have to think, even if very fleetingly and not very consciously, that its antecedent is satisfied. The rule itself, after all, has a conditional content. It doesn't call on me to just do something, but to always perform some action, if I am in a particular kind of circumstance. And it is very hard to see how such a conditional intention could guide my action without my coming to have the belief that its antecedent is satisfied. So, let us imagine, then, that I think to myself:

> Premise: This is an email that I have just received.

in order to draw the

> Conclusion: Answer it immediately!

At least in this case, then, rule-following, on the Intention model, requires *inference*: it requires the rule-follower to infer what the rule calls for in the circumstances in which he finds himself.

In this regard, though, the email case is hardly special. Since *any* rule has *general* content, if our acceptance of a rule is pictured as involving its representation by a mental state of ours, an inference will always be required to determine what action the rule calls for in any particular circumstance. On the Intention View, then, applying a rule will always involve inference.

Inference, however, as we have already seen above, is a form of rule-following par excellence. In the email case, in moving from the intention, via the premise about the antecedent, to the conclusion, I am relying on a general rule that says that from any such premises I am entitled to draw such-and-so conclusion. Since, as I have set up the example, I have construed the email rule as an imperative, this isn't quite Modus Ponens, of course, but it is something very similar:

(MP*) From 'If C, do A' and C, conclude 'do A'!

But now: If on the Intention View, rule-following always requires inference; and if inference is itself always a form of rule-following, then the Intention View would look to be hopeless: under its terms, following any rule requires embarking upon a vicious infinite regress in which we succeed in following no rule.

To see this explicitly, let us go back to the email case. On the Intention View, applying the Email Rule requires, as we have seen, having an intention with the rule as its content and inferring from it a certain course of action. However, inference, we have said involves following a rule, in this case, MP*. Now, if the Intention View is correct, then following the rule MP* itself requires having an intention with MP* as its content and inferring from it a certain course of action. And now we would be off on a vicious regress: inference rules whose operation cannot be captured by the intention-based model are presupposed by that model itself.[24]

This argument bears an obvious similarity to Lewis Carroll's famous argument in "What the Tortoise Said to Achilles."[25]

The Carrollian argument, however, is meant to raise a problem for the *justification* of our rules of inference—how can we justify our belief that Modus Ponens, for example, is a good rule of inference?

The argument I am putting forward, though, raises an even more basic problem for how it is possible to follow an inference rule of any kind, good or bad, justified or unjustified. Even if we were talking about the rule Affirming the Consequent, the problem I am pointing to would still arise.

It would seem, then, that there would be a problem with the Intention View even if we somehow managed to resolve all the other difficulties that we outlined for it. The mere combination of the Intention View and the rule-following picture of inference are sufficient for generating a problem.

Intentions and Intentional states

How should we proceed? I have been talking about the Intention View, but, of course, everything I've been saying will apply to any Intentional View. So let

---

[24] This, I believe, is the correct interpretation of Wittgenstein's remarks about needing a rule to interpret a rule. In the Kripkean framework, this is read as supposing that a rule can only be given to you as an inert sign whose meaning you would then have to divine. And this sets off an infinite regress of interpretations. However, a different way of reading Wittgenstein here is to see him as concerned not with the question: "How could an inert sign guide us, if not through the use of further rules?" But rather with the question: "How could a general content guide us, if not through the use of further rules?"

[25] See Carroll 1895. There is also a similarity to Quine's arguments in his 1976b.

me restate our problem in full generality exposing as many of our assumptions as possible.

The claim is that the following five propositions form an inconsistent set.

1. Rule-following is possible.
2. Following a rule consists in acting on one's acceptance (or internalization) of a rule.
3. Accepting a rule consists in an intentional state with general (prescriptive) content.
4. Acting under particular circumstances on an intentional state with general content involves some sort of deductive inference to what the content calls for under the circumstances.
5. Inference involves following a rule.

If my argument is correct, then one of these claims has to go.[26] The question is which one.

Giving up (1) would give us rule-following skepticism. (2) seems to be the minimal content of saying that someone is following a rule. (3) is the Intentional View. (4) seems virtually platitudinous. For how could, say, a general conditional content of the form 'Whenever C, do A' serve as your reason for doing A, unless you inferred that doing A was called for from the belief that the circumstances are C? (I shall come back to this.) (5) seems analytic of the very idea of deductive inference (more on this below).

When we review our options, the only plausible non-skeptical option seems to be to give up 3, the Intentional View. To rescue the possibility of rule-following, it seems, we must find a way of *accepting* a rule that does not consist in our having some intentional state in which that rule's requirements are explicitly represented. Wittgenstein can be read as having arrived at the same conclusion.

The full passage from *Investigations* 219 reads as follows:

"All the steps are really already taken," means: I no longer have any choice. The rule once stamped with a particular meaning, traces the lines along which it is to be followed through the whole of space.—But if something of this sort really were the case, how would it help?

No; my description only made if it was understood symbolically.—I should have said: *This is how it strikes me.*

When I obey a rule, I do not choose.

I obey the rule *blindly.*

---

[26] Notice that this argument is not only neutral on whether what is at issue are intentions as opposed to other sorts of intentional state, but also on whether what is at issue are *personal-level* intentional states as opposed to *sub-personal* content-bearing states. So long as you think that the acceptance of a rule consists in some sort of intentional state with general content and that, as a result, inference will be required to act on that state, there will be a problem—it doesn't matter whether this is thought of as occurring at the personal or the sub-personal level—more on this below.

The drift of the considerations I have been presenting seems to capture the intended point behind this passage.

Even without assuming Naturalism as an a priori constraint on the acceptability of a solution to the rule-following problem, and without assuming that mental content itself must be engendered by rule-following, it would seem that we have shown that, in its most fundamental incarnation, rule-acceptance cannot consist in the formation of a propositional attitude in which the requirements of the rule are explicitly encoded.

Such a picture would be one according to which rule-following is always fully *sighted*, always fully informed by some recognition of the requirements of the rule being followed. And the point that Wittgenstein seems to be making is that, in its most fundamental incarnation, not all rule-following can be like that—some rule-following must simply be *blind*. The argument I have presented supports this conclusion.

Rule-Following without Intentionality: Dispositions

The question is how rule-following *could be* blind. How can someone commit himself to a certain pattern in his thought or behavior without this consisting in the formation of some appropriate kind of intentional state?

The only option that seems to be available to us is the one that Kripke considers at length, that we should somehow succeed in understanding what it is for someone to accept a given rule just by invoking his or her *dispositions* to conform to the rule. If we were able to do that, we could explain how it is possible to act on a rule without inference because the relation between a disposition and its exercise is, of course, non-inferential.

Now, Kripke, as we know, gives an extended critique of the dispositional view. However, that critique has not generally been thought to be very effective; many writers have rejected it.[27] So perhaps there is hope for rule-following after all, in the form of a dispositional account.

My own view, by contrast with received opinion, is that Kripke's critique is extremely effective, although even I underestimated the force of what I now take to be its most telling strand. And so I think that it can't offer us any refuge after all, if we abandon the Intentional View.

The core idea of a dispositional account is that what it is for someone to accept the rule Modus Ponens is, roughly, for him to be disposed, for any p and q, upon believing both p and 'if p, then q,' to conclude q.

Kripke pointed out that any such dispositional view runs into two problems. First, a person's dispositions to apply a rule are bound to contain performance errors; so one can't simply read off his dispositions which rule is at work. Second, the rule Modus Ponens is defined over an infinite number of pairs of

---

[27] See, for example, Soames 1998 and Horwich 1998.

propositions. However, a person's dispositions are finite: it is not true that I have a disposition to answer q when asked what follows from any two propositions of the form p and 'if p, then q', no matter how large.

To get around these problems, the dispositionalist would have to specify ideal conditions under which (a) a thinker would not be capable of any performance errors and (b) he would in fact be disposed to infer q from *any* two propositions of the form p and 'if p, then q.'

But it is very hard to see that there are conditions under which I would be metaphysically incapable of performance errors.

And whatever one thinks about that, it's certainly very hard to see that there are ideal conditions under which I would in fact be disposed to infer q from any two propositions of the form p and 'if p, then q,' no matter how long or complex. As Kripke says, for most propositions, it would be more correct to say that my disposition is to die before I am even able to grasp which propositions are at issue.

Along with many other commentators, I used to underestimate the force of this point. The following response to it seemed compelling. A glass can have infinitary dispositions; so how come a human can't? Thus, a glass can be disposed to break when struck here, or when struck there; when struck at this angle or at that one, when struck at this location, or at that one. And so on. If a mere glass can have infinitary dispositions, why couldn't a human being?[28]

There is a difference between the two cases. In the case of the glass, the existence of the infinite number of inputs—the different places, angles and locations—just follows from the nature of the glass qua physical object. No idealization is required.

But a capacity to grasp infinitely long propositions—the inputs in the rule-following case—does *not* follow from our nature as thinking beings, and certainly not from our nature as physical beings. In fact, it seems pretty clear that we do not have that capacity and could not have it, no matter how liberally we apply the notion of idealization.

These, then, are Kripke's central arguments against a dispositional account of rule-following, and although it would take much more elaboration to completely nail these arguments down, I believe that such an elaboration can be given.[29]

But both before and after he gives those arguments, Kripke several times suggests that the whole exercise is pointless, that it should simply be *obvious* that the dispositional account is no good. Thus, he says:

To a good extent this [dispositional] reply ought to appear to be misdirected, off target. For the skeptic created an air of puzzlement as to my *justification* for responding '125' rather than '5' to the addition problem ... he thinks my response is no better than a stab in the dark. Does the suggested reply advance matters? How does it *justify* my choice of '125'? What it says is " '125' is the response you are disposed

---

[28] See the discussion in my 1989b (this volume, Chapter 1).
[29] See my *Rules and Intentionality in Nature* (forthcoming).

to give ..." Well and good, I know that '125' is the response I am disposed to give (I am actually giving it!) ... How does any of this indicate that ... '125' was an answer *justified* in terms of instructions I gave myself, rather than a mere jack-in-the-box unjustified response?

This passage can seem puzzling and unconvincing when it is read, as Kripke seems to have intended it, as directed against dispositional accounts of mental content. After all, one of the most influential views of mental content nowadays is that expressions of mentalese get their meaning by virtue of their having a certain causal role in reasoning. Could it really be that this view is so obviously false that it is not worth discussing, as Kripke suggests? And is it really plausible that the facts by virtue of which my *mentalese* symbol '+' means what it does have to *justify* me when I use it one way rather than another?

But if we see the passage as directed not at dispositional accounts of mental content but rather at dispositional accounts of personal-level rule-following, and if we substitute "rationalize" for "justify," then its points seem correct. It should be puzzling that anyone was inclined to take a dispositional account of rule-following seriously. We can see why in two stages.

First, and as I have been emphasizing, if I am following the rule Modus Ponens, then my following that rule explains and rationalizes my concluding q from p and 'if p, then q', (just as it would be true that, if I were following the rule of Affirming the Consequent, then my following that rule would explain and rationalize my inferring q from p and 'if q, then p').

Second, if I am following the rule Modus Ponens, then not only is my *actually* inferring q explained and rationalized by my accepting that rule, but so, too, is my being *disposed* to infer q. Suppose I consider a particular MP inference, find myself disposed to draw the conclusion, but, for whatever reason, fail to do so. That disposition to draw the conclusion would itself be explained and rationalized by my acceptance of the MP rule.

However, it is, I take it, independently plausible that something can neither be explained by itself, nor rationalized by itself. So, following rule R and being disposed to conform to it cannot be the same thing.

Here we see, once again, how Kripke's Meaning Assumption gets in the way of his argument: a good point about rule-following comes out looking false when it is extended to mental content.

Is Going Sub-Personal the Solution?

I emphasized from the very beginning that the notion of rule-following that appears to underwrite the rule-following picture of rational belief is a personal-level notion. *I* reason about what to believe, not a part of my brain. As a result, it is the personal-level notion with which I have been most concerned in this paper.

Someone may therefore be tempted to think that perhaps the moral of the preceding discussion is precisely that it can't be the personal-level notion that's at work in the rule-following picture, that the solution to the difficulties we have been outlining is to go sub-personal.

This suggestion resonates with what has been a robust tendency in the literature on rule-following. There are many discussions of the Intentional View that accuse it of being 'overly intellectualized' and which recommend substituting a sub-personal notion in its place.[30] It isn't very often made clear exactly what that is supposed to amount to. The preceding discussion should help us see that this is not a very useful suggestion.

In the present context, going sub-personal presumably means identifying rule-acceptance or internalization not with some person-level state, such as an intention, but with some sub-personal state. Such a state will either be an intentional state or some non-intentional state.

Let us say that it is some intentional state in which the rule's requirements are explicitly represented. Then, once again, it would appear that some inference (now, sub-personal) will be required to figure out what the rule calls for under the circumstances. And at this point the regress problem will recur. (That is what I meant by saying earlier that the structure of the regress problem seems to be indifferent as to whether the states of rule-acceptance are personal or sub-personal.)

On the other hand, we could try identifying rule-internalization with some non-intentional state. Indeed, even if the state of rule-internalization is initially identified with a sub-personal intentional state, it will ultimately, I take it, have to be identified with some sort of non-intentional state.

But then what we would have on our hands would be some version or other of a dispositional view (with the dispositions now understood sub-personally). And although we would no longer face the rationalization problem—because, presumably, sub-personal mechanisms are not called upon to rationalize their outputs—we would still face the enormous problems posed by the error and finitude objections.

In consequence, I don't believe that going sub-personal offers a satisfying solution to the problems for the notion of rule-following that we have been describing.[31]

III. CONCLUSION

We think of our reasoning as governed by rules. We worry about whether our rules are the right ones, the ones that really deliver justified belief. We worry about how we might establish that they are the right ones; and about whether there can be a fact of the matter about that.

[30] See, for example, Pollock and Cruz 1999, chapter 5.
[31] As I say, I am unable to go into these objections in detail here—they are discussed at length in my *Rules and Intentionality in Nature* (forthcoming).

This entire way of looking at matters, though, depends on our being able to vindicate its fundamental assumption, that our reasoning is governed by rules.

If the preceding arguments are correct, there is a real problem about this.

First, it is hard to give a satisfactory answer to the question: What is a rule such that following it is necessary for rational belief? Second, it is hard to explain how rule-following is so much as possible, and this difficulty arises even without our assuming either that rule-following or intentionality needs to be given a naturalistic reduction.

What are we to do?

Perhaps we should embrace rule-skepticism, denying that our reasoning is under the influence of general rules?

The trouble is that this seems not only false about reasoning in general, but also unintelligible in connection with deductive inference. It is of the essence of deductive inference that the reasons I have for moving from certain premises to certain conclusions are general ones.

So what we are contemplating, when we contemplate giving up on the rule-following picture of deductive inference, is not so much giving up on a rule-following *construal* of deductive inference as giving up on deductive inference itself. But that is surely not stable a resting point—didn't we arrive at the present conclusion through the application of several instances of deductive inference?

The only other option with respect to our second problem (I don't at the moment know what to say about the first) is to try taking the notion of fol-lowing—or applying—a rule as primitive, effectively a rejection of proposition 4 above. Notice that this goes well beyond the sort of anti-reductionist response to Kripke's arguments that I was already inclined to favor—an anti-reductionism about mental content.

It would involve a primitivism about rule-following or rule-application itself: we would have to take as primitive a *general (often conditional) content serving as the reason for which one believes something,* without this being mediated by inference of any kind. It is not obvious that we can make sense of this, but the matter clearly deserves greater consideration.[32]

---

[32] Tyler Burge urged this primitivist suggestion on me in conversation. This paper has been in the works for quite a long time. A very early version of some of its arguments appeared as my 2005b, as part of a symposium on Philip Pettit's 2002. I have benefited greatly from feedback over the intervening years from various audiences—at various seminars at NYU, the Graduate Conference at the University of Warwick, the Workshop on Epistemic Normativity at Chapel Hill, UCLA, Stony Brook, Princeton and the Transcendental Philosophy Network Workshop in London, to name just those that come to mind. I am also grateful to Shamik Dasgupta, Sinan Dogramaci, Paul Horwich, Matthew Kotzen, Christopher Peacocke, James Pryor, Josh Schechter and Stephen Schiffer for valuable comments on earlier drafts.

Part I: Suggestions for Further Reading

Blackburn, S. (1998) 'Realism and Truth: Wittgenstein, Wright, Rorty and Minimalism', *Mind* 107 (425): 157–81.
Boghossian, P. A. (1991) 'The Status of Content Revisited', *Pacific Philosophical Quarterly* 71: 264–78.
Bykvist, K. and A. Hattiangadi. (2007) 'Does Thought Imply Ought?', *Analysis* 67: 277–85.
Devitt, M. (1990) 'Transcendentalism about Content', *Pacific Philosophical Quarterly* 71: 247–63.
_____(1991) 'Transcending Transcendentalism: A Response to Boghossian', *Pacific Philosophy Quarterly* 72: 87–100.
Dillard, P. S. (1996) 'Radical Anti-Deflationism', *Philosophy and Phenomenological Research* 56 (1): 173–82.
Gibbard, A. (2005) 'Truth and Correct Belief', *Philosophical Issues* 15 (1): 338–50.
Gibson, R. (1995) 'A Note on Boghossian's Master Argument', *Philosophical Issues* 6: 222–6.
Holton, R. (2000) 'Minimalism and Truth-Value Gaps', *Philosophical Studies* 97 (2): 137–68.
Horwich, P. (1995) 'Meaning, Use and Truth', *Mind* 104: 355–68.
_____(1998) *Meaning*. Oxford: OUP.
_____(2005) 'Norms of Truth and Meaning'. In *Reflections on Meaning*, pp. 104–34. Oxford: Clarendon Press.
McManus, D. (2000) 'Boghossian, Miller and Lewis on Dispositional Theories of Meaning', *Mind and Language* 15 (4): 393–9.
Miller, A. (1997) 'Boghossian on Reductive Dispositionalism about Content: The Case Strengthened', *Mind and Language* 12 (1): 1–10.
_____(2003) 'Objective Content: Does "Belief-Holism", Show That Reductive Dispositionalism about Content Could Not Be True?' *Proceedings of the Aristotelian Society: Supplementary Volume* 77: 73–90.
Miraglia, P. (1995) 'A Note on Truth, Deflationism and Irrealism', *Sorites* 3: 48–63.
Richard, M. (1997) 'Deflating Truth', *Philosophical Issues* 8: 57–78.
Soames, S. (1997) 'The Truth about Deflationism', *Philosophical Issues* 8: 1–44.
_____(1999) *Understanding Truth*. New York: OUP.
Stoljar, D. (1993) 'Emotivism and Truth Conditions', *Philosophical Studies* 70 (1): 81–101.
Taylor, K. A. (1994) 'How Not to Refute Eliminative Materialism', *Philosophical Psychology* 7 (1): 101–25.
Tenenbaum, S. (1996) 'Realists Without a Cause: Deflationary Theories of Truth and Ethical Realism', *Canadian Journal of Philosophy* 26: 561–90.
Wilson, G. (1994) 'Kripke on Wittgenstein on Normativity', *Midwest Studies in Philosophy* 19: 366–90.
Wright, C. (1992) *Truth and Objectivity* Appendix to Chapter 6. Cambridge, MA: Harvard University Press.

Wright, C. (1993) 'Eliminative Materialism: Going Concern or Passing Fancy?', *Mind and Language* 8 (2): 316–26.

_____ (1995) 'Can There Be a Rationally Compelling Argument for Anti-Realism about Ordinary ("Folk") Psychology?', *Philosophical Issues* 6: 197–221.

Zalabardo, J. L. (1997) 'Kripke's Normativity Argument', *Canadian Journal of Philosophy* 27 (4): 467–88.

PART II
Content and Self-Knowledge

6 *Content and Self-Knowledge*

INTRODUCTION

1. This paper argues that, given a certain apparently inevitable thesis about content, we could not know our own minds. The thesis is that the content of a thought is determined by its relational properties.

The problem can be stated roughly, but intuitively, like this. We sometimes know our thoughts directly, without the benefit of inference from other beliefs. (Indeed, given a plausible internalism about justification, this claim is not merely true but necessary.) This implies that we know our thoughts either on the basis of some form of inner observation, or on the basis of nothing. But there is a difficulty either way. On the one hand, given that the content properties of thoughts are individuated in terms of their relational properties, we could not know what we think merely by looking inwards. What we would need to see, if we are to know by mere looking, is not there to be seen. And, on the other, there appear to be serious objections to the suggestion that we may know our thoughts on the basis of nothing.[1]

The paper proceeds as follows. Part I explains why we could not know our thoughts on the basis of reasoning or inference. Part II explains why we could not know them on the basis of looking. And Part III explains why we could not know them on the basis of nothing.

I consider the skeptical claim about self-knowledge to have the status of a paradox: apparently acceptable premises lead to an unacceptable conclusion. For I do not seriously envisage that we do not know our own minds. Our capacity for self-knowledge is not an optional component of our ordinary self-conception, a thesis we may be able to discard while preserving all that really matters. It is a

[1] How a contingent proposition might be known on the basis of nothing will be explained in Part III. A word also about 'inner observation': It makes no difference to the argument of this paper if you think of inner observation as amounting to traditional introspection, or if you think of it as amounting to the operation of some Armstrong-style 'brain-scanner'. What *is* crucial to inner observation models of self-knowledge is the claim that beliefs about one's own thoughts are justified by the deliverances of some internal monitoring capacity, much like beliefs about the external environment are justified by the deliverances of an external monitoring capacity (perception).

For 'brain-scanners' see Armstrong 1968. For a useful survey of various conceptions of introspection see Lyons 1986.

fundamental part of that conception, presupposed by some of the very concepts that constitute it (consider intentional action). So long as we are not able to see our way clear to abandoning that conception—and I am assuming that we have not yet been shown how to do so—there can be no question of accepting the skeptical claim.[2]

The point of advancing it, then, is not to promote skepticism but understanding: I hope that by getting clear on the conditions under which self-knowledge is not possible, we shall better understand the conditions under which it is. I have to confess, however, that at the present time I am unable to see what those conditions might be.

A couple of preliminary remarks before we proceed. First, I propose to be reasonably serious in the use of the term 'knowledge': by 'self-knowledge' I shall mean not just a *true* belief about one's own thoughts, but a *justified* one. (I do not, however, propose to be so serious as to worry about the complexities induced by Gettier-style counterexamples.) Second, I want to keep the discussion as free as possible of problematic auxiliary assumptions about the nature of thought. In particular, I do not want to assume a 'language of thought' model of thinking. I hope one of these days to write a paper entitled "The Language of Thought Hypothesis in the Philosophy of Mind." It would argue that, contrary to what many people seem to believe, a language of thought model has profound and unexpected implications for the way we think about most mental phenomena. Issues about self-knowledge, in particular, are transformed by its assumption. The reason should be evident: a language of thought model implies that there are *type-type* correlations between certain purely formal and intrinsic properties of thoughts and their semantic properties. This is a heady assumption that stands to profoundly affect the account we are able to give of our capacity to know the semantic properties of thoughts. Too heady, I think, to be assumed uncritically and, hence, too heady for the purposes of this paper.

I. THE CHARACTER OF SELF-KNOWLEDGE

Inference and Self-Knowledge

2. Many extravagant claims have been made about our capacity to know our own minds. Descartes, who was responsible for the worst excesses, taught many subsequent generations of philosophers that self-knowledge was both infallible and exhaustive. In contrast with our knowledge of other people's minds, Descartes held, our access to our own contemporaneous mental states and events could issue neither in false belief nor in ignorance.

---

[2] For arguments in support of the indispensability of the ordinary conception, see my 1990 (this volume, Chapter 2).

These famous Cartesian claims are not, of course, wholly without substance; for a certain restricted class of mental events—namely, sensations—they may even be true. For it does seem constitutive of, say, an occurrence of pain, that it register with us precisely as an occurrence of pain. And so, it seems not conceivable, in respect of facts about pain, that we should be either ignorant of their existence or mistaken about their character, just as the Cartesian doctrine requires.

But the corresponding theses about contentful or representational states carry little contemporary conviction. That we harbor a multitude of thoughts of whose existence we are unaware is a presupposition not only of Freudian theory, but of much of present-day cognitive science. And phenomena that are intelligible only if infallibility is false—self-deception, for instance—seem pervasive.

3. A Cartesian account, then, of the distinction between first-person and third-person knowledge of mind must be rejected. But we should be wary, in correcting for Cartesian excess, of recoiling too far in the opposite direction. For there remains, even after we have discarded the problematic Cartesian claims, a profound asymmetry between the way in which I know my own thoughts and the way in which I may know the thoughts of others. The difference turns not on the epistemic status of the respective beliefs, but on the manner in which they are arrived at, or justified. In the case of others, I have no choice but to *infer* what they think from observations about what they do or say. In my own case, by contrast, inference is neither required nor relevant. Normally, I know what I think—what I believe, desire, hope or expect—without appeal to supplementary evidence. Even where such evidence is available, I do not consult it. I know what I think directly. I do not defend my self-attributions; nor does it normally make sense to ask me to do so.[3]

Ryle attempted to deny all this.[4] He tried to defend the view that there is no asymmetry between first-person and third-person access to mental states. In both cases, he maintained, the process is essentially the same: ordinary inspection of ordinary behavior gives rise to the discovery of patterns in that behavior, which in turn leads to the imputation of the appropriate propositional attitudes.

The claim carries no conviction whatever. The trouble is not merely that it runs counter to all the relevant appearances, offering an implausible explanation for the knowledge we have of our thoughts. The trouble is that, for much of what we do know about our own thoughts, it can offer no explanation at all. Consider an act of entertaining a particular proposition. You think: Even lousy composers sometimes write great arias. And you know, immediately on thinking it, that that is what you thought. What explanation can the Rylean offer of this? The difficulty is not merely that, contrary to appearance and the canons of epistemic practice, he has to construe the knowledge as inferential. The difficulty is that

---

[3] Many philosophers have pointed this out. See, for example, Davidson 1987.
[4] See Ryle 1949.

he has to construe it as involving inference from premises about behavior that you could not possibly possess. Your knowledge of that occurrent thought could not have been inferred from any premises about your behavior because that thought could not yet have come to have any traction on your behavior. So it's not merely that, on the Rylean view, you would have to know inferentially what you appear to know non-inferentially. It's that you would not know at all what you seem to know unproblematically.

Any inferential conception is likely to succumb to this sort of objection. Since the epistemic norms governing ascriptions of self-knowledge do not require possession of supplementary evidence, for any item of evidence insisted on by an inference-based account—whether it involve behavior or the environment or even the causal properties of thoughts—it should be possible to describe a situation in which you know your thoughts but you do not know the item in question.

Internalism and Self-Knowledge

4. It is, actually, surprisingly little noticed that on an *internalist* conception of justification—a conception to which many philosophers remain profoundly sympathetic—knowledge of one's own mental states *has* to be non-inferential. On this view, the alternative is not merely implausible; it is incoherent. I shall explain.

The intuition that fuels internalism in the theory of justification is the thought that someone cannot count as justified in holding a certain belief if, judged from the standpoint of his own subjective conception of the situation, he may appear epistemologically irresponsible or irrational in accepting that belief. The intuition is effectively triggered by various examples in which, although a person's belief satisfies basic externalist demands—the belief is formed by a reliable belief-forming mechanism and so on—the person does not count as epistemically justified because, as far as he is concerned, he has no reason for accepting the belief and may, indeed, have reasons for rejecting it.

Consider Sam.[5] Sam believes himself to have the power of clairvoyance, though he has no reason for the belief, and some evidence—in the form of apparently cogent scientific results—against it. One day he comes to believe, for no apparent reason, that the President is in New York City. He maintains this belief, appealing to his alleged clairvoyant power, even though he is at the same time aware of a massive amount of apparently cogent evidence, consisting of news reports, allegedly live television pictures, and so on, indicating that the President is at that time in Washington, D.C. Now the President is in fact in New York City, the evidence to the contrary being part of an official hoax. Moreover, Sam does in fact have completely reliable clairvoyant power under

[5] The example is adapted from Bonjour 1985, pp. 38–40.

the conditions then satisfied, and his belief about the President did result from the operation of that power.

Is Sam justified in his belief about the President? Basic reliabilist demands are met; but the intuition persists that the belief cannot be epistemically justified because, judged from the standpoint of Sam himself, it is epistemically thoroughly irrational.

Examples such as this are at the heart of internalist dissatisfaction with externalist conceptions of justification; they motivate the requirement that, if a belief depends upon evidence, "the knower [must] grasp the connection between the evidence and what it is evidence for," if his belief is to be justified.[6]

Suppose, then, that the proposition that p depends on the proposition that q. According to internalism, if I am to be justified in believing that p, I must believe that p as a result both of my recognition that I believe that q, and that a belief that q justifies a belief that p. Spelling this out in explicit detail, we have:

1. I believe that p.
2. I believe that q.
3. The proposition that q justifies the proposition that p.
4. I know that I believe that q.
5. I know that a belief that q justifies a belief that p.
6. I believe that p as a result of the knowledge expressed in 4 and 5.

5. Now, there is, of course, a *standard* problem in holding that all knowledge of empirical propositions is inferential, that all beliefs can be justified only by reference to other beliefs. This is the problem of the regress of justification: If the belief that p is to count as justified, then the belief that q on which its justification depends must itself be justified. But if *all* beliefs can be justified only by reference to other beliefs, then the belief that q must itself be justified by reference to other beliefs. And this threatens to lapse into a vicious regress.

Any theory of justification must confront this problem. The available non-skeptical options—Foundationalism and Coherentism—are well known and need not be rehearsed here.

The point I wish to make, however, is that there is a *special* problem sustaining a thoroughly inferential conception of *self-knowledge*, one that is independent of the *standard* problem of the regress of justification.

6. In order to bring it out, waive the standard problem: let us not require that if the non-intrinsically credible proposition that p is to be justifiably believed, then it has to rest on a belief that q that is itself justified; let us simply require

---

[6] O'Connor and Carr 1982, p. 75. For a slightly more nuanced discussion of this sort of objection to externalism see my 2003a (this volume, Chapter 12). Of course, there are responses available to the externalist. I am not going to consider them here because I am not here trying to *argue* for internalism; I am just describing it. Again, for detailed discussion see Bonjour 1985.

that the belief that p be justified *relative* to the belief that q, in accordance with standard internalist requirements.

Where the subject matter of concern is knowledge of one's own beliefs, the belief that p will be a belief to the effect that I have a certain belief, say, that I believe that r. Since we are supposing that all self-knowledge is inferential, there must be a belief on which this belief rests. Let that be the belief that s. Now, what would have to be true if I am to be justified in believing that I believe that r?

Taking into account the fact that the belief in question is a belief concerning my own beliefs, the conditions that would have to be satisfied, if I am to be justified in believing that I believe that r, are these:

1'. I believe that I believe that r.
2'. I believe that s.
3'. The proposition that s justifies the proposition that I believe that r.
4'. I know that I believe that s.
5'. I know that a belief that s justifies the belief that I believe that r.
6'. I believe that I believe that r as a result of the knowledge expressed in 4' and 5'.

The problem is transparent. In order to be justified in believing that I have a certain belief, I must already know that I have some other belief (4'): In order to know that I believe that r, I must antecedently know that I believe that s. But how was knowledge of *this* belief acquired? On the assumption that all self-knowledge is inferential, it could have been acquired only by inference from yet other known beliefs. And now we are off on a vicious regress.[7]

The problem with sustaining a thoroughly inferential conception of *self-knowledge* should have been evident from the start. For the ordinary notion of being justified in believing a non-intrinsically credible empirical proposition *presupposes* self-knowledge. For it presupposes that one has grasped the fact that one's belief in that proposition bears some appropriate epistemic relation to one's other beliefs. In ordinary epistemological discussions this does not emerge as a problem because those discussions tend to focus exclusively on the justification of belief concerning the external world; they tend, understandably, to take knowledge of the beliefs themselves for granted. When such knowledge is not taken for granted, however, it emerges very clearly that not *all* knowledge of one's beliefs can be inferential. On pain of a vicious regress, it must be possible to know the content of some mental states non-inferentially.[8]

---

[7]   The regress does not particularly depend on the fact that the relation between the beliefs consists in *inference*. There are possible coherentist views according to which mediated justification consists not in inference but in 'membership' in an appropriate system of beliefs. All such views, applied to self-knowledge, are subject to the regress outlined in the text, given internalist assumptions. (I am indebted here to Crispin Wright.)

[8]   I am inclined to believe that (at least part of) what is going on in the famous passage that concludes Wittgenstein's discussion of rule-following in his *Philosophical Investigations* is an argument to this effect. The passage reads:

7. The intuitive epistemic facts indicate that knowledge of one's mental states is direct. And an internalist conception of justification implies that it has to be. There are two ways to accommodate this claim.

We may conclude, on the one hand, that self-knowledge is not inferential because it is based on some form of inner observation; or, on the other, that it is not inferential because it is based on nothing—at any rate, on nothing empirical.

How might a contingent fact be known on the basis of nothing empirical? We shall consider that question in Part III. Before that, however, I want to turn to asking whether we could know our thoughts on the basis of inner observation.

II. CONTENT AND KNOWLEDGE OF CONTENT

8. The suggestion that I know about my thoughts by being introspectively aware of them seems, from a phenomenological standpoint anyway, overwhelmingly plausible. It is not simply that I have reliable beliefs about my thoughts. I catch some of my thoughts in the act of being thought. I think: If she says that one more time, I'm leaving. And I am aware, immediately on thinking it, that that is what I thought. Can 'inner awareness' provide the right explanation for how I know my thoughts?

There are many aspects to this question. An exhaustive treatment would distinguish carefully between occurrent events—fleeting thoughts, sudden fancies—and standing states—fixed beliefs, stable desires—and would worry about the epistemological ramifications of that distinction. It would also distinguish between the distinct attitudes that one may sustain toward a given content—judging, believing, desiring, entertaining—and explore any corresponding epistemic differences. Here, however, I shall not be concerned with these important nuances. For my worry is that, given certain currently prevailing orthodoxies about content, it is impossible to see how *any* contentful state could be known on the basis of inner observation.

The difficulty stems from the contemporary commitment to a relationist conception of content: the view that the content properties of mental states and events are determined by, or supervenient upon, their *relational* properties. Intuitively, the difficulty seems clear: how could anyone be in a position to know his thoughts merely by observing them, if facts about their content are determined

---

It can be seen that there is a misunderstanding here from the mere fact that in the course of our argument we give one interpretation after another; as if each one contented us at least for a moment, until we thought of yet another standing behind it. What this shows is that there is a way of grasping a rule that is *not* an *interpretation*. ... (*PI*: 201)

The textual evidence strongly indicates that Wittgenstein uses the term 'interpretation' to mean 'hypothesis as the meaning of.' Read this way, the passage says that the moral of the rule-following 'paradox' is that there must be a way of grasping the content of a mental event without having to form hypotheses as to its content. This is not the occasion to say what else might be going on in that passage or to defend this reading in greater detail.

by their relational properties? Articulating the intuitive problem in explicit detail is the task of the present part.

Anti-Individualism and Self-Knowledge

9. The commitment to relationism is evident, of course, in *wide* or *anti-individu-alistic* conceptions of thought content. According to such views, many of a person's thought contents are necessarily dependent on relations that that person bears to the physical or, in some cases, social environment. The view is supported by a series of now-famous thought experiments. Their strategy is to show that two individuals who are molecule-for-molecule duplicates of each other, may nevertheless think different thoughts if their environments differ from each other in certain specified ways. Thus, Putnam has argued that *part* of what makes it true that some of my thoughts involve the concept *water*, is that it is typically *in re* H_2O that I token those thoughts; a duplicate of mine, who grew up in an indistinguishably similar environment except that in it the liquid that filled the lakes and swimming pools consisted of XYZ and not H_2O, would not have the concept *water* but some other concept, *twater*. Similarly, Tyler Burge has argued that part of what makes it true that some of my thoughts involve the concept *arthritis* is that I live in, and defer to, a community in which the concept of arthritis is used in a certain way; a duplicate of mine, who grew up in an indistinguishably similar community except that in it the use of the concept was extended so as to cover all rheumatoid ailments, would not have the concept *arthritis* but some other concept, *tharthritis*.

10. Now, doesn't it follow from such anti-individualistic views that we cannot know our thoughts in a direct, purely observational manner? The following line of reasoning might seem to lead rather swiftly to that conclusion. To know my water thoughts, I would have to know that they involve the concept *water* and not the concept *twater*. But I could not know whether my thought involves the concept *water* or the concept *twater* without investigating my environment. For what I would need to know is whether it was typically *in re* H_2O or typically *in re* XYZ that I token my thoughts; and I certainly would have to investigate my environment in order to know that. I could hardly know such facts by mere introspection. It would seem to follow, therefore, that I could not know the contents of my thought purely observationally: I would have to *infer* what I think from facts about my environment.

  This line of reasoning is no doubt too swift. As it stands it appears to be making problematic assumptions about the conditions required for knowledge.[9] Consider perceptual knowledge. Someone may know, by looking, that he has a dime in his hand. But it is controversial, to put it mildly, whether he needs to

---

[9] This point is made in Burge 1988.

know all the conditions that make such knowledge possible. He need not have checked, for example, that there is no counterfeit money in the vicinity, nor does he need to be able to tell the difference between a genuine dime and every imaginable counterfeit that could have been substituted. The ordinary concept of knowledge appears to call for no more than the exclusion of "relevant" alternative hypotheses (however exactly that is to be understood); and mere logical possibility does not confer such relevance.

Similar remarks apply to the case of self-knowledge. And so, since under normal circumstances the *twater* hypothesis is not a relevant alternative, we ought not to assume, as the swift argument evidently does, that we could not know our actual thought contents unless we are able to discriminate between them and their various twin counterparts.

11. The swift argument, however, suggests a slower and more convincing argument for the same conclusion. For it seems fairly easy to describe scenarios in which the twin hypotheses *are* relevant alternatives, but in which they are, nevertheless, not discriminable non-inferentially from their actual counterparts.

Imagine that twin-earth actually exists and that, without being aware of it, S undergoes a series of switches between earth and twin-earth. Most anti-individualists agree that, if a person were to remain in each situation long enough, that person would eventually acquire the concepts appropriate to that situation.[10] There are two ways to imagine the final outcome. On the one hand, we may imagine that after a series of such switches, S ends up with *both* earthian and twin-earthian concepts: thoughts involving both *arthritis* and *tharthritis* are available to him. Or, alternatively, we may imagine that with every such slow switch a wholesale displacement of S's resident concepts takes place, so that at any given time either the earthian or the twin-earthian concepts are available to him, but not both.

The story is usually told, I believe, in the second of these two ways; though so far as I can tell, it is perfectly coherent—and a lot more interesting—to tell it the other way. Still, in the interests of keeping matters as simple as possible, I shall follow tradition and imagine only the second version.[11] I invite you to

---

[10] Burge and Davidson are explicit about this.

[11] The first version of the slow switching story involves questions that admit of no easy answer. Suppose both earthian and twin-earthian thoughts are simultaneously available to you. And suppose you think a thought that you would express with the words "I have arthritis." How is it determined whether this particular thought token involves the concept *arthritis* or the concept *tharthritis*? (This is not a question about how you would *know* whether it involved the one or the other; it's a question about what *makes it true* that it involves the one and not the other.) There seems to be no simple answer. It certainly does not seem right to say, for reasons that underlie the intuition that quick switching wouldn't suffice for change of content, that it is simply a function of the environment in which the thought is tokened. Nor are there other obvious dimensions of difference to appeal to: *ex hypothesi*, thoughts with the different contents would have exactly the same functional roles, the same linguistic expression and the same associated qualitative episodes (if any).

consider, then, a thinker S, who, quite unawares, has been shuttled back and forth between earth and twin-earth, each time staying long enough to acquire the concepts appropriate to his current situation, and at the expense of the concepts appropriate to his previous situation.

What does S know? By assumption, he is not aware that the switches have taken place and nothing about his qualitative mental life or his perceived environment tips him off. Indeed, S may not even be aware of the existence of twin-earth or of the dependence of content on environment. As far as S is concerned, he has always lived on earth. If someone were to ask him, just after one set of twin-earthian concepts has been displaced by a set of earthian ones, whether he has recently thought thoughts involving an arthritis-like concept distinct from *arthritis*, S would presumably say "no." And yet, of course, according to the anti-individualist story, he has. His knowledge of his own past thoughts seems very poor, but not presumably because he simply can't *remember* them. Could it be because he never knew them?

Let us in fact confront that question directly. Does S know what he is thinking while he is thinking it? Suppose he is on twin-earth and thinks a thought that he would express with the words "I have arthritis." Could he know what he thought? The point to bear in mind is that the hypothesis that he thought *I have arthritis* is now a relevant alternative. He, of course, is not aware of that, but that doesn't change matters. Epistemic relevance is not a subjective concept. Someone may not be aware that there is a lot of counterfeit money in his vicinity; but if there is, the hypothesis that the dime-looking object in his hand is counterfeit needs to be excluded before he can be said to know that it is a dime. Similarly, S has to be able to exclude the possibility that his thought involved the concept *arthritis* rather than the concept *tharthritis*, before he can be said to know what his thought is. But this means that he has to *reason* his way to a conclusion about his thought; and reason to it, moreover, from evidence about his external environment which, by assumption, he does not possess. How, then, can he know his thought at all?—much less know it directly?[12]

Individualist Content and Self-Knowledge

12. Ever since Putnam first invented twin-earth, philosophers have expressed concern about the compatibility of wide individuation with the direct character of self-knowledge.[13] In the previous section I have tried to show that these

---

[12] It is no objection to this argument to point out that, on *this* way of telling the switching story, S cannot even frame the hypothesis he is called upon to exclude. Someone may not have the concept of counterfeit money, but if there is a lot of counterfeit money in his vicinity, then he must be able to exclude the hypothesis that the coin in his hand is counterfeit before he can be said to know that it is a dime. The fact that he cannot so much as frame the relevant hypothesis does not absolve him of this requirement. In any case, any residual worries on this score can be averted, if necessary, by telling the switching story in the alternative way outlined in the text.

[13] See, for example, Andrew Woodfield's remarks in the "Introduction" to his 1982, p. viii. See also Brueckner 1986.

concerns are in order, that there is indeed a problem reconciling the thesis with the intuitive facts. As I shall try now to explain, however, the problem about self-knowledge was there all along and the recent emphasis on *widely* individuated content betrays a misunderstanding: even if no external factors were involved in fixing mental content, on any currently acceptable account of the internal determinants, the difficulty about self-knowledge would still remain.

The point is that according to currently prevailing orthodoxy, even the internal (or narrow) determinants of a mental event's content are relational properties of that *event* (although they are, of course, intrinsic properties of the *thinker* in whom the events occur.)

An example of a properly non-relationist conception of content is provided by the imagistic theory of the British Empiricists. According to this theory, thinking the thought that p involves entertaining an image that represents that p. And the facts in virtue of which an image represents a particular state of affairs are said to depend exclusively on the intrinsic properties of the image. Neither tenet is considered plausible today. Thinkings are not imagings; and, in any case, the representational properties of images are not determined by their intrinsic properties.

Indeed, according to contemporary conviction, there is *no* property intrinsic to a mental event—certainly no *naturalistic* intrinsic property—that could serve as the complete determinant of that event's representational content. In effect, the only idea around about what narrow properties of an event might fix its content is the suggestion that it is some subset of the event's *causal* properties. The central functionalist idea here is that the content of a mental event is determined by that event's causal role in reasoning and deliberation and, in general, in the way the event interacts with other events so as to mediate between sensory inputs and behavioral outputs. On the assumption, then, that no external factors are involved in content individuation, the facts in virtue of which a thought is a thought about *water*, as opposed to a thought about *gin*, have to do with the thought's causal properties: thoughts with causal role R are thoughts about water, whereas thoughts with causal role R′ are thoughts about gin.

Consider now a particular episode of thinking *water is wet*. How, on the dominant functionalist picture, might I know that that is what I thought? To know that I just had a *water* thought, as opposed to a *gin* thought (which, unlike a *twater* thought counts as a relevant alternative even in the absence of special circumstances) I would have to know, it seems, that my thought has the causal role constitutive of a *water* thought, as opposed to one constitutive of a *gin* thought. But it doesn't seem possible to know a thought's causal role directly. The point derives from Hume's observation that it is not possible to ascertain an item's causal properties non-inferentially, by mere inspection of its intrinsic properties; discovering them requires observation of the item's behavior over time.

But, again, this would appear to imply that I would have to *reason* my way to a thought's content; and reason to it, moreover, from facts about its causal role that I do not necessarily possess. How, then, could I know my thoughts at all?—much less know them directly?

Knowledge of relations

13. It might be suggested that the appearance of a difficulty here is being generated by appeal to a false principle: namely, that in order to know a mental event one must know how things stand with respect to the conditions that individuate that event.[14]

The cogency of the argument would certainly be at risk if such a principle were being assumed. For it is clearly not in general true that to know whether an object x has a property P one has to know how things stand with respect to the facts on which P supervenes. For example, the roundness of this coin in my hand supervenes on a mass of facts concerning the arrangement of molecules at its boundary; but I do not need to know those facts in order to know that the coin is round.

It is fortunate for my argument, therefore, that it assumes no such principle. What it does assume is different and considerably more plausible. Namely this: That you cannot tell by mere inspection of an object that it has a given *relational* or *extrinsic* property. This principle is backed up by appeal to the following two claims, both of which strike me as uncontestable. That you cannot know that an object has a given relational property merely by knowing about its *intrinsic* properties. And that mere inspection of an object gives you at most knowledge of its intrinsic properties. Uncontestable or not, it may yet seem that there are exceptions to the principle that an extrinsic property can never be detected by mere inspection.

Consider monetary value. Being a dime is not an intrinsic property of an object: for something to be a dime it must bear a number of complicated relations to its economic and social environment. And yet, we seem often able to tell that something is a dime purely observationally, by mere inspection of its intrinsic properties. Counterexample.

Not quite. The reason an extrinsic property seems, in this case, ascertainable by mere inspection, is due to the fact that possession of that property is correlated with possession of an intrinsic property that is ascertainable by mere inspection. The reason that the coin's dimehood seems detectable by mere inspection derives from the fact that its having the value in question is neatly encoded in several of its purely intrinsic properties: in the phrase "ten cents" that is inscribed on it, and in several other of its size, shape, and design characteristics.

To see clearly that it is only because of this feature that we are able to "inspect" the coin's value properties, consider a monetary system in which *all* coins, regardless of value, share their intrinsic properties: they are all minted of

---

[14] See Burge 1988, p. 651. See also his 1986.

precisely the same metal, are all precisely of the same shape, size, and design. As far as their intrinsic properties are concerned, nothing serves to distinguish between coins of different value. Nevertheless, the coins are not all of equal value; and, let us suppose, what determines a coin's value is the mint it was minted at: coins minted at "five cent" mints are worth five cents, those at "ten cent" mints, ten cents, and so on. It should be obvious that the value of *these* coins is not ascertainable by mere inspection; one would have to know something about their historical properties.

If this is right, it shows that our normal ability to "inspect" monetary value cannot help explain our ability to know our thought contents directly. First, because the feature that helps explain our knowledge in the former case—the correlation between the coin's monetary value and possession of certain intrinsic properties—does not obtain in the latter: facts about a thought token's content are not correlated with any of that token's purely intrinsic properties.[15] And second, because even if this were not true, that would still not explain how we might know our thoughts directly. For the process by which we know the coin's value is not really inspection, it's inference: you have to deduce that the coin is worth ten cents from your knowledge of its intrinsic properties plus your knowledge of how those intrinsic properties are correlated with possession of monetary value. And our knowledge of thought is not like that.

III. IS SELF-KNOWLEDGE A COGNITIVE ACHIEVEMENT?

14. Many philosophers would agree, I think, with the conclusion of the previous part: that if we had to know our thoughts on the basis of inner observation, then we couldn't know our thoughts. It has certainly become very popular to claim that an observational model of self-knowledge is mistaken. Thus Burge:

If one thinks of one's relation to the subject matter of basic self-knowledge on an analogy to one's relation to objects of empirical investigation, then the view that one's thoughts (the subject matter) are dependent for their natures on relations to the environment will make it appear that one's knowledge of one's thoughts cannot be any more direct or certain than one's knowledge of the environment. ... This line of reasoning is deeply misconceived.[16]

Donald Davidson has sounded a similar theme:

I can tell by examining my skin what my private or 'narrow' condition is, but nothing I can learn in this restricted realm will tell me that I am sunburned. The difference between referring to and thinking of water and referring to and thinking of twater is like the difference between being sunburned and one's skin being in exactly the same condition through another cause. The semantic difference lies in

---

[15] This would be false if a language of thought hypothesis were true.
[16] Burge 1988, p. 660.

the outside world, beyond the reach of subjective or sublunar knowledge. So the argument might run.

This analogy, between the limited view of the skin doctor and the tunnel vision of the mind's eye, is fundamentally flawed.[17]

But it is not as if, in opposing an observational model of self-knowledge, these philosophers are suggesting that knowledge of thought is inferential. The claim is, rather, that the correct way to explain the direct and authoritative character of self-knowledge is to think of it as based on nothing—at any rate, on nothing empirical.

Cognitively Insubstantial Judgments

Ordinarily, to know some contingent proposition you need either to make some observation, or to perform some inference based on some observation. In this sense, we may say that ordinary empirical knowledge is always a *cognitive achievement* and its epistemology always *substantial*. How could a judgment about a contingent matter of fact count as knowledge and yet not be a cognitive achievement? Or, to put the question another way, how could a contingent proposition be known directly, and yet not through observation?

Consider the judgment *I am here now*. Any token of this contingent judgment would be true and justified. But, in contrast with ordinary empirical judgments, the thinker is not required to possess any evidence for his judgment; he needs only to think it. The judgment is true and justified as soon as thought. The thinker counts as knowing something thanks not to the possession of any empirical evidence on his part, but simply courtesy of the concepts involved.

Consider another example. Suppose that the Kantian thesis, that experience of the world as containing substances is a precondition for experiencing it at all, is correct. It would follow, on such a view, (and ignoring for present purposes the distinction between experiencing and knowing), that knowledge that the (experienced) world contains substances is knowledge that is cognitively insubstantial. To know the fact in question a thinker is not required to possess any particular item of empirical evidence; he needs merely to experience. The truth of, and warrant for, the belief are secured, not by evidence, but by the satisfaction of certain very general conditions on experience. The thinker counts as knowing something thanks not to the possession of any evidence on his part, but simply courtesy of those general facts.

A third example. According to some philosophers, certain self-regarding judgments are essentially self-verifying. Antecedent to the judgment that I am jealous, for example, there may be no fact of the matter about whether I am;

---

[17] Davidson 1987, p. 453.

but thinking it makes it so.[18] The judgment that I am jealous, when made, is, therefore, both true and justified. But, again, no evidence is required for the judgment. To know the fact in question, I am not required to possess any particular item of empirical evidence; I need merely to make the judgment. I count as knowing something thanks not to the possession of any evidence on my part, but simply courtesy of the self-verifying nature of the judgment involved.

These examples illustrate three different kinds of contingent judgment which one may be justified in making even in the absence of any empirical evidence. The warrant for such judgments derives from other sources: from the meanings of the concepts involved, or from the satisfaction of certain general conditions, or from the judgment-dependent character of the phenomena being judged. Whatever the source, no observation, or inference based on observational premises, is required or relevant. These judgments, when known, constitute knowledge that is based on nothing empirical. In my terms, they are not cognitive achievements and are subject, therefore, to an insubstantial epistemology.[19]

The relevance of such judgments ought to be clear. So long as knowledge of thought is construed as dependent on evidence, it seems impossible to understand how we could know our thoughts. That is what the argument of the previous two parts amounts to. If, however, self-regarding judgments could be understood along cognitively insubstantial lines—as the sorts of judgment which, for one reason or another, might be known without empirical evidence—then we might be able to explain how we know our thoughts, consistent with the admission that we do not know them on the basis of observation, or of inference based on observation. Could self-knowledge be, in this way, cognitively insubstantial?

Cognitively Insubstantial Self-Knowledge

15. It is hard to see how it could be. Knowledge that is not a cognitive achievement would be expected to exhibit certain characteristics—characteristics that are notably absent from self-knowledge. For instance, and unlike ordinary empirical knowledge, you would not expect cognitively insubstantial knowledge to

---

[18] Jealousy is being used here merely for illustrative purposes. For reasons that are touched upon briefly below (see note 23), I actually rather doubt that judgments about jealousy are self-verifying in the sense bruited in the text.

[19] Wittgenstein remarked, famously, that:

It cannot be said of me at all (except perhaps as a joke) that *I know* I am in pain. What is it supposed to mean—except perhaps that I *am* in pain? (*PI*: 246)

The remark has struck most philosophers as extremely implausible. A truth it may harbor, however, is that if (as seems right) it is constitutive of being in pain that one know that one is, then knowing that one is cannot count as a cognitive achievement; one doesn't count as being in pain unless one knows it. As against Wittgenstein, I am not sure that this point is best captured by denying that judgments about pain constitute 'knowledge.'

be subject to direction: how much you know about your thoughts should not depend on how much *attention* you are paying to them, if you do not know your thoughts on the basis of evidence. And yet it does seem that, within bounds anyway, self-knowledge can be directed: one can decide how much attention to direct to one's thoughts or images, just as one can decide how much attention to pay to objects in one's visual field.[20]

Or consider the fact that some adults are better than others at reporting on their inner states; and that most adults are better than children. How is this to be explained if self-knowledge is not to be thought of as an information-sensitive capacity that may be subject to cultivation or neglect?

The most important consideration, however, against an insubstantial construal of self-knowledge derives not so much from these observations but from a claim they presuppose: namely, that self-knowledge is both fallible and incomplete. In both the domain of the mental and that of the physical, events may occur of which one remains ignorant; and, in both domains, even when one becomes aware of an event's existence, one may yet misconstrue its character, believing it to have a property it does not in fact possess. How is this to be explained? I know of no convincing alternative to the following style of explanation: the difference between getting it right and failing to do so (either through ignorance or through error) is the difference between being in an epistemically favorable position with respect to the subject matter in question—being in a position to garner the relevant evidence—and not. To put this point another way, it is only if we understand self-knowledge to be a cognitive achievement that we have any prospect of explaining its admitted shortcomings.

There is an irony in this, if it's true. Since Descartes, self-knowledge has been thought to present special philosophical problems precisely because it was held to be immune to cognitive deficit. The assumption was that we knew—or anyway had some idea—how to explain *imperfect* cognitive mechanisms; what seemed to elude explanation was a cognitive faculty that never erred. This line of thought seems to me to be exactly backwards. If Descartes's hyperbolic claims were right—if self-knowledge really were immune to error and ignorance—the temptation to explain it in an epistemologically deflationary way would be overwhelming. As it is, however, the Cartesian claims are incorrect and the epistemology of self-knowledge, thereby, substantial.

16. Strange to discover, then, that deflationary accounts of self-knowledge appear to be gaining widespread acceptance.[21] I have already mentioned some general reasons for being suspicious of such accounts. In the remainder of this paper I

---

[20] This observation is made in Mellor 1978.

[21] See Burge 1988, Davidson 1987, and Heil 1988.

An interesting proposal, that seems to me to fall somewhere in between a substantial and an insubstantial conception as defined here, is outlined by Crispin Wright in his 1989. The proposal deserves extensive separate treatment. For a brief discussion see my 1989b (this volume, Chapter 1).

propose to look at Burge's provocative proposal in detail, outlining the specific ways in which, as I see it, it fails as an account of self-knowledge.

Burge: Self-Knowledge and Self-Verification

17. According to Burge, it is a fundamental error to think that self-knowledge is a species of cognitive achievement. As he puts it, it is a mistake to think that, in order to know a thought, one must know a lot about it. Rather,

[t]he source of our strong epistemic right, our justification, in our basic self-knowledge is not that we know a lot about each thought we have. ... It is that we are in the position of thinking those thoughts in the second-order, self-verifying way.[22]

How is this to be understood?

Consider the following judgment about what I am thinking:

I judge: I am thinking that writing requires concentration.

In such a judgment, Burge points out, the subject matter of the judgment is not merely contingently related to the thoughts one thinks about it. The judgment is self-referential and self-verifying. The second-order judgment to the effect that I'm thinking that writing requires concentration could not exist unless I were to think, through that very thought, that writing requires concentration. The thought I am making a judgment about is self-referentially fixed by the judgment itself; and the judgment is thereby self-verifying. At least in this sort of case, then, it appears that one need know nothing about a thought in order to know that one has thought it; one need only think the thought as part of a second-order thought that asserts its occurrence. Since such thoughts are, as Burge correctly points out, logically self-verifying, they are guaranteed to be true as soon as thought. Hence, they would appear to constitute authoritative and non-inferential knowledge of thought, the relational character of the properties that determine thought content notwithstanding.

Burge calls this sort of self-verifying, self-regarding judgment *basic self-knowledge*. Let us start with the following question: how much of direct self-knowledge is basic self-knowledge? How well does Burge's paradigm explain the general phenomenon?

18. We may begin by noting that it does not at all explain our knowledge of our *standing* mental states. Judgments concerning such states, for example,

I judge: I *believe* that writing requires concentration

or

I judge: I *desire* that writing require concentration

---

[22] Burge 1988, p. 660.

are not self-verifying. I need not actually believe that writing requires concentration in order to think the first thought, nor actually desire that it require concentration to think the second. These self-regarding judgments do not conform to Burge's paradigm. This would appear to be a serious problem. After all, we do know about our beliefs and desires in a direct and authoritative manner, and Burge's proposal seems not to have the resources to explain how.

How does his proposal fare in connection with *occurrent* events? In this domain, too, its applicability seems rather limited. Self-regarding judgments about what I occurrently desire or fear, for example, are manifestly not self-verifying, in that I need not actually desire or fear any particular thing in order to judge that I do. Thus, it may be that

I judge: I fear that writing requires concentration

without actually fearing that it does. The judgment is not self-verifying.

The best possible case for Burge's purposes will involve a self-regarding judgment about a mere thinking or entertaining of a proposition—a judgment of a the form

I judge: I think that writing requires concentration

And even here, the judgment will only prove self-verifying if the time at which the judgment is made is *absolutely coincident* with the time at which the thought being judged about is thought. In other words, the second-order judgment will be self-verifying only if it literally incorporates the very thought about which it is a judgment. It is only under this very special condition that the thinking of the proposition in question is presupposed by the very act of making a judgment about it; and, hence, only under this very special condition that the judgment is self-verifying.[23] If, for example, the judgment concerned an act of entertaining a proposition that preceded the act of making judgment by even the smallest interval of time, as in

I judge: I just now thought that writing requires concentration

then, since it need not be true that I had that thought *then* in order to make this judgment *now*, such a judgment would not be self-verifying and, hence, would constitute a species of self-knowledge that is not subject to Burge's deflationary paradigm.

But is it not precisely knowledge of this form—knowledge of what one has thought immediately after one has thought it—that we think of as central to our capacity for self-knowledge? We are struck by our ability to know, non-inferentially and authoritatively, that a certain mental event has occurred,

---

[23] This explains why second-order judgments about sudden wants or momentary frights cannot be self-verifying: these events are not mental performatives in the required sense. They cannot be brought about by the mere thinking of a second-order judgment; hence, they cannot be incorporated into a second-order judgment in the way required for self-verification.

immediately on its having occurred. We think: Writing requires concentration. And then we know, directly and unproblematically, that that is what we thought. A first-order thought occurs. And we are then able, without the benefit of inference, to form a correct judgment about what thought that was. The second-order judgment in these central cases is not self-verifying. Such cases are not instances of "basic self-knowledge" in Burge's sense. How does his proposal help explain how they are possible? The fact that, *had* the thought been part of a second-order judgment, then that judgment would have been self-verifying, does not help explain how we are able to know what thought it was, given that it *wasn't* part of such a judgment. First-order thoughts that are not part of second-order thoughts are directly knowable. Arguably, acts of knowing such thoughts are paradigm cases of self-knowledge. And Burge's proposal seems incapable of explaining how they are possible.

19. Still, even if Burge's proposal does not explain the central cases, does it not supply us with at least *one* case in which a thought is known directly despite the relational nature of its individuation conditions? And isn't that enough to dislodge our intuition that relationism is irreconcilable with directness?

If Burge's self-verifying judgments were instances of genuine knowledge, then they would indeed dislodge the problematic intuition. But I am not convinced that they are.

Consider again the case of the person who undergoes a series of slow switches between earth and twin-earth. Burge observes:

In the former situation, the person may think "I am thinking that water is a liquid." In the latter situation, the person may think "I am thinking that twater is a liquid." In both cases the person is right and as fully justified as ever. The fact that the person does not know that a switch has occurred is irrelevant to the truth and justified character of these judgments. Of course, the person may learn about the switches and ask "Was I thinking yesterday about water or twater?"—and yet not know the answer. Here knowing the answer may sometimes depend on knowing empirical background conditions. But such sophisticated questions about memory require a more complex story.[24]

These remarks strike me as puzzling. They amount to saying that, although S will not know tomorrow what he is thinking right now, he does know right now what he is thinking right now. For any given moment in the present, say t1, S is in a position to think a self-verifying judgment about what he is thinking at t1. By Burge's criteria, therefore, he counts as having direct and authoritative knowledge at t1 of what he is thinking at that time. But it is quite clear that tomorrow he won't know what he thought at t1. No self-verifying judgment concerning his thought at t1 will be available to him then. Nor, it is perfectly clear, can he know by any other non-inferential means. To know what he thought

---

[24] Burge 1988, p. 659.

at t1 he must discover what environment he was in at that time and how long he had been there. But there is a mystery here. For the following would appear to be a platitude about memory and knowledge: if S knows that p at t1, and if at (some later time) t2, S remembers everything S knew at t1, then S knows that p at t2.

Now, let us ask: *why* does S not know today whether yesterday's thought was a *water* thought or a *twater* thought? The platitude insists that there are only two possible explanations: either S has forgotten or he *never* knew. But surely memory failure is not to the point. In discussing the epistemology of relationally individuated content, we ought to be able to exclude memory failure by stipulation. It is not as if thoughts with widely individuated contents might be easily known but difficult to remember. The only explanation, I venture to suggest, for why S will not know tomorrow what he is said to know today, is not that he has forgotten but that he never knew. Burge's self-verifying judgments do not constitute genuine knowledge. What other reason is there for why our slowly transported thinker will not know tomorrow what he is said to know directly and authoritatively today?[25]

In sum, Burge's self-verifying judgments seem to me neither to explain the central cases, nor to provide particularly compelling examples of special cases in which a relationally individuated thought is known non-inferentially.

Conclusion

20. In this paper, I have attempted to map out the available theoretical options concerning self-knowledge. And I have argued that none of the options work. It seems to me that we have a serious problem explaining our ability to know our thoughts, a problem that has perhaps not been sufficiently appreciated. As I said in the introduction, however, the point of the exercise is not to promote skepticism, but understanding. I am confident that one of the options will work; but I think we need to think a lot harder before we are in a position to say which one.[26]

---

[25] Obviously, this barely scratches the surface of the various issues that crop up here. A proper discussion would include, among other things, an account of what Burge's self-verifying judgments *do* constitute, if not a species of knowledge. Limitations of space prevent me from taking matters further in this paper.

[26] For valuable comments on an earlier draft, or for helpful discussion of the issues, I am very grateful to Jennifer Church, Jerry Fodor, Barry Loewer, David Velleman, Crispin Wright, and Stephen Yablo.

7 *The Transparency of Mental Content*

INTRODUCTION

Michael Dummett once wrote:

It is an undeniable feature of the notion of meaning—obscure as that notion is—that meaning is *transparent* in the sense that, if someone attaches a meaning to each of two words, he must know whether these meanings are the same.[1]

As the surrounding discussion makes clear, Dummett's claim isn't merely the fairly weak thesis that, for any two expressions in a person's repertoire, it must be possible for that person to come to know whether or not they mean the same. Rather, the claim is that it must be possible for that person to come to know such a fact purely *introspectively*, without the benefit of further empirical investigation—a priori, as I shall also occasionally put it.

Dummett doesn't say much about the basis for his conviction that 'transparency' in this sense—*epistemic transparency* as I shall sometimes call it, to distinguish it from the *referential* variety—is "an undeniable feature of the notion of meaning." He gives the impression of finding the claim too obvious to need arguing. In this respect, I believe, he follows in the footsteps of Frege and Russell, both of whom gave epistemic transparency a pivotal, if unargued, role in their respective theories of linguistic and mental content.

In another paper, I hope to discuss this historical point. In this paper, however, my concern will be purely philosophical and, then, only with *mental* content. I believe that the notion of epistemic transparency does play an important role in our ordinary conception of mental content and I want to say what that role is. Unfortunately, the task is a large one; here I am able only to begin on its outline.

I shall proceed somewhat indirectly, beginning with a discussion of *externalist* conceptions of mental content. I shall show that such conceptions violate epistemic transparency to an extent that has not been fully appreciated. Subsequently, I shall look at the implications of this violation and at the reconstructive project that a rejection of transparency entails. I am inclined to think it

---

[1] Dummett 1978, p. 131.

unlikely that we will get a conception of propositional content that underwrites epistemic transparency. But I am concerned that we have not fully appreciated the role that transparency currently plays and the work that would need to be done were we to discard it.

EXTERNALISM, SELF-KNOWLEDGE AND TRANSPARENCY

The minimal intended significance of the Twin Earth thought experiments may be put like this: Either mental contents are not individuated individualistically, or they are not individuated in terms of their truth conditions.

Thus, consider Oscar and twin Oscar; they are alike in all intrinsic, non-relational respects. But whereas Oscar grows up in a physical environment which contains H_2O, twin Oscar grows up in an environment which contains XYZ. And widespread intuition appears to have it that whereas Oscar's utterance of 'Water is wet' expresses a thought that is true if and only if H_2O is wet, twin Oscar's utterance of that sentence expresses a thought that is true if and only if XYZ is wet. Hence, either the contents of the two thoughts are not individuated individualistically or they are not individuated in terms of their truth conditions.[2]

Thus, consider also Bert and twin Bert; they are alike in all intrinsic, non-relational respects. But whereas Bert grows up in, and defers to, a community in which the word 'arthritis' is used to apply only to a certain kind of inflammation of the joints, twin Bert grows up in, and defers to, a community in which 'arthritis' is used to apply to all rheumatoid ailments, even to those that might occur in the thigh. And widespread intuition has it that whereas Bert's utterance of 'I have arthritis in my thigh' expresses a thought that is true if and only if he has arthritis in his thigh (and, hence, can never be true), twin Bert's utterance of that sentence expresses a thought that is true if and only if he has (some other disease) tharthritis in his thigh (and, hence, may occasionally be true). As before, the moral would appear to be: Either the mental contents of the two thoughts are not individuated individualistically or they are not individuated in terms of their truth conditions.[3] Let us call the former view *externalism*, and the latter *individualism*.

According to externalism, then, the psychologically relevant contents of a subject's intentional states are individuated in part by certain sorts of facts about the physical and/or social environment in which he happens to be situated.[4] And although this would appear to undermine the claim that we can have

---

[2] See Putnam 1975a.

[3] See Burge 1979. Burge, of course, regards externalism to be the correct moral of the thought experiments.

[4] Throughout this paper, I shall use 'externalism about mental content' to refer only to the sorts of dependence on external factors that are encouraged by the Putnam and Burge thought experiments. Any number of other sorts of dependence are also imaginable, but I take it that no case has been made for taking them seriously as models of *our* propositional attitudes.

purely introspective, non-empirical access to the contents of our thoughts, we are assured by an increasing number of philosophers that this appearance is illusory: there is in fact no conflict between an externalist conception of mental content and introspective self-knowledge. I want to begin with the question, On what is this confidence based?

It is based on a thought that is succinctly expressed by Davidson:

Showing that there is no conflict [between externalism and knowledge of content] is basically simple. It depends on realizing that whatever is responsible for the contents of our thoughts, whether known or not, is also responsible for the content of the thought that we have the thought.[5]

How exactly should we understand Davidson's thought here?

Let's assume, without loss of generality, that we think in a language of thought (in fact, I'll pretend that we think in English. This will make the exposition easier but is not required for anything that's to follow: similar claims could have been made without the assumption that psychological states possess syntactic structure). With the convenient assumption in place, we may say that Peter believes that **p** just in case Peter has a token of a sentence S, which means that **p**, in his belief box; and Peter desires that **q** just in case Peter has a token of a sentence Q, which means that **q**, in his desire box; and so on for the other attitudes.

It is now easy to give a completely general elaboration of Davidson's thought. For since externalism is guaranteed to be entirely neutral on the matter, we may safely assume that there are *syntactic* mechanisms which ensure that when, and only when, a token of the sentence S enters Peter's belief box, then *ceteris paribus*, so does a token of the sentence 'I believe S'. And so, provided that the embedded and unembedded tokens of S may always be counted upon to express the same content, Peter's second-order belief will always report correctly on the content of his first-order belief, the externalist nature of content individuation notwithstanding. Hence, and in this sense, externalism is shown to be consistent with authoritative first-person knowledge of thought content. This is, I think, the best and simplest way to develop the idea that Davidson expresses.[6]

Now, there are, I think, a number of questions that might be raised about this proposal. For instance: can we in fact always count on the embedded and unembedded occurrences of S to express the same content? (As we shall presently see, there may be special reasons for doubting the reliability of this covariation under externalist assumptions.) Also: the envisaged proposal would appear at best to ensure the availability of *reliable* beliefs about content, not *knowledge*; and there are some tricky questions about justification that need answering. But I am not going to pursue either of these lines of questioning

---

[5] "Reply to Burge," unpublished ms.

[6] Though I certainly don't wish to *assume* that Davidson himself would develop it along these lines. For a similar proposal see Lepore and Loewer 1986.

here; for present purposes, I wish simply to grant the claim that externalism is consistent with the sort of knowledge of content envisaged by this elaboration of Davidson's idea. My point will rather be that the kind of self-knowledge that is thereby secured falls short—way short—of the kind of self-knowledge we normally think of ourselves as possessing.

Let us grant the claim that, for any sentence S in my belief box, I can form a correct second-order belief about its content by prefixing the words 'I believe ... ' to that very sentence. It is important to observe, however, that no other epistemic capacity is thereby grounded. For instance, suppose I have two sentences P and Q in my belief box that are *identical* in content; it needn't follow that I will know, or be able to a priori come to know, that they are, and this despite my being said to know what the contents of P and Q are individually. Nor, similarly, does it follow that if I have two sentences Q and R in my belief box that are *distinct* in content, that I will know, or be able to a priori come to know, that they are; and this despite my being said to know what the contents of Q and R are individually. In fact, it doesn't even follow from the sort of knowledge that is underwritten by the proposal, that I will know, or be able to a priori come to know, whether two distinct tokens of the *same* sentence type S express the same·or distinct contents. To put the point concisely, the proposal does nothing to reconstruct the intuitive idea that we know the contents of our thoughts in the sense that we can introspectively *discriminate* between them, that we can tell them apart from each other: it doesn't by itself underwrite the epistemic transparency of mental content.

EXTERNALISM, TRANSPARENCY AND THE SEMANTICS OF TRAVEL

The thesis of the epistemic transparency of content may be usefully broken up into two parts: (a) If two of a thinker's token thoughts possess the same content, then the thinker must be able to know a priori that they do; and (b) If two of a thinker's token thoughts possess distinct contents, then the thinker must be able to know a priori that they do. Call the first the thesis of the *transparency of sameness* and the second the thesis of the *transparency of difference*.

Now, it is fairly easy to show that externalist contents do not satisfy the transparency of sameness. Kripke's notorious Frenchman, Pierre, already shows this for the special case of *Millian* contents (themselves, of course, a species of externalist content).[7] The details are well enough known that I need not rehearse them here. A plausible story culminates in Pierre having two expressions—'Londres' and 'London'—which refer to the same city without, however, his realizing that they do. The thought he expresses with

---

[7] See Kripke 1988.

London is pretty

is the same as the thought he expresses with

Londres is pretty;

but this fact is unavailable to introspection alone.

We need a different sort of case, however, to illustrate the general claim that even a non-Millian, referentially opaque content would fail the transparency of sameness, if it were individuated externalistically. Brian Loar has described a case which may be adapted to just this purpose.[8]

Paul, an English speaker, has been raised by a French nanny in a sheltered way. She speaks English with Paul, but amuses herself by referring to the cats around them as "chats" and never as "cats." Paul, satisfying the usual competence and deference constraints on concept possession, is to be credited with beliefs involving the concept cat. In particular, the belief he would express with "All chats have tails" would be the belief that all cats have tails.

Now, Paul occasionally sees his parents, who speak of animals called "cats." Because on those occasions, no cats or pictures of cats are ever present, Paul does not realize that cats are his familiar "chats." However, Paul's parents tell him quite a lot about cats and in particular that all cats have tails. On this basis, it is again true of Paul that the belief he would express with "All cats have tails" would be the belief that all cats have tails.[9]

Intuitively, however, it is quite clear that Paul will not be able to tell a priori that the belief he expresses with "All chats have tails" is the same belief that he expresses with "All cats have tails."

So much, then, by way of illustrating externalism's violation of the transparency of sameness. What has not been generally appreciated, however, is that externalism also allows for a coherent description of the *converse* case: two tokens of a thinker's language of thought belonging to the *same* syntactic type have *distinct* meanings, but the thinker is in principle not in a position to know a priori that they do. These converse cases, illustrating externalism's violation of the transparency of difference, are, I believe, important even for issues beyond the ones presently at hand.[10]

To see *one* way in which such converse cases might arise we need to think—harder perhaps than is common in the literature—about the semantics of so-called 'one-world traveling cases'. Suppose that Earth and Twin Earth are part of the actual world and that Peter, a normal, competent adult Earthling, is

---

[8] See Loar 1988. As I explain below, Loar himself uses his example to illustrate a different thesis.

[9] Loar himself uses the case to argue for individualism about thought content. His idea is to concede that the beliefs would be *reported* as the externalist claims, while still maintaining that their psychologically relevant contents would be individualistically individuated.

[10] The assumption that there could not be disambiguated tokens of an ambiguous word type in the language of thought is widespread in the philosophy of mind. See, for example, Fodor 1981, p. 227.

suddenly and unwittingly transported to Twin Earth. An accidental tourist, Peter goes to sleep one night at home and wakes up in twin home in twin bed. He suffers no discernible disruption in the continuity of his mental life. Here on Twin Earth, Peter happily lives out the rest of his days, never discovering the relocation that he has been forced to undergo. How should we think about the semantics of Peter's thoughts?

Well, one intuition that is shared by practically everyone who has thought about these cases is that, after a while (how long is unclear), some tokens of, say, 'water' in Peter's language of thought will shift from meaning **water** and will come to mean **twater**. Thus, to quote just one example, Tyler Burge writes:

The thoughts would not switch as one is [quickly] switched from one actual situation to another twin actual situation. The thoughts would switch only if one remained long enough in the other situation to establish environmental relations necessary for new thoughts. So quick switching would not be a case in which thoughts switched ...
But slow switching could be such a case.[11]

Viewed from an externalist perspective, it's hard to deny the force of the intuition that Burge is expressing here. We imagine Peter moving to Twin Earth and staying there for a while. Over time he thinks to himself a variety of thoughts that he expresses with sentences like:

I won't go swimming today; the water is too cold.

Or:

There's too much water in this whiskey.

It seems very plausible that these expressions of beliefs about one's present environment, expressions of current desires and current intentions, are expressions of thoughts that involve the concepts **twater**, not **water**.

So it seems right to say that some tokens of 'water' will shift from meaning **water** to meaning **twater**. But it seems to me equally compelling to say that certain *other* tokens of 'water' *won't* shift. Specifically, it seems to me that those tokens of 'water' occurring in *memories*, and in *beliefs about the past* based upon them, will retain their Earthly interpretations, despite being tokened on Twin Earth. Such thoughts, unlike, for instance, beliefs with undated general contents, or thoughts about one's present surroundings, are caused and sustained by *previous* perceptions long gone. In the normal case, they owe little, if anything, to current perceptions and cognitive transactions with one's environment. From a purely intuitive standpoint, they would be expected to retain their Earthly interpretations, despite the admitted shift in their syntactic cousins. After all, why should mere *travel* from one place to another obliterate one's capacity to have certain memories. Normal tourism doesn't have such an

---

[11] Burge 1988, p. 652.

effect; why should travel to another planet with somewhat unusual geographical properties?

Consider an example. While still on Earth, Peter goes hiking in the mountains of northern New Zealand. Here he comes across Lake Taupo and is startled to see the famous tenor Luciano Pavarotti floating on its pristine waters. They talk amiably for a while and Peter goes off flushed with excitement.

Understandably enough, this experience of Peter's gives rise to many subsequent memories on his part, and to beliefs based upon them. Consider the ones that are tokened while he is still on Earth, many years prior to his trip to Twin Earth. There can be no question about their content. They are about Pavarotti and Lake Taupo and water.[12] In fact, I take it, they would be about Pavarotti even in a possible world in which Pavarotti has a twin living in Los Angeles who Peter doesn't know about but whom he subsequently meets. Even after he does so, the memories of the encounter on Lake Taupo, and the beliefs based upon them, would continue to be about Pavarotti, not Twin Pavarotti.

Well, some years go by and Peter is moved surreptitiously to Twin Earth and becomes happily ensconced there. Eventually, some of the tokens of his mental names come to refer to the twin counterparts of the familiar Earthly figures, and some of the tokens of his general terms come to express twearthly properties: some tokens of 'Pavorotti' will come to refer to twin Pavarotti and some tokens of 'water' will come to mean **twater**.[13]

One day, perhaps while reading a schedule of upcoming events, Peter is moved to reminisce about the occasion when he saw Pavorotti swimming in the waters of Lake Taupo. He calls up vivid and accurate representations of the scene. Of course, he takes himself to be remembering scenes involving the singer he is reading about now. But he isn't. His memories, intuitively, are about the Earthly Pavarotti, the Earthly Lake Taupo, and Earthly water, previous perceptions of which are the sustaining cause of his later ability to recall what the scene looked like and how it felt.

In the situation described, Peter's externally individuated thought tokens are not epistemically transparent to him. In particular, Peter's language of thought contains token expressions that possess different semantic values, despite being of the same syntactic type. And yet, clearly, Peter does not know that they do. Tokens of 'Pavarotti', 'water', and 'Lake Taupo', in sentences expressing memories and beliefs about that memorable occasion, will mean Pavarotti, water and Lake Taupo, respectively; whereas other tokens of that type, in sentences expressing beliefs about his current environment, or current desires, will intuitively mean twater and twin Pavarotti. From the inside, however, there will be

---

[12] In this example, I am not taking a stand on whether the intuitive semantics of proper names is Millian or not. I intend the example to work on either reading.

[13] Obviously, my Twin Earth is richer than Putnam's in containing counterparts for many more objects, properties and people than his.

no indication of this: as far as Peter is concerned, they will appear to express precisely the same contents.[14]

Externalism, then, would appear to be robustly inconsistent with the epistemic transparency of thought contents: thoughts that have the same content may look to introspection to have distinct contents (as in Pierre and Paul), and thoughts that have distinct contents may look to introspection to have the same content (as in Peter). Externalist contents fail, in other words, to possess the feature that Dummett proclaimed "undeniable." What problem, if any, does this pose?

I shall argue that the problem is this. We don't just ascribe thoughts to a person in order to say something descriptively true of him. We use such ascriptions for two related purposes: on the one hand, to enable assessments of his rationality and, on the other, to explain his behavior. As these matters are currently conceived, a thought must be epistemically transparent if it is to play these roles. Without transparency, our conceptions of rationality and of rational explanation yield absurd results. We manifest our recognition of this fact by barring *de re* thoughts—thoughts which intuitively lack epistemic transparency—from figuring in assessments of rationality and psychological explanation. However, if we abandon transparency even for *de dicto* thoughts, and hence in effect altogether, then we must either jettison the notion of rationality and with it the practice of psychological explanation that it underwrites, or we must show these notions can be refashioned so as not to yield absurd results. The problem is that the first suggestion is wild and there appears to be no obviously satisfactory way of implementing the second.

THE APRIORITY OF LOGICAL PROPERTIES AND DE RE THOUGHTS

We may usefully begin with a discussion of *de re* beliefs. By a '*de re* belief' I shall mean, *by stipulation*, a belief that is individuated by the objects it is about. Such beliefs are typically reported with the use of an 'of-clause', rather than a 'that-clause', as in,

Jane believes *of* the piano that it is ugly,

and their content is given by a *Millian* proposition. Clearly, and in contrast with fully conceptualized, referentially opaque *de dicto* beliefs, it is both necessary and sufficient for the distinctness of two *de re* beliefs applying the same predicate that they concern distinct objects. I should emphasize here that I am not presupposing, for the purposes of this discussion, either that this account

---

[14] Ideally, this example would be described at much greater length and would include a discussion of various objections and replies. For some further discussion see my 1992a, Schiffer 1992, and my 1992b.

explicates the 'intuitive' notion of *de re* belief, if there is such a thing, or even that there actually are *de re* beliefs in this stipulated sense. I am only interested in the question what would be true of such beliefs, if there were any.

Well, one claim that is often made in connection with such thoughts is nicely expressed by Burge:

individual entities referred to by [referentially] transparently occurring expressions, and, more generally, entities (however referred to or characterized) *of* which a person holds his beliefs do not in general play a direct role in characterizing the nature of the person's mental state or event. *The difference [between such entities] does not bear on Alfred's mind in any sense that would immediately affect explanations of Alfred's behavior or assessment of the rationality of his mental activity.* ... Moreover, it seems unexceptionable to claim that the obliquely occurring expressions in propositional attitude attributions are critical for characterizing a given person's mental state. Such occurrences are the stuff of which explanations of his actions and assessments of his rationality are made.[15]

Burge's striking claim here is that *de re* beliefs, in contrast with fully conceptualized, referentially opaque, *de dicto* beliefs, don't enter into *assessments of a subject's rationality or psychological explanations of his behavior*. Here, for the purposes of further illustration, is Jerry Fodor making a similar point (Fodor's emphasis is on psychological explanation):

Suppose I know that John wants to meet the girl who lives next door, and suppose I know that this is true when "wants to" is construed opaquely. Then, given even rough-and-ready generalizations about how people's behaviors are contingent upon their utilities, I can make some reasonable predictions (guesses) about what John is likely to do: he's likely to say (viz., utter), "I want to meet the girl next door." He's likely to call upon his neighbor... .

On the other hand, suppose that all I know is that John wants to meet the girl next door where "wants to" is construed [referentially] transparently; i.e., all I know is that it's true of the girl next door that John wants to meet her. Then there is little or nothing that I can predict about how John is likely to proceed. And this is *not* just because rough-and-ready psychological generalizations want *ceteris paribus* clauses to fill them in ... .[16]

What reasons do Burge and Fodor offer in support of their respective claims? Burge, actually, has very little to say on the matter (though in fairness to him, I should point out that the essay from which the citation is drawn is largely concerned with other questions). And the exact interpretation of what Fodor has to say would take us too far afield. So without concerning myself overmuch with why these authors believe that *de re* beliefs are unfit for the purposes of content-based psychology, let me offer my own explanation. Let's begin with the question about rationality.

---

[15] Burge 1982, p. 99; my emphasis.
[16] Fodor 1981, pp. 234–5.

Suppose that Jane sees a wholesome-looking apple. She thinks *de re* of the apple that it is wholesome. That is, she comes to believe the Millian proposition

<apple₁, is wholesome>.

She subsequently sees the same apple with its blemished side exposed. She thinks *de re* of this apple that it is not wholesome. That is, she comes to believe the Millian proposition

<apple₁, is not wholesome>.

Two things are true of Jane in this case. First, her *de re* beliefs about the apple logically contradict each other: the (Millian) proposition subtended by the one is **p** and the one subtended by the other is **not-p**. And, second, she cannot recover from this condition on an a priori basis; to discover that the beliefs contradict each other she would have to learn an empirical fact, namely, that the apple involved in the first thought is identical to the apple involved in the second. That the two thoughts logically contradict each other is not introspectively accessible to her.[17]

Clearly, a similar case can be described to illustrate the fact that the logical *consistency* of Millian propositions is also not necessarily introspectively accessible. In general, then, the point is that the logical properties of *de re* propositions are not knowable a priori. The question is: How might this fact help explain why *de re* beliefs are unfit for the purpose of assessments of rationality?

THE APRIORITY OF LOGICAL PROPERTIES AND NORMS OF GOOD REASONING

The answer derives from our conception of the nature of rationality and, in particular, of what it is for someone to be a good *reasoner*. What does a person have to do in order to count a good reasoner? Clearly, it is not at all a question of knowing empirical facts, of having lots of justified true beliefs about the external world. Rather, it is a matter of being able, and of being disposed, to make one's thoughts conform to the principles of logic on an a priori basis.[18] A surreptitiously envatted brain—transplanted from its normal adult body into a vat and attached to a computer that seamlessly duplicated and continued its previous course of experience—could be as good a *reasoner* as

---

[17] I am assuming here, and in the rest of this paper, that logical properties are, in the first instance, properties of *propositions*, not of the sentences which express them. I cannot defend this assumption here, except to say that it seems to me incredible to suppose that we cannot, in point of principle, evaluate a languageless creature's logical abilities. I hope to discuss this issue at greater length elsewhere.

[18] Notice that I am talking primarily about 'good reasoning,' rather than 'rationality' more widely construed. I take good reasoning to involve norms concerning the manipulation of propositions already at hand; I leave it open whether rationality involves something more.

it ever was, despite the sharp escalation in the number of its false beliefs about the external world. Or so, at any rate, our conception of rationality requires us to think.

So, rationality is a function of a person's ability and disposition to conform to the norms of rationality on an a priori basis; and the norms of rationality are the norms of logic. We may, if we wish, put matters in a far less committal way: let's say that being *minimally* rational is a matter of being able to *avoid* obvious violations of the principles of logic, given enough time to reflect on the matter and so on. But even relative to this very minimal notion of rationality we would appear to have stumbled onto a problem. For according to this view, our Jane, who innocently believed of one and the same apple that it is both wholesome and not wholesome, would appear to stand convicted of irrationality: she believes a pair of Millian propositions that contradict each other, but she is unable to recover from this predicament on an a priori basis, no matter how long she may be given to reflect on the matter. But, intuitively, there is nothing irrational about her. Therefore, either our conception of rationality is mistaken or we have to find some other systematic and non-arbitrary way of absolving Jane's cognitive behavior. Obvious conservative solution: Bar an agent's *de re* thoughts from entering into assessments of her rationality. The ban on contradictory belief and invalid inference is preserved, but only in application to *de dicto* beliefs, just as Burge says.

THE APRIORITY OF LOGICAL PROPERTIES
AND PSYCHOLOGICAL EXPLANATION

Precisely parallel considerations explain why *de re* thoughts are also unfit for the purposes of *psychological explanation*. Since rationality is taken to consist in the ability and disposition to conform to the principles of logic on an a priori basis, *any* rational subject, regardless of his external conditions, may be expected to obey certain laws (or counterfactual-supporting generalizations): namely, those generalizations that mirror the introspectively obvious logical consequences of a person's propositional attitudes. Thus, our ordinary psychological practice of explaining and predicting behavior is built upon appeal to such laws as this:

> If **S** occurrently believes **p** and occurrently intends to **F** if **p**, and if **S** has no independent reason for not **F**'ing, then **S** will intend to **F** or, at the very least, will be disposed to intend to **F**.

> If **S** intends to **F** iff **p**, but does not believe **p**, but merely **q** instead, (where **p** and **q** are logically independent propositions), then **S** will not intend to **F**.

The trouble is that perfectly rational subjects will *not* obey these generalizations, when they are construed as quantifying over *de re* thoughts.

Thus, suppose that Jack intends to call the FBI whenever he is within 50 feet of a spy. And let's suppose that he believes of the dean of his College that he is a spy. The dean in fact is currently seated next to him at the beach, disguised as a lifeguard. So, *de re*, he believes of the 'lifeguard' seated next to him, that he is a spy. Yet he doesn't budge. Yet Jack would appear to be a perfectly rational person.

The elementary generalizations upon which the practice of psychological explanation depends fail to hold for *de re* thoughts. Therefore, either there is something wrong with our conception of rationality and, hence, with the generalizations that it underwrites, or we must find some way of justifying our belief in these generalizations, consistent with their failing to hold in this case. Obvious conservative solution: Except a subject's *de re* thoughts from psychological explanations of his behavior. The elementary generalizations on which psychological practice depends are preserved, but only in application to *de dicto* beliefs, just as Burge and Fodor say.

It seems to me, then, that we have before us the general answer to the question: What considerations might underwrite Burge's claim that *de re* thoughts are unfit for the purposes of assessments of rationality and psychological explanation? The answer is that both these enterprises require that the logical properties of the propositional attitudes they manipulate be knowable a priori; and the logical properties of *de re* thoughts aren't. (Again, I don't claim that this is the answer that Burge himself would give.)

REFERENCE AND EPISTEMIC TRANSPARENCY

Why, though, are the logical properties of referentially individuated thoughts—whether these be *de re* thoughts normally so-called, or thoughts involving Millian proper names—not knowable a priori? What makes these thoughts special in this regard?

The answer, of course, is that the logical properties of referentially individuated thoughts fail to be a priori just because these thoughts fail to be epistemically transparent. It is precisely because—and only because—a subject is unable to tell a priori whether the thought he expresses with

> Tully is bald

is the same as the thought he would express with

> Cicero is bald

that he is unable to tell whether the thought he would express with

> Tully is bald and Cicero isn't

is or is not a contradiction, on a Millian construal. Referential transparency entails epistemic opacity.

It is worth noticing in this connection that violations of the transparency of sameness and violations of the transparency of difference induce different sorts of logical defect. A thinker for whom the transparency of sameness is false may well fail, as we have seen, to be able to tell a priori that a given proposition is in fact a logical consequence of other propositions that he believes. That it is such a consequence is a fact he will be able to discover only a posteriori, by learning some empirical facts.

Thus, Pierre both believes that

> He lives in London

and believes that

> If he lives in London ('Londres'), he lives in the same city as Oscar Wilde lived.

Yet he is unable to draw the conclusion that he lives in the same city as Oscar Wilde lived in.

Such a thinker, however, need not be supposed ever to actually reason invalidly. It is consistent with the falsity of the transparency of sameness, in other words, that all the simple inferences that look a priori to such a thinker to be valid, are valid; what is falsified is the claim that all the simple inferences that are valid, will necessarily so look.

On the other hand, a thinker who suffers from the converse defect—failure of the transparency of difference—will suffer from the converse failing. For such a thinker, certain inferences may well look valid, when they in fact are not. And that they are not is a fact he will be able to discover only a posteriori, by learning some empirical facts.

Peter provides an appropriate example. Since his language of thought contains token expression that differ in semantic value *despite* being of the same syntactic type, he will be tempted to think that certain inferences are instances of, e.g., *modus ponens*, when they in fact aren't. Thus, he might muse to himself as follows:

> Whoever floats on water, gets wet.

This thought, by virtue of expressing a general quantified proposition, is to be regarded as having Twearthly content, i.e. as being about twin-floating and twin water. Now, however, he combines it with a memory belief that he would express with the sentence

> Pavarotti once floated on water

to conclude

> Pavarotti once got wet.

The inference will seem valid to him; but it arguably isn't. The second premise, by virtue of expressing a memory belief that is rooted in an Earthly experience, will be about Earthly floating and Earthly water. True premises, aided by a failure of univocity that Peter is in principle not in a position to introspect, will combine to produce a false conclusion.

Returning to the main line of argument, we see, then, that the *fundamental* answer to the question: Why are *de re* thoughts *unsuitable* for the purposes of assessments of rationality and psychological explanations, is this: It's because *de re* contents (and Millian propositions quite generally) are not epistemically transparent. By contrast, fully conceptualized *de dicto* thoughts, nowhere subject to co-referential substitution, are supposed to be, as Burge rightly says, "the stuff of which explanations of his actions and assessments of his rationality are made."

If the diagnosis on offer is correct, however, this contrast can hold up only if fully conceptualized *de dicto* thoughts *are* transparent. But as Loar's example of Paul and my example of Peter show, fully conceptualized *de dicto* contents will themselves fail to be epistemically transparent—and hence will themselves fail to be suitable for the purposes of psychological explanation and assessments of rationality—if they are individuated externalistically in the manner that Burge advocates. On what basis, then, does Burge distinguish between them? Why are externalistically individuated, and, hence, *non-transparent, de dicto* thoughts held to be suitable for the purposes of rational psychology, when *de re* thoughts are conceded not to be?

THE APRIORITY OF LOGICAL PROPERTIES AND THE INTRODUCTION OF SENSE

It seems to me that once epistemic transparency is identified as a semantically significant thesis, its role in a variety of important disputes in the philosophy of language and mind becomes obvious. I shall discuss two of these: the role it has played in the canonical argument for the thesis that names have *sense* and not merely reference, and the role it plays in generating Kripke's puzzle about belief.

Beginning with the former, many philosophers would probably resist the claim that transparency plays a part in the canonical argument motivating a non-Millian view of names, because they would resist the claim that there is any such *argument*. Most philosophers write as if it's merely obvious—and, hence, in need of no argument—that someone might be in a state truly described by

(1) Mary believes that Ali was a champ

but not thereby in a state truly described by

(2) Mary believes that Clay was a champ.

It's worth seeing, however, that it isn't merely obvious. It becomes compelling, as I shall now argue, only when one makes the assumption, left implicit by Frege, that beliefs involving proper names are fit for the purposes of assessments of rationality and hence must be epistemically transparent. It is only under the terms of this assumption that one gets an argument for the referential opacity of proper names in the first place.[19]

For consider how a belief in referential opacity is typically motivated. We are given a case which goes like this: Mary sincerely asserts 'Ali was a champ.' She also sincerely asserts 'Clay was not a champ.' She asserts these sentences even though it is clear that, as she is using the names 'Ali' and 'Clay' they refer to one and the same legendary boxer. Now, given the following principle for reporting beliefs

Jones' sincere assertion of 'p' expresses his belief that **p**

we may conclude that

(1) Mary believes that Ali was a champ

and that

(3) Mary believes that Clay was not a champ.

It is important to notice, however, that nothing *so far* bars us from supposing that beliefs involving names *are* referentially transparent, and, hence, that (1) is equivalent to

(2) Mary believes that Clay was a champ.

For all that this would entail is that Mary has contradictory beliefs, a state of affairs that is, presumably, perfectly possible. We need to be given a reason why an ascription of contradictory beliefs is unacceptable in the present instance. Otherwise, we would have no case illustrating, and consequently no argument for, the referential opacity of beliefs involving names. What is that reason?

We get such a reason only if we insist that beliefs involving proper names must be fit for the purposes of assessments of rationality and psychological explanation, and hence must have logical properties that are knowable a priori—must, that is, be transparent. Armed with such an assumption the argument for referential opacity is finally enabled. For the assumption insists that the attribution of a contradictory pair of beliefs involving proper names is acceptable only if the fact that they contradict each other is a priori available to the subject to whom they are attributed. Yet it seems perfectly clear in this case that no matter how much Mary might search her own mind, she won't discover that the belief she expresses with 'Ali was a champ' is referentially (and, hence, on a Millian construal, logically) inconsistent with the belief that she expresses with 'Clay was not a champ.' With the insistence in place, then, it follows, that (1) and (3) could not be attributing logically contradictory beliefs and, hence, that (1) is not equivalent to (2). If we ignore, as Frege himself evidently did, views that attempt to accommodate this result by analyzing belief in terms of a

---

[19] Here I follow a point made by Kripke in his 1988.

three-place relation, we get Frege's conclusion: there must be a level of semantic description of beliefs involving names other than the referential.

KRIPKE'S PUZZLING PIERRE

We may observe the very same dialectic at work in Kripke's famous Pierre case. In one scenario (I won't discuss the other), Pierre assents both to

>   Londres is pretty

and to

>   London is not pretty.

Kripke argues that, in this case, there is no saying what it is that Pierre believes, no satisfactory belief ascription. His overall idea is to protect *Millian* theories from the charge that they generate absurd belief ascriptions, by showing that parallel absurdities can be generated solely from principles constitutive of belief as such, and without reliance on distinctively Millian principles (for example, substitutivity):

> When we enter into the area exemplified by ... Pierre, we enter into an area where our normal practices of interpretation and attribution of belief are subjected to the greatest possible strain, perhaps to the point of breakdown. So is the notion of the *content* of an assertion, the *proposition* it expresses.[20]

But is it really true that we are unable to say what it is that Pierre believes in the case as described? Why can't we say, applying our disquotational principle, that Pierre believes *both* that London is pretty and that London is not pretty? Kripke writes:

> ... there seem to be insuperable difficulties with this alternative as well. We may suppose that Pierre ... is a leading philosopher and logician. He would *never* let contradictory beliefs pass. And surely anyone, leading logician or no, is in principle in a position to notice and correct contradictory beliefs if he has them... . [Pierre] cannot be convicted of inconsistency: to do so is incorrect.[21]

Here we see the assumption of epistemic transparency playing an explicit role: Pierre cannot be ascribed contradictory beliefs because "anyone ... is in principle in a position to notice and correct contradictory beliefs if he has them"; and yet in this case it is clear that he will not be able to do so. But the blame ought not to be placed on the very idea of belief or propositional content as such, at least not in the first instance. Rather, the source of the problem lies in the fact that Kripke is working both with the requirement that content be transparent and with a notion

---

[20] Kripke 1988, p. 135.
[21] Kripke 1988, p. 122.

of propositional content that falsifies that assumption. The impression of a puzzle is generated by keeping two conflicting elements at play at the same time. No wonder, then, that no satisfactory belief ascription to Pierre is forthcoming.

A SIMPLE SOLUTION?

Our story thus far has unfolded as follows. We have the view that rationality, or at any rate, good reasoning, is the disposition to conform to the principles of logic on an *a priori* basis. This view, in conjunction with a non-transparent conception of propositional content, yields highly counterintuitive results. Our willingness to exclude *de re* thoughts in particular, and Millian thoughts in general, from the province of rationality-based psychology manifests our recognition of this fact. It commits us to the assumption, unless we are to forego rationality-based psychology altogether, that *de dicto* contents are epistemically transparent.

Yet most of us adhere to conceptions of propositional content, chief among them *externalist* conceptions of propositional content, that have it as a consequence that *de dicto* contents are not transparent. We cannot have it both ways. We must either reject such conceptions of propositional content, or we must show how to refashion the idea of reasoning so that it no longer consists in the disposition to conform to logic on an a priori basis.

But isn't there in fact a simple way of refashioning the idea of reasoning that will take care of the problem cases?[22] Well, how would it go?

We can't just say: A person is absolved for believing a contradiction provided that he doesn't—or can't—'see' that it's a contradiction. Irrationality often consists in precisely such failure. We want in some sense to capture the fact that Pierre or Peter or Paul are *blameless* for not seeing the contradictions that the stories attribute to them. The question is how is that to be done? The only proposal I can think of is this: A thinker is to be absolved for believing a contradiction, provided that the contradictory character of the proposition he believes is inaccessible to mere *a priori* reflection on his part.

The trouble is that, against the background of a non-transparent conception of propositional content, any contradictory proposition will satisfy that description. Since on a non-transparent conception, it is precisely not available to mere a priori reflection that a given belief is a belief in a contradiction, practically any contradictory belief will be absolvable under the terms of this proposal. The only exceptions will be those beliefs of which it is simultaneously true (i) that they are beliefs in contradictions, (ii) that the subject *believes* them to be beliefs in contradictions, and (iii) which he nevertheless refuses—mysteriously enough—to change his mind about. Any such subject would undoubtedly count as exemplifying a form of extreme irrationality; but he could hardly be considered the normal case.

---

[22] In discussions of this paper, I have often encountered the impression that there may be.

CONCLUSION

There is a pervasive tension between our conception of rationality and the practice of psychological explanation it underwrites, on the one hand, and currently dominant conceptions of mental content, on the other. The former presuppose what the latter deny. One or the other conception must be reconsidered.[23, 24]

---

[23] After writing this paper, I came across two discussions of epistemic transparency—Millikan 1993 and Owens 1990. Both writers agree that the notion has played an important role in traditional discussions, yet both advocate that it be eliminated: they concur in seeing a belief in transparency as a mere residue of a 'Cartesian' conception of mind, Millikan calling it the "last myth of the given." However, neither writer satisfactorily explains, in my view, how the crucial notions of reasoning and rationality are to be plausibly refashioned in its absence.

[24] This paper is extracted from a longer unpublished manuscript, much of which dates back to 1987. Some portions of the present paper overlap with portions of my 1992a. For helpful reactions either to this paper, or to the material in the larger manuscript, I am grateful to Jennifer Church, Barry Loewer, Stephen Schiffer, David Velleman and Crispin Wright; participants in seminars at Princeton and Michigan; and audiences at St. Andrews, Stony Brook, Campinas and Oxford.

8 *What the Externalist Can Know A Priori*[1]

Even after much discussion, it remains controversial whether an externalism about mental content is compatible with a traditional doctrine of privileged self-knowledge. By an externalism about mental content, I mean the view that what concepts our thoughts involve may depend not only on facts that are internal to us, but on facts about our environment. It is worth emphasizing, if only because it is still occasionally misperceived, that this thesis is supposed to apply at the level of sense and not merely at that of reference: what *concepts* we think in terms of—and not just what they happen to pick out—is said by the externalist to depend upon environmental facts. By a traditional doctrine of privileged self-knowledge, I mean the view that we are able to know, without the benefit of empirical investigation, what our thoughts are in our own case. Suppose I entertain a thought that I would express with the sentence 'Water is wet'. According to the traditional doctrine, I can know without empirical investigation (a) that I am entertaining a thought; (b) that it has a particular conceptual content, and (c) that its content is that water is wet.

Let us call someone who combines an externalist view of mental content with a doctrine of privileged self-knowledge a *compatibilist*. In this paper, I will present a *reductio* of compatibilism; in particular, I intend to argue that, if compatibilism were true, we would be in a position to know certain facts about the world a priori, facts that no one can reasonably believe are knowable a priori. Whether this should be taken to cast doubt on externalism or on privileged self-knowledge is not an issue I will attempt to settle in this paper. Anti-compatibilist arguments with this general form have been attempted in the past, but I believe that those earlier efforts have misstated the case that needs to be made.[2] Before we get into the details, however, it will be useful to outline certain semantical preliminaries.

---

[1] This paper was originally presented at a meeting of the Aristotelian Society, held in the Senior Common Room, Birkbeck College, London, on Monday, 24th February, 1997 at 8.15 p.m

[2] See, for example, McKinsey 1991, and the effective response in Brueckner 1992. This style of anti-compatibilist argument is to be distinguished from the 'traveling case' arguments discussed in my 1989a, pp. 5–26 (this volume, Chapter 6).

I. SEMANTICAL PRELIMINARIES

In the case of a general term—for instance 'water'—I recognize a three-fold distinction between its extension, its referent, and its meaning. A term's extension is just the set of actual things to which it correctly applies. In the case of 'water,' it is all the bits of water existing anywhere in the universe. Since we know that those bits of water are just aggregates of H_2O molecules, we may also say that the extension of 'water' consists in the set of all aggregates of H_2O molecules that exist anywhere (including those aggregates that we may never encounter).

By a term's referent, I mean the property that it denotes. In the case of 'water' it will be natural to say that its referent is the property of being water. It is possible to wonder whether it would be equally correct to say that it is the property of being H_2O. That depends on whether the property of being water may be identified with the property of being H_2O, an example of an interesting question in the theory of properties, but not one that I need to settle for present purposes. What is important here is to be able to distinguish between a term's extension and its referent, so that we are able to say that a term may express a property that nothing actually has. I think of a sentence's *truth condition* as the proposition it expresses; and I think of the proposition it expresses as composed out of the referents denoted by its terms. Thus, the truth condition of the sentence 'Water is wet' is the proposition made up out of the property of being water and the property of being wet and which says that anything that has the one has the other.

I distinguish between the property that the term 'water' denotes and its *meaning*. The terms 'water' and 'H_2O' may have the same referent, but they do not have the same meaning. What do I mean by the meaning of a term? I wish to be as neutral about this as possible and not to presuppose any particular view. I will let the reader decide to what extent I have succeeded in my neutrality.

Finally, I identify a word's meaning with the concept it expresses, and so I take the meaning of the sentence 'Water is wet' to give the content of the belief that a literal assertoric use of the sentence would express. I use quotes to name words and underlining to name the concept those words express: thus, water is the concept expressed by 'water'. Now, for the argument.

II. EXTERNALISM AND TWIN EARTH

Abstractly speaking, externalism is easily enough defined. It is simply the view that facts external to a thinker's skin are relevant to the individuation of (certain of) his mental contents. So stated, externalism does not commit one to any specific form of dependence of mental contents on external facts, just to some form of dependence or other.

However, philosophers who embrace externalism don't do so because they regard it as a self-evident truth. They embrace it, rather, because their intuitive responses to a certain kind of thought experiment—Putnamian Twin Earth fantasies—appear to leave them little choice.[3] And that sort of thought experiment motivates externalism only by motivating a specific form of dependence of mental contents on external facts. In particular, it underwrites the claim that, in the case of an atomic, natural kind concept C, the substance actually picked out by C enters into the individuation of C. To put the claim another way: the substances with which a person actually interacts help determine what atomic, natural kind concepts, if any, that person has.[4]

To see this, let us remind ourselves how the Putnam thought experiment is supposed to work. Whereas Oscar, an ordinary English speaker, lives on Earth, his molecular and functional duplicate, Toscar, lives on Twin Earth, a planet just like Earth except that the liquid that fills its lakes and oceans, while indistinguishable from Earthly water in all ordinary circumstances, is not H_2O but some other substance with a different chemical composition—call it XYZ. Going by whatever criteria are relevant to such matters, water and twin water are distinct kinds of substance, even though a chemically ignorant person would be unable to tell them apart. Now, widespread intuition appears to have it that, whereas Oscar's tokens of 'water' apply exclusively to H_2O, Toscar's tokens of 'water' apply exclusively to XYZ. Widespread intuition appears to have it, in other words, that Oscar's and Toscar's 'water' tokens have distinct extensions. If this intuition is sustained, then that implies either that their 'water' concepts are not individuated individualistically or that they are not individuated in terms of their referents. For Oscar and Toscar are molecular and functional duplicates of each other: they are alike in all internal respects (up to intentional description). Yet the referents of their concepts differ. Hence, either those concepts don't determine what they refer to in some context-independent way (they are not individuated in terms of their referents) or they do determine what they refer to and so are not individuated individualistically.

It is worth emphasizing that a Twin Earth experiment by itself does not get you all the way to an externalism about concepts; it only gets you as far as this disjunction. It is possible to respond to the experiment, and to the intuitions it generates, by opting for the individualistic disjunct and abandoning the idea that concepts are individuated in terms of their referents. That is the response favoured by so-called 'narrow content' theorists. To get an argument for concept

---

[3]　In this paper, I will be restricting myself to externalist theses that are motivated by Putnamian Twin Earth experiments concerning natural kind concepts. In particular, I want to put aside for present purposes externalist theses that are motivated by the influential Burge-style thought experiments involving deference to the usage of linguistic communities. I believe that an argument parallel to the one given in this paper can be mounted for those sorts of externalism as well, but will not argue for this here.

[4]　By the schema 'x individuates y', I just mean that if the value of 'x' had been different, the value of 'y' would have been different, too. By itself, this doesn't tell us anything about what the value of 'y' is for any particular value of 'x'. More on this below.

externalism you need not only Twin Earth intuitions, you also need to insist that any notion of mental content deserving of the name has to be individuated in terms of its truth conditions, has to determine the conditions for its truth or satisfaction in some context-independent way. Given this further assumption, there is then no option but to say that Earthly and Twin Earthly tokens of 'water' express distinct concepts—water in the case of the former, and let us say, twater in the case of the latter.

Let us make explicit, then, the various presuppositions involved in using the TE thought experiment as a basis for concept externalism. First, and least controversially, water and twater have to be thought of as distinct substances, distinct natural kinds; otherwise, it won't be true that Oscar's word 'water' and Toscar's word 'water' have distinct extensions and referents. Second, the word 'water'—whether on Earth or on Twin Earth—must be thought of as aiming to express a natural kind concept; otherwise, the fact that water and twater are distinct natural kinds will not be semantically relevant. Third, Oscar and Toscar have to be thought of as chemically indifferent, as having no views about the chemical composition of the liquid kinds around them; otherwise, they won't end up as functional duplicates of each other in the way that the experiment requires. Fourth, the concepts expressed by the Earthly and Twearthly tokens of 'water' have to be thought of as atomic concepts, not compound concepts that are compositionally built up out of other concepts in well-defined ways. For example, the experiment presupposes that water can't be thought of as capable of being defined as: A tasteless, odourless liquid that flows in the rivers and faucets. For if it were a compositional concept of that sort, its extension would be determined by the extension of its ingredient parts. Hence, a conclusion to the effect that water and twater have different extensions would have to proceed differently than it does in Putnam's original experiment, by showing that one of the *ingredients* of water—the concept expressed by 'liquid', for example—has a different extension from that expressed by its Twin counterpart. Finally, and as I have recently noted, concepts must be thought of as individuated in terms of their referents.

III. THE ARGUMENT

Now, let us suppose that Oscar—our prototypical Twin Earth subject—is a compatibilist. I claim that Oscar is in a position to argue, purely a priori, as follows:

1. If I have the concept water, then water exists.
2. I have the concept water.

Therefore,

3. Water exists.

Since the conclusion is clearly not knowable a priori, one of the premises in Oscar's evidently valid reasoning had better either be false or not knowable a priori. The question is: Can Oscar, qua compatibilist, safely count on one or the other claim? I shall argue that he cannot, that he is committed to both premises (1) and (2) and to their being knowable a priori. If I am right, then the compatibilist is committed to the manifestly absurd conclusion that we can know a priori that water exists.

Now, the a priori knowability of premise (2) just *is* the view that I have called the doctrine of privileged self-knowledge, so we don't have to spend any time debating its dispensability for compatibilism. The only real question concerns premise (1), to an extended discussion of which I now turn.

IV. PERHAPS: WATER IS NOT REQUIRED FOR <u>WATER</u>

Two possible objections need to be considered. On the one hand, an opponent might wish to reject the first premise out of hand, on the grounds that it isn't necessary, on an externalist view, that water exist for someone to have the concept <u>water</u>. On the other, he might wish to argue that, although it is true that water is required for <u>water</u> on an externalist view, that fact is not knowable a priori. Which, if any, of these two alternative strategies is available to the compatibilist? Let us begin with a discussion of the first.

How might Oscar have acquired the concept <u>water</u> without actually interacting with some water, according to a Twin Earth externalist? He couldn't have acquired it merely by virtue of its internal functional role, for his duplicate shares that functional role and yet is said not to have the concept <u>water</u>. And he couldn't have acquired it by theorizing that the liquid around him is H_2O, for it is stipulated that Oscar is no chemist and has no specific views about the microstructure of water.

An externalist could claim that Oscar might have acquired <u>water</u> from other speakers who have the concept. This suggestion harbours a number of difficulties which limitations of space prevent me from discussing here.[5] Even if it were ultimately sustained, however, its impact on the argument I'm pursuing would be minimal—it would simply force us to slightly complicate the absurd conclusion that I have claimed the compatibilist is in a position to derive a priori. Instead of (3), we would now have the equally unpalatable disjunction:

3′. If I have the concept <u>water</u>, then either water exists or other speakers who have the concept <u>water</u> exist.[6]

---

[5] Part of what I have in mind here is that not all speakers could reason in this way, for some of them must have acquired the concept without any help from others. But it would be a needless distraction to go into this now.

[6] It is interesting to note that here we are in agreement with Tyler Burge, if not on the apriority of the disjunction, then at least on its truth, as far as externalism is concerned:

For now, however, I propose to set aside this complication and say, simply, that if Twin Earth externalism is true, then contact with water is required for possession of the concept water.

V. WATER IS REQUIRED FOR WATER, BUT THAT FACT IS NOT A PRIORI

The most important challenge to the line of argument I'm pursuing derives not from opposition to the truth of this claim, but from opposition to its alleged apriority. This opposition can be stated in a number of related ways; I shall present the strongest version I can think of.

According to the externalist, we know that water is required for possession of the concept water because we know, roughly, that 'water' is one of those words on which a Twin Earth experiment can be run. But doesn't our knowledge that a given word is Twin Earth-eligible rest on empirical information? Compatibilists are very fond of saying that it does;[7] however, it is rare to find their reasons explicitly spelled out. Where exactly do empirical elements intrude into the TE experiment? Let us look at this in some detail. What conditions does a word have to meet if it is to be TE-eligible?

As we have seen, it has to be a word that expresses an atomic concept. It also has to aim to name a natural kind. Furthermore, the user of the word must be indifferent about the essence of the kind that his word aims to name, he must be chemically indifferent. But aren't all these conditions available a priori to the user of the word? More to the point, wouldn't a compatibilist have to hold that they are?

The answer is perfectly straightforward, it seems to me, in the case of the latter two conditions. Whether or not a person has beliefs about the microstructure of the kinds around him, and whether or not he intends one of his words to name one of those kinds, are matters that not only seem intuitively a priori, but that a believer in privileged access would have to hold are a priori. Notice that we are not asking whether the word actually names a natural kind, but only whether its user intends it to do so. And according to the doctrine of privileged access, the contents of one's intentions and beliefs are available to one a priori.

It might be thought, however, that the question about atomicity is somewhat more delicate. For is it so clear that facts about compositionality are a priori? Haven't we, as philosophers, often been in the unhappy position of assuming that

---

What seems incredible is to suppose that [Oscar], in his relative ignorance and indifference about the nature of water, holds beliefs whose contents involve the notion, even though neither water nor communal cohorts exist.

See his 1982, p. 116.

[7] Tyler Burge has urged this in conversation; for a statement in print, see Brueckner 1992.

a concept was compositional, investing a lot of effort in seeking its definition, only to conclude that it has none, that it must be deemed atomic after all?

It is important not to conflate a priority with ease. A fact may be a priori but very difficult to uncover, as the example of any number of mathematical or logical theorems might illustrate. We need not claim that facts about atomicity are easy, only that they are not empirical. And in fact it is hard to see how they could be otherwise. What sense can we make of the idea that knowledge of whether a concept is internally structured might depend on empirical information about the external world?

So far, then, we have not come across a TE-eligibility criterion that could plausibly be claimed not to be available a priori. We are now about to consider another criterion, however, which, if it really were a criterion, would definitely make TE-eligibility an empirical matter. The criterion is this: In addition to *aiming* to express a natural kind, a word must *actually* name a natural kind, if it is to be Twin Earth-eligible. One cannot run a TE thought experiment on a word that aims, but fails, to name a kind.[8]

In support of this claim someone might offer the following. Putnam's original experiment is carried out on a term—'water'—in full knowledge that it does refer to a kind, namely, H_2O. That knowledge plays a central role in the experiment. Twin Earth by itself doesn't speak to what we should say about a term that doesn't name a natural kind. So, for all that Twin Earth overtly commits us to, actually naming a natural kind is a condition on TE-eligibility and that is certainly not a condition that is available a priori. True, Twin Earth teaches us that water is required for the word 'water' to express the concept water, such an objector would concede; but we only learn this because we know—empirically—that water is the kind actually named by 'water'. Hence, TE-eligibility is not a priori.

Now, I think that this objection, as stated, isn't correct; buried within it, however, is another objection that is considerably more challenging. The reason this particular objection doesn't succeed is that it is quite clear that we *can* run a TE experiment on a word that doesn't actually name a natural kind. Suppose we had such a word, W, on Earth. Then, to get a successful TE experiment, all you need to do is describe a Twin situation in which, although the users of the word type W are functional and molecular duplicates of their counterparts on Earth, W does name a kind in the Twin situation. Provided intuition still has it that the extension of Earthly tokens of W are different from the extension of the Twin tokens of W—which of course they will be since the extension of the former will be empty and the extension of the latter won't be—the experiment will succeed.

Now, however, the objector would appear to be in a position to pose a more difficult challenge. For if this is in fact right, and we can run TE experiments

---

[8] I am grateful to my colleague John Gibbons for helping me see the need to confront this objection and the general line of argument that it opens up.

even on terms that fail to refer, then how do we know a priori that water is required for 'water' to express <u>water</u>? We can't infer that claim merely from the fact that 'water' is TE-eligible, for we have established that even empty terms are TE-eligible. Maybe <u>water</u> is the concept that 'water' expresses when it fails to name a natural kind, when there is no water for it to name. If we can be said to know that water is required for <u>water</u>, we know that only by virtue of our knowledge that 'water' does name a natural kind, namely, water. And that, of course, is something that we could only have come to know empirically. Hence, our knowledge that water is required for <u>water</u> is not a priori.

Here, finally, we come across the most important challenge to the line of argument I've been pursuing. It will be interesting to uncover the reason why it doesn't ultimately protect compatibilism from the charge of absurdity.

VI. THE EMPTY CASE

I want to approach a response to this objection somewhat indirectly, by focusing on the following question: What should a Twin Earth externalist say about the case where a word aiming to name a natural kind fails to do so? Two sorts of scenario might lead to such an outcome. On the one hand, a word like 'water' may fail to name a natural kind because the liquids to which it is competently applied don't form a natural kind, but rather a heterogeneous motley. On the other hand, a term may fail to name a kind because there fails to be anything at all out there—motley or otherwise—to which it could correctly be said to apply. Here I want to concentrate on the second more extreme sort of case because it throws the issues of interest into sharper relief.

So let us imagine a planet just like ours in which, although it very much seems to its inhabitants that there is a clear, tasteless and colourless liquid flowing in their rivers and taps and to which they confidently take themselves to be applying the word 'water', these appearances are systematically false and constitute a sort of pervasive collective mirage. In point of actual fact, the lakes, rivers and taps on this particular Twin Earth run bone dry. All of this may seem very far-fetched, and no doubt it is. However, the scenario described is not substantially different—except in point of pervasiveness—from what has actually turned out to be true in the case of such terms as 'phlogiston' and 'caloric'; and, anyway, the point isn't to describe a genuine possibility. Rather, it is to inquire how a particular semantical theory proposes to treat cases of reference failure and whether it is committed to treating such cases in a particular way. What *concept*, if any, should a Twin Earth externalist say would be expressed by tokens of the word 'water' on this Dry Earth?

Some may think the answer to be obvious. Since externalism is the view that the concept expressed by a word is individuated in part by the referent of that word, then it follows, does it not, that if the word has no referent that it expresses no concept?

This reasoning would be far too hasty. It confuses the claim that a concept is individuated in terms of its referent, with the claim that the existence of the concept depends on the existence of a referent. To put matters in terms of a familiar technical vocabulary, it confuses externalist individuation with object-dependence. All that Twin Earth externalism is committed to, strictly speaking, is the claim that, if the referent of a given word were different, the concept it would then express would be different, too. And that is consistent with the claim that the word would express a concept in a case where it fails to refer, provided that the concept it would there express is different from any it would express in a case where it does refer. To say it again, externalist individuation, in the sense in which Twin Earth externalism is committed to it, is just the view that, if two words differ in their referents, then they also differ in the concepts they express; strictly speaking, that is consistent with a word's expressing some concept or other even when it fails to have a referent.

But what concept should we say 'water' expresses under the conditions described, in which there fails to be any natural kind for it to refer to? We may consider options under two main headings: compound and atomic.

We could try saying that under the envisioned dry conditions, 'water' expresses a suitable compound concept made up in the familiar way out of other available concepts. Which compound concept? Most plausibly, I suppose, something like: the clear, tasteless, colourless liquid that flows in the taps and the rivers around here and .... It won't matter much for the purposes of this argument how precisely this proposal is fleshed out. On any such view, the word 'water' will contribute a complex property to the proposition expressed by whole sentences involving it, one which, as a matter of contingent fact, nothing in that environment possesses.

Intuitively, this seems to me to be a plausible view of the matter. When I think of a group of people just like us, applying the word 'water' confidently to something that appears to them to be a clear, colourless, tasteless liquid in their environment, when in fact there is no such liquid in their environment, I feel tempted by the sort of error theory of their linguistic behaviour that the present proposal delivers. It seem plausible to me to say that what these people mean by the word 'water' is this clear, colourless, tasteless liquid etc., which, however and unfortunately, is not to be found in their environment.

The problem is that it is very difficult to see how such a view could be available to the Twin Earth externalist. Remember, the TE externalist is committed, for reasons detailed earlier, to holding that 'water' expresses an *atomic* concept under conditions where it has a non-empty extension, whether that extension be H_2O or XYZ or whatever. That is one of the presuppositions of the Twin Earth experiment. But, then, how can the very same word, with the very same functional role, express an atomic concept under one set of external conditions and a compound, decompositional concept under another set of external conditions? A concept's compositionality is exclusively a function, its internal 'syntax', and can't be contingent upon external circumstances in the way that the present proposal would require.

Let me forestall a possible misunderstanding of this point. My argument here is not that, if the compatibilist were to embrace the compound notion, that would undermine his commitment to privileged access. For although it is true that embracing the compound option for 'water' on Dry Earth, while being committed to its atomicity on Earth, would have the effect of making facts about compositionality come out a posteriori, that would not flout any doctrine of privileged access that I have defined.

Nor is my argument here that the compound option is unacceptable because it runs into conflict with the independently plausible claim that facts about compositionality are a priori, although, as I noted above, that is something I believe and would be prepared to defend.

In fact, my argument here is not epistemic at all, but rather metaphysical. The compound option requires the externalist to say that one and the same word, with one and the same functional role, may express an atomic concept under one set of external circumstances and a compound decompositional concept under another set of external circumstances. But it is hard to see how the *compositionality* of a concept could be a function of its external circumstances in this way. Compositionality, as I understand it, can only be a function of the internal syntax of a concept; it can't supervene on external circumstances in the way that the compound proposal would require. (This is especially clear on a 'language of thought' picture of mental representation, but is independent of it.)

How do things look with the other main class of available options, that according to which the empty tokens of 'water' express an atomic concept? On this branch, too, we need to answer the question: Which atomic concept will that be, according to the TE externalist?

The externalist will know quite a lot about which concepts it cannot be: in particular, he will know that it cannot be identical with any of the concepts that are expressed by non-empty tokens of 'water'. To suppose otherwise would contradict his overriding commitment to individuating a concept in terms of its referent. But can he tell us, in line with his overriding commitment, what concept *is* expressed by the empty tokens of 'water'?

Unfortunately, there would appear to be a compelling argument showing that the externalist will not be able to say what atomic concept is expressed by the non-referring tokens of 'water', because by his own lights there can't be such a concept. Let me explain.

We have seen that one of the assumptions that is needed to transform a TE experiment into an argument for externalism is the assumption that concepts have context-independent conditions of satisfaction, or, in the case of thought contents, context-independent conditions of truth. So let us ask this: What are the satisfaction conditions for 'water' on Dry Earth, to what sorts of liquid does it apply? By assumption, of course, the actual extension of 'water' is empty on Dry Earth, so there is no liquid in its actual environment to which it applies. But the question I am asking is consistent with the word's actual extension being empty, and consistent even with its extension being empty in all worlds. What I want to know is: What proposition—what truth condition—is expressed by sentences of the form, 'Water is wet', for example, as uttered on Dry Earth? What is it that gets said? Never mind if such sentences are ruled false in the actual world, or even in all worlds.

On the line we are currently investigating, the answer has to be that there is no fact of the matter what truth condition is expressed by sentences involving 'water' on Dry Earth, for there is no fact of the matter what property is denoted by those tokens of 'water'. Since there is no natural kind at the end of the relevant causal chain leading up to uses of 'water' on Dry Earth, there is no fact of the matter what the referent of 'water' is and so no fact of the matter what proposition is expressed by sentences involving it.

But on an externalist view, this admission is fatal to the claim that there is a concept there in the first place, for an externalism about concepts is fuelled in part by the conviction that thought contents must possess context-invariant conditions of satisfaction or, as appropriate, of truth. If, in a given context, there is no fact of the matter what the referent of a given concept is, then to that extent there is also no fact of the matter what the concept is.

We have looked at two possible tacks that an externalist might take regarding empty tokens of 'water', and we have found them both to be irremediably problematic. Letting the empty tokens express a compound concept, while having the virtue of supplying the word with a property to refer to, runs directly into conflict with the externalist's commitment to the atomicity of 'water'. Evading this problem by letting the word express an atomic concept, on the other hand, runs into direct conflict with the externalist's commitment to the idea that concepts must possess determinate, context-independent, conditions of satisfaction.

What then is the externalist to say about the empty case? The answer would appear to be that he has to say just what the proponent of object-dependence said he should say all along—namely, that the empty tokens simply don't express a determinate concept. That turns out to be the right thing to say not because TE externalism is conceptually equivalent to object-dependence, but because TE externalism, in conjunction with its other commitments, entails object-dependence.

VII. THE ARGUMENT COMPLETED

If this is right, then the compatibilist is in a position to conclude—via purely a priori reasoning—that if a term expresses a concept in the first place, that it must have a non-empty extension. Moreover, privileged access assures him that he will be able to tell a priori whether or not a given term does express a concept, and indeed, if it does, which one. In particular, our friend Oscar will be able to tell non-empirically that his term 'water' expresses a concept, and in particular that it expresses the concept <u>water</u>. Putting these two bits of information together, he is in a position to conclude, a priori, that water must have existed at some time. And that, we are all agreed, is not something he ought to be able to do.[9, 10]

---

[9] To generate our problem for the compatibilist we have had to assume that when Oscar reasons as we have described, his a priori warrant for the premises of his argument transmits, across the a priori known entailment, to the entailed conclusion. Recently, some philosophers have taken to questioning whether this principle is correct. Aren't there cases, they have asked, where although A is known a priori, and although A is known a priori to entail B, nevertheless B is not known a priori. See, for example, the interesting paper by Martin Davies (1997). I have to say that I would be very surprised if there turned out to be any such cases that survived scrutiny. However, defending this claim in full generality is something that deserves separate treatment and will have to be left for another occasion. Here, I will settle for discussing one such case that has been suggested to me (by Stephen Schiffer). Consider the following inference:

If I have toothache, then teeth exist.

I have toothache.

Therefore,

Teeth exist.

I have defined 'a priori knowledge' as 'knowledge that is obtained without empirical investigation'. Relative to this (admittedly vague and informal) characterization, don't the premises of this argument come out a priori? Can't I know that I have toothache without empirical investigation? And, also, that if I have toothache then that I have teeth? However, the conclusion of this argument is clearly not a priori. Therefore, there must be something wrong with the transmission of warrant principle that we have been assuming.

   My perhaps predictable reply is that it is not at all clear that the premises of the toothache argument are a priori, relative to the intended notion of 'a priori'. That we are in pain, and even that we are in a particular kind of phenomenologically classifiable pain (a 'toothachey' pain)—these matters seem clearly a priori. But there is no intuitive reason to believe, it seems to me, that we can know a priori that we have toothache, if that is supposed to mean, as it evidently does in the objection under consideration, that we have an ache *in a tooth*. Imagine a toothless person insisting that he has toothache; would we have to defer to his alleged a priori access to that fact?

[10] Earlier versions of the argument of this paper were presented to my seminar on 'Self-Knowledge' at Princeton in the Spring of 1991, to my seminar on 'Mental Content' at the University of Michigan in the Spring of 1992, and to the plenary session of the Conference on Self-Knowledge at the University of St. Andrews in August of 1995. I am grateful to those audiences for helpful comments and reactions. I am especially grateful to Anthony Brueckner and Stephen Schiffer for detailed comments on a previous draft and to John Gibbons and Christopher Peacocke for numerous helpful conversations on the general topic.

Part II: Suggestions for Further Reading

Bernecker, S. (1998) 'Self-Knowledge and Closure'. In *Externalism and Self-Knowledge*, edited by P. Ludlow and N. Martin, pp. 333–49. Stanford CA: CSLI Publications.

—— (2004) 'Memory and Externalism', *Philosophy and Phenomenological Research* 69 (3): 605–32.

Boghossian, P. A. (1998) 'Reply to Commentators', *Philosophical Issues* 9: 253–60.

Brown, J. (1999) 'Boghossian on Externalism and Privileged Access', *Analysis* 59 (1): 52–9.

Brueckner, A. (1997) 'Externalism and Memory', *Pacific Philosophical Quarterly* 78: 1–12.

Burge, T. (1998) 'Memory and Self-Knowledge'. In *Externalism and Self-Knowledge*, edited by P. Ludlow and N. Martin. Stanford CA: CSLI Publications, 1998.

Butler, K. (1997) 'Externalism, Internalism, and Knowledge of Content', *Philosophy and Phenomenological Research* 57 (4): 773–800.

Chase, J. (2001) 'Is Externalism about Content Inconsistent with Internalism about Justification?', *Australasian Journal of Philosophy* 79 (2): 227–46.

Corbí, J. E. (1998) 'A Challenge to Boghossian's Incompatibilist Argument', *Philosophical Issues* 9: 231–42.

Davies, M. (2000) 'Externalism and Armchair Knowledge'. In *New Essays on the A Priori*, edited by P. Boghossian and C. Peacocke, pp. 384–414. Oxford UK: OUP.

Favley, K. (2003) 'Memory and Knowledge of Content', In *New Essays on Semantic Externalism and Self-Knowledge*, edited by S. Nuccetelli, pp. 219–40. Cambridge, MA: MIT Press.

—— and J. Owens. (1994) 'Externalism, Self-Knowledge, and Scepticism', *Philosophical Review* 103 (1): 107–37.

Fernandez, J. (2004) 'Externalism and Self-Knowledge: A Puzzle in Two Dimensions', *European Journal of Philosophy* 12 (1): 17–37.

Gertler, B. (2004) 'We Can't Know A Priori That H_2O Exists: But Can We Know That Water Does?', *Analysis* 64 (1): 44–7.

Goldberg, S. C. (1997) 'Self-Ascription, Self-Knowledge, and the Memory Argument', *Analysis* 57 (3): 211–19.

—— (1999) 'Word-Ambiguity, World-Switching, and Knowledge of Content: Reply to Brueckner', *Analysis* 59 (3): 212–17.

—— (1999) 'The Relevance of Discriminatory Knowledge of Content', *Pacific Philosophical Quarterly* 80: 136–56.

—— (2005) 'The Dialectical Context of Boghossian's Memory Argument', *Canadian Journal of Philosophy* 35 (1): 135–48.

—— (2003) 'What Do You Know When You Know Your Own Thoughts?' In *New Essays on Semantic Externalism and Self-Knowledge*, edited by S. Nuccetelli, pp. 241–56. Cambridge, MA: MIT Press.

—— (2005) 'An Anti-Individualistic Semantics for 'Empty' Natural Kind Terms', *Grazier Philosophische Studien* 70: 147–68.

Haukioja, J. (2006) 'Semantic Externalism and *A Priori* Self-Knoweldge', *Ratio* XIX: 169–75.

Kraay, K J. (2002) 'Externalism, Memory, and Self-Knowledge', *Erkenntnis* 56 (3): 297–317.

Loar, B. (1998) 'Is There a Good Epistemological Argument Against Concept-Externalism?', *Philosophical Issues* 9: 213–17.

Ludlow, P. (1995) 'Externalism, Self-Knowledge, and the Prevalence of Slow Switching', *Analysis* 55 (1): 45–9.

——(1995) 'Social Externalism, Self-Knowledge, and Memory', *Analysis* 55 (3): 157–9.

——(1997) 'On the Relevance of Slow Switching', *Analysis* 57 (4): 285–6.

——(1995) 'Social Externalism and Memory: A Problem?' *Acta Analytica: Psychology and Philosophy* 14: 69–76.

——and N. Martin. (1998) 'Introduction'. In *Externalism and Self-Knowledge*, edited by P. Ludlow and N. Martin, pp. 1–16. Stanford CA: CSLI Publications, 1998.

——(1999) 'First Person Authority and Memory'. In *Interpretations and Causes: New Perspectives on Donald Davidson's Philosophy*, edited by M. De Caro. Dordrecht: Kluwer, 1999.

McLaughlin, B. and M. Tye. (1998) 'Externalism, Twin Earth, and Self-Knowledge'. In *Knowing Our Own Minds*, edited by C. Wright, B. C. Smith and C. Macdonald, pp. 285–320. Oxford, UK: OUP.

Moran, R. (2001) *Authority and Estrangement*, Chapter 1. Princeton NJ: Princeton University Press.

Moya, C. J. (1998) 'Boghossian's Reductio of Compatibilism', *Philosophical Issues* 9: 243–51.

Nagasawa, Y. (2002) 'Externalism and the Memory Argument', *Dialectica* 56 (4): 335–46.

Noonan, H. W. (2004) 'Against Absence-Dependent Thoughts', *Analysis* 64 (281): 92–3.

Sawyer, S. (2003) 'Sufficient Absences', *Analysis* 63: 202–8.

Schiffer, S. (1992) 'Boghossian on Externalism and Inference', *Philosophical Issues* 2: 29–37.

Smith, A. (2003) 'Semantic Externalism, Authoritative Self-Knowledge, and Adaptation to Slow Switching', *Acta Analytica: Philosophy and Psychology* 18: 71–87.

Spicer, F. N. C. (2004) 'On the Identity of Concepts, and the Compatibility of Externalism and Privileged Access'. *American Philosophical Quarterly* 41 (2): 155–68.

Stoneham, T. (1999) 'Boghossian on Empty Natural Kind Concepts', *Proceedings of the Aristotelian Society* 99: 119–22.

Strueber, K. R. (2002) 'The Problem of Self-Knowledge', *Erkenntinis* 56: 269–96.

Vahid, H. (2003) 'Content Externalism and the Internalism/Externalism Debate in Justification Theory', *European Journal of Philosophy* 11 (1): 89–107.

Warfield, T. A. (1992) 'Privileged Access and Externalism are Compatible', *Analysis* 52: 232–7.

_____(1995) 'Knowing the world and Knowing Our Minds', *Philosophy and Phenomenological Research* 55 (3): 525–45.

_____(1997) 'Externalism, Privileged Self-Knowledge, and the Irrelevance of Slow Switching', *Analysis* 57 (4): 282–4.

Yablo, S. (1998) 'Self-Knowledge and Semantic Luck', *Philosophical Issues* 9: 219–29.

PART III
Content and the A Priori

9 *Analyticity Reconsidered*[1]

I

This is what many philosophers believe today about the analytic/synthetic distinction: In his classic early writings on analyticity—in particular, in "Truth by Convention," "Two Dogmas of Empiricism," and "Carnap and Logical Truth" —Quine showed that there can be no distinction between sentences that are true purely by virtue of their meaning and those that are not. In so doing, Quine devastated the philosophical programs that depend upon a notion of analyticity—specifically, the linguistic theory of necessary truth, and the analytic theory of a priori knowledge.

Quine himself, so the story continues, went on to espouse far more radical views about meaning, including such theses as meaning-indeterminacy and meaning-skepticism. However, it is not necessary, and certainly not appealing, to follow him on this trajectory. As realists about meaning, we may treat Quine's self-contained discussion in the early papers as the basis for a profound *insight* into the nature of meaning facts, rather than any sort of rejection of them. We may discard the notions of the analytic and the a priori without thereby buying in on any sort of unpalatable skepticism about meaning.

Now, I don't know precisely how many philosophers believe all of the above, but I think it would be fair to say that it is the prevailing view. Philosophers with radically differing commitments—including radically differing commitments about the nature of meaning itself—subscribe to it: whatever precisely the correct construal of meaning, so they seem to think, Quine has shown that it will not sustain a distinction between the analytic and the synthetic. Listen, for example, to Bill Lycan:

It has been nearly forty years since the publication of "Two Dogmas of Empiricism." Despite some vigorous rebuttals during that period, Quine's rejection of analyticity still prevails—in that philosophers en masse have either joined Quine in repudiating the "analytic/synthetic" distinction or remained (however mutinously) silent and made no claims of analyticity.

[1] This is a shorter, and somewhat modified, version of my 1997. I am grateful to Blackwell, and to the editors, for permission to use some of that material here.

This comprehensive capitulation is somewhat surprising, in light of the radical nature of Quine's views on linguistic meaning generally. In particular, I doubt that many philosophers accept his doctrine of the indeterminacy of translation...

Lycan goes on to promise that in his paper, he is going to

make a Quinean case against analyticity, without relying on the indeterminacy doctrine. For I join the majority in denying both analyticity and indeterminacy. ...[2]

Now, my disagreement with the prevailing view is not total. There is *a* notion of 'truth by virtue of meaning'—what I shall call the metaphysical notion—that *is* undermined by a set of indeterminacy-independent considerations. Since this notion is presupposed by the linguistic theory of necessity, that project fails and must be abandoned.

However, I disagree with the prevailing view's assumption that those very same considerations also undermine the analytic explanation of the a priori. For it seems to me that an entirely distinct notion of analyticity underlies that explanation, a notion that is epistemic in character. And in contrast with the metaphysical notion, the epistemic notion can be defended, I think, provided that even a minimal realism about meaning is true. I'm inclined to hold, therefore, that there can be no effective Quinean critique of the a priori that does not ultimately depend on Quine's radical thesis of the indeterminacy of meaning, a thesis that, as I've stressed, many philosophers continue to reject.

All of this is what I propose to argue in this paper. I should emphasize right at the outset, however, that I am not a historian and my interest here is not historical. Think of me rather as asking, on behalf of all those who continue to reject Quine's later skepticism about meaning: Can something like the analytic explanation of the a priori be salvaged from the wreckage of the linguistic theory of necessity?

BELIEF, APRIORITY AND INDETERMINACY

We need to begin with some understanding—however brief and informal—of what it is to believe something and of what it is for a belief to count as a priori knowledge. Let's work with a picture of belief that is as hospitable as possible to Quine's basic outlook. According to this 'linguistic' picture, the objects of belief are not propositions, but rather interpreted sentences: for a person **T** to believe that **p** is for **T** to hold true a sentence **S** which means that **p** in **T**'s idiolect.[3]

---

[2] Lycan 1991.

[3] As I say, I am going to work with this linguistic picture out of deference to my opponents. I would prefer to work with a propositionalist picture of belief, according to which the objects of belief are propositions in the technical sense—mind- and language-independent, asbtract objects which have their truth conditions essentially. Most of the crucial notions developed in this paper, and much of the argument involving them, can be translated, with suitable modifications, into this propositionalist framework.

Against this rough and ready background, we may say that for **T** to know that **p** is for **T** to justifiably hold **S** true, with a strength sufficient for knowledge, and for **S** to be true. And to say that **T** knows **p** a priori is to say that **T**'s warrant for holding **S** true is independent of outer, sensory experience.[4] The interesting question in the analysis of the concept of apriority concerns this notion of warrant: what is it for a belief to be justified independently of outer sensory experience?

On a minimalist reading, to say that the warrant for a given belief is a priori is just to say that it is justified, with a strength sufficient for knowledge, without appeal to empirical evidence.[5] On a stronger reading, it is to say that *and* that the justification in question is not defeasible by any future empirical evidence.[6] Which of these two notions is at issue in the present debate?

My own view is that the minimal notion forms the core of the idea of apriority and, hence, that it would be achievement enough to demonstrate its possibility. However, in this paper I will aim to provide the materials with which to substantiate the claim that, under the appropriate circumstances, the notion of analyticty can help explain how we might have a priori knowledge even in the strong sense. A defense of the strong notion is particularly relevant in the present context, for Quine seems to have been most skeptical of the idea of empirical indefeasibility.

Before proceeding, we should also touch briefly on the notion of meaning-indeterminacy. In chapter Two of *Word and Object*, Quine argued that, for any language, it is possible to find two incompatible translation manuals that nevertheless perfectly conform to the totality of the evidence that constrains translation. This is the famous doctrine of the indeterminacy of translation. Since Quine was furthermore prepared to assume that there could not be facts about meaning that are not captured in the constraints on best translation, he concluded that meaning facts themselves are indeterminate—that there is, strictly speaking, no determinate fact of the matter as to what a given expression in a language means. This is the doctrine that I have called the thesis of the indeterminacy of meaning.

An *acceptance* of meaning-indeterminacy can lead to a variety of *other* views about meaning. For instance, it might lead to an outright eliminativism about meaning. Or it might be taken as a reason to base the theory of meaning on the notion of likeness of meaning, rather than on that of sameness of meaning.[7] In this

---

[4] The inclusion of the word "outer" here is partly stipulative. I have always found it natural to regard a priori knowledge as encompassing both knowledge that is based on no experience as well as knowledge that is based purely on *inner* experience.

[5] In the interests of brevity, I shall henceforth take it as understood that "justification" means "justification with a strength sufficient for knowledge."

[6] Even this strong notion is not as demanding as many have supposed. For instance, it is consistent with a belief's being a priori in the strong sense that we should have *pragmatic* reasons for dropping it from our best overall theory. For illuminating discussion of the modesty of the notion of the a priori see Wright 1984a, and Hale 1986, ch. 6.

[7] See Harman 1973.

paper, I am not concerned with the question what moral should be drawn from the indeterminacy thesis, on the assumption that it is true; nor am I concerned with whether the indeterminacy thesis is true. I am only concerned to show that a skepticism about epistemic analyticity cannot stop short of the indeterminacy thesis, a thesis that, as I have stressed, most philosophers agree in rejecting.

ANALYTICITY: METAPHYSICAL OR EPISTEMOLOGICAL?

Traditionally, three classes of statement have been thought to be the objects of a priori knowledge: logical statements, mathematical statements and such 'conceptual truths' as, for example, that all squares are four-sided. The problem has always been to explain what could justify us in holding such statements true on a priori grounds.

The history of philosophy has known a number of answers to this problem, among which the following has had considerable influence: We are equipped with a special evidence-gathering faculty of *intuition*, distinct from the standard five senses; by exercising this faculty, we are able to know a priori such truths as those of mathematics and logic.

The central impetus behind the *analytic* explanation of the a priori is a desire to explain the possibility of a priori knowledge without having to postulate such a special faculty, one that has never been described in satisfactory terms. The question is: How could a factual statement **S** be known a priori by **T**, without the help of a special evidence-gathering faculty?

Here, it would seem, is one way: *If mere grasp of* **S**'s **meaning by** *T* **sufficed** *for* *T*'s *being justified in holding* **S** *true*. If **S** were analytic in this sense, then, clearly, its apriority would be explainable without appeal to a special faculty of intuition: mere grasp of its meaning by **T** would suffice for explaining **T**'s justification for holding **S** true. On this understanding, then, 'analyticity' is an overtly *epistemological* notion: a statement is 'true by virtue of its meaning' provided that grasp of its meaning alone suffices for justified belief in its truth.

Another, far more *metaphysical* reading of the phrase 'true by virtue of meaning' is also available, however, according to which a statement is analytic provided that, in some appropriate sense, it *owes its truth value completely to its meaning*, and not at all to 'the facts.'

Which of these two possible notions has been at stake in the dispute over analyticity? There has been a serious unclarity on the matter. Quine himself tends to label the doctrine of analyticity an epistemological doctrine, as for example in the following passage from "Carnap and Logical Truth":

the linguistic doctrine of logical truth, which is an epistemological doctrine, goes on to say that logical truths are true purely by virtue of the intended meanings, or intended usage, of the logical words.[8]

[8] Quine 1976a, p. 110.

However, his most biting criticisms seem often to be directed at what I have called the metaphysical notion. Consider, for example, the object of disapproval in the following famous passage, a passage that concludes the official discussion of analyticity in "Two Dogmas":

It is obvious that truth in general depends on both language and extralinguistic fact. The statement 'Brutus killed Caesar' would be false if the world had been different in certain ways, but it would also be false if the word 'killed' happened rather to have the sense of 'begat'. Thus one is tempted to suppose in general that the truth of a statement is somehow analyzable into a linguistic component and a factual component. Given this supposition it next seems reasonable that in some statements the factual component should be null; and these are the analytic statements. But for all its a priori reasonableness, a boundary between analytic and synthetic statements simply has not been drawn. That there is such a distinction to be drawn at all is an unempirical dogma of empiricists, a metaphysical article of faith.[9]

Now, I think that there is no doubt that many of the proponents of the analytic theory of the a priori, among them especially its positivist proponents, intended the notion of analyticity to be understood in this metaphysical sense; very shortly I shall look at why.

Before doing that, however, I want to register my wholehearted agreement with Quine that the metaphysical notion is of dubious explanatory value and possibly also of dubious coherence. Fortunately for the analytic theory of the a priori, it can be shown that it need have nothing to do with this discredited idea.

THE METAPHYSICAL CONCEPT

What could it possibly mean to say that the truth of a statement is fixed exclusively by its meaning and not by the facts? Isn't it in general true—indeed, isn't it in general a truism—that for any statement S,

S is true iff for some p, S means that p and p?

How could the *mere* fact that S means that **p** make it the case that S is true? Doesn't it also have to be the case that **p**? As Harman has usefully put it (he is discussing the sentence 'Copper is copper'):

what is to prevent us from saying that the truth expressed by "Copper is copper" depends in part on a general feature of the way the world is, namely that everything is self-identical.[10]

The proponent of the metaphysical notion does have a comeback, one that has perhaps not been sufficiently addressed. If he is wise, he won't want to deny

[9] Quine 1953, pp. 36–7.
[10] Harman 1967, p. 128. I am grateful to Paul Horwich for emphasizing the importance of this point.

the meaning-truth truism. What he will want to say instead is that, in some appropriate sense, our meaning **p** by **S** *makes it the case that* **p**.

But this line is itself fraught with difficulty. For how can we make sense of the idea that something is made true by our meaning something by a sentence?

Consider a sentence of the form 'Either **p** or not **p**'. It is easy, of course, to understand how the fact that we mean what we do by the ingredient terms fixes what is expressed by the sentence as a whole; and it is easy to understand, in consequence, how the fact that we mean what we do by the sentence determines whether the sentence expresses something true or false. But as Quine points out, that is just the normal dependence of truth on meaning. What is far more mysterious is the claim that the *truth of what the sentence expresses* depends on the fact that it is expressed by that sentence, so that we can say that what is expressed wouldn't have been true at all had it not been for the fact that it is expressed by that sentence. Are we really to suppose that, prior to our stipulating a meaning for the sentence

Either snow is white or it isn't

it wasn't the case that either snow was white or it wasn't? Isn't it overwhelmingly obvious that this claim was true *before* such an act of meaning, and that it would have been true even if no one had thought about it, or chosen it to be expressed by one of our sentences? Why, if this idea is as problematic as I have claimed it to be, did it figure so prominently in positivist thinking about analyticity?

Much of the answer derives from the fact that the positivists didn't merely want to provide a theory of a priori knowledge; they also wanted to provide a reductive theory of necessity. The motivation was not purely epistemological, but metaphysical as well. Guided by the fear that objective, language-independent necessary connections would be both metaphysically and epistemologically odd, they attempted to show that all necessities could be understood to consist in linguistic necessities, in the shadows cast by conventional decisions concerning the meanings of words. Conventional linguistic meaning, by itself, was supposed to generate necessary truth; a fortiori, conventional linguistic meaning, by itself, was supposed to generate truth. Hence the play with the metaphysical concept of analyticity.

But this is, I believe, a futile project. In general, I have no idea what would constitute a better answer to the question: What is responsible for generating the truth of a given class of statements? than something bland like 'the world' or 'the facts'; and, for reasons that I have just been outlining, I cannot see how a good answer might be framed in terms of meaning, or convention, in particular.

So I have no sympathy with the linguistic theory of necessity or with its attendant Conventionalism. Unfortunately, the impression appears to be wide-spread that there is no way to disentangle that view from the analytic theory of the a priori; or, at a minimum, that there is no way to embrace the epistem-ic concept of analyticity without also embracing its metaphysical counterpart. I don't know whether Gil Harman believes something of the sort; he certainly gives the impression of doing so in his frequent suggestions that anyone deploying the notion of analyticity would have to be deploying both of its available readings simultaneously:

It turned out that someone could be taught to make the analytic-synthetic distinction only by being taught a rather substantial theory, a theory including such principles as that meaning can make something true and that knowledge of meaning can give knowledge of truth.[11]

One of the main points of the present paper is that these two notions of analyticity are distinct and that the analytic theory of the a priori needs only the epistemological notion and has no use whatsoever for the metaphysical one. We can have an analytic theory of the a priori without in any way subscribing to a Conventionalism about anything. It is with the extended defense of this claim that much of the present essay is concerned.

THE EPISTEMOLOGICAL CONCEPT

Turning, then, to the epistemic notion of analyticity, we immediately confront a serious puzzle: How could any sentence be analytic in this sense? How could mere grasp of a sentence's meaning justify someone in holding it true?

Clearly, the answer to this question has to be *semantical:* something about the sentence's meaning, or about the way that meaning is fixed, must explain how its truth is knowable in this special way. What could this explanation be?

In the history of the subject, two different sorts of explanation have been especially important. Although these, too, have often been conflated, it is crucial to distinguish between them.

One idea was first formulated in full generality by Gottlob Frege. According to Frege, a statement's analyticity (in my epistemological sense) is to be explained by the fact that it is *transformable into a logical truth by the substitution of synonyms for synonyms.* When a statement satisfies this semantical condition, I shall say that it is 'Frege-analytic'.[12]

Now, it should be obvious that Frege-analyticity is at best an *incomplete* explanation of a statement's epistemic analyticity and, hence, of its apriority. For suppose that a given sentence **S** is Frege-analytic. How might this fact

---

[11] Harman 1994, p. 47. See also his 1967.

[12] See Frege 1950, section 3. (Some may regard the attribution of precisely this notion to Frege controversial. What matters to me is not who came up with the idea, but rather the philosophical role it has played.)

My use of the term 'analytic' in connection with Frege's *semantical* notion as well as with the preceding epistemic and metaphysical concepts may be thought ill-advised. But I do so deliberately, to highlight the fact that the term has been used in the literature in general, and in Quine in particular, to stand for all three different sorts of notion, often without any acknowledgement of that fact. This terminological promiscuity has undoubtedly contributed to the confusion surrounding discussions of this issue.

explain its analyticity? Clearly, two further assumptions are needed. First, that facts about synonymy are knowable a priori; and second, that the truths of logic are. Under the terms of these further assumptions, a satisfying explanation goes through. Given its Frege-analyticity, **S** is transformable into a logical truth by the substitution of synonyms for synonyms. Facts about synonymy are a priori, so it's a priori that **S** is so transformable. Furthermore, the sentence into which it is transformable is one whose truth is itself knowable a priori. Hence, **S**'s truth is knowable a priori.

Frege tended not to worry about these further assumptions, for two reasons. First, Frege thought it obviously constitutive of the idea of meaning, that meaning is transparent—that any competent user of two words would have to be able to know a priori whether or not they meant the same. Second, Frege also thought it obvious that there could be no substantive epistemology for logic—a fortiori, not one that could explain its apriority. As a consequence, he was happy to take logic's apriority for granted. For both of these reasons, he didn't worry about the fact that an explanation of apriority in terms of Frege-analyticity simply leaned on these further assumptions without explaining them.

I think the jury is still out on whether Frege was right to take these further assumptions for granted. There is certainly a very strong case to be made for the transparency of meaning.[13] And there are well-known difficulties providing a substantive epistemology for something as basic as logic, difficulties we shall have occasion to further review below. Nevertheless, because we cannot simply assume that Frege was right, we have to ask how a complete theory of the a priori would go about filling in the gaps left by the concept of Frege-analyticity.

I shall have very little to say about the first gap. The question whether facts about the sameness and difference of meaning are a priori cannot be discussed independently of the question what meaning is, and that is not an issue that I want to prejudge in the present context. On some views of meaning—for example, on certain conceptual role views—the apriority of synonymy is simply a by-product of the very nature of meaning facts, so that no substantive epistemology for synonymy is necessary or, indeed, possible. On other views—for example, on most externalist views of meaning—synonymy is not a priori, so there is no question of a sentence's Frege-analyticity fully explaining its epistemic analyticity.

Since this issue about the apriority of synonymy turns on questions that are currently unresolved, I propose to leave it for now. As we shall see, none of the analyticity-skeptical considerations we shall consider exploit it in any way. (Quine never argues that the trouble with Frege-analyticity is that synonymies are a posteriori.)

Putting aside, then, skepticism about the apriority of synonymy, and, for the moment anyway, skepticism about the very existence of Frege-analytic

---

[13] For some discussion see my 1994b (this volume, Chapter 7).

sentences, let us ask quite generally: What class of a priori statement would an account based on the notion of Frege-analyticity *fail* to explain?

Two classes come to mind. On the one hand, a priori statements that are not transformable into logical truths by the substitution of synonyms for synonyms; and, on the other hand, a priori statements that are trivially so transformable.

Taking the first class first, there do appear to be a significant number of a priori statements that are not Frege-analytic. For example:

> Whatever is red all over is not blue.
> Whatever is colored is extended.
> If x is warmer than y, then y is not warmer than x.

These statements appear not to be transformable into logical truths by the appropriate substitutions: the ingredient descriptive terms seem not to be decomposable in the appropriate way.

The second class of recalcitrant statements consists precisely of the truths of logic. The truths of logic satisfy, of course, the conditions on Frege-analyticity. But they satisfy them trivially. And it seems obvious that we can't hope to explain our warrant for belief in the truths of logic by appealing to their analyticity in this sense: knowledge of Frege-analyticity presupposes knowledge of logical truth and so can't explain it.

How, then, is the epistemic analyticity of these recalcitrant truths to be explained? As we shall see below, the solution proposed by Carnap and the middle Wittgenstein turns on the suggestion that they are to be viewed as *implicit definitions* of their ingredient terms. When a statement satisfies this semantical condition, I shall sometimes say that it is 'Carnap-analytic'. However, before proceeding to a discussion of Carnap-analyticity, I want to re-examine Quine's famous rejection of the much weaker concept of Frege-analyticity.[14]

II

"TWO DOGMAS" AND THE REJECTION
OF FREGE-ANALYTICITY

For all its apparent limitations, the concept of Frege-analyticity is not without interest. Even though Quine made it fashionable to claim otherwise, the sentence "All bachelors are male," *does* seem to be transformable into a logical truth by the substitution of synonyms for synonyms and that fact *does* seem to have something important to do with its apriority. If, then, appearances are not misleading here, and a significant range of a priori statements are Frege-analytic,

---

[14] What follows is a compressed discussion of Frege-analyticity. For a fuller treatment see my 1997.

then the problem of their apriority is *reduced* to that of the apriority of logic and synonymy and, in this way, a significant economy in explanatory burden is achieved.

It was, therefore, an important threat to the analytic theory of the a priori to find Quine arguing, in one of the most celebrated articles of this century, that the apriority of no sentence could be explained by appeal to its Frege-analyticity, because no sentence of a natural language could *be* Frege-analytic.

It has not been sufficiently appreciated, it seems to me, that "Two Dogmas," is exclusively concerned with this weaker notion of Frege-analyticity, and not at all with the more demanding project of explaining the apriority of logic. But this is made very clear by Quine:

Statements which are analytic by general philosophical acclaim are not, indeed, far to seek. They fall into two classes. Those of the first class, which may be called *logically true*, are typified by:

(1) No unmarried man is married.

The relevant feature of this example is that it is not merely true as it stands, but remains true under any and all reinterpretations of 'man' and 'married'. If we suppose a prior inventory of *logical* particles ... then in general a logical truth is a statement that remains true under all reinterpretations of its components other than the logical particles.

But there is also a second class of analytic statements, typified by:

(2) No bachelor is married.

The characteristic of such a statement is that it can be turned into a logical truth by putting synonyms for synonyms. (pp. 22–3)

Quine goes on to say very clearly:

Our problem ... is analyticity; and here the major difficulty lies not in the first class of analytic statements, the logical truths, but rather in the second class, which depends on the notion of synonymy. (p. 24)

Most of the rest of TD is devoted to arguing that no good sense can be made of such analyticities of the 'second class'.

None of this would make any sense unless Quine were intending in "Two Dogmas" to be restricting himself solely to the notion of Frege-analyticity. Of course, it is the point of two other important papers of his—"Truth by Convention" and "Carnap and Logical Truth"—to argue that there is no non-trivial sense in which *logic* is analytic. We will turn to that issue in due course. Relative to the Fregean notion, however, the logical truths are trivially analytic; and so, given his apparent desire to restrict his attention to that notion in TD, he simply concedes their 'analyticity' in the only sense he takes to be under discussion.

What he wishes to resist in TD, he insists, is merely the claim that there are any *non-trivial instances of Frege-analyticity*.[15]

SKEPTICAL THESES ABOUT ANALYTICITY

What form does Quine's resistance take? We may agree that the result being advertised isn't anything modest, of the form: There are fewer analyticities than we had previously thought. Or, there are some analytic truths, but they are not important for the purposes of science. Or anything else of a similar ilk. Rather, as a very large number of Quine's remarks make clear, the sought-after result is something ambitious to the effect that the notion of Frege-analyticity is, somehow or other, not cogent. TD's many admirers have divided on whether to read this as the claim that the notion of Frege-analyticity does not have a well-defined, determinate factual content, or whether to read it merely as claiming that, although it has an intelligible content, it is necessarily uninstantiated. I'll call the first claim a *Non-factualism* about analyticity:

(NF)   No coherent, determinate property is expressed by the predicate 'is analytic' (or, since these are correlative terms, the predicate 'is synthetic'); consequently, no coherent factual claim is expressed by sentences of the form 'S is analytic' and 'S is synthetic.'

And the second an *Error Thesis* about analyticity:

(ET)   There is a coherent, determinate property expressed by 'is analytic', but it is necessarily uninstantiated; consequently, all sentences of the form 'S is analytic' are necessarily false.[16]

---

[15] Exegetically, this does leave us with a few puzzles. First, TD does contain a brief discussion of the implicit definition idea, under the guise of the notion of a "semantical rule." Given that, why does Quine insist that he intends only to discuss the notion of Frege-analyticity? Second, the notion of a semantical rule is discussed only in connection with non-logical truths: since, however, the deployment of this idea would be exactly the same in the logical case, why is the analyticity of logic expressly excluded? Third, given that the analyticity of logic is expressly excluded, on what basis does Quine allow himself to draw morals about logic's revisability towards the end of TD? I think there is no avoiding the conclusion that, on this and other related issues (see below), TD is confused. It would, in fact, have been surprising if these rather tricky problems had all been in clear focus in Quine's pioneering papers.

[16] In this context, nothing fancy is meant by the use of such expressions as 'property' and 'proposition'. For present purposes they may be understood in a thoroughly deflationary manner.

I have sometimes been asked why I consider just this particular weakening of a non-factualist thesis, one that involves, problematically from Quine's official point of view, a modal notion? Why not rather attribute to him the following *Very Weak Thesis:*

(VWT)   There is a coherent, determinate property expressed by 'is analytic', but *as a matter of fact*, it has never been instantiated; consequently, all tokens of the sentence 'S is analytic' have been false up to now.

Regardless, however, of how TD's skepticism about Frege-analyticity is understood, I don't see how either thesis can plausibly stop short of a radical indeterminacy about meaning.[17]

NON-FACTUALISM ABOUT FREGE-ANALYTICITY

Let's begin with the non-factualist version. To say that there is no such property as the property of Frege-analyticity is essentially to say that, for *any* sentence, there is no fact of the matter as to whether it is transformable into a logical truth by the substitution of synonyms for synonyms. Presumably, this itself is possible only if, either there is no fact of the matter as to what counts as a logical truth, or no fact of the matter as to when two expressions are synonymous. Since the factuality of logic is not in dispute, the only option is a non-factualism about synonymy.

But, now, how can there fail to be facts about whether any two expressions mean the same—even where these are drawn from within a *single* speaker's idiolect, so that no questions of *inter*linguistic synonymy arise? Wouldn't this have to entail that there are no facts about what each expression means individually? Putting the question the other way: Could there be a fact of the matter about what each expression means, but no fact of the matter about whether they mean the same?[18]

Let's consider this question first against the background of an unQuinean relational construal of meaning, according to which an expression's meaning something is a relation **M** between it and its meaning, the meaning **C**. Someone who held that a non-factualism about synonymy could co-exist with a determinacy about meaning would have to hold that, although it might be true that some specific word—say, "cow"—bears some specific relation **M** to some specific meaning **C**, there is no fact of the matter about whether some *other* word—some other orthographically identified particular—bears precisely the same relation to precisely the same meaning.

But how could this be? How could it conceivably turn out that it is intelligible and true to say that "cow" bears **M** to **C**, and not merely false but *nonfactual* to say that some other word—"vache" as it may be—also does? What could be so special about the letters "c", "o", "w"?

There are two reasons. First, the VWT is not a philosophically interesting thesis and, second, it could not have been argued for on the basis of a *philosophy* paper—i.e., on the sorts of a priori grounds that Quine offers. So although Quine may not be entitled to precisely the ET, I am going to ignore that and not hold it against him.

[17] In my 1990 (this volume, Chapter 2) I discuss in more depth the nature of Error-theories and non-factualist views, and in particular their application to semantic concepts.

[18] This question was first asked by Grice and Strawson in their 1956. Grice and Strawson didn't sufficiently stress, however, that Quine was committed to a skepticism even about *intra*linguistic synonymy, and not just about *inter*linguistic synonymy, for the theory of apriority doesn't care about the interlinguistic case.

The answer, of course, is that there is nothing special about them. If it is factual that one word bears **M** to **C,** it is surely factual that some other word does. Especially on a relational construal of meaning, it makes no sense to suppose that a determinacy about meaning could coexist with a non-factualism about synonymy.

The question naturally arises whether this result is forthcoming *only* against the background of a relational construal of meaning. I think it's quite clear that the answer is 'No'. To see why, suppose that instead of construing meaning facts as involving relations to meanings we construe them thus: "cow" means *cow* just in case "cow" has the monadic property **R**—a history of use, a disposition, or whatever your favorite candidate may be. Precisely the same arguments go through: it remains equally difficult to see how, given that "cow" has property **R,** it could fail to be factual whether some other word does.

THE ERROR THESIS ABOUT FREGE-ANALYTICITY

I think, then, that if a plausible skepticism about Frege-analyticity is to be sustained, it cannot take the form of a non-factualism. Does an Error thesis fare any better? According to this view, although there are determinate facts about which sentences are transformable into logical truths by the appropriate manipulations of synonymy, this property is necessarily uninstantiated: it is nomically impossible for there to be any Frege-analytic sentences. Our question is: Does at least this form of skepticism about Frege-analyticity avoid collapse into the indeterminacy doctrine?

Well, I suppose that if we are being very strict about it, we may have to admit that it is barely *logically possible* to combine a denial of indeterminacy with an Error thesis about synonymy, so that we can say that although there are determinate facts about what means what, it is impossible for any two things to mean the same thing. But is such a view plausible? Do we have any reason for believing it? I think not.

Let's begin with the fact that even Quine has to admit that it is possible for two *tokens of the same orthographic type* to be synonymous, for that much is presupposed by his own account of logical truth.[19]

What about two tokens of different types? Here again, our own argument can proceed from Quine's own admissions. For even Quine concedes that two expressions can mean the same thing, provided that they are explicitly stipulated to mean the same thing.[20] So his skepticism about synonymy has to boil down to the following somewhat peculiar claim: Although there is such a thing as the property of synonymy; and although it can be instantiated by pairs of tokens of the same orthographic type; and although it can be instantiated by pairs of

[19] See Strawson 1971, p. 117.
[20] See the discussion of stipulative definitions in TD. For further discussion see my 1997.

tokens of distinct orthographic types, provided that they are related to each other by way of an explicit stipulation; it is, nevertheless, in principle impossible to generate instances of this property in some other way, via some other mechanism. For example, it is impossible that two expressions that were introduced independently of each other into the language, should have been introduced with exactly the same meanings.

But what conceivable rationale could there be for such a claim? As far as I am able to tell, there is precisely one argument in the literature that is supposed to provide support for it. It may be represented as follows:

> Premise: Meaning is radically holistic in the sense that: "What our words mean depends on *everything* we believe, on *all* the assumptions we are making."[21]

Therefore,

> Conclusion: It is very unlikely that, in any given language, there will be two words of distinct types that mean exactly the same thing.

I am inclined to agree that this argument (properly spelled out) is valid, and so, that if a radical holism about meaning were true, then synonymies between expressions of different types would be rare.

However, I note that "rare" does not mean the same as "impossible," which is the result we were promised. And, much more importantly, I am completely inclined to disagree that TD provides any sort of cogent argument for meaning holism in the first place.

It's easy to see why, if such a radical meaning holism were true, synonymies might be hard to come by. For although it is not unimaginable, it is unlikely that two words of distinct types will participate in *all* of the same beliefs and inferences. Presumably there will always be some beliefs that will discriminate between them—beliefs about their respective shapes, for example. But what reason do we have for believing that *all* of a word's uses are constitutive of its meaning?

Many Quineans seem to hold that the crucial argument for this intuitively implausible view is to be found in the concluding sections of TD. In those concluding sections, Quine argues powerfully for the epistemological claim that has come to be known as the Quine–Duhem thesis: confirmation is holisitic in that the warrant for any given sentence depends on the warrant for every other sentence. In those concluding sections, Quine also assumes a Verificationist theory of meaning, according to which the meaning of a sentence is fixed by its method of confirmation. Putting these two theses together, one can speedily arrive at the view that a word's meaning depends on *all* of its inferential links to other words, and hence at the thesis of meaning-holism.[22]

---

[21] Harman 1973, p. 14; emphasis in the original.

[22] Recent formulations of this argument may be found in Fodor 1987, pp. 62ff; Fodor and Lepore 1991a, pp. 37ff; and Devitt 1995, p. 17. None of the authors mentioned approve of the argument.

This, however, is not a very convincing train of thought. First, and not all that importantly, this couldn't have been the argument that *Quine* intended against Frege-analyticity, for this argument for meaning holism is to be found in the very last pages of TD, well after the rejection of Frege-analyticity is taken to have been established.

Second, and more importantly, the argument is not very compelling because it depends crucially on a verificationism about meaning, a view that we have every good reason to reject, and which has in fact been rejected by most contemporary philosophers.

Finally, and perhaps most importantly, any such holism-based argument against the possibility of synonymy would need to be supported by something that no one has ever provided—a reason for believing that yielding such an intuitively implausible result about synonymy isn't itself simply a *reductio* of meaning holism.[23]

III

THE ANALYTICITY OF LOGIC

If the preceding considerations are correct, then there is no principled objection to the existence of Frege-analyticities, and, hence, no principled objection to the existence of statements that are knowable a priori if logical truth is.[24] But what about logical truth? Is it knowable a priori? And, if so, how?[25]

In the case of some logical truths, the explanation for how we have come to know them will be clear: we will have deduced them from others. So our question concerns only the most elementary laws of sentential or first-order logic. How do we know a priori, for example, that all the instances of the law of non-contradiction are true, or that all the instances of modus ponens are valid?

As I noted above, Frege thought it obvious that there could be no substantive answer to such questions; he was inclined, therefore, to take appearances at face value and to simply *assume* the apriority of logic.

What Frege probably had in mind is the following worry. 'Explaining our knowledge of logic' presumably involves finding some *other* thing that we know, on the basis of which our knowledge of logic is to be explained. However, regardless of what that other thing is taken to be, it's hard to see how the use of logic is to be avoided in moving from knowledge of that thing to knowledge

---

[23] A further TD-based argument for meaning holism, this time invalid, will be considered further below, in connection with the discussion of the thesis of Implicit Definition.

[24] As before, subject to the proviso about the apriority of synonymy.

[25] I am ignoring for now the class of a priori truths that are neither logical nor Frege-analytic. As we shall see, the very same strategy—implicit definition—that can be applied to explain our knowledge of logic can be applied to them as well.

of the relevant logical truth. And so it can come to seem as if any account of
how we know logic will have to end up being vacuous, presupposing that we
have the very capacity that's to be explained.

Michael Dummett has disputed the existence of a real problem here. As he
has pointed out, the sort of circularity that's at issue isn't the gross circularity
of an argument that consists of including the conclusion that's to be reached
among the premises. Rather, we have an argument that purports to prove the
validity of a given logical law, at least one of whose inferential steps must be
taken in accordance with that law. Dummett calls this a "pragmatic" circularity.
He goes on to claim that a pragmatic circularity of this sort will be damaging
only to a justificatory argument that

is addressed to someone who genuinely doubts whether the law is valid, and is
intended to persuade him that it is. ... If, on the other hand, it is intended to satisfy
the philosopher's perplexity about our entitlement to reason in accordance with such
a law, it may well do so.[26]

The question whether Dummett's distinction fully allays Frege's worry is a large
one, and I can't possibly hope to settle it here. If something along these general
lines can't be made to work, then *any* explanation of logic's apriority—or
aposteriority, for that matter—is bound to be futile, and the Fregean attitude
will have been vindicated.

However, the question that particularly interests me in the present essay is this:
Assuming that the very enterprise of explaining our knowledge of logic isn't
shown to be hopeless by Frege's straightforward argument, is there any *special*
reason for doubting an explanation based on the notion of analyticity? Quine's
enormously influential claim was that there is. I shall try to argue that there isn't—
that, in an important sense to be specified later on, our grasp of the meaning of
logical claims can explain our a priori warrant for holding them true (provided
that the Fregean worry doesn't defeat all such explanations in the first place).

THE CLASSICAL VIEW AND IMPLICIT DEFINITION

It's important to understand, it seems to me, that the analytic theory of the
apriority of logic arose indirectly, as a by-product of the attempt to explain in
what a grasp of the meaning of the logical constants consists. Alberto Coffa
lays this story out very nicely in his recent book.[27]

What account are we to give of our grasp of the logical constants, given that
they are not to be explicitly definable in terms of *other* concepts? Had they been

---

[26] Dummett 1991, p. 202.

[27] Coffa 1991, ch. 14. In the next three paragraphs, I follow the general contours of the account
that Coffa puts forward. However, the formulations are mine and they differ in important respects
from Coffa's, as we shall see further on.

explicitly definable, of course, we would have been able to say—however plausibly—that we grasp them by grasping their definitions. But as practically anybody who has thought about the matter has recognized, the logical constants are not explicitly definable in terms of other concepts, and so we are barred from giving that account. The question is, what account are we to give?

Historically, many philosophers were content to suggest that the state of grasping these constants was somehow primitive, not subject to further explanation. In particular, such a grasp of the meaning of, say, 'not', was to be thought of as prior to, and independent of, a decision on our part as to which of the various sentences involving 'not' to count as true. We may call this view, following Wittgenstein's lead, the doctrine of

Flash-Grasping: We grasp the meaning of, say, 'not' "in a flash"—prior to, and independently of, deciding which of the sentences involving 'not' are true.

On this historically influential picture, Flash-Grasping was combined with the doctrine of Intuition to generate an epistemology for logic:

Intuition: This grasp of the concept of, say, negation, along with our intuition of its logical properties, explains and justifies our logical beliefs involving negation—e.g., that 'If not not p, then p' is true.

As Coffa shows, this picture began to come under severe strain with the development of alternative geometries. Naturally enough, an analogous set of views had been used to explain the apriority of geometry. In particular, a flash-grasp of the indefinables of geometry, along with intuitions concerning their necessary properties, was said to explain and justify belief in the axioms of Euclidean geometry.

However, with the development of alternative geometries, such a view faced an unpleasant dilemma. Occupying one horn was the option of saying that Euclidean and non-Euclidean geometries are talking about the *same* geometrical properties, but disagreeing about what is true of them. But this option threatens the thesis of Intuition: If in fact we learn geometrical truths by intuition, how could this faculty have misled us for so long?

Occupying the other horn was the option of saying that Euclidean and non-Euclidean geometries are talking about *different* geometrical properties— attaching different meanings to, say, 'distance'—and so not disagreeing after all. But this option threatens the doctrine of Flash-Grasping. Suppose we grant that a Euclidean and a non-Euclidean geometer attach different meanings to 'distance'. In what does the difference in the respective psychological states consist? Officially, of course, the view is that one primitive state constitutes grasp of Euclidean distance, and another that of non-Euclidean distance. But absent some further detail about how to tell such states apart and the criteria that govern their attribution, this would appear to be a hopelessly ad hoc and non-explanatory maneuver.

The important upshot of these considerations was to make plausible the idea that grasp of the indefinables of geometry consists precisely in the adoption of one set of truths involving them, as opposed to another. Applied to the case of logic, it generates the semantical thesis that I shall call

Implicit definition: It is by arbitrarily stipulating that certain sentences of logic are to be true, or that certain inferences are to be valid, that we attach a meaning to the logical constants. More specifically, a particular constant means that logical object, if any, which makes valid a specified set of sentences and/or inferences involving it.

Now, the transition from this sort of implicit definition account of grasp, to the analytic theory of the apriority of logic, can seem pretty immediate. For it would seem that the following sort of argument is now in place:

1. If logical constant **C** is to mean what it does, then argument-form **A** has to be valid, for **C** means whatever logical object in fact makes **A** valid.
2. **C** means what it does.

Therefore,

3. **A** is valid.

I will return to various questions regarding this form of justification below.[28] For now I want to worry about the fact that neither Carnap nor Wittgenstein was content merely to replace Flash Grasping with Implicit Definition. Typically, both writers went on to embrace some form of anti-realism about logic. Intuitively, the statements of logic appear to be fully factual statements, expressing objective truths about the world, even if necessary ones, and even if (on occasion) highly obvious ones. Both Carnap and Wittgenstein, however, seemed inclined to deny such an intuitive realism about logic, affirming in its place either the thesis of logical Non-Factualism or the thesis of logical Conventionalism, or, on occasion, both theses at once.

By *logical* Non-Factualism,[29] I mean the view that the sentences of logic that implicitly define the logical primitives do not express factual claims and, hence, are not capable of genuine truth or falsity. How, on such a view, are we to think

---

[28] Readers who are acquainted with my 1994a will be aware that I used to worry that Implicit Definition could not generate a priori knowledge because of the falsity of something I called "The Principle." The Principle is the thesis that it follows from a sentence's being an implicit definer that that sentence is true. This is a tangled issue that I cannot fully discuss here. I will have to settle for a few brief remarks. I stand by the letter of what I said in the earlier paper. However, *part of* the problem there highlighted for the theory of the a priori is taken care of here by a reformulation of the thesis of Implicit Definition; another part is taken care of by a reformulation of the relation between Implicit Defintion and the a priori; and, finally, a residual problem, not discussed in this paper, is met by the section entitled "A Pragmatic Solution" in my 1997. Readers for whom this footnote reads darkly may ignore it in its entirety.

[29] Not to be confused with the non-factualism about Frege-analyticity discussed earlier in the paper.

of their semantic function? On the most popular version, we are to think of it as prescriptive, as a way of expressing a rule concerning the correct use of logical expressions. By contrast, logical Conventionalism is the view that, although the sentences of logic are factual—although they can express truths—their truth values are not objective, but are rather determined by our conventions.

Despite this important difference between them, there is an interesting sense in which the upshot of both views is the same, a fact that probably explains why they were often used interchangeably and why they often turn up simultaneously in the analytic theory of logic. For what both views imply is that, as between two different sets of decisions regarding which sentences of logic to hold true, there can be no epistemic fact of the matter. In short, both views imply an epistemic relativism about logic. Conventionalism implies this because it says that the truth in logic is up to us, so no substantive disagreement is possible; and Non-Factualism implies this because it says that there are no truths in logic, hence nothing to disagree about.

Nevertheless, for all this affinity of upshot, it should be quite plain that the two views are very different from each other—indeed, incompatible with each other. Conventionalism is a factualist view: it presupposes that the sentences of logic have truth values. It differs from a realist view of logic in its conception of the *source* of those truth values, not on their existence. Therefore, although it is possible, as I have noted, to find texts in which a rule-prescriptivism about logic is combined with Conventionalism, that can only be a confusion.

The important question is: Why did the proponents of Implicit Definition feel the need to go beyond it all the way to the far more radical doctrines of Non-Factualism and/or Conventionalism? Whatever problems it may eventually be discovered to harbor, Implicit Definition seems like a plausible candidate for explaining our grasp of the logical constants, especially in view of the difficulties encountered by its classical rival. But there would appear to be little that prima facie recommends either Non-factualism or Conventionalism. So why combine these dubious doctrines with what looks to be a plausible theory of meaning?

Apparently, both Carnap and Wittgenstein seem to have thought that the issue was forced, that Implicit Definition entailed one or the other anti-realist thesis. It seems quite clear that Carnap, for example, believed that Implicit Definition brought Conventionalism immediately in its wake; and Quine seems to have agreed. What separated them was their attitude towards Conventionalism. Carnap embraced it; Quine, by contrast, seems to have been prepared to reject any premise that led to it; hence his assault on the doctrine of Implicit Definition.

But if this is in fact the correct account of Quine's motivations, then they are based, I believe, on a false assumption, for neither form of anti-realism about logic follows from the thesis of Implicit Definition.

I will proceed as follows. First, I will argue that Implicit Definition, properly understood, is completely independent of any form of anti-realism about logic. Second, I will defend the thesis of Implicit Definition against Quine's criticisms.

Finally, I will examine the sort of account of the apriority of logic that this doctrine is able to provide.

IMPLICIT DEFINITION AND NON-FACTUALISM

Does Implicit Definition entail Non-Factualism? It is certainly very common to come across the claim that it does. Coffa, for instance, writes that from the new perspective afforded by the doctrine of Implicit Definition, the basic claims of logic are

our access to certain meanings, definitions in disguise, devices that allow us to implement an explicit or tacit decision to constitute certain concepts. ... From this standpoint, necessary claims do not tell us anything that is the case both in the world and in many others, as Leibniz thought, or anything that is the case for *formal* reasons, whatever that might mean, or anything that one is forced to believe due to features of our mind. They do not tell us anything that is the case; so they had better not be called claims or propositions. Since their role is to constitute meanings and since (apparently) we are free to endorse them or not, it is better to abandon the old terminology (a priori "principles", "laws," etc.) that misleadingly suggests a propositional status and to refer to them as "rules."[30]

I have no desire to engage the exegetical issues here; as far as I can tell, the middle Wittgenstein seems very much to have been a non-factualist about the implicit definers of logic, just as Coffa says. What I dispute is that it *follows* from the fact that a given sentence Q is being used to implicitly define one of its ingredient terms, that Q is not a factual sentence, not a sentence that "tells us anything that is the case." These two claims seem to me to be entirely independent of each other.

To help us think about this, consider Kripke's example of the introduction of the term 'meter'. As Kripke imagines it, someone introduces the term into his vocabulary by stipulating that the following sentence is to be true:

[1] Stick **S** is a meter long at **t**.

Suppose that stick **S** exists and is a certain length at **t**. Then it follows that 'meter' names that length and hence that [1] says that stick **S** is that length at **t**, and since it is that length at **t**, [1] is true.

Knowing all this may not be much of an epistemic achievement, but that isn't the point. The point is that there appears to be no inconsistency whatsoever between claiming that a given sentence serves to implicitly define an ingredient term and claiming that that very sentence expresses something factual.

Similarly, I don't see that there is any inconsistency between supposing that a given logical principle—for instance, the law of excluded middle—serves

---

[30] Coffa 1991, pp. 265–6.

to implicitly define an ingredient logical constant, and supposing that that very sentence expresses a factual statement capable of genuine truth and falsity.[31]

IMPLICIT DEFINITION AND CONVENTIONALISM

So far I have argued that it is consistent with a sentence's serving as an implicit definer that that very sentence come to express a fully factual claim, capable of genuine truth and falsity. Perhaps, however, when implicit definition is at issue, the truth of the claim that is thereby fixed has to be thought of as conventionally determined? Does at least Conventionalism follow from Implicit Definition?[32]

It is easy to see, I suppose, why these two ideas might have been run together. For according to Implicit Definition, 'if, then', for example, comes to mean the conditional precisely by my assigning the truth value True to certain basic sentences involving it, for example, to

If, if **p** then **q**, and **p**, then **q**.

And in an important sense, my assigning this sentence the value True is arbitrary. Prior to my assigning it that truth value, it didn't have a complete meaning, for one of its ingredient terms didn't have a meaning at all. The process of assigning it the value True is simply part of what fixes its meaning. Had I assigned it the value False, the sentence would then have had a *different* meaning. So, prior to the assignment there couldn't have been a substantive question regarding its truth value. And after the assignment there couldn't be a substantive question as to whether that assignment was correct. In this sense, then, the sentence's truth value is arbitrary and conventional. Doesn't it follow, then, that Implicit Definition entails Conventionalism?

Not at all. All that is involved in the thesis of Implicit Definition is the claim that the conventional assignment of truth to a sentence determines what claim that sentence expresses (if any); such a view is entirely silent about what (if

---

[31] Someone may object that the two cases are not relevantly analogous. For the meter case is supposed to be a case of the *fixation of reference*, but the logical case an instance of the fixation of meaning. Doesn't this difference between them block the argument I gave?

I don't see that it does. First, the two cases really are disanalogous only if there is an important difference between meaning and reference; yet, as is well known, there are many philosophers of language who are inclined to think that there isn't an important such difference. Second, it seems to me that even if we allowed for a robust distinction between meaning and reference, the point would remain entirely unaffected. Whether we think of an implicit definer as fixing a term's reference directly, or we think of it as first fixing its meaning, which then in turn fixes its reference, seems to me entirely irrelevant to the claim that Implicit Definition does not entail Non-Factualism. As long as both processes are consistent with the fixation of a factual claim for the sentence at issue—as they very much seem to be—the important point stands.

[32] Certainly many philosophers seem to have thought so. Richard Creath, for example, sympathetically expounds Carnap's view that the basic axioms of logic implicitly define the ingredient logical terms by saying that on this view "the postulates (together with the other conventions) create the truths that they, the postulates express." See his 1992.

anything) determines the truth of the claim that is thereby expressed—a fortiori, it is silent about whether our conventions determine it.

Think here again of Kripke's meter stick. If the stick exists and has such-and-so length at **t**, then it is conventional that 'meter' names that length and, therefore, conventional that [1] expresses the proposition stick *S has such-and-so length at t*. However, that stick **S** has that length at **t** is hardly a fact generated by convention; it presumably had that length prior to the convention, and may continue to have it well after the convention has lapsed.[33]

I anticipate the complaint that the entailment between Implicit Definition and Conventionalism is blocked only through the tacit use of a distinction between a sentence and the proposition it expresses, a distinction that neither Carnap nor Quine would have approved.

Such a complaint would be mistaken, however. The argument I gave relies not so much on a distinction between a sentence and a proposition in the technical sense disapproved of by Quine, as on a distinction between a sentence and *what it expresses*. And it is hard to see how any adequate philosophy of language is to get by without some such distinction.[34] Even on a deflationary view of truth, there is presumably a distinction between the *sentence* 'Snow is white' and that which makes the sentence true, namely, snow's being white. And the essential point for my purposes is that it is one thing to say that 'Snow is white' comes to express the claim that snow is white as a result of being conventionally assigned the truth value True; and quite another to say that snow comes to be white as a result of our conventions. The first claim is Implicit Definition (however implausibly applied in this case); and the other is Conventionalism. Neither one seems to me to entail the other.

QUINE AGAINST IMPLICIT DEFINITION: REGRESS

As I noted above, I am inclined to believe that erroneous opinion on this score has played an enormous role in the history of this subject. I conjecture that had Quine felt more confident that Implicit Definition could be sharply distinguished from Conventionalism, he might not have felt so strongly against it.

In any event, though, whatever the correct explanation of Quine's animus, we are indebted to him for a series of powerful critiques of the thesis of

---

[33] This point is also forcefully made in Salmon 1993 and Yablo 1992b.

[34] Notice that conventionalists themselves need to make crucial use of such a distinction when they describe their own position, as in the passage cited above from Creath:

the postulates (together with the other conventions) create the truths that they, the postulates, express.

As Hilary Putnam pointed out some time ago, it's hard to see how distinctive content is to be given to Conventionalism without the use of some such distinction. For a conventionalism merely about linguistic expressions is trivial. A real issue is joined only when the view is formulated as a claim about the truths expressed. See his 1975b.

Implicit Definition, critiques that have persuaded many that that thesis, and with it any explanation of the apriority of logic that it might be able to ground, are fundamentally flawed. We must now confront Quine's arguments.

According to Implicit Definition, the logical constants come to have a particular meaning in our vocabulary by our conventionally stipulating that certain sentences (or inferences) involving them are to be true. For instance, let us assume that the meaning for 'and' is fixed by our stipulating that the following inferences involving it are to be valid:

[2]
$$\frac{\text{A and B}}{\text{A}} \qquad \frac{\text{A and B}}{\text{B}} \qquad \frac{\text{A, B}}{\text{A and B}}$$

Now, Quine's first important criticism of this idea occurs in his early paper 'Truth by Convention'.[35] As Quine there pointed out, there are an infinite number of instances of schema [2]. Consequently, the inferences of this infinitary collection could not have been conventionally stipulated to be valid singly, one by one. Rather, Quine argued, if there is anything at all to this idea, it must be something along the following lines: We adopt certain general conventions from which it follows that all the sentences of the infinitary collection are assigned the value Valid. Such a general convention would presumably look like this:

> Let all results of putting a statement for 'p' and a statement for 'q' in 'p and q implies p' be valid.

However, the trouble is that in order to state such a general convention we have had, unavoidably, to use all sorts of logical terms—'every', 'and', and so on. So the claim, essential to the proposal under consideration, that all our logical constants acquire their meaning via the adoption of such explicitly formulated conventional assignments of validity must fail. Logical constants whose meaning is not fixed in this way are presupposed by the model itself.[36]

This argument of Quine's has been very influential; and I think that there is no doubt that it works against its target as specified. However, it is arguable that its target as specified isn't the view that needs defeating.

---

[35] Quine's argument here is offically directed against a Conventionalism about logical truth, that is, against the idea that logical truth is determined by our conventions. This idea we have already rejected in our discussion of the metaphysical concept of analyticity. However, Quine attacks Conventionalism *by* attacking the semantical thesis of Implicit Definition. Hence, the need for the present discussion.

[36] Quine claims that this argument may also be put as follows: The claim that the sentences of logic lack assignment of truth value until they are conventionally assigned such values must fail. For logic is needed in order to infer from a formulated general convention that the infinitely many instances of a given schema are true. Hence, sentences of logic whose truth value is not fixed as the model requires, are presupposed by the model itself.

It's unclear to me that this is a formulation of precisely the same argument. However, to the extent that it is distinct, it is also addressed by the proposal I put forth below.

For, surely, it isn't compulsory to think of someone's following a rule **R** with respect to an expression **e** as consisting in his *explicitly stating* that rule in so many words in the way that Quine's argument presupposes. On the contrary, it seems far more plausible to construe **x**'s following rule **R** with respect to **e** as consisting in some sort of fact about **x**'s *behavior* with **e.**

In what would such a fact consist? Here there are at least a couple of options. According to a currently popular idea, following rule **R** with respect to **e** may consist in our being disposed to conform to rule **R** in our employment of **e,** under certain circumstances. On this version, the notion of rule-following would have been *reduced* to a certain sort of dispositional fact. Alternatively, one might wish to appeal to the notion of following a given rule, while resisting the claim that it can be reduced to a set of naturalistically acceptable dispositional facts. On such a non-reductionist version, there would be facts about what rule one is following, even if these are not cashable into facts about one's behavioral dispositions, however optimal.

For myself, I am inclined to think that the reductionist version won't work, that we will have to employ the notion of following a rule unreduced.[37] But because it is more familiar, and because nothing substantive hangs on it in the present context, I will work with the reductionist version of rule-following. Applied to the case we are considering, it issues in what is widely known in the literature as a "conceptual role semantics."

According to this view, then, the logical constants mean what they do by virtue of figuring in certain inferences and/or sentences involving them and not in others. If some expressions mean what they do by virtue of figuring in certain inferences and sentences, then some inferences and sentences are *constitutive* of an expression's meaning what it does, and others aren't. And any CRS must find a systematic way of saying which are which, of answering the question: What properties must an inference or sentence involving a constant C have, if that inference or sentence is to be constitutive of C's meaning?

QUINE AGAINST IMPLICIT DEFINITION: CONSTITUTIVE TRUTH

Now, Quine's second objection to Implicit Definition can be put by saying that there will be no way of doing what I said any CRS must do—namely, systematically specify the meaning-constituting inferences. Quine formulated this point in a number of places. Here is a version that appears in "Carnap and Logical Truth":

if we try to warp the linguistic doctrine of logical truth into something like an experimental thesis, perhaps a first approximation will run thus: *Deductively irresoluble disagreement as to a logical truth is evidence of deviation in usage (or meanings)*

---

[37] For discussion see my 1989b and 2008 (this volume, Chapters 1 and 5 respectively).

of words. ... [However] the obviousness or potential obviousness of elementary logic can be seen to present an insuperable obstacle to our assigning any experimental meaning to the linguistic doctrine of elementary logical truth. ... For, that theory now seems to imply nothing that is not already implied by the fact that elementary logic is obvious or can be resolved into obvious steps.[38]

Elsewhere, Quine explained his use of the word "obvious" in this connection thus:

In "Carnap and Logical Truth" I claimed that Carnap's arguments for the linguistic doctrine of logical truth boiled down to saying no more than that they were obvious, or potentially obvious—that is, generable from obvieties by obvious steps. I had been at pains to select the word 'obvious' from the vernacular, intending it as I did in the vernacular sense. A sentence is obvious if (a) it is true and (b) any speaker of the language is prepared, for any reason or none, to assent to it without hesitation, unless put off by being asked so obvious a question.[39]

Quine's important point here is that there will be no substantive way of distinguishing between a highly obvious, non-defining sentence and a sentence that is an implicit definer. Both types of sentence—if in fact both types exist—will have the feature that any speaker of the language will be prepared to assent to instances of them, "for any reason or none." So in what does the alleged difference between them consist? How is distinctive content to be given to the doctrine of Implicit Definition?[40]

Now, there is no doubt that this is a very good question; and the impression that it has no good answer has contributed greatly to the rejection of the doctrine of Implicit Definition. Jerry Fodor and Ernie Lepore, for example, base the entirety of their recent argument against a conceptual role semantics on their assumption that Quine showed this question to be unanswerable.[41]

If Quine's challenge is allowed to remain unanswered, then the threat to the analytic theory of the a priori is fairly straightforward. For if there is no fact of the matter as to whether **S** is a sentence that I must hold true if **S** is to mean

---

[38] Quine 1976a, p. 105.

[39] Quine 1975, p. 206.

[40] For all its influence, it is still possible to find the force of the Quinean point being underestimated by the friends of Implicit Definition. Christopher Peacocke, for example, in a recent, subtle defense of an inferential role semantics claims that what makes the inferences involving the logical constants constitutive is that a thinker finds those inferences "primitively compelling" and does so because they are of those forms. He goes on to explain:

To say that a thinker finds such instances primitively compelling is to say this: (1) he finds them compelling; (2) he does not find them compelling because he has inferred them from other premises and/or principles; and (3) for possession of the concept in question ... he does not need to take the correctness of the transitions as answerable to anything else. (Peacocke 1992a, p. 6)

I think it is plain, however, that these conditions are insufficient for answering the Quinean challenge: a non-constitutive, though highly obvious, form of inference may also be found compelling because of its form, and not on the basis of inference from anything else. So these conditions cannot be what distinguish between a constitutive and a non-constitutive inference.

[41] See Fodor and Lepore 1991b.

what it does, then there is no basis on which to argue that I am entitled to hold **S** true without evidence.

But that would seem to be the least of our troubles, if Quine's argument is allowed to stand. For what's threatened is not only the apriority of logical truths but, far more extremely, the *determinacy* of what they claim. For as I've already pointed out, and as many philosophers are anyway inclined to believe, a conceptual role semantics seems to be the *only* plausible view about how the meaning of the logical constants is fixed. It follows, therefore, that if there is no fact of the matter as to which of the various inferences involving a constant are meaning-constituting, then there is also no fact of the matter as to what the logical constants themselves mean. And that, again, is just the dreaded indeterminacy of meaning on which the critique of analyticity was supposed not to depend.

The simple point here is that if the only view available about how the logical constants acquire their meaning is in terms of the inferences and/or sentences that they participate in, then any indeterminacy in what those meaning-constituting sentences and inferences are will translate into an indeterminacy about the meanings of the expressions themselves. This realization should give pause to any philosopher who thinks he can buy in on Quine's critique of implicit definition without following him all the way to the far headier doctrine of meaning-indeterminacy.

There has been a curious tendency to miss this relatively simple point. Jerry Fodor seems a particularly puzzling case. For Fodor holds all three of the following views. (1) He rejects indeterminacy, arguing forcefully against it. (2) He follows Quine in rejecting the notion of a meaning-constituting inference. (3) He holds a conceptual role view of the meanings of the logical constants. As far as I am able to judge, however, this combination of views is not consistent.[42]

Part of the explanation for this curious blindness derives from a tendency to view Quine's argument as issuing not in an indeterminacy about meaning, but, rather, in a *holism* about it. In fact, according to Fodor and Lepore, the master argument for meaning holism in the literature runs as follows:

A. Some of an expression's inferential liaisons are relevant to fixing its meaning.
B. There is no principled distinction between those inferential liaisons that are constitutive and those that aren't. (The Quinean result)

Therefore,

C. All of an expression's inferential liaisons are relevant to fixing its meaning. (Meaning Holism)

Fearing this argument's validity, and seeing no way to answer Quine's challenge, they spend their whole book trying to undermine the argument's first

---

[42] For Fodor's views on the mentioned issues, see his 1987 and his 1994.

premise, namely, the very plausible claim that at least *some* of an expression's inferential liaisons are relevant to fixing its meaning.[43]

But they needn't have bothered, for I don't see how the master argument could be valid in the first place. The claim that *all* of an expression's inferential liaisons are constitutive of it cannot cogently follow from the claim that it is *indeterminate* what the constitutive inferences are. If it's *indeterminate* what the constitutive inferences are, then it's genuinely *unsettled* what they are. And that is inconsistent with saying that they are *all* constitutive, and inconsistent with saying that *none* are constitutive and inconsistent with saying that some specified subset are constitutive.

Fodor and Lepore are not alone in not seeing the problem here. Let me cite just one more example. In his comments on an earlier version of the present paper, Gil Harman says:

Can one accept Quine's argument against analyticity without being committed to the indeterminacy of meaning? Yes and no. By the "indeterminacy of meaning" might be meant an indeterminacy as to which of the principles one accepts determine the meanings of one's terms and which simply reflect one's opinions about the facts. Clearly, Quine's argument against analyticity is committed to that sort of indeterminacy. [However] that by itself does not imply full indeterminacy in the sense of Chapter Two of *Word and Object*.[44]

As Harman correctly says, Quine has to deny that there is a fact of the matter as to which of **T**'s principles determine the meanings of his terms and which simply reflect **T**'s opinions about the facts—that, after all, is just what it is to deny that there are facts about constitutivity. However, Harman insists, this denial in no way leads to the indeterminacy thesis of Chapter Two of *Word and Object*.

But this is very puzzling. Against the background of a conceptual role semantics, according to which the meaning of **T**'s term **C** is determined precisely by a certain subset of the principles involving **C** that **T** accepts, an indeterminacy in what the meaning-determining principles are will automatically lead to an indeterminacy in what the meaning is—in the full sense of chapter Two of *Word and Object*. If a subset (not necessarily proper) of accepted principles is supposed to determine meaning; and if there is no fact of the matter as to which subset that is; then there is, to that extent, no fact of the matter as to what meaning has been determined.

I think there is really no avoiding the severe conclusion that meaning is indeterminate, if the Quinean challenge to constitutivity is allowed to remain unanswered. I'm inclined to think, therefore, that anyone who rejects radical indeterminacy of meaning must believe that a distinction between the

---

[43] See Fodor and Lepore 1991a.

[44] Harman, "Comments on Boghossian," APA Symposium on Analytic Truth, Boston, MA, December 1994. Since published as Harman 1996.

meaning-constituting and the non-meaning-constituting can be drawn. The only question is how.

Well, that is not the task of the present paper. Although there are some good ideas about this, I don't have a fully thought-through proposal to present just now.[45] My main aim here is not to *solve* the fundamental problem for a conceptual role semantics for the logical constants; rather, as I have stressed, it is to show that, against the background of a rejection of indeterminacy, its insolubility cannot be conceded.

Pending the discovery of other problems, then, it seems open to us to suppose that a plausible theory of meaning for the logical constants is given by something like the following:

> A logical constant **C** expresses that logical object, if any, that makes valid its meaning-constituting inferences.

IMPLICIT DEFINITION, JUSTIFICATION AND ENTITLEMENT

Now, how does any of this help vindicate the analytic theory of the apriority of logic, the idea that logic is epistemically analytic? Let us consider a particular inference form, **A**, in a particular thinker's (**T**) repertoire; and let's suppose that that inference form is constitutive of the meaning of one of its ingredient constants **C**. How, exactly, might these facts help explain the epistemic analyticity of **A** for **T**?

To say that **A** is epistemically analytic for **T** is to say that **T**'s knowledge of **A**'s meaning alone suffices for **T**'s justification for **A**, so that empirical support is not required. And it does seem that a conceptual role semantics can provide us with a model of how that might be so. For given the relevant facts, we would appear to be able to argue as follows:

1. If **C** is to mean what it does, then **A** has to be valid, for **C** means whatever logical object in fact makes **A** valid.
2. **C** means what it does.

Therefore,

3. **A** is valid.

Now, it is true that this is tantamount to a fairly broad use of the phrase "knowledge of the meaning of **A**," for this knowledge includes not merely knowledge of what **A** means, strictly so-called, but also knowledge of how that meaning is fixed. But this is, of course, both predictable and unavoidable: there was never any real prospect of explaining apriority merely on the basis of a knowledge of propositional content. Even Carnap realized that one needed to

---

[45] For a good start, see Peacocke 1992a.

know that a given inference or sentence had the status of a 'meaning postulate'.

But isn't it required, if this account is to genuinely explain **T**'s a priori justification for the basic truths of logic, that **T** know the premises a priori as well? Yet, it hasn't been shown that **T** can know the premises a priori.

It is quite correct that I have not attempted to show that the relevant facts about meaning cited in the premises are knowable a priori, although I believe that it is intuitively quite clear that they are. I have purposely avoided discussing all issues relating to knowledge of meaning facts. My brief here has been to defend epistemic analyticity; and this requires showing only that certain sentences are such that, *if* someone knows the relevant facts about their meaning, *then* that person will be in a position to form a justified belief about their truth. It does not require showing that the knowledge of those meaning facts is itself a priori (although, I repeat, it seems quite clear to me that it will be).[46]

Isn't it a problem for the aspirations of the present account that a thinker would have to use modus ponens to get from the premises to the desired conclusion? Not if Dummett's distinction between pragmatic and vicious circularity is credited with opening a space for an epistemology for logic, as discussed above.

Finally, how could such an account possibly hope to explain the man in the street's justification for believing in the truths of logic? For such a person, not only would the relevant meaning facts be quite opaque, he probably wouldn't even be capable of framing them. Yet such a person is obviously quite justified in believing the elementary truths of logic. Thus, so our objector might continue, this sort of account cannot explain our ordinary warrant for believing in logic; at best, it can explain the warrant that sophisticates have.

I think that, strictly speaking, this objection is correct, but only in a sense that strips it of real bite. Philosophers are often in the position of articulating a warrant for an ordinary belief that the man in the street would not understand. If we insist that a person counts as justified only if they are aware of the reason that warrants their belief, then we will simply have to find another term for the kind of warrant that ordinary folk often have and that philosophers seek to articulate. Tyler Burge has called it an "entitlement":

The distinction between justification and entitlement is this. Although both have positive force in rationally supporting a propositional attitude or cognitive practice, and in constituting an epistemic right to it, entitlements are epistemic rights or warrants that need not be understood by or even be accessible to the subject. ... The unsophisticated are entitled to rely on their perceptual beliefs. Philosophers may articulate these entitlements. But being entitled does not require being able to justify reliance on these resources, or even to conceive such a justification. Justifications, in the narrow sense, involve reasons that people have and have access to.[47]

---

[46] For a discussion of why the second premise is a priori see my 1997.
[47] Burge 1993.

When someone is entitled, all the facts relevant to the person's justification are already in place, so to say; what's missing is the reflection that would reveal them.

Just so in the case at hand. If a conceptual role semantics is true, and if **A** is indeed constitutive of **C**'s meaning what it does, then those facts by themselves constitute a warrant for **A**; empirical support is not necessary. **A** can only be false by meaning something other than what it means. But these facts need not be known by the ordinary person. They suffice for his entitlement, even if not for his full-blown justification. This full-blown justification can be had only by knowing the relevant facts about meaning.

CONCLUSION

Quine helped us see the vacuity of the metaphysical concept of analyticity and, with it, the futility of the project it was supposed to underwrite—the linguistic theory of necessity. But I don't see that those arguments affect the epistemic notion of analyticity that is needed for the purposes of the theory of a priori knowledge. Indeed, it seems to me that epistemic analyticity can be defended quite vigorously, especially against the background of a realism about meaning.

On the assumption that our warrant for believing in elementary logical truths cannot be explained, the outstanding problem is to explain our a priori knowledge of conceptual truths. For this purpose, the crucial semantical notion is that of Frege-analyticity. I have argued that this notion is bound to be in good standing for a meaning realist.

If the project of explaining logic is not ruled hopeless, then I have tried to show how the doctrine that appears to offer the most promising account of how we grasp the meanings of the logical constants—namely, Implicit Definition—can explain the epistemic analyticity of our logical beliefs and, hence, our a priori warrant for believing them. As long as we are not prepared to countenance radical indeterminacy, we should have every confidence that this form of explanation can be made to work.[48]

---

[48] I am grateful to a number of audiences—at MIT, CUNY Graduate Center, Michigan State, the University of Chicago, the SOFIA Conference on Tenerife, the Chapel Hill Colloquium, Dartmouth College, London University and Oxford University. An earlier version of this paper was presented at the NEH Institute on the "Nature of Meaning," held at Rutgers University in the summer of 1992. It was there that I first became aware that Christopher Peacocke has been thinking along somewhat similar lines about the a priori—see his 1993a, presented at the Rutgers conference. Although there are a number of differences between our approaches, and although Peacocke's focus is not on the notion of analyticity, I have benefited from discussing these matters with him. I also benefited from presenting a version of this paper as part of a symposium on Analytic Truth, involving Gil Harman, Burton Dreben and WVO Quine, at the 1994 Eastern Division meetings of the APA. I am especially grateful to Hartry Field, Elizabeth Fricker, Gary Gates, Gil Harman, Barry Loewer, Bill Lycan and Stephen Schiffer for their detailed comments on previous versions of this paper. Special thanks are due to Bob Hale and Crispin Wright for their patience and for their very helpful reactions to several different drafts. For other helpful discussion and commentary, I want to thank Ned Block, Albert Casullo, Jennifer Church, Richard Creath, Jerry Fodor, Allan Gibbard, Paul Horwich, Tom Nagel, Neil Tennant, Peter Unger, David Velleman, Stephen Yablo and Norma Yunez.

10 *Epistemic Analyticity: A Defense*

SUMMARY

The paper is a defense of the project of explaining the a priori via the notion of meaning or concept possession. It responds to certain objections that have been made to this project—in particular, that there can be no epistemically analytic sentences that are not also metaphysically analytic, and that the notion of implicit definition cannot explain a priori entitlement. The paper goes on to distinguish between two different ways in which facts about meaning might generate facts about entitlement—inferential and constitutive.

EPISTEMIC VS. METAPHYSICAL ANALYTICITY

In an earlier paper—"Analyticity Reconsidered"—I attempted to do two things: salvage a notion of analyticity from Quine's widely accepted critique of that notion and show how it might be able to do serious work in the epistemology of a priori knowledge.[1]

Salvaging analyticity, I argued, depends crucially on distinguishing between a metaphysical and an epistemic version of that concept. According to the *metaphysical* notion, a sentence is analytic if it owes its truth entirely to its meaning and without any contribution from the 'facts.' By contrast, I took a sentence to be *epistemically* analytic if grasp of its meaning can suffice for justified belief in the truth of the proposition it expresses.

I believe that Quine was deeply right to insist that there are no metaphysically analytic sentences. However, I argued, first, that the considerations that militate against metaphysical analyticity do not extend to epistemic analyticity and, second, that it is possible to provide a model of how some sentences might be epistemically analytic.

While I continue to believe that these claims are true, I have also come to think that "Analyticity Reconsidered" was less clear than it needed to be

---

[1] See my 1996 (this volume, Chapter 9). A longer version containing some further discussion of Quine and an appendix on knowledge of meaning appeared as my 1997.

about the exact nature of the relation between meaning facts and entitlement. In particular, at the time of writing that paper, I did not delineate sufficiently clearly the difference between *inferential* and *constitutive* construals of the relation between meaning and entitlement. In this paper, I explain in what that difference consists and how it bears on the project of the analytic theory of the a priori. In the course of the exposition, I attempt to respond to various criticisms that have been made of that project and of my particular way of pursuing it.

Before proceeding, it is worth emphasizing that although I follow tradition in construing analyticity as a property of linguistic items, that feature of the presentation of the view is entirely optional. For example, I will talk of grasp of the meaning of a sentence as sufficing for justified belief in the proposition it expresses; but I could equally well have talked simply about grasp of a proposition p as sufficing for justified belief in p. Thus, too, I will talk about words being synonymous with each other; but I could equally well have talked about concepts being identical to one another. Finally, I will talk of holding some sentences true, as a condition of meaning some specific proposition by them; but I could equally well have talked of believing some propositions as a condition of having some of their ingredient concepts. Although I find it convenient for expository purposes to assume that we think in a language (which I will pretend is in fact English), no central issue hangs on that assumption.

So, playing along with this linguistic picture, and assuming that T's believing that p is constituted by T's accepting a sentence S which means that p, let us ask: Why should it matter whether or not there are epistemically analytic sentences—sentences such that grasp of their meaning can suffice for justified belief in the truth of the proposition they express?

The interest of the epistemically analytic derives from the thought that it might help explain how there could be factual propositions known a priori. To see how this might work, let us first distinguish between three different things that one might mean by the phrase "grasp of meaning."

In one sense, a thinker T grasps S's meaning just in case T means some determinate thing or other by his use of S. Call this notion of grasp "mere grasp of meaning." In a second sense, T grasps S's meaning when he can correctly and knowledgeably *state* what S means. In this sense, it is not enough that T mean something by S—he must also have second-order knowledge of what S means. Call this notion of grasp "knowledge of meaning." In the third and most demanding sense, T's grasping S's meaning implies not only that T is able to state S's meaning knowledgeably but also that he understands that meaning well enough to know whether or not it means the same as some other sentence. Call this "understanding of meaning."

As we shall see, different models of epistemic analyticity employ one or more of these notions of grasp of meaning. And although these notions differ from each other in significant ways, they share the following property: each of them has been thought to be attainable without the benefit of empirical knowledge. Given this assumption, it becomes easy to see how the existence of epistemically analytic sentences might contribute to demystifying the phenomenon of a priori knowledge.

In a minute we shall look in detail about how such meaning-justification connections are to be construed, but I first want to take up an objection to the idea that there could be epistemically analytic sentences that are not metaphysically analytic. The objection has been pressed by Eric Margolis and Stephen Laurence:

After all, if p really is an independent fact that makes S true, then just knowing that S means that p couldn't suffice for the needed justification; one would also need to be justified in believing that p. In other words, so long as the truth of S isn't merely a matter of what it means, then grasping its meaning can only be (at best) part of the story about why one is justified in holding it to be true.[2]

If we try to turn the hunch that Margolis and Laurence are giving expression to here into an argument, we would need to rely on the following epistemic principle:

So long as the truth of S isn't merely a matter of F, but is also a function of G, then being justified in believing F can only be (at best) part of the story about why one is justified in holding S to be true; one would also need to be justified in believing G.

But this is not in general a sound epistemic principle. The truth of the sentence "This is water" isn't merely a matter of how some substance looks or feels; it is also a matter of its being H_2O. However, it doesn't follow that I could never be justified in holding some stuff to be water without my first being justified in believing it to be H_2O.

At least as far as this particular argument is concerned, I see no reason to doubt that there could be epistemically analytic sentences that are not, per impossibile, also metaphysically analytic.

EXPLAINING EPISTEMIC ANALYTICITY: SYNONYMY

The real problem with the epistemically analytic lies not in demonstrating its independence from the metaphysically analytic; it lies, rather, in explaining how any sentence *could be* epistemically analytic. How might grasp of the meaning of a sentence S suffice for justified belief in the truth of the proposition S expresses?

Let us start with the chestnut "All bachelors are unmarried males." How might grasp of the meaning of this sentence by a speaker suffice for his being justified in believing the proposition it expresses?

One route from meaning to justification that philosophers have often had in mind, without bothering to spell it out, would imagine our thinker reasoning as follows:

[2] Margolis and Laurence 2001, p. 294.

1. "All bachelors are unmarried males" means that All bachelors are unmarried males. (By knowledge of S's meaning)
2. Since "bachelor" just means "unmarried male," "All bachelors are unmarried males" is synonymous with "All unmarried males are unmarried males." (By understanding of meaning)
3. "All unmarried males are unmarried males" means that all unmarried males are unmarried males. (By knowledge of S's meaning)
4. If sentence F is synonymous with sentence G, then F is true iff G is true. (Conceptual knowledge of the link between meaning and truth)
5. Therefore, "All bachelors are unmarried males" is true iff all unmarried males are unmarried males.
6. All unmarried males are unmarried males. (By knowledge of logic)
7. Therefore, "All bachelors are unmarried males" is true.
8. Therefore, all bachelors are unmarried males.

The template that this bit of reasoning instantiates may be represented as follows:

1. S means that P. (Knowledge of meaning)
2. S is synonymous with S'. (Understanding of meaning)
3. S' means that Q, where Q is some logical truth. (Knowledge of meaning)
4. If F is synonymous with G, then F is true iff G is true. (Conceptual link between meaning and truth)
5. Therefore, S is true iff Q.
6. Q (Logic)
7. Therefore, S is true. (Deductive reasoning)
8. Therefore, P. (Deductive reasoning)

Let us call this the "Synonymy Template" and the model of a priori knowledge that it presents the "Synonymy Model." If someone in possession of justification for the premises of this argument actually runs through it, I will say that he is *justified* in believing P; if someone is merely *able* to run through such an argument without actually doing so, I will say that he is *entitled* to P.[3]

Quine, of course, objected that the notion of synonymy on which this model relies is not sufficiently well defined to do serious explanatory work. However, as I argued in "Analyticity Reconsidered," no Meaning Realist can afford to accept Quine's argument.

I think that the Synonymy Model is correct so far as it goes: it correctly explains the structure of our knowledge of *some* a priori truths—of those 'conceptual' truths, namely, that are transformable into logical truths by the substitution of synonyms for synonyms (sentences that in "Analyticity Reconsidered" I called "Frege-analytic"). However, the Synonymy Model is obviously not a *complete* story about how grasp of meaning might generate entitlement, and this in several respects.

---

[3] This invokes Tyler Burge's well-known distinction between justification and entitlement. See Burge 1993.

First, it relies on a piece of a priori conceptual knowledge at premise 4—connecting meaning and truth—that it cannot explain.

Second, it relies on a priori knowledge of logical principles that it cannot explain, and this in two ways. First, it relies on the thinker's knowing that a certain principle is a truth of logic; second, it relies on the thinker's being able justifiably to infer in accordance with deductive rules of logic, so that the thinker is able knowledgeably to move from the premises to the conclusion of the Template.

Finally, it seems quite clear that there will be *other* propositions, beyond the ones mentioned thus far, that the Synonymy Model will be unable to account for. For there do seem to be a considerable number of a priori propositions that are expressed by sentences that are not transformable into logical truths by the substitution of synonyms for synonyms. For example,

- Whatever is red all over is not blue.
- Whatever colored is extended.
- If x is warmer than y, then y is not warmer than x.

If meaning-based explanations of the a priori are to be complete, a meaning-based explanation must be found for the apriority of each of these other types of proposition.

EXPLAINING EPISTEMIC ANALYTICITY: IMPLICIT DEFINITION

As I explained in "Analyticity Reconsidered," one of the central ideas in this connection is that of Implicit Definition (ID). I will look in detail here at the case of logic, postponing to another occasion a description of how ID explanations of apriority might be extended to the other cases we described.

As a first approximation, we may explain the idea of ID, as applied to logic, thus:

It is by stipulating that certain sentences of logic are to be true, or that certain inferences are to be valid, that we attach a meaning to the logical constants.

For example, one might think that:

It is in part by stipulating that
    It is not the case that both P and not P
is to be true, that someone comes to mean negation by 'not.'

Or, to pick another example that will feature further below:

It is in part by stipulating that all inferences of the form
    p
    If p, then q

Therefore, q

are to be valid that someone comes to mean *if* by 'if.'

In considering implicit definitions, we must bear in mind that they come in two varieties: explicit and implicit. An *explicit* implicit definition involves an explicit stipulation by a thinker that a given sentence S(f) is to be true if its ingredient term f is to mean what it does. In the *implicit* variety, it is somehow tacit in that person's behavior with the term f that S(f) is to be true if f is to mean what it does.

Later on I will come back to what it might mean for an implicit definition to be itself implicit. For now, let us operate with the explicit version and ask: how would S(f)'s being an implicit definer for f help explain how grasp of S(f)'s meaning might suffice for justified belief in its truth?

One suggestion, though as we shall see, not ultimately the favored one, would mimic the Synonymy Model by supplying an argument template that a thinker will be in a position to perform as a result of grasping the meaning of S(f).[4]

1. S(f) means that P (By knowledge of meaning)
2. If S(f) means that P, S(f) is true (By knowledge of the contents of one's stipulations)
3. Therefore, S(f) is true
4. If S(f) means that P, then S(f) is true iff P (By knowledge of the link between meaning and truth)
5. S(f) is true iff P
6. Therefore, P

Call this the "Implicit Definition Template" and the model of the a priori that it presents the "Implicit Definition" Model.[5]

KNOWLEDGE OF MEANING AND IMPLICIT DEFINITION

Several philosophers have objected to this model of the a priori. The main recurring complaint has been nicely expressed by Kathrin Glüer:

... let P be the proposition that S(f) expresses. On Boghossian's account, it seems to me, being justified in believing that S(f) means P *presupposes* being justified in believing P. Of course, it then *follows* from being justified in believing that S(f) means P that I am justified in believing P. However, believing P cannot be justified in this way; for knowledge of the meaning of the sentence already requires such justification and, therefore, cannot provide it.[6]

---

[4] This seems to me a better representation of the relevant template than what I offered in my 1996 (this volume, Chapter 9), but it is not materially different.

[5] An example of an a priori that this model might plausibly be taken to explain is the proposition *Vixens are female foxes*.

[6] Glüer 2003, p. 57.

Laurence Bonjour makes a similar point when he says:

Thus, for example, one might stipulate that the sentence '40@8 = 5' is to count as a (partial) implicit definition of the symbol '@'. This, along with other stipulations of the same kind, might prove a useful way of conveying that '@' is to stand for the operation of long division (assuming that the other symbols in the sentence are already understood). But if this is the right account of implicit definition, then the justification of the proposition that 40 divided by 8 is equal to 5 (as opposed to that of the linguistic formula '40@8 = 5') is not a result of the implicit definition, but is rather presupposed by it: if I were not justified in advance, presumably a priori, in believing that forty divided by eight is equal to five, I would have no reason for interpreting '@' in the indicated way.[7]

According to Bonjour and Glüer, if S(f)'s expressing P is fixed via the stipulation that S(f) is to be true, one cannot be justified in believing that S(f) expresses P without *first* being justified in believing that P is true. If that is right, then the Implicit Definition Template could not explain how someone could acquire a priori warrant for the belief that P, since warranted belief in P would be presupposed by anyone running an argument of that form.

This is a surprising objection. As I noted towards the beginning of this paper, most philosophers simply assume that meaning facts are first-person accessible in some privileged way, regardless of what the supervenience base for meaning facts is taken to be. For example, many philosophers believe that even if facts about meaning and concept possession were to supervene on facts that are *external* to the mind that that would have no tendency to undermine our privileged access to first-person facts about meaning.

Now, it is an interesting question whether these many philosophers are right to make this assumption. I, for one, have worried about whether we genuinely understand how first-person access to meaning is possible, especially if meaning is externally determined. I am not a skeptic about such access; I simply believe that we don't really understand how it works.

Bonjour and Glüer, however, write neither as skeptics about privileged access, nor in the service of raising a question about how such access should ultimately be understood. They write as though there is reason to think that in the *special* case where meaning is fixed by implicit definition, there is a problem with the assumption of privileged access. In that case, they assert, someone cannot be said to know that S means that P without first knowing that

a) if S means that P, then S has to be true and that

b) P is true.

But they have supplied us with no special reason to think that, if S's meaning is fixed via implicit definition, the usual assumption of privileged access must be suspended.

[7] Bonjour 1988, pp. 50–1.

This point is only strengthened when we reflect that the only plausible version of ID is not the explicit one with which we have been working so far, but rather the implicit one.

It is rare for a term to be introduced via some explicit stipulation. And in the special case that interests us—the case of the logical constants—it is not only rare but incoherent. As Quine pointed out, if the logical constants are to be thought of as having their meaning fixed by implicit definitions, that meaning cannot be thought of as fixed by explicit implicit definitions, since the logical constants will have to be presupposed in any statement of the stipulations by which we might seek to fix their meanings (see Quine 1976b). Rather, if there is to be anything at all to the idea of ID as applied to logic, it must be that the logical constants have their meaning fixed by our *tacitly* regarding some of the inferences involving them as valid, or by our *tacitly* regarding some of the sentences involving them as true. It's a good question what this sort of tacit stipulation amounts to—many a conceptual role semantics has struggled with that question. But it is a question to which there has to be an answer if, as seems likely, our only hope of explaining how we come to grasp the concepts of the logical constants is through the idea of ID.

But do Bonjour and Glüer really wish to say that if the meaning of 'and' is fixed by a thinker's being disposed to use it according to its standard introduction and elimination rules that he cannot be said to know what 'and' means without first knowing that

'A and B' implies A?

If this particular style of objection is to be sustained, we need to be given a special reason for thinking that where a conceptual role semantics is concerned, there the usual assumption of privileged access must be rejected. But I don't see that we have been given any such reason.

IMPLICIT DEFINITION AND ENTITLEMENT:
THE CONSTITUTIVE MODEL

However, there are several other difficulties with the suggestion that the ID Template gives a fundamental account of the entitlement that implicit definition is able to provide.

First, there continues to be a reliance on the link between meaning and truth at step 4. Even if we can correctly say that we know that

If S means that P then S is true iff P

because we have stipulated it to be true, we cannot hope to explain *why* the stipulation grounds the knowledge via the Implicit Definition Template, because that template relies on our knowledge of that link.

Second, no such argument template could possibly hope to explain in what our entitlement to *reason* according to certain deductive rules consists, since— once again—it presupposes such reasoning.

Finally, if we are operating with the more promising *tacit* version of implicit definition rather than with the version according to which our stipulations are explicit, there is the problem that we can no longer rely on its *following* from the fact that S(f) is an implicit definer of f that S(f) is true. For how is it going to be implicit in someone's behavior with S(f) that it is acting as an implicit definer? Presumably, by S(f)'s being used in a certain way—most plausibly, by its being held to be true come what may. But the point is that there is all the difference in the world between saying that a certain sentence must be held true, if it is to mean this, that or the other, and saying that it *is* true.[8] But it's actually being true is what premise 2 of the ID Template requires. What these problems suggest, therefore, if implicit definition is to be a genuine source of a priori entitlement, is that there must be a different way in which implicit definitions can generate entitlement other than by supplying premises from which the truth of various propositions may somehow be derived.

Call this premise-and-derivation model, on which we have been concentrating so far, the *inferential* conception of how meaning generates entitlement. On the contrasting *constitutive* model, the thinker doesn't start with some premise about some sentence S's meaning from which he deduces that S is true. Rather, the mere fact that the thinker grasps S's meaning entails that the thinker is justified in holding S to be true. Or, if we focus on inferences rather than sentences: the mere fact that the thinker grasps inference rule R's meaning entails that the thinker is justified in inferring according to R. How would this work?

In the two papers that follow, two related though distinct answers to this question are explored.[9]

---

[8] This point was first made in my 1994a.

[9] When originally published this paper went on to develop one of these answers. I have omitted this material here because much of it overlaps with my 2003a (this volume, Chapter 12). Those passages that don't overlap have been added as an appendix to that chapter. I am grateful to Stephen Schiffer for comments on an earlier version of this paper.

11 *How are Objective Epistemic Reasons Possible?*

INTRODUCTION

Epistemic relativism has the contemporary academy in its grip. Not merely in the United States, but seemingly everywhere, most scholars working in the humanities and the social sciences seem to subscribe to some form of it. Even where the label is repudiated, the view is embraced. Sometimes the relativism in question concerns truth, sometimes justification. The core impulse appears to be a relativism about *knowledge*. The suspicion is widespread that what counts as knowledge in one cultural, or broadly ideological, setting need not count as knowledge in another.

While it is true that these views are often very poorly laid out and argued for, I found myself surprised, on reflection, at the extent to which a relativism about justification—as opposed to one concerning truth—may be seen to be a natural, if ultimately ill-advised, response to a real problem. For there is a serious difficulty seeing how there could be objectively valid reasons for belief, a difficulty that has perhaps not been adequately faced up to in the analytic tradition.

In this essay, I aim to explain what the problem is; to say why relativism, and its sophisticated cousin, non-factualism, are unpalatable solutions to it; and to try to point the way forward.

I

THE PROBLEM

I take it for granted that we aim to have true beliefs and that we attempt to satisfy that aim by having *justified* beliefs. Let us represent a thinker as possessing a certain set of beliefs and a certain set of rules—epistemic rules—that specify how to modify those beliefs in response to incoming evidence. An example of such a rule may be:

(ER1) If lighting conditions are good, etc, and it visually seems to you as if there is a cat in front of you, then believe that there is a cat in front of you.

Another example:

(ER2) If you are justified in believing that p, and justified in believing that 'If p, then q', then believe q or give up one of the other beliefs.

By saying that a thinker has and operates according to these rules I don't mean that the thinker grasps these rules as propositions. I mean that he *follows* these rules, and that this shows up in his behavior, however exactly that is to be analyzed. It will do no harm, for present purposes, to think of rule-following as a disposition to rule-conform under appropriately idealized circumstances.[1]

Now, epistemic rules are rules and as such make no claims. They are rules of obligation governing belief. But the point of saying that we aim to have justified beliefs is to say that their function is to so modify belief that what results from their application is always a justified belief in the circumstances. In adopting (ER1) as our rule of belief modification, in other words, we are implicitly committed to the truth of a corresponding *epistemic principle*:

(EP1) If S is in good lighting conditions and etc, then if it visually appears to S that there is an x in front of him, then S would be prima facie justified in believing that there is an x in front of him.[2]

Similarly for (ER2):

(EP2) If S is justified in believing p and is justified in believing 'If p then q', and S infers q from those premises, then S is prima facie justified in believing q.

Against this backdrop, the thesis of the objectivity of reasons can be stated as the claim that there is an objective fact of the matter which epistemic principles are true, and, consequently, which sets of rules a thinker ought to employ to shape his beliefs, if he is to arrive at beliefs that are genuinely justified.

We certainly act as though we believe in the objectivity of reasons. We don't behave as though anything goes in the way of belief, suggesting that we operate with a specific set of epistemic rules. And we don't hold that others are at liberty to operate with whatever epistemic rules they like.

---

[1] For discussion, though, see my 1989b and 2008 (this volume, Chapters 1 and 5 respectively).

[2] As James Van Cleve points out, any epistemic principle has the following form:

(EP) If a belief of type B is based on a reason of type R then the belief is justified.

On a foundationalist view (and adopting Van Cleve's terminology), such principles will include both *generation* principles and *transmission* principles. Generation principles specify circumstances under which a belief is justified independently of its logical relations to other beliefs; transmission principles specify under what circumstances the warrant for a given belief transmits to other beliefs. On a coherentist view, epistemic principles will largely consist of some sort of hybrid of these two, assuming the form: If P coheres with the system of propositions accepted by S, then P is justified for S. This is analogous to a generation principle in that its antecedent does not mention any term of epistemic appraisal, but analogous to a transmission principle in that its antecedent specifies relations to other proposition. See Van Cleve 1979. For the sake of concreteness, in this essay I will assume that epistemic principles always take the form characteristic of foundationalism; but the arguments will apply to either type of epistemic system.

The problem for the objectivity of reasons can now be stated succinctly, in the form of the following *reductio*:

1. Assume that there are objective facts about which epistemic principles are true.
2. If there are objective facts about which epistemic principles are true, these facts should be knowable: it ought to be possible to arrive at justified beliefs about them.
3. It is not possible to know which epistemic principles are objectively true, therefore
4. There are no objective facts about which epistemic principles are true.

THE SECOND PREMISE

This is not the strong and implausible claim that, if S is to know anything, he must know the underlying epistemic principles to which he is committed. To learn by observation that there is a cat in front of me does not require me first to know that observation justifies perceptual beliefs.

It is rather the much weaker claim that, if there are objective facts about epistemic principles that are true, there should be humanly accessible circumstances under which those facts can be known. And this much weaker claim seems to me almost not to require argument. If there are such facts, why should they be in principle unknowable?

My claim here does not stem from a generalized verificationism: for any fact, if it is to obtain, it must be knowable. I am perfectly happy to admit that there might be facts about the world that are not accessible to creatures such as ourselves. What I don't see is how this could apply to the sort of epistemic fact currently under consideration. There is no intuitive sense in which such epistemic facts are analogous to evidence-transcendent or undecidable facts of a more familiar variety—those four consecutive sevens in the decimal expansion of pi, for example. Rather, what is at issue are facts of the form encoded in (EP1) and (EP2). It would be peculiar, to say the least, if truths of this type were in principle unknowable. It would certainly be peculiar for us to *suppose* that they are unknowable. For in what could our confidence that there are such facts consist, if we simultaneously take it that we cannot know what they are?

Prima facie, indeed, a much stronger claim seems plausible: not merely that these facts are knowable, but that they are, at least in large measure, *known*. For are we seriously to suppose that we don't know what it takes to justify a belief or a claim? If we don't, should we not be far more diffident about putting forward any claim, including the claim that we don't know which epistemic principles are true? Although, as I have conceded, it does not logically follow from S's knowing something that he knows which epistemic principles are true, it does seem to be true that, if S is a sufficiently *self-conscious* knower, he must *assume* that he knows which epistemic principles are true. So there is at least something pragmatically problematic about claiming that we don't know, and can't know, which epistemic principles are true.

A further source of support for the claim that we know comes from the nearly universal agreement about which epistemic principles are true. With the exception of certain postmodern thinkers—and in their case they merely pretend to believe otherwise—nearly everyone agrees that observation generates justification for certain sorts of belief and that deductively valid inferences transmit the justification attaching to their premises to their conclusions. What better explanation could there be for this practically universal agreement than that there are objective facts about what the correct principles are and that these facts are relatively obvious?

If we wished we could go further and plausibly claim not only that these facts are known, but that they are known *a priori*. For we don't seem to have learnt from experience that deductively valid arguments transmit justification, nor it seems, could we have.[3]

Nevertheless, for the purposes of this argument, I will rely only on the weaker claim that, if there are correct epistemic principles, they are knowable.

THE THIRD PREMISE

Why should there be any difficulty in knowing which they are? Having emphasized how widely known they seem to be, how do we now contrive a difficulty about knowing them in the first place? Unfortunately, it is not too difficult to say what the problem is.

Let's concentrate, for now, on deductive reasoning. As I said, we modify our beliefs according to:

(ER2) If you are justified in believing that p, and justified in believing that 'If p, then q', then you should either believe q or give up one of the other beliefs.

In subscribing to ER2, we are evincing our acceptance of the rule of inference modus ponens:

$$\text{(MPPR) p, q} \rightarrow \text{q/q.}$$

Some might choose to regard acceptance of MPPR as simply *consisting* in an acceptance of ER2; others might prefer to regard MPPR as the more basic and hence as *leading* to an acceptance of ER2. It won't matter for my purposes how the relation between these rules is conceived.

In the interests of keeping matters as simple as possible, let us restrict ourselves to propositional logic and let us suppose that we are working within

---

[3] For discussion, see my 2000.

a system in which MPPR is the only *fundamental*, underived, rule of inference. In that case, S's fundamental transmission principle becomes our familiar:

(EP2) If S is justified in believing p and is justified in believing 'If P then q', and S infers q from those premises, then S is prima facie justified in believing q.

And this principle will in turn be true provided that a certain logical fact obtains, namely:

$$\text{(MPP) } p, p \rightarrow q \text{ imply } q.$$

Now, if S is to know that his fundamental transmission principle is true, he must, at a minimum, be justified in believing that MPP is true. So our question about the knowability of epistemic principles becomes: Is it possible for S to be justified in believing that all arguments of the form modus ponens are necessarily truth-preserving?[4] (I am not at the moment concerned with how thinkers such as ourselves are *actually* justified, but only with whether it makes sense to suppose that we could be.)

When we look at the available options, however, it seems hard to see how we could be justified in believing something as basic as MPP. For in what could such a justification consist? It would have to be either inferential or non-inferential. And there look to be serious problems of principle standing in the way of either option.

NON-INFERENTIAL JUSTIFICATION

For us to be non-inferentially justified in believing something we would have to be justified in believing it either on the basis of some sort of observation or on the basis of nothing.

But what sort of observation could possibly serve as the basis for the belief that all arguments of the form MPP are truth-preserving? Henry Kyburg has given voice to a temptation that we must all have felt at some point:

I think that in some sense ... our justification of deductive rules must ultimately rest, in part, on an element of deductive intuition: we *see* that *modus ponens* is truth-preserving—that is simply the same as to reflect on it and fail to see how it can lead us astray.[5]

It is possible to discern two distinct thoughts in this short passage, although Kyburg seems to want to equate them. One is that we can simply *see* that MPP is truth-preserving. The other is that, try as we might, we cannot see any way in which it could fail us.

---

[4] Some philosophers distinguish between the *activity* of giving a justification and the *property* of being justified. My question involves the latter, more basic, notion: Is it possible for our logical beliefs to have the property of being justified?

[5] Kyburg 1965. It is cited in van Cleve 1984.

Neither thought seems particularly helpful. As for the first thought, in any sense of "see" that I can make sense of, we cannot just *see* that MPP is valid. To be sure, the idea that we possess a quasi-perceptual faculty—going by the name of "rational intuition"—the exercise of which is supposed to give us direct insight into necessary truths has been historically influential. It would be fair to say, however, that no one has succeeded in saying what this faculty really is nor how it manages to yield the relevant knowledge. "Intuition," or "clear and distinct perception," seem like names for the mystery we are addressing, rather than solutions to it.[6]

As for the second thought, when we say that we cannot see or conceive a counterexample to some general claim—for example, to the claim that all arguments of the form modus ponens are truth-preserving—we cannot plausibly mean that we have some direct, non-ratiocinative ability to detect whether such an example exists. The only thing we can legitimately mean is that a more or less elementary piece of *reasoning* shows that there cannot be any such counterexample. The "reflecting" on the matter that Kyburg mentions is mediated by reasoning. We think: A conditional statement is true provided that if its antecedent is true so is its consequent. Suppose, then, that a particular conditional statement is true and that so is its antecedent. Then it simply has to be the case that its consequent is true. Hence, there can be no counterexample.

Talk of "conceiving" and "seeing" here are just thin disguises for a certain familiar style of logical reasoning. This is not, of course, to condemn it. But it is to emphasize that its acceptability as an epistemology for *logic* turns on the acceptability of an inferential account more generally.

DEFAULT REASONABLE BELIEFS

But perhaps it is a mistake to think that some positive act of observation or imagining is required, if a belief is to be justified non-inferentially. According to an increasingly influential line of thought, certain beliefs are simply "default reasonable," reasonable in and of themselves, without any supporting justification from either observation or argument. In particular, the fundamental logical beliefs have this feature.[7] It is reasonable to believe them, but *not* because there is some positive *ground* by virtue of which they are reasonable. If believed, they are reasonably believed, period.

I am not implacably opposed to the idea that there might be beliefs that are reasonable on the basis of nothing, especially if this is understood to mean simply that they are beliefs that are *presumptively but defeasibly justified*. It is possible that this will prove to be the best description of the epistemology of

---

[6] Laurence Bonjour, in his 1998, attempts to defend a "rational right" view of the a priori. For critical discussion, see my 2001b.

[7] See Field 2000.

our first-person knowledge of the contents of our own minds. What I don't see, however, is how this idea could plausibly apply to the case at hand, to the *generalization* that all inferences of a certain form are necessarily truth-preserving.

If the notion of default reasonableness is to play a significant role in the theory of knowledge, there has to be some principled way of saying which beliefs are default reasonable and why. What is needed, in other words, is a *criterion* for determining whether a belief qualifies for that status and an *explanation* for why satisfaction of that criterion is sufficient for it. Which beliefs are default reasonable and what is it about them that gives them this special standing? This insistence does not contravene the root idea that, in the case of a default reasonable belief, there is no *ground* that makes it reasonable; for it is consistent with a belief's having that status that there be a criterion by virtue of which it has that status and an explanation for why it has it.

The trouble with default reasonable beliefs is that there do not seem to be very many plausible answers to these questions: it is hard to see what condition could plausibly qualify a belief for default reasonable status.

One idea that might seem initially promising concerns the class of self-fulfilling beliefs: beliefs that are such that, having them guarantees that they are true. Surely these beliefs count as default reasonable if any do. Tyler Burge has discussed such beliefs in connection with the phenomenon of authoritative self-knowledge. For example, the belief—With this very thought I am thinking that water is wet—looks to be self-fulfilling: thinking it logically guarantees its truth.[8]

It would, however, be a mistake to think that being logically self-confirming is sufficient for default reasonableness. A guarantee of truth is not in itself a guarantee of reasonableness; and it is reasonableness that's at issue. What is missing from a merely self-confirming thought is some knowledge, however trivial, on the part of the thinker that the thought *is* self-confirming. But such knowledge would transform the source of the reasonableness to an inference based on that knowledge and we would now no longer have anything that is reasonable by default.

A second thought, more directly connected to the thinker's justification, has it that a default reasonable belief is any belief which, by virtue of being pre-supposed in any justification that a thinker might give, is neither justifiable nor refutable for that thinker. But this suggestion has two implausible consequences. First, it entails that what is default reasonable has to be relativized to individual thinkers, for different thinkers may build their epistemic systems around different claims. Second, it has the consequence that some very implausible claims would come out as default reasonable for someone if they happened to be presupposed by that person's epistemic system. For example, suppose that someone takes as basic the *negation* of the law of non-contradiction; on this view, we would have to say that the negation of that law is default reasonable

---

[8] See Burge 1988. I discuss Burge's view in more detail in my 1989a (this volume, Chapter 6).

for him, because, by assumption, it will be neither justifiable nor refutable for that person.

A third suggestion has it that the beliefs that are default reasonable are those beliefs that a thinker finds "self-evident"—that is, that he is disposed to find plausible simply on the basis of understanding them and without any further support or warrant. But this proposal, too, would seem to be subject to the previous two objections. Once again, it is entirely possible that two people will find very different propositions "self-evident," and that some of those will include propositions that are intuitively highly implausible.

Nor would it help to strengthen the requirement so that it concerns those beliefs that actually *are* self-evident, as opposed to those that merely *seem* self-evident. Here the problem is that no one seems to me to have shown how this notion is to be spelled out. In particular, no one has supplied a criterion for distinguishing those propositions that *are* self-evident from those that—like the parallel postulate in Euclidean geometry or the proposition that life cannot be reduced to anything biological—merely *seemed* self-evident to many people for a very long time.

By contrast, there is one form of explanation that seems to me have some promise. There may be beliefs that are such that, having those beliefs is a condition for having one of the concepts ingredient in them. Thus, Christopher Peacocke has written of a special case

... in which it is written into the possession conditions for one or more concepts in [a] given principle that to possess those concepts, the thinker must be willing to accept the principle, by reaching it in [a particular] way.[9]

The special case that Peacocke has in mind concerns our belief in the validity of the basic truths of deduction. Under the terms of our assumptions, then, the idea would be that it is written into the possession conditions for conditional, that to possess it a thinker would have to believe that all arguments of the form MPP are truth-preserving.

If this were true, then, it seems to me, it would be correct to say that the belief that MPP is truth-preserving is default reasonable. For if it really were part of the possession condition for a given concept that to possess it one had to believe a certain proposition containing it, then that would explain why belief in that proposition is presumptively but defeasibly justified. If it really were a precondition for being able to so much as *entertain* any thought involving the concept *phlogiston* that one *believe* that phlogiston is a substance, then it would seem to me right to say that the belief that phlogiston is a substance is presumptively reasonable, subject to defeat by other considerations. It seems wrong to call the belief in question unreasonable when having it is a precondition for having any thoughts about it—including thoughts about its reasonableness.

---

[9] Peacocke 2000.

Unfortunately, it is not remotely plausible that anyone possessing the concept of conditional would have to have the *belief* that MPP is valid. One can have and reason with conditional without so much as having the concept of logical implication. At most what the theory of concept possession would license is that *inferring* according to MPPR is part of the possession condition for conditional, not the *belief* that MPP is valid. But what we are after now is the justification for the belief. (Henceforth, to avoid unnecessary prolixity, I will drop the distinction between the labels, 'MPP' and 'MPPR'. I will talk simply about the difference between believing that MPP is valid and reasoning according to MPP.)

INFERENTIAL JUSTIFICATION: RULE-CIRCULARITY

This brings us, then, to the inferential path. Here there are a number of distinct possibilities, but they would all seem to suffer from the same master difficulty: in being inferential, they would have to be *rule-circular*. If MPP is the only underived rule of inference, then any inferential argument for MPP would either have to use MPP or use some other rule whose justification depends on MPP. And many philosophers have worried, legitimately, that a rule-circular justification of a rule of inference is no justification at all.

Thus, it is tempting to suppose that we can give an a priori justification for modus ponens on the basis of our knowledge of the truth-table for 'if, then'. Suppose that p is true and that 'if p, then q' is also true. By the truth-table for 'if, then', if p is true and if 'if p, then q' is true, then q is true. So q must be true, too. As is clear, however, this justification for MPP must itself take at least one step in accord with MPP.

But why should this be considered a problem? While it may be immediately obvious that a grossly circular justification—one that includes among its premises that which it is attempting to prove—is worthless it is not equally obvious that the same is true of a merely rule-circular justification. What intuitive constraint on justification does a rule-circular justification violate? It will be useful to approach this question by looking first at what is wrong with a grossly circular justification and to examine subsequently to what extent these problems afflict mere rule-circularity as well.

There are at least two things wrong with a grossly circular argument. First, it assumes that which it is trying to prove and that, quite independently of any further consequences, seems wrong. An argument is put forward with the intent of justifying—earning the right to believe—a certain claim. But it will only do so if it proceeds from premises that are justified. If, however, the premise is also the conclusion, then it is simply helping itself to the claim that the conclusion is justified, instead of earning the right to it. And this maneuver offends against the very idea of proving something or arguing for it. As we are prone to say, it begs the question.

A second problem is that by allowing itself the liberty of assuming that which it is trying to prove, a grossly circular argument is able to prove absolutely anything, however intuitively unjustifiable. Let us call the first problem the problem of "begging the question" and the second that of "bad company."[10] Is a merely rule-circular justification subject to the same or analogous worries?

It is not obvious that a rule-circular argument begs the question, for what we have is an argument that is circular only in the sense that, in purporting to prove the validity of a given logical law, it must take at least one step in accordance with that law. And it is not immediately clear that we should say that an argument relies on its implicated rule of inference in the same way as we say that it relies on its premises.

Well, perhaps not in the *same* way, but it is not difficult to motivate a worry on this score. One clear way of doing so is to look at the role that a rule-circular argument might play in a dialectical context in which it is being used to silence a *sketpic's* doubt about its conclusion.

Suppose that you doubt some claim C, and I am trying to persuade you that it's true. I offer you an argument A in its support. In general, in such a context, you could question A's cogency either by questioning one of its premises or by questioning the implicated rule of inference R. If you were to proceed by challenging R, then I would have to defend R and my only option would appear to be to try to defend my *belief* that R is truth-preserving.

Now suppose that the context in question is the special case where C is the proposition that R is truth-preserving and my argument for C is rule-circular in that it employs R in one of its steps. Here it very much looks as if I have begged the question: I have certainly begged *your* question. You doubt MPP. I give you an argument in support of MPP that uses MPP. Alert enough to notice that fact, you question my argument by reiterating your doubts about MPP. I defend my argument by asserting that MPP is truth-preserving. In this dialectical sense, a rule-circular argument might be said to beg the question.

At a minimum, then, the skeptical context discloses that a rule-circular argument for MPP would beg a skeptic's question about MPP and would, therefore, be powerless to quell his doubts about it. In doing this, however, it reveals yet another sense in which a worry might arise about a rule-circular argument. An argument relies on a rule of inference. As the skeptical scenario highlights, one's reliance on such a rule might be questioned. But, quite apart from whether it is questioned, in what does one's entitlement to rely on that rule consist, if not in one's entitlement to the *belief* that the rule is truth-preserving? And if it does consist in that, how can a rule-circular argument in support of belief in MPP confer warrant on its conclusion? In relying on a step in accord with MPP, in the course of an argument for MPP, one would be leaning on the very conclusion one is allegedly trying to prove.

---

[10] I owe the term "bad company" to Crispin Wright.

Under the general heading of a worry about begging the question, then, I want to distinguish two problems: First, to say in what the entitlement to use a rule of inference consists, if not in one's justified belief that that rule is truth-preserving. Second, to say how a rule-circular argument can confer warrant on its conclusion even if it is powerless to move the relevant skeptic.

What about the problem of bad company? Prima facie, anyway, there looks to be a big difference between a grossly circular argument, on the one hand, and a rule-circular argument on the other, so far as their potential to positively rationalize belief is concerned. A grossly circular argument is guaranteed to succeed, no matter what proposition it is attempting to rationalize. A similar charge could not be made against a merely rule-circular argument: the mere license to use an inferential step in accord with modus ponens, for example, does not *in and of itself guarantee* that a given argument will succeed in demonstrating the validity of modus ponens. Appropriate premises from which, by (as it might be) a single application of MPP, we can get the general conclusion that MPP is truth-preserving, may simply not exist. In general, it is a non-trivial fact that a given rule of inference is self-supporting in this way.

While this point is strictly correct, however, the fact is that unless constraints are placed on the acceptability of rule-circular arguments, it will nevertheless be true that we will be able to justify all manner of absurd rules of inference. We must confront the charge that unconstrained rule-circular justifications keep bad company.

Consider someone who has somehow come to adopt the unreflective practice of inferring according to Prior's introduction and elimination rules for the 'tonk' connective:

(I) A/A tonk B; (E) A tonk B/B

If we suppose that we are allowed to *use* inferences in accord with these rules in mounting a justification for them, then it would seem that we could justify them as follows:[11]

'P tonk Q' is true iff 'P' is true tonk 'Q' is true	Meaning Postulate
P	Assumption
'P' is true	2, T-scheme
'P' is true tonk 'Q' is true	3, tonk-introduction
'P tonk Q' is true	4, 1, biconditional-elimination
P tonk Q	5, T-scheme
If P, then P tonk Q	6, logic

[11] The example is Crispin Wright's, drawn from his commentary on a related paper at the Stirling Conference on Naturalism, April 1997.

Here line 7 expresses a canonical statement of tonk-introduction dependent just on the meaning postulate in line 1. So this template is available to explain how someone for whom inference in accordance with tonk introduction was already part of their unreflective practice could arrive at an explicit justification for it. And an exactly corresponding example could be constructed to yield a "justification" for the principle of tonk-elimination.

Or consider the following example.[12] Let R* be the rule that, for any P, P, *therefore* All snow is white. Now, we seem to be in a position to mount a justification for it along the following lines. Pick any proposition P:

1. P	Assumption
2. All snow is white	1, R*
3. If P, then All snow is white	Conditional Weakening

Therefore, the inference from P to all snow is white is truth-preserving. Since this is independent of the particular proposition P that is chosen, then, for any proposition P, the inference from P to "All snow is white" is truth-preserving, i.e., R* is valid.

Prima facie, then, there look to be serious objections to supposing that a rule-circular justification can confer any sort of warrant on its conclusion.

HOW TO RESPOND?

If the preceding considerations are correct, it's a serious question how there could be objectively correct deductive transmission principles. And this result by itself would deal a powerful blow to the objectivist pretensions of the concept of knowledge. If there are no objectively correct facts about how one ought to reason deductively, much of what we take to be knowledge would not be binding on those who would prefer to reason differently.

But the true situation is probably worse even than this. For given the inevitable involvement of deductive reasoning in any account of how we might know the correctness of *non-deductive* epistemic principles, the problem is likely to be global: it will be difficult to see how there could be objectively correct epistemic principles of any sort.

I don't have the space to argue for this general claim in detail here. In outline, this is how the argument would go. All the points about the inadequacy of observational or default reasonableness accounts would carry over to the non-deductive case. That means that any justification for the principles governing non-deductive reasoning would have to be inferential. As inferential, they would either have to be non-deductive or deductive, or a mixture of the two. If

---

[12] Due to Marcus Giaquinto.

non-deductive, then the justification would be rule-circular and so subject to a version of the worries just outlined. If deductive, then ditto. If a mixture, then ditto.

To put matters another way, it seems to me that all we really need, in order to raise a serious problem about the possibility of objectively correct epistemic principles, is the simple and seemingly inescapable claim that *reasoning* of some sort will be involved in any putative knowledge that we might have of any high-level epistemic claim. Once that simple thought is in place, seemingly insuperable problems are upon us virtually immediately.

How should we respond? For obvious reasons, we can't just say that there are no objectively correct principles and leave it at that. We cannot but think that some beliefs are more justified than others, and that fact entails that we cannot but think that some epistemic principles are preferable to others. But how are we to make sense of this preference, if we are not allowed to think that some principles are objectively correct and others aren't?

There look to be two options: we can either treat judgments about justification as capable only of relative truth, or we can treat them expressively, as not expressing genuinely truth-evaluable propositions in the first place. On the first view, we accommodate the result that there are no objective facts about justification by appealing only to relative facts about it; on the second view, we accommodate it by not appealing to any facts at all. I will start with a discussion of the relativist option.[13]

II

RELATIVISM

Against the backdrop of the problem for objectivism just outlined, a relativism about justification can seem almost forced. There appears to be no way to justify one set of epistemic principles over another except by the use of those very epistemic principles. However, depending on what principles we begin with, distinct sets of principles will come out looking correct. In response, it seems very natural to say that there can be no such thing as *the* objectively correct epistemic principles. There is just where we start, and how we find it natural to reason.[14]

---

[13] Why not consider instead a relativism or non-factualism about logic itself, rather than about justification? The reason is that these views are well known to be hopeless. A relativism about logic is just a version of a conventionalism about it, a view decisively defeated in Quine 1976b. And as I have argued in my 2000, those objections carry over straightforwardly to a non-factualist construal of logic.

[14] Some may find this thought expressed in Wittgenstein's remark: "If I have exhausted the justifications I have reached bedrock, and my spade is turned. Then I am inclined to say: 'This is simply what I do'." *Philosophical Investigations*, para. 217.

There are, of course, a number of ways in which such a relativism about justification might be elaborated, but the core idea is this: whether, under the appropriate circumstances, a given body of information supports a particular belief isn't some absolute relation between the information and the belief but is rather to be understood as obtaining only relative to some further parameter—the epistemic principles accepted by a community: whereas the objectivist thinks that some proposition P can simply be justified (by the evidence, under the appropriate conditions, all this henceforth suppressed), the relativist thinks that we can only cogently talk about P's being justified relative to a communal epistemic practice C, for variable C.

On the relativist's view, in other words, there is, in our usual of attributions of justification a hidden reference to a relation that obtains between the claim being put forward and the speaker's own community, a reference that his analysis purports to reveal, in just the way that Russell's famous analysis of definite descriptions purported to disclose a hidden reliance on existential quantification:

(J) For any speaker S asserting that P is justified, S is making a judgment of the form: P is justified relative to S's communal principles C.[15]

As for the communal norms themselves, there can be no question of their being justified or correct. They are what they are.

Now, philosophical tradition has it that relativism so understood is subject to a decisive dilemma. Either the relativist is putting forward his view as objectively justified or only as relatively justified, justified for his community. If it's the former, then the view refutes itself, for there would then be, by its own admission, at least one proposition that is objectively justified (and if there is that one, is it really plausible that there shouldn't be others?). If, however, he insists that it is meant to be justified only in a relative sense, only justified for his community, then why do we as non-relativists need to worry about it?

The argument I have just presented is nearly as old as philosophy itself.[16] Objectivists seem to find it decisive, whereas relativists are prone to dismiss it as worthless, a clever bit of logical trickery that has no real bearing on the issues at hand.

It's hard to see how the relativist's attitude here is to be vindicated: there is absolutely nothing illicit about self-refutations of this sort. In fairness, however, it is important to note that this famous argument does suffer from three significant weaknesses.

First, the argument is a self-refutation argument of a *pragmatic* variety, and the point is that such an argument proceeds not by uncovering a genuine

---

[15] The relativist could also be understood as arguing not that we already speak this way, but that we ought to, if we are to speak cogently.

[16] It can be found in Plato's *Theaetetus*, and in Thomas Nagel's 1996.

contradiction in the target view, but by uncovering a contradiction between *asserting* the view and the view's content. It follows, therefore, that we cannot say, merely on the basis of the argument, that we have demonstrated the *falsity* of the claim that all justification is relative, but only that such a claim would not be assertible or believable.

Another limitation that self-refutation arguments of a pragmatic variety are subject to is that they depend on a particular vocabulary for describing the activity of knowledge—for example, on the propriety of describing the activity of knowledge in terms of the notions of *assertion* and *belief*. But perhaps these are not the right concepts for the description of cognitive activity, as some eliminativists have claimed.[17] Perhaps this whole way of describing what we do, when we seek knowledge, will be replaced by some other set of terms. What would be the value of our pragmatic refutation then? Obviously, if the notion of asserting something, or of believing it, were replaced by some other way of thinking about knowledge—shmasserting and shmelieving, for example—it would be irrelevant that there is an inconsistency between *asserting* or *believing* that all justification is relative and the claim that it is. What we would need to do is find an inconsistency between shmasserting that all justification is relative and the claim that it is.

A third problem for the argument is perhaps the most serious. If the relativist opts for the horn of saying that J is meant to be justified only relative to his community, he has not yet committed himself to the view that that community is identical with the community of relativists. For all we are entitled to assume, he may mean that J is justified for a community that includes non-relativists and, hence, that it is equally justified for them. So we are not immediately entitled to say that, if he adopts that horn, we are entitled to ignore him.

For instance, the anti-objectivist argument that I presented in Part I relies only on ordinary and widely accepted epistemic norms. If the relativist motivates his view by appealing to that argument, we can hardly dismiss him by saying that his view is justified only relative to relativists. His view would appear to have been motivated for all of us.

There are certainly things that can be said in reply to these objections. In response to the first objection we may point out that it is highly significant that a view is not coherently assertible or believable. If we know a view to be not coherently believable, we know that we cannot take it seriously as a possible candidate for truth.

In response to the second objection, one can say two things. The first is that no one has come close to saying what an alternative to classical epistemology would look like, no one has provided the slightest guidance as to how we are to think of our basic cognitive activities if not in terms of the notions of asserting, claiming, saying, believing and the like. And the second is that it's very

---

[17] See, for example, Churchland 1984.

hard to see how any putative replacement would be able to evade the sorts of consideration that the pragmatic refutation employs, given how austere those considerations actually are. Surely, any replacement epistemology will have to have some notion that plays the same role as our notion of a reason for believing something; and for any such notion we will be able to run a version of the argument that we deployed above.

But it is hard to see what to say in response to the third objection, it seems to me. The epistemic norms that are relied upon in the anti-objectivist argument of Part I are ordinary norms that beg no question against the objectivist. With what right, then, does the objectivist claim the freedom simply to ignore the relativism that they seem to motivate?

At least as traditionally formulated, then, the classical pragmatic refutation of relativism seems to me to be far from decisive. Unfortunately for the relativist, however, there is a different way of formulating the objection to his view that evades these difficulties. To bring it out, let me introduce a notion—that of being 'epistemically blameless.' If someone is epistemically blameless in believing something then it makes no sense to criticize him for believing it. I intend this to be an absolute notion, by contrast with the relativist's relative notion of justification.

Consider next a community C, and a given state of information I that C finds itself in. If justificatory relativism is true, then, even while keeping the state of information I fixed, it is *possible* for C to believe *any* proposition P that it wants, and be blameless. All C has to do is adopt whatever epistemic norm sanctions P under I. Since, according to the relativist, there can be no higher facts about which epistemic principles it would be correct to adopt, C can adopt any epistemic principle it wants and be blameless. Since, for any P, there will be some set of principles that will sanction believing it, any state of information is consistent with blameless belief in *any* proposition, if relativism is true.

In particular, C can blamelessly adopt epistemic norms that prohibit a relativism about justification. Indeed, because it can adopt whatever epistemic norms it wants, it can keep most of the ordinary norms in place and simply accept certain exceptions to them, whatever it takes to selectively prohibit whatever view it doesn't like, including relativism. By the relativist's own lights, there can be no objection to this maneuver.

The original hunch behind the classical pragmatic anti-relativist argument is that relativism may be blamelessly rejected. That hunch is now vindicated by our reformulated anti-relativist argument. But more than that, we see that, at least on this straightforward way of formulating a relativism about justified belief, relativism does indeed lead to an unacceptable form of 'anything goes.' On its own terms, any state of information is consistent with blameless belief in any proposition, given only appropriate (and guaranteed to be blameless) adjustments in the epistemic system.

NON-FACTUALISM ABOUT JUSTIFICATION

The question is: Would we do better if we accommodated an anti-objectivism about justification not in relativist terms but in *expressivist* ones?

Allan Gibbard has developed just such an expressivist theory of judgments of rationality; adapted to the present case it would yield something like the following view: When someone says that 'x is a justified belief' they are not attributing any sort of property to it at all, relational or otherwise; rather, they are *expressing* their acceptance of a system of norms that permits that belief under those circumstances.[18]

Now, it might appear at first glance that this is a considerable improvement over a relativist construal of justification. Since, in saying that a belief is justified, we are not attributing any sort of property to it, but merely expressing our acceptance of a system of norms that permits it; and since we don't as a matter of fact accept epistemic norms that permit believing anything, it looks as though the consequence that one can believe anything one likes and be blameless is blocked. Unfortunately, I shall argue that this appearance is illusory and that a non-factualism about justification is subject to much the same sort of objection as an outright relativism about it.

To see why, let's imagine that I come across someone—call him AR—who holds a view I consider utterly unjustified: for example, that there is a space-ship trailing the comet Hale-Bopp that is going to come down and swoop him away. What can be my attitude towards such a person, given a Gibbard-style expressivism? I can express my acceptance of a system of norms that forbids that belief, all right, but that seems to leave something important out. If I tell AR that his belief that p is irrational and unjustified, I am not merely expressing my acceptance of a system of norms that forbids it; I am claiming to see some-thing that he is not, namely, that p ought not to be believed, given the available evidence. I am saying (roughly): I do not believe p; you should not either.

Gibbard tries to account for the normativity of such judgments by invoking a classic expressivist resource: the conversational demand. In saying that x is unjustified, he says, I am expressing my acceptance of a system of norms that forbids x and adding: Do so as well!

In and of itself, however, this does not capture the claim that I appear to be making when I claim that I am justified and AR isn't, for even someone who is simply browbeating his interlocutor can issue a conversational demand. To browbeat someone is to issue a conversational demand whilst knowing that one is not entitled to do so. So the question is: with what *right* do I insist that someone accept my view and abandon his, on non-factualist views of justification? Could not AR insist, with equal right, that I abandon my view in favor of his? Indeed,

[18] Gibbard 1990.

as a non-factualist, would not I have to recognize that our claims to normative authority here are perfectly symmetrical, thereby undermining any hold I might have had on the thought that I am justified and he is not? And is not this a version of the sort of relativism expressivism was supposed to avoid?

Now, AR's belief about alien spaceships may arise in a number of different ways. He may share all my epistemic norms on the fixation of belief and he may be very good at reasoning from those norms and the available evidence to the relevant conclusions. He may simply not be aware that there is not a scintilla of evidence that there is a spaceship trailing Hale-Bopp. In that case, there is no difficulty accounting for my demand that he give up his view in favor of mine. Knowing that his problem stems simply from an ignorance of the relevant facts, I can coherently ask that he take my reasoning as proxy for his own. And he, for his part, would be entirely reasonable in taking me up on my invitation.

Then, again, AR's curious belief may derive not from his ignorance of any item of evidence but from his poor abilities at reasoning: he may be bad at moving from the epistemic norms that we share and the evidence to the appropriate conclusions. Here, again, there is no difficulty accounting for the normative authority that I claim. Given that we share the relevant norms, I can again ask him to take my reasoning as proxy for his own.

But suppose that the difference between AR's beliefs and mine stems not from such mundane sources but rather from a deep-seated difference in the fundamental epistemic norms to which we subscribe, norms for the fixation of belief that are not derived from any others. In calling his view irrational, then, I am in effect demanding that he give up *his* fundamental epistemic norms in favor of the ones that I employ. And the question I am asking is: With what right do I do this, on a non-factualist view?

As an objectivist, I would have no trouble explaining my attitude here. Since, as an objectivist, I take there to be a fact of the matter which fundamental norms are correct, and since I take myself to know what they are, I can easily explain why I am insisting that my interlocutor give up his norms in favor of mine. Of course, my interlocutor, convinced of the correctness of his own norms, may make a similar demand on me. If the norms are fundamental, this may well result in an impasse, a disagreement from which neither of us can be budged by argument. But it would at least make sense that there *is* a disagreement here and that we should be issuing (potentially ineffective) conversational demands on each other. But what explanation can the non-factualist offer of these matters?

The non-factualist may reply that there is no difficulty here. After all, he will say, the epistemic norms that I accept are unconditional: they apply to someone whether or not that person is inclined to accept them.

There seem to me to be two problems with this reply, however, one with the assumption that I accept unconditional norms in the first place, the other with my insistence that someone else also accept them.

First, if a non-factualism about justification is correct, with what right do I accept epistemic norms that are unconditional, so that they apply to someone whether or not they accept them?[19] If there really are no perspective-independent facts about which epistemic norms are correct, with what right do I accept norms that apply to people whether or not they accept them? Should not an appropriate sensitivity to the fact that there is nothing that makes my norms more correct than anyone else's result in my being hesitant about accepting norms that apply to others regardless of whether they are also inclined to accept them?

Second, and putting this first problem to one side, on what basis do I insist that AR give up his unconditional norms in favor of mine? I accept a particular set of fundamental norms, he accepts another. By assumption, the norms in dispute are fundamental, so there is no neutral territory on which the disagreement can be adjudicated. Furthermore, on the non-factualist view, there are no facts about which fundamental epistemic norms are correct and which ones are not. So, on what basis do I insist that he give up his norms in favor of mine?

The expressivist thinks he can evade the clutches of an unpalatable relativism by claiming that talk about a belief's being justified expresses a state of mind rather than stating anything. But this stratagem does not long conceal the view's inevitable relativistic upshot, which can now be restated in terms of the problem of normative authority. If no evidential system is more correct than any other, then I cannot coherently think that a particular belief is blameworthy, no matter how crazy *it* may be, so long as that belief is grounded in a set of fundamental epistemic norms that permit it, no matter how crazy *they* may be.

To repeat: the point here is not about suasive *effectiveness*. I do not mean that the realist about justification will have an easier time persuading anyone of anything. In fact, it is quite clear that there are lots of extreme positions from which no one can be dislodged by argument, whether confronted by a realist or an expressivist (this is a point to which we will have occasion to return).

The issue is rather about having the resources with which to think certain thoughts coherently. By virtue of believing that there are objective facts about what justifies what, the realist can coherently think that a particular epistemic system is mistaken. The non-factualist, however, cannot.

In a sense, the difficulty should have been evident from the start. For the root problem is with the claim with which the expressivist about justification must begin, that there is nothing that epistemically privileges one set of epistemic principles over another. Once that basic thought is in place, it becomes impossible to evade some sort of relativistic upshot. It doesn't matter whether the basic thought is embedded in an expressivist or a non-expressivist framework.

---

[19] David Velleman has emphasized this point to me.

III

VINDICATING RULE-CIRCULARITY: WARRANT TRANSFER

Where do we stand? In Part I, we saw that there are powerful considerations in favor of thinking that there could not be objectively valid epistemic reasons. In Part II, on the other hand, we saw that there appears to be no palatable way to accommodate this result. Unless we are to be mired in paradox, then, we have to find some way of vindicating the claim that we *can* know what the correct epistemic principles are. And if we are to do that we have to find some way of vindicating rule-circular justifications—of defending them from the objections that they beg the question and keep bad company—for so far as I can see, that can be our only route to knowing them. That is the idea I propose to explore in this third and final part.

If rule-circular arguments are in fact capable of transferring warrant from their premises to their conclusions, we should expect this result to flow in some natural way from the conditions that govern warrant transfer quite generally. So let's begin with the general question: Under what conditions does an argument transmit the warrant for its premises to its conclusion?

One condition seems clear enough: the thinker, S, must be justified in believing the premises p. Beyond that, however, matters get less straightforward. It will be instructive to start with an incorrect, overly rich account of what is required in order to try to converge on something more plausible. In his article, "Epistemic Circularity,"[20] William Alston considers, without fully endorsing, a version of the following account (I have modified it in small ways). S's belief that p *confers* warrant on his belief that q just in case:

(A) S is justified in believing the premises, p.
(B) p and q are logically related in such a way that if p is true, that is a good reason for supposing that q is at least likely to be true.
(C) S knows, or is justified in believing that the logical relation between p and q is a specified in (B).
(D) S infers q from p because of his belief specified in (C).

The conditions are intended to be singly necessary and jointly sufficient for the inference to warrant the conclusion.

Now, one problem that I wish to set aside concerns the sufficiency of these conditions. Crispin Wright and others have remarked that there are important cases where one's knowledge that p depends on one's prior knowledge that q, and in those cases it would be wrong to claim transfer of warrant from premises to conclusion.[21] We may assume, however, that this problem has been

---

[20] Alston 1986.
[21] Wright, manuscript.

accommodated by the stipulation that knowledge of the premises be suitably independent. The problem I will be interested in concerns the *necessity* of these conditions, specifically that of (C). It is easy to appreciate why.

If C were a correct necessary condition on warrant transfer, then it would follow immediately that there could be no such thing as a rule-circular justifica- tion. For C requires that, in order to use an argument employing a given rule to support the claim that that rule is truth-preserving, one already has to know that that rule is truth-preserving. And that would make the rule-circular justification otiose: the knowledge arrived at would already be presupposed.

Fortunately, however, it can readily be seen that C is intuitively too strong.

One problem with it we have already had occasion to note in connection with the passage cited from Peacocke above: it is far too sophisticated a requirement. A child who reasoned:

- If he were hiding behind that tree, he wouldn't have left his bicycle leaning on it
- But it is leaning on it
- So, he must be hiding behind some other tree

would, other conditions permitting, have reasoned his way to a justified con- clusion. But such a child would not have beliefs about logical entailment. He wouldn't even have the ingredient (meta-logical) concepts.

A second, more severe, problem is suggested by Lewis Carroll's observations in his note "What the Tortoise Said to Achilles."[22] There are a number of ways of reading that famous argument, of course, and it is not clear which, if any, of them, Carroll actually had in mind. But on one suggestive reading, its moral is precisely that condition (C) is too strong, if there is to be any such thing as transfer of warrant by argument.[23]

According to the propositional picture, one can only be justified in inferring a given conclusion from a given premise according to a given rule R, if one knows that R has a particular logical property, say that it is truth- preserving.

So, for example, no one simply reasoning from the particular proposition p and the particular proposition 'if p, then q' to the proposition q could ever be justified in drawing the conclusion q; in addition, the thinker would have to know that his premises necessitate his conclusion. Let us suppose that the thinker does know this, whether this be through some act of rational insight or otherwise. How should we represent this knowledge? We could try:

$$\text{Necessarily} : p \rightarrow ((p \rightarrow q) \rightarrow q)) \quad (1)$$

Some may feel it more appropriate to represent it meta-logically, thus:

$$p, p \rightarrow q \text{ logically imply } q \quad (2)$$

---

[22] Carroll 1895.

[23] James van Cleve also suggests that as the moral of the Lewis Carroll argument; but the argument he outlines is distinct from the one I shall present. See his 1984.

The question is: However the knowledge in question is represented, how does it help justify the thinker in drawing the conclusion q from the premises with which he began?

The answer might seem quite simple. Consider (1). Doesn't knowledge of (1) allow him to appreciate that the proposition that q follows logically from the premises, and so that the inference to q is truth-preserving and so justified?

In a sense, the answer is obviously 'Yes', knowledge of (1) does enable an appreciation of just that fact. But it doesn't do so automatically, but only via a transition, a transition, moreover, that is of a piece with the very sort of transition it is attempting to justify.

1. $p \rightarrow ((p \rightarrow q) \rightarrow q)$
2. p
3. $(p \rightarrow q) \rightarrow q$
4. $p \rightarrow q$
5. Therefore, q

As is transparent, any such reasoning would itself involve at least one step in accord with modus ponens.

What about representing the knowledge in question as in (2)? The problem recurs. To know that p and $p \rightarrow q$ logically imply q is just to know that if p and $p \rightarrow q$ are true, then q must be true. Once more, there is an easy transition from this knowledge to the knowledge that q must be true, given that p is true and that $p \rightarrow q$ is true. But the facility of this transition should not obscure the fact that it is there and that it is of the same kind as the transition that it is attempting to shore up.

If, therefore, we insist that the original inference from p and $p \rightarrow q$ to q was unjustified unless supported by the propositional knowledge represented either by (1) or by (2), then we commit ourselves to launching an unstoppable regress. Bringing any such knowledge to bear on the justifiability of the inference would itself require justified use of the very same sort of inference whose justifiability the general knowledge was supposed to secure.

What this Lewis Carroll-inspired argument shows, it seems to me, is that at some point it must be possible to use a rule in reasoning in order to arrive at a *justified* conclusion, without this use needing to be supported by some knowledge about the rule that one is relying on. It must be possible simply to *move* between thoughts in a way that generates justified belief, without this movement being grounded in the thinker's justified belief about the rule used in the reasoning.

Condition (C), we are agreed then, must go. But do we simply scratch it out and remain content with the external condition mentioned in (B)? And, what, exactly should that external condition be?

If we look at the external condition described by Alston, we notice something striking: it is thoroughly unhelpful. It says: If inferring q from p is to provide a good reason for believing q, then p and q must be so related that p's being true is a good reason for believing q to be true. That verges on the platitudinous. Can we do better?

What about the suggestion that p and q be so related that the inference from p to q is reliably truth-preserving? That won't do, for it leaves out the inductive case. What about saying that p and q be so related that the probability of q given p be reliably high? The trouble with this suggestion is that it is not clear that we have a grip on this that is other than in terms of subjective probability. And if that is right, then the suggestion collapses back into the unhelpful proposal just considered.

However, even if there were an external condition that was both helpful and general enough to cover the requisite range of cases, it's clear, it seems to me, that it would not be sufficient to explain under what conditions arguments transfer warrant. Henceforth, and for the remainder of this essay, I shall concentrate on the deductive case, leaving a treatment of induction for another occasion. (The extension of the ideas of this paper to the inductive case involve questions to which I currently have no settled answers.)

The reason why not is familiar from discussions of reliabilist conceptions of justification more generally. The mere fact that a particular inference is truth-preserving bears no intuitive link to the thinker's *entitlement* to it. There are infinitely many hopelessly complicated truth-preserving inferences that it would be absurd to suppose are justifiably performed just because they are truth-preserving.

For example, any inference of the form

If x, y, z, and n are numbers and n is greater than 2

then

$$x^n + y^n \text{ is not equal to } z^n$$

is, as we now know, reliably truth-preserving. But it would be absurd to suppose that anyone making that inference, whether or not they knew anything about Andrew Wiles' proof of Fermat's last theorem, would be drawing a justified conclusion.

Someone may object: "Of course that would not be enough. It is only in the fundamental cases, where the inference cannot be broken down into further steps, that mere truth-preservation is sufficient for warrant transfer. In non-fundamental or derived cases, actual recognition that the rule is truth-preserving may well be required."

It is difficult to see, however, how this qualification is to be motivated. Why should it matter, one way or the other, whether the inference is fundamental or not? How do we explain why it is only in cases that are fundamental that truth-preservation is sufficient for justification? The missing intuitive link between the external condition and the entitlement may be especially vivid in cases where the inferred conclusion is one that the thinker is not already entitled to; but the point would appear to hold quite generally.

We find ourselves in a familiar philosophical predicament, looking for a satisfying intermediate position between two unpalatable extremes. We cannot say that all that's required, for a deductive inference to be justified is that it be truth-preserving. But we cannot supply the missing ingredient, on pain of regress, by requiring that the thinker know that his inference is of a truth-preserving sort. So what are we to do? Can we make sense of the idea that a thinker is entitled to reason in a particular way, without this involving—incoherently—that the thinker know something about the rule involved in his reasoning?

We can, I think, if a natural, indeed virtually inevitable suggestion, is true: namely, that our logical words (in the language of thought) mean what they do by virtue of their inferential role, that 'if, then', for example (or more precisely, its mentalese equivalent) means what it does by virtue of participating in some inferences and not in others. If this is correct, and if, as is overwhelmingly plausible, it is by virtue of its role in *fundamental* (i.e., underived) inference that the conditional means what it does, then we have an immediately compelling answer to the question: how could someone be entitled to reason according to MPP without having a positive belief that entitles him to it. If fundamental inferential dispositions fix what we mean by our words, then, as I shall now try to show, we are entitled to act on those dispositions prior to and independently of having supplied an explicit justification for them.

The satisfying intermediate position concerning warrant transfer, I therefore want to propose, is that in the case of fundamental inference the implicated rule must be meaning-constituting. Unlike the purely external requirement of truth-preservation, this view explains why the thinker is entitled to the rule; and yet unlike the impossible internalism, it does so without requiring that the thinker know that the rule is truth-preserving.

EXTERNALISM, INTERNALISM, INFERENCE, JUSTIFICATION

It is beyond the scope of this essay to defend the correctness of this account of inferential warrant in the detail that it requires. But in order to begin to get a sense of why it might be on the right track, it will be necessary to look briefly at the notion of justification more generally, and at the controversy about 'externalist' versus 'internalist' construals of it.

The issue can be usefully approached by considering an objection to the view I'm proposing that was put to me by Crispin Wright:

Boghossian's reaction to the simple externalist account betrays an interest in reflectively appreciable warrant—warrant that makes a phenomenologically appreciable impact, as it were. But he does not connect his own proposal with such impacts;

and it is not clear how the connection might be made. If it cannot be, one might as well stick with simple externalism.[24]

Wright's point can be restated in the form of a dilemma. Either the account is trying to reconstruct an externalist warrant, or an internalist one. If an externalist one, then the account in terms of meaning-constitution has no obvious advantage over simple truth-preservation; if an internalist one, then it is not clear that the demand is satisfied: a rule's being meaning-constituting does not necessarily have any "appreciable phenomenological impact."

I intend my account to capture a broadly *internalist* notion of warrant, and so I embrace the second horn of the bruited dilemma. To see why that characterization is correct, however, and why my account *does* satisfy the constraints appropriate to an internalist notion, we have to look at how that distinction is properly conceived.

Start with a crude externalism about justified belief (and put aside worries about how reliability is to be defined): a belief is justified just in case it is produced by a reliable belief-forming mechanism. If I reject a crude externalism—and I do—it is because I was convinced by some familiar examples—Bonjour's Samantha, Casper, Maud and Norman and Lehrer's TrueTemp—that it is false. These examples show conclusively, I think, that mere reliability is not sufficient for justification.[25]

If we look at these examples, we find their structure to be this: a subject's belief that p is produced by a reliable mechanism but the belief is, nevertheless, in some strongly intuitive sense, epistemically irresponsible. And our response to such cases is that, under those circumstances, the subject cannot count as justified. It appears to be a condition on someone's being epistemically justified that they *not be epistemically irresponsible* in forming their belief.

What makes a belief epistemically irresponsible? An inspection of the examples seems to suggest a uniform answer: the *absence* of a reflectively appreciable warrant for the belief (which can sometimes assume the form of the *presence* of a reflectively appreciable warrant for its negation). A steady diet of such examples has encouraged philosophers simply to *identify* possession of an internalist warrant—and hence warrant as such—with the possession of a reflectively appreciable item of information that justifies the belief, and that is in effect what Wright does in his formulation of the dilemma.

Understandable as this identification may be, it is not justified by the considerations that have been adduced by internalists. For all that the examples show, it is possible that there is some *other* way in which a belief might be responsibly

---

[24] The objection is from a draft of a commentary on an earlier version of this paper delivered at the Pacific Division meetings of the APA, Albuquerque, NM, in April of 2000.

[25] Bonjour 1985, Lehrer 1990.

held—or at least held not irresponsibly—other than by being supported by some reflectively appreciable warrant. All that the examples actually teach us is that being justified cannot coexist with being epistemically irresponsible. They don't—and can't—teach us that the *only* way to avoid epistemic irresponsibility requires support from a reflectively appreciable warrant.

As I have already indicated in my discussion of default reasonableness, I think that beliefs that are meaning- or concept-constituting can be held responsibly even in the absence of a reflectively appreciable warrant for them. This is particularly compelling in the case that is the focus of the present discussion—justifiable inference. There are two key related points.

First, if it is really true that someone's being disposed to reason according to modus ponens is a necessary condition of their having any logical concepts at all, and so of being able to reason in any shape manner or form, there can be no intuitive sense in which their disposition to reason according to modus ponens can be held to be irresponsible, even in the absence of a reflectively appreciable warrant that justifies it. If you doubt that this is true, try to construct a Bonjour-style case that will make it seem intuitively irresponsible for someone to reason according to modus ponens, without *first* having satisfied themselves that the inference form is truth-preserving, when their doing so is a precondition of their being able to engage in any reasoning whatsoever.

Second, if my Lewis Carroll-inspired argument is correct, we know that, at least in the most basic cases, no richer warrant—nothing that would count as a phenomenologically appreciable belief about the rule, for example—could so much as be coherent. At some point, as that argument shows, it must be possible simply to *move* to a justified conclusion. But that fact should not be taken to imply that in that range of cases we have to settle for a merely externalist warrant. The core distinction between externalism and internalism in the theory of justification is properly characterized in terms of the notion of epistemic responsibility. Fundamental inferences that are meaning-constituting are not epistemically culpable, even if they are not supported by reflectively appreciable warrants. To demand more of a thinker is to demand the provably impossible.

BEGGING THE QUESTION (2): REPLY

So far in this part of the paper, we have been looking at what we should say to the general question: Under what conditions is an argument warrant-transferring? And the answer, based purely on general considerations, has been that, in the most basic cases, the relied upon rule should be meaning-constituting.

If this answer is correct, though, it points the way forward with our question concerning the legitimacy of rule-circular justifications. For it answers the second part of the problem about begging the question: how could we be entitled to use a particular rule of inference independently of being entitled to believe that that rule is valid? So long as the rule-circular justification at issue involves a meaning-constituting rule, there can be no question of our entitlement to reason in accordance with it, even in the absence of a reflectively appreciable belief that justifies it.

What about the problem of bad company? To see how the very same resources can supply a solution to this further set of problems, we need to further explore the idea of a conceptual role semantics.

CONCEPTUAL ROLE SEMANTICS

When we say that meaning is determined by conceptual role, how exactly should this be understood?

On one view, every possible conceptual role determines some meaning or other. But we know this not to be a plausible view, on purely meaning-theoretic grounds. That is the minimal lesson of Arthur Prior's 'tonk' example.[26]

Prior imagined a connective governed by the following introduction and elimination rules:

A/A tonk B   A tonk B/B.

The specification defines a conceptual role; but what meaning does it determine? If we said that there is one, then we would have to hold that there is a thinkable proposition expressed by sentences of the form 'A tonk B'. If there were such a thinkable proposition, then there would have to be a way the world is when the proposition is true. How, though, must the world be if 'A tonk B' is to be true? Since the sentence is compound, its truth value will depend on the truth values of its ingredient sentences A and B. But we can readily see that there can be no consistent assignment of truth value to sentences of the form 'A tonk B' given the introduction and elimination rules for 'tonk'.

Given those rules, both

A → A tonk B

and

A tonk B → B

have to come out tautologous, for any A or B. It is impossible to satisfy that demand. Pick an A that's true and a B that's false. Then, for the first conditional to come out true, 'A tonk B' has to be true. However, given that B is false, 'A tonk B' has to be false if the second conditional is to come out true. So there can be no determinate way the world has to be, if 'A tonk B' is to come out true.[27]

---

[26] Prior 1960.
[27] Peacocke 1992b, p. 802.

But we don't need actual inconsistency to make the point that not every conceptual role determines a meaning. Consider, for example, the following connective 'shmand'. Its introduction and elimination rules are exactly like those for conjunction, except that the sentence that occupies the 'A' position is restricted to a length of 25 letters.

A (<25), B/A shmand B   A (<25) shmand B/A (<25)

A (<25) shmand B/B

What proposition would be expressed by sentences of the form 'A shmand B'? How would the world have to be if this sort of proposition is to be true? Clearly, there is no determinate answer to that question.[28]

For purely meaning-theoretic reasons, then, we should deny that every conceptual role determines a meaning. We should insist that a conceptual role determines a meaning for an expression only if it manages to contribute in some determinate way to determining how the world would have to be if sentences involving the expression are to be true. Put in other words, the way to understand a conceptual role theory of the logical constants is to see them as subject in part to the implicit stipulation:

Let x express that meaning, if any, whose semantic value makes a particular class of inferences truth-preserving. If there is no such value, then there is no such meaning.[29]

BAD COMPANY: REPLY

Now, if that is the correct way to think of a conceptual role semantics, then the problem of bad company takes care of itself. If, in a given fundamental rule-circular justification, there is a meaningful inference to begin with, then it is guaranteed to be truth-preserving, for a rule of inference doesn't get to determine a meaning unless it is truth-preserving. As a result, the problem of bad company does not arise: it is impossible, intelligibly, to justify a non-truth-preserving rule, such as the tonk rules or R*.

The key insight is that, just as there are objective constraints on what is true, so there are objective constraints on what we can mean. This is something that we have reason to accept entirely independently of our epistemological investments. A conceptual role semantics, by virtue of its ties to the notion of justification, transforms this constraint on meaning into a constraint on justification

---

[28] Christopher Peacocke gives a similar example in his 1993b. Peacocke has long urged that a conceptual role semantics be understood in this restrictive truth-theoretic way. Although my route into these issues is distinct from his, I find myself in agreement with much of what Peacocke has to say about the logical constants and the role of meaning in justification.

[29] See my 1997.

that simultaneously vindicates the possibility of rule-circular justifications while staving off the threat of an unpalatable relativism.[30]

BEGGING THE SKEPTIC'S QUESTION

It is time now to turn to the final problem I outlined for a rule-circular justification, its incapacity to move the appropriate skeptic. The point at issue is prefigured in Dummett's discussion when he says that rule-circularity will be damaging only to a justificatory argument that

is addressed to someone who genuinely doubts whether the law is valid, and is intended to persuade him that it is. ... If, on the other hand, it is intended to satisfy the philosopher's perplexity about our entitlement to reason is accordance with such a law, it may well to do. The philosopher does not seriously doubt the validity of the law and is therefore prepared to accept an argument in accordance with it. He does not seek to be persuaded of the conclusion; what he is seeking is an *explanation* of its being true.[31]

Before inquiring into the significance of this, let us make sure that we do not underestimate all that a rule-circular justification is capable of accomplishing. First, it is not at all similar to a grossly circular argument in that it is not trivially guaranteed to succeed. For one thing, the relevant premises from which, by (as it might be) a single application of the rule the desired conclusion is to follow, may not be available. For another, not all rules are self-supporting. Second, the rule-circular argument for MPP asks in effect that it be granted that *one* application of MPP and from that it promises to deliver the conclusion that MPP is *necessarily* truth-preserving—truth-preserving in *any possible* application. That seems like a significance advance. Finally, this one application will itself be one to which we are entitled if, as seems plausible, MPP is meaning-constituting.

For all that, it is nevertheless true that if we were confronted by a skeptic who *doubted* the validity of MPP in *any* of its applications, we could not use this argument to rationally persuade him. Doubting the rule, he would rightly reject this particular argument in its favor. Since, by assumption, we have no other sort of argument to offer him, it seems that we are powerless to persuade him of the rightness of our position. The question is: What is the epistemic significance of this fact?

Could we not say to him: "Look, MPP is meaning-constituting. If you reject it then you simply mean something different by 'if, then' and therefore there is no real disagreement after all." But if our skeptic were playing his cards right, he would deny that MPP is meaning-constituting. To persuade him otherwise

---

[30] I suspect that it is Wittgenstein's failure to appreciate the point that not every conceptual role determines a meaning that led to the relativistic-sounding passages of the *Remarks on the Foundations of Mathematics*.

[31] Dummett 1991.

we would have to offer him an argument and that argument would in turn have to use MPP. And then we would be right back where we started, faced with the question: What is the epistemological significance of the fact that we are unable to persuade the skeptic about MPP?

In the passage cited above, Dummett seems to think that its significance lies in the way in which it highlights a distinction between two distinct projects: quelling the skeptic's doubts versus *explaining* to a non-skeptic why MPP is valid.

But I do not really understand what it would be to explain *why* a given logical law is true. What could it mean except something along the lines of a conventionalism about logical truth, an account which really does aspire to explain *where* logical truth comes from? As any reader of Quine's "Truth By Convention," will be aware however, there are decisive objections to conventionalism, objections that probably generalize to any explanatory project of that form.[32]

The question that we need to be asking, I think, is rather this: Can we say that something is a real *reason* for believing that p if it cannot be used to answer a skeptic about p? Is it criterial for my having a genuine reason for believing that p that I be able to use it to persuade someone who doubts whether p?

Well, in fact, we *are* very drawn to the idea that if I am genuinely justified in believing that p, then, in principle, I ought to be able to bring you around as well—or, at the very least, I ought to be able to take you some distance towards rational belief in p. Of course, you may not understand the warrant that I have; or, being more cautious than I, you may not assign it the same weight that I do. But, prescinding from these and similar considerations, how could I be genuinely justified in believing something and yet be totally unable to have any sway with you? As Thomas Nagel puts it in his recent book *The Last Word*:

To reason is to think systematically in ways that anyone looking over my shoulder ought to be able to recognize as correct. It is this generality that relativists and subjectivists deny.[33]

Notice how naturally it comes to Nagel to equate the claim that *there are* objectively valid reasons, reasons that would apply to anyone anywhere, with the *epistemic* claim that anyone exposed to them ought to be able to *recognize* them as reasons.

There is a principle behind this thought, one that we may call the "principle of the universal accessibility of reasons": If something is a genuine reason for believing that p, then, subject to the provisos just made, its rationalizing force ought to be accessible from any epistemic standpoint.

I think that this principle has played a very large role in our thinking about justification. It is what explains, it seems to me, why the theory of knowledge

---

[32] See Quine 1976b. For further discussion, see my 2000.
[33] Nagel 1996, p. 5.

is so often centered on a refutation of *skepticism*. We take it to be criterial of our having a genuine warrant for a given proposition that we be in a position to refute a skeptic about p.

If my discussion has been on the right track, however, then one of its main lessons is that this principle is false. For consider: We cannot accept the claim that we have no warrant whatsoever for the core logical principles. We cannot conceive what such a warrant could consist in (whether this be a priori or a posteriori) if not in some sort of inference using those very core logical principles. So, there must be genuine warrants that will not carry any sway with a skeptic. Answering the skeptic about modus ponens cannot be criterial for whether we are warranted in believing modus ponens.

To put this point another way: we must recognize a distinction between two different sorts of reason—suasive and *non-suasive reasons*. And we have to reconcile ourselves to the fact that in certain areas of knowledge, logic featuring prominently among them, our warrant can be at most non-suasive, powerless to quell skeptical doubts.

It seems to me that this is a conclusion that we have reason to accept entirely independently of our present concern with knowledge of logic, that there are many other compartments of knowledge in which our warrant can be at most non-suasive. One such area concerns our knowledge of the existence of other minds; another concerns our knowledge of the external world. I think that in both of these areas it is very unlikely that we will be able to provide warrants for our belief that would be usable against a determined and level-headed skeptic.[34]

The correct project in epistemology is to show how knowledge is possible. It is not the refutation of arbitrarily extreme skeptics.

CONCLUSION

A central problem for the possibility of objectively valid epistemic principles has to do with explaining how we might know what they are: how could there be any if our only means of access to them is via rule-circular reasoning? I hope to have shown that, if the notion of justification and its transfer across argument is understood correctly, rule-circular justifications can be vindicated.

The case is constructed on the basis of several independently plausible elements. First, that a plausible construal of warrant transfer has it that, in the most basic cases, warrant is transferred only across inferences that are meaning-constituting. Second, that if an inferential disposition is meaning-constituting then it is a fortiori reasonable, reasonably used independently of any belief about its properties. Third, that something can be a warrant for something even if it is powerless to bring about a determined skeptic.

---

[34] In related though distinct contexts, similar points are made both in Alston 1986, and in James Van Cleve 1979.

Putting all this together allows us to say that we are justified in our fundamental epistemic beliefs in spite of the fact that we can produce only rule-circular arguments for them. The price is that we have to admit that we cannot use this form of argument to silence skeptical doubts. It is arguable, however, that with respect to matters that are as basic as logic and principles of justification, that was never in prospect anyway.[35]

[35] For helpful comments, I would like to thank Christopher Peacocke, Josh Schechter, Stephen Schiffer and the audience at the Pacific APA meetings in Albuquerque, NM in April 2000. I am especially grateful to Crispin Wright for agreeing to comment on that occasion and for numerous stimulating conversations on this and related topics. Some sections of this paper overlap with parts of my 2000.

12 *Blind Reasoning*[1]

ABSTRACT The paper asks under what conditions deductive reasoning transmits justification from its premises to its conclusion. It argues that both standard externalist and standard internalist accounts of this phenomenon fail. The nature of this failure is taken to indicate the way forward: basic forms of deductive reasoning must justify by being instances of 'blind but blameless' reasoning. Finally, the paper explores the suggestion that an inferentialist account of the logical constants can help explain how such reasoning is possible.

I. THE QUESTION

I'm in the mood for some music; what, I wonder, is on offer today in Carnegie Hall? A quick check of the schedule reveals that Martha Argerich is scheduled to play on the 20th. As a result, I come to believe that:

(1) If today is the 20th, then Martha Argerich is playing today in Carnegie Hall.

A glance at the calendar reveals that in fact:

(2) Today is the 20th.

With these two beliefs in place, I move immediately to the conclusion that:

(3) Martha Argerich is playing today in Carnegie Hall.

And I pick up the phone.

If, prior to making this modus ponens inference, I already believed (presumably with only a low level of confidence) that Martha Argerich was playing today in Carnegie Hall, then the inference looks to have strengthened whatever justification I had for that belief. If, prior to making the inference, I had no views about who was playing today in Carnegie Hall, the inference looks to have augmented my beliefs with a further justified belief. Whichever scenario obtained,

---

[1] This paper was presented at a meeting of the Joint Session of the Mind Association and the Aristotelian Society in Belfast, July 2001, and was first published as my 2003a. The presentation was followed by a reply by Timothy Williamson, published as his 2003.

how did my two premises contribute to justifying the conclusion that I drew on their basis? Under what conditions does an inference transfer justification in this way?

Clearly, at the very least, the following two conditions must be satisfied. First, the thinker must be justified in believing the premises. Second, his justification for believing the premises must not depend on his being *antecedently* justified in believing the conclusion.

Equally clearly, though, these conditions do not suffice for the inference to transfer justification. In addition, the premises must bear an appropriate relation to the conclusion they ground. And my question is: What is that relation?

In this paper, I am going to restrict myself to asking this question about *deductive* inference, leaving it an open question to what extent what is said here generalizes to other cases of justification- or warrant-transfer.[2] In a deductive inference, the thinker takes his premises to justify his conclusion in part because he takes them to necessitate it.[3]

II. INFERENTIAL EXTERNALISM

The simplest possible answer to our question is this:

(Simple Inferential Externalism): A deductive inference performed by S is warrant-transferring just in case (a) S is justified in believing its premises (b) S's justification for believing its premises is suitably independent of his justification for believing the conclusion, and (c) the implicated pattern of inference is valid—necessarily such as to move S from truth to truths.[4]

This can't be a good answer: large numbers of inferences that we are in no intuitive way justified in performing satisfy the stipulated conditions. For example: it is easy for me to be justified in believing any particular claim of the form:

x, y, z, and n are whole numbers and n is greater than 2.

---

[2] Even with this restriction in place, the paper covers a lot of ground rather quickly. I am aware that many of its claims need more detailed support than is possible within present limits. My aim is to offer a broad view of the terrain with the hopes of distinguishing the dead ends from the promising pathways.

[3] It's a tricky question how this 'taking' is to be understood, but I can't pause to consider the matter here. In this paper, I shall use the terms 'justification,' 'warrant' and 'entitlement' interchangeably.

[4] I shall soon be contrasting this externalist conception of inference with a diametrically opposed internalist conception. The idea of converging onto the (hopefully) correct view of inference by picking a course between these two traditionally opposed extremes was first suggested in my 2001a (this volume, Chapter 11). In his commentary on that paper, Crispin Wright suggested the labels 'simple internalism' and 'simple externalism' for the traditionally opposed extremes, labels which I am happy now to modify and adopt. See Wright 2001.

I should emphasize that I am asking *by virtue of what facts* a deductive inference transfers warrant, and not just under what conditions it does so.

If I inferred from this proposition that:

$$x^n + y^n \text{ is not equal to } z^n$$

I would have performed an inference that is, as we now know, reliably truth-preserving. But it would be absurd to suppose that anyone making such an inference would be drawing a justified conclusion, whether or not they knew anything about Andrew Wiles's proof of Fermat's last theorem or had checked each individual inequality. Being valid (in conjunction with the other two conditions) clearly does not *suffice* for being warrant-transferring, even if it may be necessary.[5]

A number of philosophers seem to believe that this objection can be easily met. All we need to do, they say, is to restrict the Reliabilist claim to those inferences that are sufficiently 'simple'.[6]

But what could 'simple' possibly mean here if not something like: an inference whose validity it is easy to 'take in'? If that isn't what 'simple' means, why should an inference's simplicity be relevant to the question of justification? If that is what 'simple' means, then it's this presumed 'taking in' that's doing the relevant explanatory work, and not the assumed reliability of the simple inference. In a moment, we will consider views according to which an inference is entitling just in case the thinker can 'take in' its validity, but this is not where such views belong.

The counterexamples to Simple Inferential Externalism echo a broader class of objections to Reliabilist accounts of justification more generally. Since many of these examples are so well known, I will not discuss them here in detail except to say this. I am not so impressed with those counterexamples that rely on the subject's having a justified belief to the effect that some reliable belief-forming method of his is not reliable; I think a Reliabilist can handle those cases by imposing a 'no-undermining belief' condition. But I am inclined to regard as decisive those counterexamples in which the reliability of the relevant method is *not* subjectively undermined—either because the subject has no *justified* belief about its reliability, or because he has no belief about it at all. Laurence Bonjour has described just such a case.

Norman, under certain conditions which usually obtain, is a completely reliable clairvoyant with respect to certain kinds of subject matter. He possesses no evidence or reasons of any kind for or against the general possibility of such a cognitive power or for or against the thesis that he possesses it. One day Norman comes to believe that the President is in New York City, though he has no evidence either for or against this belief. In fact the belief is true and results from his clairvoyant power under circumstances in which it is completely reliable.[7]

---

[5] I shall come back to the question whether it is necessary.

[6] I have often encountered this suggestion in conversation; I didn't manage to track down a published reference.

[7] See Bonjour 1985, p. 41.

Our robust response to this case is that Norman is not justified. And a plausible and widely-accepted diagnosis of our response is that we are reluctant to regard someone as justified in holding a given belief if they are being epistemically *irresponsible* in holding that belief. Being justified is, at least in part, a matter of being epistemically blameless.

What lesson should we draw from these counterexamples? The moral seems almost forced. We need to ensure that being justified excludes being epistemically blameworthy. Mere reliability doesn't do that. How is that to be ensured except by insisting that, if a subject is to be justified in believing some proposition p, he must have to hand a *reflectively accessible* warrant for the proposition that p?

It looks, in other words, as though the counterexamples to Reliabilism motivate an *Access Internalism* about justification: S is justified in having the belief that p only if S is in a position to know,[8] by reflection alone, that he has a warrant for the belief that p. If S is to have genuine justification, it must be a reflectively *transparent* justification.[9]

III. INFERENTIAL INTERNALISM

If we go along with this diagnosis of the failure of Reliabilism and apply it to the case we are focusing on—the case of warrant transfer by deductive inference—the thought would then be that, in a deductive inference, the subject must be in a position to know by reflection alone that his premises provide him with a good reason for believing the conclusion, if his inference is to justify his conclusion. Call this

(Simple Inferential Internalism): A deductive inference performed by S is warrant-transferring just in case (a) S is justified in believing its premises (b) S's justification for believing its premises is suitably independent of his justification for believing the conclusion, and (c) S is able to know by reflection alone that his premises provide him with a good reason for believing the conclusion.

There are any number of problems with this idea. Take the case of our original Argerich modus ponens (MPP) inference, from (1) and (2) to (3). What would it be for S to be able to know by reflection alone that his premises provide him with a good reason for believing the conclusion?

Since we are dealing with a deductive inference, the most natural suggestion is that S would know this epistemic fact only if he knew that his premises

---

[8] In insisting on knowledge here, as opposed merely to justified belief, I follow standard presentations of Internalism, though my arguments will depend only on the weaker condition.

[9] Note that what I am calling 'Access Internalism' is the weaker of the two possible versions of Internalism: it requires only that the epistemic fact be reflectively accessible, if the person is to be justified, not that the person actually have accessed it.

necessitate his conclusion. So the question becomes: How might S be in a position to know by reflection alone that p and 'p → q' imply q?

There look to be two options: inferential and non-inferential. The inferential route, which would include empirical and broadly pragmatic accounts of knowledge of logical implication, may be ruled out immediately.

The point is a subtle one. It's not that there is necessarily a problem with rule-circular justifications of meta-logical claims. Indeed, I have elsewhere argued that, if we are to have knowledge of basic logical or meta-logical truths at all, it must be via rule-circular reasoning.[10] However, in the present context, where knowledge of the validity of MPP is supposed to be a component in the justification that we have for *reasoning* according to MPP, an inferential route to knowledge of the validity would be completely useless. The very sort of reasoning whose justification is at issue would have been presupposed.

What about the non-inferential options? If a given item of knowledge is non-inferential, then it is either justified by observation alone or it is justified by nothing.

For reasons that I don't have the space to rehearse here, it seems to me very implausible that one can be said to know the general proposition that any argument of the form MPP is valid on the basis of nothing, as though all one would have to do to be justified in believing such an ambitious proposition is simply to believe it.[11] If there is to be any hope for the non-inferential option, it must lie along the observational branch.

IV. RATIONAL INSIGHT

Clearly, what is at issue is not ordinary empirical observation. Rather, the idea is that we are equipped with a special capacity for non-empirical observation, a capacity whose exercise is capable of yielding insights into necessary truths. That we have such a capacity has recently been defended by Laurence Bonjour.

When I carefully and reflectively consider the ... inference ... in question, I am able simply to see or grasp or apprehend ... that the conclusion of the inference must be true if the premises are true. Such a rational insight, as I have chosen to call it, does not seem to depend on any particular sort of criterion or any further discursive or ratiocinative process, but is instead direct and immediate.[12]

In finding the idea of rational insight attractive, Bonjour joins a venerable tradition, one that stretches from Plato through Leibniz to Gödel. Why, then, does the idea have so few supporters these days?

[10] See my 2000 and 2001a (this volume, Chapter 11).
[11] See my 2001a (this volume, Chapter 11).
[12] Bonjour 1998, pp. 106–7.

The single most influential consideration against rational insight theories can be quite simply stated: no one has been able to explain, clearly enough, in what an act of rational insight could intelligibly consist. No one denies, of course, that we can *think about* properties and relations, including logical properties and relations, and that, as a result, we can reason our way to general conclusions about them, just as we can reason our way to conclusions about other topics. The question is whether we can be said to have some sort of *non-discursive, non-ratiocinative, insight* into their natures, an insight that would disclose immediately, and without the help of any reasoning whatsoever, that all instances of MPP are truth-preserving.

Bonjour does not succeed in convincing us that there is. On reading his book, one can't help but be struck by how little progress a resolute and resourceful defender of rational insight was able to make.

There are many issues that could be discussed with profit; here I have space only to raise the fundamental issue of cognitive access. What sort of relation obtains between a thinker and a property, when the thinker has 'rational insight' into its nature? Or, to pick a more immediately relevant example, what relation obtains between a thinker and the conditional, when the thinker has a rational insight into its nature, when he is simply able to *see* that when his MPP premises are true so must be its conclusion?

The analogy with sense perception encourages us to think that the relation between the thinker and the conditional is causal. But that is impossible since the conditional is just an abstract object. Bonjour wrestles with this issue and comes up with a three-part response.

The first is to downplay the analogy with sense perception. The second is to propose the revival of an Aristotelian conception of mental content, according to which when we think about a given property—triangularity, for example—that very property itself is *instantiated* in our thought. Finally, Bonjour suggests assimilating rational insight to a form of introspective examination of that thought content.

His proposal raises more questions than it answers. First, we are not really told how the property of triangularity could be instantiated by my thoughts without their being—absurdly—triangular as a result. Second, we are not told how this neo-Aristotelian conception of mental content would help, even if it were not mystifying. Suppose my thoughts about a particular triangle do instantiate the property of triangularity. How does this help explain how I am able to directly divine the nature of triangularity without the help of any reasoning whatsoever? The belief that the sum of the interior angles of any triangle is 180 degrees and the belief that it is 320 degrees both instantiate triangles. Why is the first justified and the second not?

We are left staring at the problem with which we began, rather than feeling that we have been placed on the path to real understanding.

V. RATIONAL INSIGHT AND CARROLLIAN CIRCULARITY

Even if we waived worries about the very cogency of the capacity for rational insight, however, it's not clear how rational insight into the validity of MPP could help vindicate Simple Inferential Internalism, and this for reasons that are reminiscent of Lewis Carroll's famous note 'What the Tortoise Said to Achilles.'[13]

According to Simple Inferential Internalism, a thinker's move to (3) on the basis of (1) and (2) counts as justified only if he is in a position justifiably to believe that his inference is valid. Let us suppose, for the sake of argument, that a capacity for rational insight explains how he is in a position justifiably to believe that, if his MPP premises are true, then so must be his conclusion. How might this explanation go?

For obvious reasons, it's not plausible to think of this capacity for rational insight as operating on individual inferences one by one, generating for each of them the insight that if its premises are true, then so is its conclusion. Rather, we suppose that rational insight equips the thinker to arrive at the wholly general insight that MPP is valid, that is that:

For all p, q: Necessarily: If both p and 'p $\rightarrow$ q', then q.

Now, however, we need to ask how such a justified belief in the validity of all arguments of the form MPP could help a thinker be justified in performing any *particular* MPP inference, for example, the Argerich inference with which we began.

To bring this knowledge to bear on the justifiability of that inference will, it would seem, require the thinker first to establish its relevance to that inference, by reasoning as follows:

(i) Any inference of the form MPP is valid.
(ii) This particular inference, from (1) and (2) to (3) is of MPP form.

Therefore,

(iii) This particular inference from (1) and (2) to (3) is valid.[14]

Rational insight, we are conceding, gets us as far as the general propositional knowledge that all arguments of MPP form are valid. However, to bring this knowledge to bear on the justifiability of any particular inference will require the thinker to be able justifiably to infer the validity of that particular inference

---

[13] Carroll 1895.
[14] This argument was originally presented in my lecture at the Pacific APA in Albuquerque in April 2001.

from the validity of all arguments of MPP form. And this will require him to be able to reason according to MPP justifiably.

Now, however a fatal circularity looms. To infer from (1) and (2) to (3) justifiably, I must be able justifiably to believe that the inference from (1) and (2) to (3) is valid. To be able justifiably to believe that this inference is valid, I must be able justifiably to infer that it is valid from the general proposition that all inferences of its form are valid. To be able justifiably to infer that it is valid from the general proposition that all inferences of its form are valid, I must be able justifiably to infer according to MPP. So, on the picture on offer, my inference from (1) and (2) to (3) will count as justifying only if I am already able to infer according to MPP justifiably. The very ability we are trying to explicate is presupposed by the internalist account on offer.

At this point, an internalist might be tempted by the following thought. So long as we are being so concessive about rational insight, why can't we grant thinkers rational insight into the validity of *specific* inferences, and not require that this be derived from some general knowledge of the validity of all inferences of the form MPP. Perhaps this more general knowledge could be arrived at later, by using the knowledge gained through these acts of individual insight?

It's important to appreciate that this manoeuvre will not help overcome Simple Inferential Internalism's difficulties with the problem of circularity. For, once again, we can ask how my knowledge of the validity of the inference from (1) and (2) to (3) is supposed to bear on my warrant to infer (3)?

According to Simple Inferential Internalism, this inference will be justified only if I am able justifiably to believe that that my premises provide me with a good reason for drawing the conclusion. But it is very hard to see, once again, how my putatively justified judgment that my premises entail my conclusion could bear on my entitlement to draw the conclusion in anything other than inferential form, thus:

(iv) This particular inference from (1) and (2) to (3) is valid.
 (v) If an inference is valid, then anyone who is justified in believing its premises and knows of its validity is justified in inferring its conclusion.

Therefore,

 (vi) Anyone who is justified in believing the premises of this inference is justified in inferring its conclusion.
(vii) I am justified in believing the premises (1) and (2).

Therefore,

(viii) I am justified in inferring (3).[15]

---

[15] The idea that Internalism suffers from the difficulties outlined in the preceding two arguments was first presented in my 2001a (this volume, Chapter 11). In that paper, though, I followed Carroll in supposing that the inference to which the internalist is committed is an inference from knowledge of the validity of the MPP inference, along with its premises, P and 'If P, then Q,' to the original

Even if we conceded, then, that we have rational insight into the validity of specific inferences, we do not escape the threat of circularity that afflicts the internalist account. Once again, an ability to infer justifiably according to MPP is presupposed.

Commenting on an earlier presentation of this argument, Crispin Wright observes:

It is clear how the simple internalist must reply to Boghossian. To staunch her view against all threat of Carrollian regress, she must insist that recognition of the validity of a specific inference whose premises are known provides a warrant to accept a conclusion not by providing additional information from which the truth or warrantedness of the conclusion may be inferred, but in a direct manner … In effect, and paradoxically, her view must be that warrants acquired by inference are, in a way, a subspecies of non-inferential warrant in general: that an appreciation that a conclusion follows from warranted premises confers, when it does, a warrant for an acceptance of that conclusion in no less direct a fashion than that in which a visual appreciation of the colour of the sky confers warrant for the belief that it is blue.[16]

I agree with Wright that this represents the only escape route available to the simple internalist. Wright himself does not endorse it, or even present it as an especially attractive option. He claims for it only that it remains undefeated by the sorts of considerations adduced so far.

No doubt there remains scope for discussion. But it is very difficult to see, it seems to me, how the inferential case is to be plausibly assimilated to the admittedly non-inferential warrant provided for the belief that the sky is blue by the observation of a blue sky under favourable circumstances.

Admittedly, we don't have very refined ways of deciding when a warrant for a particular belief is direct and when it is fundamentally inferential in nature. What we seem to operate with is a rough-and-ready criterion which says in effect: when the gap between the content of an apparent observation and the content of the belief that it is supposed to justify is too large, the justification must be inferential in nature, even if that may not be apparent from its presentation in everyday conversation.

So, for example, in response to the question 'How do you know it is going to rain?' I may simply point to the dark and threatening clouds. But as everyone would agree, the observation of the dark and threatening clouds doesn't justify the belief in rain all by itself, but only by way of an inference in which the content of that observation serves as a premise. The gap between the content of

---

target conclusion Q. In his commentary on my paper, Crispin Wright suggested that this second anti-internalist argument would be more effective if it claimed not that the internalist is committed to inferences to the target conclusion itself, but rather to the conclusion: the inference to Q is justified. I am not entirely persuaded that Wright's is a better way of running this second argument; but I am persuaded that it raises fewer distracting objections than my original presentation, and so I adopt it for the purposes of this paper.

[16] Wright 2001, pp. 79–80.

the observation and the content of the belief it is supposed to ground is simply too large.

Similarly, I say, in the case before us. The gap between the content of the apparent observation

If (1) and (2) are true, then (3) must be true

and the belief:

I am justified in believing (3)

is simply too large for the warrant to be direct, even if in most conversational contexts the inference could be left unsaid.[17]

To sum up. In order to ensure that a thinker's inference from particular MPP premises to a particular MPP conclusion not be blameworthy, the simple inferential internalist insisted that the inference's justifiedness be transparent to the thinker—the thinker has to be in a position reflectively to appreciate that his inferring this conclusion from these premises is justified. But this runs into two major problems. First, it requires us to take seriously a notion of rational insight, a notion that no one has been able to render respectable. Second, and even if we waived this first worry, the aimed-for transparency will still be unattainable, since the only way to attain it will require that the thinker use such knowledge as rational insight is able to afford him as the basis for an inference to the justifiedness of his conclusion. So no matter how concessive we are about rational insight and about the knowledge of logical implication that it is supposed to engender, there seems to be no way to satisfy the transparency insisted upon by Simple Inferential Internalism.

VI. BLIND YET BLAMELESS INFERENCE: DEFLATIONARY OPTIONS

The question is where we go from here. Simple Inferential Externalism is false. Simple Inferential Internalism, construed as requiring some form of reflectively accessible warrant, is unsatisfiable. We know, furthermore, that we cannot say that deductive inferences do not transfer warrant; that would be not merely implausible but self-undermining. Hence, unless we are to admit that our epistemic system is subject to deep and crippling paradox, there had better be a stable and coherent account of what the conditions for warrant transfer are.

In searching for a solution, we must respect the following facts. On the one hand, the failure of Simple Inferential Internalism teaches us that it must be possible for certain modes of reasoning to be entitling without our knowing, or

---

[17] What if we imagined that we are able to gain rational insight not only into the validity of specific inferences but directly into their justifiedness? Not only is this unimaginable but I believe that a Carroll-style problem will arise for it as well. I hope to elaborate on this elsewhere.

being able to know, anything about them. I'll put this by saying that it must be possible for certain inferences to be *blind* but justifying.[18]

On the other hand, the counterexamples to Reliabilism teach us that the way *not* to accommodate this phenomenon is through Simple Inferential Externalism. So our question is: How should we construe warrant transfer consistent both with Simple Internalism's and Simple Externalism's falsity?

If there is to be a way forward, the following had better be true: the anti-Reliabilist examples, properly understood, don't really motivate Access Internalism, even though they seem to do so. Rather, they motivate something weaker which *can* be reconciled both with the falsity of Reliabilism and with the falsity of Access Internalism. What could that intermediate position be?

The minimal lesson of the anti-Reliabilist examples, as we saw, is that being justified cannot coexist with being epistemically blameworthy. To get from here to Access Internalism you need to assume furthermore that what *makes* a belief epistemically blameworthy is the *absence* of a reflectively appreciable warrant for it. And although all the known examples uniformly support this construal, it's not actually forced. For all that the examples show, in other words, it is possible that there should be some *other* way in which a belief might be held blamelessly other than by being supported by some reflectively appreciable warrant.

Some philosophers are inclined to think that there isn't much of a problem here because they think that it isn't all that hard to be epistemically blameless. Gilbert Harman, for example, thinks that just about any belief, or method for forming beliefs, that one cares to have is blameless, at least initially. He writes:

What I take to be the right theory of justification goes something like this (Goodman, 1995; Quine, 1960a; Quine and Ullian, 1978; Rawls, 1971). In deciding what to believe or what to do, you have to start where you are with your current beliefs and methods of reasoning. These beliefs and methods have a privileged status. You are justified in continuing to accept them in the absence of a serious specific challenge to them, where the challenge will typically involve some sort of conflict in your overall view. Conflict is to be resolved by making conservative modifications in your overall view that makes your view more coherent in certain ways. Your goal in resolving conflict is to reach what Rawls calls a 'reflective equilibrium', in which your various views are not in tension with each other … The

---

[18] The allusion here is to Wittgenstein's remark at *Philosophical Investigations* 219:

When I obey a rule, I do not choose.
I obey the rule *blindly*. (219)

One of Wittgenstein's fundamental insights, it seems to me, was to realize that we must be capable of a form of blameless reasoning that did not depend on any other cognitive state of the thinker's and, in particular, not on anything analogous to sight. As he put the matter in *On Certainty*:

Giving grounds, however, justifying the evidence, comes to an end—but the end is not certain propositions' striking us immediately as true, i.e., it is not a kind of *seeing* on our part; it is our *acting*, which lies at the bottom of the language game.

crucial point is that, to a first approximation, continuing to accept what you accept does not require justification. What requires justification is making changes in your view.[19]

On this view, which Harman dubs 'General Conservatism', we have a quick and painless answer to our question. We are now justified in using MPP because MPP is one of the methods with which we 'start' and we have, so far, encountered no incoherence in our overall view to which the best response would have been to reject or modify it.

The principal thought behind general conservatism is an 'innocent until proven guilty' model of epistemic justification. It doesn't matter what beliefs or methods one starts with—they are all *prima facie* justified. What matters is how one changes one's view in response to a developing incoherence.

But this is all very misleading, for the notion of 'coherence', is empty unless it embeds a specific conception of logical consequence and logical consistency. (Actually, it would probably have to include not just that but conceptions of probabilistic consistency, and a great deal more, but I'll let that pass.)[20] That in effect implies, however, that talk about 'coherence' *presupposes* an answer to our question, rather than providing one. You need to have figured out which deductive rules are justifying in order to have a substantive coherence theory rather than the other way around.

This brings us to the second 'deflationary' answer to our question: a *list*. You want to know which inference patterns are permitted to be blind? These ones: Modus Ponens, Non-Contradiction, and a few others. Don't ask *why* it is precisely these inference patterns that are sanctioned. There is no deep answer to that question; there is just the list.

What makes this brand of deflationary answer unsatisfactory is that it is hard to believe that the property of being warrant-transferring is simply a primitive property that an inference pattern either has or fails to have. Surely, if an inference pattern is warrant-transferring there must be some property by virtue of which it is warrant-transferring. And our question is: What, in the most basic cases, in which reflectively available support is not possible, could that property be?

VII. BLIND YET BLAMELESS INFERENCE: CONCEPT CONSTITUTION

An important question—which I don't wish to prejudge for present purposes—is whether the validity of the inference is a *necessary condition* on warrant transfer.

---

[19] Harman 2003, pp. 25–6.
[20] See, for example, Bonjour 1985, ch. 5, for a discussion of coherence conceptions of justification.

What I will be exclusively concerned with in the remainder of this paper is the question of blamelessness.

The 'inflationary' answer to that question that I want to explore may be roughly formulated as follows (we'll see how to refine it later):

A deductive pattern of inference P may be blamelessly employed, without any reflective appreciation of its epistemic status, just in case inferring according to P is a precondition for having one of the concepts ingredient in it.

Now, in some sense this is a very old answer to our question. It falls into what may broadly be called 'analytic' explanations of the a priori. Previous versions of such views, however, have suffered, I believe, in two respects.[21] First, they did not adequately distinguish between questions concerning our entitlement to certain logical beliefs, and questions concerning our entitlement to certain belief-forming methods of inference (like the one I have dubbed MPP). Second, they did not adequately explain what concept-constitution has to do with the epistemology of blind inference. In both of these respects, I hope here to do a little better.

Prima facie, there is a difficulty seeing how appeal to concept constitution can help with our question. What is the connection supposed to be?

The thought is this. Suppose it's true that my taking A to be a warrant for believing B is constitutive of my being able to have B-thoughts (or A-thoughts, or both, it doesn't matter) in the first place. Then doesn't it follow that I could not have been epistemically blameworthy in taking A to be a reason for believing B, even in the absence of any reason for taking A to be a reason for believing B? For how could I have had *antecedent* information to the effect that A is a good reason for believing B, if I could not so much have had a B-thought without taking A to be a reason for believing B in the first place? If inferring from A to B is required, if I am to be able to think the ingredient propositions, then it looks as though so inferring cannot be held against me, even if the inference is blind.

Applied to the case of deductive inference before us, then, the thought would be that we would have an explanation for the blameless blindness of MPP if it's constitutive of having the concept *conditional* that one take p and 'p → q' as a reason for believing q.

Now, of course, the idea that, in general, we come to grasp the logical constants by being disposed to engage in some inferences involving them and not in others, is an independently compelling idea. And the thought that, in particular, we grasp the conditional just in case we are disposed to infer according to MPP is an independently compelling thought. So, if the meaning-entitlement connection that I've gestured at is correct, it looks as though we are in a position to mount an explanation of the blameless blindness of MPP that we were after.

---

[21] See, for example, Peacocke 1993a.

VIII. PROBLEMS FOR THE MEANING-ENTITLEMENT CONNECTION

Unfortunately, matters are not quite so straightforward. If we spell out the principle underlying the meaning-based explanation of blameless blindness gestured at, it would be this:

(Meaning-Entitlement Connection, or MEC): Any inferential transitions built into the possession conditions for a concept are *eo ipso* entitling.

And the trouble is that, at least as stated, there seem to be clearcut counter-examples to the MEC: it doesn't in general seem true that if my taking A as a reason for believing B is constitutive of my believing B, that this *automatically* absolves me of any charge of epistemic blameworthiness. For there seem to be clear cases where the acceptance of some inference is written into the possession of a given concept but where it is also clear that the inference isn't one to which the thinker is entitled.

One famous illustrative case is Arthur Prior's connective 'tonk'.[22] To possess this concept, Prior stipulated, a thinker must be willing to infer according to the following introduction and elimination rules:

(Tonk) $$\frac{A}{A \text{ tonk } B} \qquad \frac{A \text{ tonk } B}{B}$$

Obviously, no one could be entitled to infer any B from any A; but this entitlement appears to flow from the possession conditions for 'tonk' along with the MEC.

A similar conclusion can be drawn from the case of racist or abusive concepts, for example the concept *boche* discussed by Dummett.[23] Plausibly, a thinker possesses the concept *boche* just in case he is willing to infer according to the following rules:

(Boche) $$\frac{x \text{ is German}}{x \text{ is boche}} \qquad \frac{x \text{ is boche}}{x \text{ is cruel}}$$

Yet no one is entitled—let alone simply as the result of the introduction of a concept into the language—to the view that all Germans are cruel. How should we think about such cases?

Robert Brandom has this to say about *boche*-like concepts:

The use of any concept or expression involves commitment to an inference from its grounds to its consequences of application. Critical thinkers, or merely fastidious ones, must examine their idioms to be sure that they are prepared to endorse and so defend the appropriateness of the material inferential commitments implicit in the

---

[22] Prior 1960.
[23] Dummett 1973, p. 454.

concepts they employ...The proper question to ask in evaluating the introduction and evolution of a concept is not whether the inference embodied is one that is already endorsed, so that no new content is really involved, but rather whether the inference is one that *ought* to be endorsed. The problem with 'boche' is not that once we explicitly confront the material inferential commitment that gives the term its content it turns out to be novel, but that it can then be seen to be indefensible and inappropriate—a commitment we cannot become entitled to.[24]

From the standpoint of a proponent of the MEC, there is nothing in this passage that helps protect it from the threatening examples. It's no answer to the challenge they pose to observe that whatever entitlement concept possession gives rise to, it can be defeated by further considerations. No one should expect more than a defeasible entitlement, even from concept possession; and what's implausible in the case of 'tonk' and 'boche' is that there is any entitlement there at all, defeasible or no.

If we are to save the MEC, it seems to me that we must do one or both of two things: either restrict it to certain concepts from which entitlement really does flow, or restrict what we count as a genuine concept. I will advocate doing the former.

The latter strategy is suggested by the work of Christopher Peacocke who has long urged that we should require that the meaning-constituting rules of a genuine concept be truth-preserving.[25] If we adopt this requirement, we can say that what's wrong with both 'tonk' and 'boche' is precisely that there is no concept that those terms express, for there is no reference for 'tonk' and 'boche' that's capable of making all of their constitutive rules truth-preserving.

While this might seem to yield the right result for 'tonk' it doesn't yield the right result for 'boche': it's hard to believe that racists who employ boche-like concepts fail to express complete thoughts.

And even if we were to put this complaint to one side, it seems clear that truth-preservation alone will not suffice for dealing with our problem about the MEC.

Imagine someone theorizing about water and coming to believe, for whatever reason, that the way in which it is correct to say that water is composed of H_2O is that there is some *other* stuff that composes water and that *it* is composed of H_2O.[26] So he introduces a term—'aqua'—to name this stuff and he stipulates that it is to be governed by the following introduction and elimination rules:

(Aqua) $\dfrac{\text{x is water}}{\text{x is aqua}}$ $\dfrac{\text{x is aqua}}{\text{x is } H_2O}$

Unlike the case of 'boche', we have no independent reason for thinking that these rules are not truth-preserving. But there is clearly something fishy about

[24] Brandom 2000, pp. 70–2.
[25] See Peacocke 1993b. I myself took this line in my 2001a (this volume, Chapter 11), so the present paper represents a change of heart.
[26] For the purposes of this example, I am assuming that composition is not identity.

this concept. And however one feels about that, there is certainly a problem for the MEC, given only the resources that we've been accorded so far: for no one could think that the mere act of introducing the concept *aqua* into one's repertoire could give one a priori entitlement to the inference from x's being water to x's being H_2O.

Or consider the concept *flurg* individuated by the following introduction and elimination rules:

x is an elliptical equation	x is flurg
x is flurg	x can be correlated with a modular form

It turns out to be a result that Wiles had to prove on the way to proving Fermat's Last Theorem that every elliptical equation can be correlated with a modular form (the Taniyama-Shimura conjecture). Once again, therefore, we have no independent reason to think that these introduction and elimination rules are not necessarily truth-preserving. But it's hard to see that one is a priori entitled, merely on the basis of introducing the term 'flurg', to the Taniyama-Shimura conjecture. So there is still a problem for the claim that entitlement flows from meaning-constitution, given only the requirement that a concept's introduction and elimination rules be truth-preserving.

IX. DEFECTIVE CONCEPTS AND BLAMELESS INFERENCE

I would like to propose a different diagnosis of what has gone wrong with concepts such as *aqua* and *flurg*, one that doesn't depend on denying that they constitute genuine thinkable contents.

That denial can be sustained, I believe, in the case of 'tonk', but that is a rather extreme case. No one can actually possess the concept allegedly expressed by 'tonk', because it isn't possible for someone to follow the rules that are constitutive of that connective. For to follow those rules one would have to be prepared to infer anything from everything, and that is no longer recognizable as belief or inference. But no such extreme claim can be made with respect to all the other examples that have been causing problems for the hypothesized connection between meaning and entitlement.

Start with the example of 'aqua'. The theorist who has conceived the need to introduce a term for the concept *aqua* has come to hold the following *theory*: 'There is some stuff, distinct from water, that composes water and that is itself composed of H_2O. Let me call it "aqua".' Such a theorist already believes in water and H_2O, we may suppose. He has come to hold an additional belief about the world, namely, that it contains another substance, one that is related to water and H_2O in the specified way.

Now, the way we have written down the inferential rules for 'aqua' essentially amounts to insisting that, in order to have the concept *aqua* you must be prepared to *believe* this little *aqua* theory. Given that you already believe in water and

H₂O, the only way for you to acquire the concept *aqua*, on this account of its inferential rules, requires you to *believe* that there is such a thing as aqua. One cannot so much as have the concept of *aqua* without being prepared to believe that there is such a thing.

And although it seems to me that one *can* define and then think in terms of such a concept, it does seem like an epistemically questionable thing to do. Even if the aqua theorist were *certain* that there is such a thing as aqua, he should want the concept he expresses by that term to leave it open whether there is. He should allow for the conceptual possibility that he is mistaken; and he should certainly allow others intelligibly to disagree with him about aqua's existence. The concept itself should not be designed in such a way that, only those who believe a certain creed are allowed to possess it.

Ordinary scientific terms in good standing—'neutrino' for example—are held to have just this feature, of intelligibly allowing for disagreement about their extension. Thus, we don't think of the rules which correspond to our possession of the concept *neutrino* as consisting in the propositions that would actually be believed by a proponent of neutrino theory, but rather as corresponding only to what someone would be willing to believe who was *conditionalizing* on the truth of neutrino theory.

If we follow Russell, Ramsey, Carnap and Lewis, and represent neutrino theory

T(neutrino)

as the conjunction of the two propositions

(S) (∃x) Tx

and

(M) (∃x) Tx → T(neutrino)

then the point is that we think of possession of the concept *neutrino* as requiring someone to affirm only M and not S as well.[27]

Now, someone could certainly introduce a concept that did not have the conditionalized structure that I've claimed is actually true of *neutrino*, but which consists rather in the inferences that are characteristic of neutrino theory unconditionalized. Call this *neutrino₊*. Such a person would insist that it is a condition on having *his* concept of neutrino that one be willing to endorse the characteristic claims and inferences of neutrino theory, and not merely the conditionalized claim captured in (M). But, for the reasons previously articulated, there would be something epistemically *defective* about this concept, even if its constitutive rules turned out to be truth-preserving.

---

[27] This paragraph follows Paul Horwich's discussion of the conditional nature of semantic stipulation in his 2000. I ignore various complexities that a thorough discussion of the representation of scientific theories would require.

Flurg, aqua and *neutrino*$_+$, then, all suffer from the same problem: they are all unconditional versions of a concept, when only its conditionalized version would be epistemically acceptable. I don't think we should put this by saying that they are not real concepts. Concepts are relatively cheap. But they are *defective* concepts. They are structured in such a way that perfectly reasonable questions about their extensions are foreclosed.

Under what conditions is only a conditionalized version of a concept acceptable? Here I want to make two claims: one bold, one sober.

(Bold) Whenever both a conditional and an unconditional version of a given concept are available, it is the conditional version that ought to be used. Given the availability of both versions, the unconditional version counts as epistemically defective.

(Sober) In the case of some concepts, only the unconditionalized version will be available.

Start with Bold. Whenever a conditionalized version of a concept is available, that is the version that ought to be used. In those contexts, an unconditionalized version would be defective.

The argument for this is quite straightforward and recapitulates the considerations we have just been looking at. You don't ever want the *possession conditions* for a concept to foreclose on the possible falsity of some particular set of claims about the world, if you can possibly avoid it. You want the possessor of the concept to be able coherently to ask whether there is anything that falls under it, and you want people to be able to disagree about whether there is.

If in a certain range of cases, however, it is logically impossible to hold the governing theory at arm's length then, in those cases, obviously, it can hardly be a requirement that one do so. But in all those cases where that is possible, it ought to be done.

What about Sober? It should be clear, given the kind of conditionalization that is in view here, that not every meaningful term in a language can be thought of as expressing a concept that conditionalizes on the existence of an appropriate semantic value for it. Take the case of 'flurg'. The stipulation that would correspond to a conditional version for 'flurg' would amount roughly to this:

If there is a property which is such that, any elliptical equation has it, and if something has it, then it can be correlated with a modular form, then if x has that property, x is flurg.

The corresponding introduction and elimination rules that would specify the possession condition for it would therefore be:

$$\frac{(\exists F)\,[T(F)\ \&\ Fx]}{x \text{ is flurg}}$$

and

$$\frac{\text{x is flurg}}{(\exists F)\,[\text{T(F) \& Fx}]}$$

As this makes clear, the only thinkers who could follow such rules—and, hence, the only thinkers who may be seen as implicitly conditionalizing on the existence of an appropriate semantic value for 'flurg'—are those who (a) possess a basic set of logical constants and (b) are able to refer to and quantify over properties in particular, and semantic values, more generally.

It follows, therefore, that conditional counterparts for one's primitive logical constants will not be available and hence that one could hardly be blamed for employing their unconditionalized versions. In particular, if the conditional is one of your primitive logical constants, you couldn't conditionalize on the existence of an appropriate truth function for it, for you would need it in order to conditionalize on anything. In such a case, there is no alternative but to accept 'conditional theory'—modus ponens in effect—if you are so much as to have the conditional concept. It thus couldn't be epistemically irresponsible of you just to go ahead and infer according to modus ponens without conditionalizing on the existence of an appropriate truth function for it—that is simply not a coherent option in this case.

What is the full range of those concepts for which conditional counterparts would not be available? To answer this question, one would need to have a clear view of what the minimal logical resources are that are needed to conditionalize in the envisaged answer on the truth of an arbitrary theory, and I don't have a systematic theory of that to present at the moment. What does seem clear, though, is that some set of basic logical constants would have to be presupposed and that is enough to get me the result that inference in accord with their constitutive rules can be entitling even though blind.

If we go back to the MEC, then, it seems clear what we should say: Any rules that are written into the possession conditions for a *non-defective* concept are a fortiori entitling.

With that in hand, we have the answer to our question: how could MPP premises warrant MPP conclusions while being blind? Answer: they do, because they are written into the possession conditions for the conditional, and the conditional is a non-defective concept.

X. CONCLUSION

If we are to make sense of the justified employment of our basic logical methods of inference, we must make sense of what I have called *blind but blameless* reasoning—a way of moving between thoughts that is justified even in the absence of any reflectively appreciable support for it.

In this paper, I have attempted to sketch the outlines of an account of this phenomenon, one that avoids the pitfalls both of an overly austere Reliabilism and an overly intellectualized Internalism. The account seeks to revive and exploit two traditionally influential thoughts: first, that following certain inferential rules is constitutive of our grasp of the primitive logical constants; and, second, that if certain inferential rules are constitutive of our grasp of certain concepts, then we are *eo ipso* entitled to them, even in the absence of any reflectively appreciable support.[28]

APPENDIX[29]

In his response to this paper, Timothy Williamson objected to this line of reasoning as follows:

Although $\exists$ and $\rightarrow$ occur in the Carnap sentence $\exists F T(F) \rightarrow T(Neutrino)$, in place of that sentence Boghossian could have used the rule that allows one to infer *T(Neutrino)* directly from any premise of the form *T(A)*. That rule is formulated without reference to the logical operators in the object-language, but is interderivable with the Carnap sentence once one has the standard rules for $\exists$ and $\rightarrow$. ... Logical operators may of course occur in the theory *T* itself, although Boghossian does not appeal to that point. In any case, it seems insufficiently general for his argument, since for some less highly theoretical concepts than *neutrino*, the analogue of the theory *T* for conditionalization may consist of some simple sentences free of logical operators.   (Williamson 2003, p. 287)

Of course, I did not mean to suggest that one could simply read off the Carnap sentence that existential quantification and conditional would be presupposed by any conditionalization, though no doubt my presentation was overly elliptical. In the cases of most central interest, the affirmation of the Carnap sentence would be *implicit* in the thinker's behavior and could not be supposed to amount to an explicit belief from which one could simply read off the ingredient conceptual materials.

To see whether we could have nothing but conditionalized concepts, we have to ask whether it is possible for someone to implicitly affirm the Carnap sentence for, e.g., boche, without possessing any of the logical concepts with which we would explicitly conditionalized our concepts.

We have agreed that for someone to affirm T(boche) implicitly is for them to be willing to infer according to the following introduction and elimination rules:

[28] For valuable comments on previous drafts I am grateful to Gregory Epstein, Kit Fine, Paul Horwich, Stephen Schiffer, Joshua Schechter and Crispin Wright; and to audiences at the Quine Conference in Berlin, the Summer School in Analytic Philosophy in Parma, the SOFIA Conference in Veracruz, and the colloquia series at Smith College and the University of Toronto.

[29] The material in this appendix originally appeared as the last few pages of my 2003b (this volume, Chapter 10).

Gx/Bx Bx/Cx.

Now, the question is: What would it be for a thinker to implicitly conditionalize his affirmation of T(boche) on the existence of an appropriate semantic value for these rules? Williamson says that this could be adequately captured by picturing the conditionalizing thinker as operating according to the following rule:

$$\frac{T(A)}{T(boche)}$$

But what this seems to me to say is something very different from what is needed. A thinker operating according to Williamson's rule is like someone who already has the concept boche but is now simply relabeling it with the word 'boche.' Whereas what I want to capture is the idea of someone who is only prepared to infer according to the boche rules because they antecedently believe that

There is a property F, such that $Gx \rightarrow Fx$ and $Fx \rightarrow Cx$

And I don't see how their reasoning could depend on that without their having, at a minimum, the conceptual materials that make up the antecedent of the Carnap sentence, including the quantificational apparatus and the conditionals that make up the statement of the theory.

If all of this is right, it follows that conditional counterparts for one's primitive logical constants will not be available and hence that one could hardly be blamed for employing their unconditionalized versions. In particular, you couldn't conditionalize on the existence of an appropriate truth function for the conditional, for you would need it in order to conditionalize on anything. In such a case, there is no alternative but to accept "conditional theory"—modus ponens and Conditional Proof, in effect—if you are to so much as have the conditional concept. It thus couldn't be epistemically irresponsible of you to just go ahead and infer according to MPP without conditionalizing on the existence of an appropriate truth function for it—that is simply not a coherent option in this case.

Part III: Suggestions for Further Reading

Casalegno, P. (2004) 'Logical Concepts and Logical Inferences', *Dialectica* 58 (3): 395–411.

Ebert, P. A. (2005) 'Transmission of Warrant-Failure and the Notion of Epistemic Analyticity', *Australasian Journal of Philosophy* 83 (4): 505–21.

Enoch, D. and J. Schechter. (2006) 'Meaning and Justification: The Case of Modus Ponens', *Noûs* 40 (4): 687–715.

Fodor, J. and E. Lepore. (2006) 'Analyticity Again'. In *The Blackwell Guide to the Philosophy of Language*, edited by M. Devitt, pp. 114–30. Malden MA: Blackwell.

Glüer, K. (2003) 'Analyticity and Implicit Definition', *Grazier Philosophische Studien* 66: 37–60.

Hale, B. and C. Wright. (2001) *The Reason's Proper Study*. Oxford UK: OUP.

Harman, G. 1996. 'Analyticity Regained?', *Noûs* 30: 392–400.

Horwich, P. (2000) 'Stipulation, Meaning, and Apriority', In *New Essays on the A Priori*, edited by P. Boghossian and C. Peacocke, pp. 150–69. Oxford UK: OUP.

———(2005) 'Meaning Constitution and Epistemic Rationality', In *Reflections on Meaning*, pp. 134–73. Oxford UK: OUP.

Liz, M. (1995) 'Meaning, Realism, and the Rejection of Analyticity', *Sorites*: 51–80.

Margolis, E. and S. Laurence. (2001) 'Boghossian on Analyticity', *Analysis* 61 (4): 293–302.

Okasha, S. (2002) 'How to be a Selective Quinean', *Dialectica* 56 (1): 37–47.

Philie, P. (2005) 'Meaning-Scepticism and Analyticity', *Dialectica* 59 (3): 357–65.

Tennant, N. (2005) 'Rule-Circularity and the Justification of Deduction', *Philosophical Quarterly* 55 (221): 625–48.

Williamson, T. (2003) 'Understanding and Inference', *Proceedings of the Aristotelian Society: Supplementary Volume* 77: 249–93.

Wright, C. (2001) 'On Basic Logical Knowledge', *Philosophical Studies* 106 (1): 41–85.

———(2004) 'Intuition, Entitlement and the Epistemology of Logical Laws', *Dialectica* 58 (1): 155–75.

PART IV
Color: Concepts and Properties

13 *Colour as a Secondary Quality*

With J. David Velleman.

THE GALILEAN INTUITION

Does modern science imply, contrary to the testimony of our eyes, that grass is not green? Galileo thought it did:

Hence I think that these tastes, odors, colors, etc., on the side of the object in which they seem to exist, are nothing else than mere names, but hold their residence solely in the sensitive body; so that if the animal were removed, every such quality would be abolished and annihilated. Nevertheless, as soon as we have imposed names on them, particular and different from those of the other primary and real accidents, we induce ourselves to believe that they also exist just as truly and really as the latter.[1]

The question whether Galileo was right on this score is not really a question about the content of modern scientific theory: aside from some difficulties concerning the interpretation of quantum mechanics, we know what properties are attributed to objects by physics. The question is rather about the correct understanding of colour concepts as they figure in visual experience: how do objects appear to be, when they appear to be green? Galileo seems to have found it very natural to say that the property an object appears to have, when it appears to have a certain colour, is an intrinsic qualitative property which, as science teaches us, it does not in fact possess.

Subsequent philosophical theorizing about colour has tended to recoil from Galileo's semantic intuition and from its attendant ascription of massive error to ordinary experience and thought. Thus, in a recent paper Sydney Shoemaker has written:

[S]ince in fact we apply color predicates to physical objects and never to sensations, ideas, experiences, etc., the account of their semantics recommended by the Principle of Charity is one that makes them truly applicable to tomatoes and lemons rather than to sense experiences thereof.[2]

---

[1] Galilei 1842, p. 333 (as translated by Burtt 1954, p. 85).
[2] Shoemaker 1990, p. 110.

Should a principle of charity be applied in this way to the interpretation of the colour concepts exercised in visual experience? We think not. We shall argue, for one thing, that the grounds for applying a principle of charity are lacking in the case of colour concepts. More importantly, we shall argue that attempts at giving the experience of colour a charitable interpretation either fail to respect obvious features of that experience or fail to interpret it charitably, after all. Charity to visual experience is therefore no motive for resisting the natural, Galilean response to a scientific understanding of light and vision. The best interpretation of colour experience ends up convicting it of widespread and systematic error.[3]

CHARITABLE ACCOUNTS OF COLOUR EXPERIENCE

According to the principle of charity, the properties that objects are seen as having, when they are seen as coloured, must be properties that they generally have when so perceived. Two familiar interpretations of visual experience satisfy this principle.

The Physicalist Account

The first of these interpretations begins with the assumption that what objects appear to have, when they look red, is the physical property that is normally detected or tracked by that experience. Since the physical property that normally causes an object to be seen as red is the property of having one out of a class of spectral-reflectance profiles—or one out of a class of molecular bases for such

---

[3] One might be tempted to dissolve the conflict between the Galilean view and the charitable view of colour experience by rejecting a presupposition that they share. Both sides of the conflict assume that the properties mentioned in our descriptions of visual experience are properties that such experience represents objects as having. The only disagreement is over the question whether the colour properties that are thus attributed to objects by visual experience are properties that the objects tend to have. One might claim, however, that visual experience does not attribute properties to objects at all; and one might bolster one's claim by appeal to a theory known as adverbialism. According to adverbialism, the experience of seeing a thing as red is an event modified by some adverbial property—say, a seeing event that proceeds red-thing-ly. Not all adherents of adverbialism are committed to denying that such an experience represents an object as having a property; but adverbialism would indeed be useful to one who wished to deny it. For adverbialism would enable one to say that the phrase 'seeing a thing as red' describes a seeing event as having some adverbial property rather than as having the content that something is red. One could therefore contend that the question whether things really have the colour properties that they are seen as having is simply ill-formed, since colour properties figure in a visual experience as adverbial modifications of the experience rather than as properties attributed by the experience to an object.

Our view is that this extreme version of adverbialism does unacceptable violence to the concept of visual experience. Seeing something as red is the sort of thing that can be illusory or veridical, hence the sort of thing that has truth-conditions, and hence the sort of thing that has content. The content of this experience is that the object in question is red; and so the experience represents an object as having a property, about which we can legitimately ask whether it is a property that objects so represented really tend to have.

profiles—the upshot of the present interpretation is that seeing something as red is seeing it as reflecting incident light in one of such-and-such ways, or as having surface molecules with one of such-and-such electron configurations.[4]

Now, we have no doubt that experiences of an object as having a particular colour are normally correlated with that object's possessing one of a class of spectral-reflectance profiles. But to concede the existence of such a correlation is not yet to concede that membership in a spectral-reflectance class is the property that objects are seen as having when they are seen as having a particular colour. Indeed, the claim that visual experience has this content yields unacceptable consequences.

In particular, this claim implies that one cannot tell just by looking at two objects whether they appear to have the same or different colours. For according to the physicalist interpretation, which colour one sees an object as having depends on which spectral-reflectance class one's visual experience represents the object as belonging to; and which spectral-reflectance class one's experience represents an object as belonging to depends on which spectral-reflectance profiles normally cause experiences of that sort. Hence in order to know whether two objects appear to have the same colour, under the physicalist interpretation, one must know whether one's experiences of them are such as result from similar spectral-reflectance profiles. And the latter question cannot be settled on the basis of the visual experiences alone: it calls for considerable empirical enquiry. The physicalist interpretation therefore implies that knowing whether two objects appear to have the same colour requires knowing the results of empirical enquiry into the physical causes of visual experiences.

But surely, one can tell whether two objects appear similarly coloured on the basis of visual experience alone. To be sure, one's experience of the objects will not necessarily provide knowledge of the relation between their actual colours. But the physicalist account implies that visual experience of objects fails to provide epistemic access, not just to their actual colour similarities, but to their apparent colour similarities as well. And here the account must be mistaken. The apparent colours of objects can be compared without empirical enquiry into the physical causes of the objects' visual appearances; and so the properties that objects appear to have, when they appear coloured, cannot be identified with the physical properties that are detected or tracked by those appearances.

Dispositionalist Accounts

We turn, then, to another class of theories that respect the principle of charity in application to colour experience. These theories are united under the name of dispositionalism. All of them are based, in one way or another, on the claim that the concept of colour is such as to yield a priori truths of the following form:

---

[4] Armstrong 1968; Smart 1975 (as cited by Peacocke 1984, n. 5).

(i) x is red if and only if x appears red under standard conditions.[5]

Different versions of dispositionalism interpret such biconditionals differently and apply them to the vindication of colour experience in different ways.

Applying the Biconditionals: the Direct Approach

Perhaps the most direct way to argue from the dispositionalist biconditionals to the veridicality of colour experience is to point out that the biconditionals assert, as a priori truths, that there are conditions under which things appear to have a colour if and only if they actually have it, and hence that there are conditions under which colour experience is veridical. The possibility of global error in colour experience is thus claimed to be excluded a priori by the very concept of colour.

We think that this version of dispositionalism misappropriates whatever a priori truth there may be in the relevant biconditionals. We are prepared to admit that the concept of colour guarantees the existence of privileged conditions for viewing colours, conditions under which an observer's colour experiences or colour judgements are in some sense authoritative. But colour experiences and colour judgements may enjoy many different kinds of authority, some of which would not entail that objects have the properties that colour experience represents them as having.

Even philosophers who regard colour experience as globally false, for example, will nevertheless want to say that some colour experiences are correct in the sense that they yield the colour attributions that are generally accepted for the purposes of describing objects in public discourse. Of course, such a claim will yield slightly different biconditionals, of the following form:

(ii) x is to be described as red if and only if x appears red under standard conditions.

Our point, however, is that (ii) may be the only biconditional that is strictly true, and that (i) may seem true only because it is mistaken for (ii). If biconditional (ii) expresses the only genuine a priori truth in the vicinity, then the authority of experiences produced under standard conditions may consist in no more than there being a convention of describing objects in terms of the colours attributed to them in such experiences. As we shall argue at the end of this paper, such a convention may be perfectly justifiable even if all colour experience is, strictly speaking, false. Hence the intuitive support for biconditionals like (i) may not be such as to ground a vindication of colour experience.

In order for the dispositionalist biconditionals to vindicate colour experience, they must mean, not just that convention dictates describing objects in terms

---

[5] The final clause of this biconditional is often formulated so as to specify not only standard conditions but a standard observer as well. But the observer's being standard can itself be treated as a condition of observation; and so the distinction between observer and conditions is unnecessary.

of the colours that they appear to have under standard conditions, but also that objects actually have the properties that they thereby appear to have. And we see no reason for regarding this stronger claim as an a priori truth.

Applying the Biconditionals as Content-specifications

Another way of arguing from dispositionalist biconditionals to the veridicality of colour experience is to interpret the biconditionals as specifying the content of that experience. This argument proceeds as follows.

The first premiss of the argument says that the property that objects are represented as having when they look red is just this: a disposition to look red under standard conditions. The second premiss says that many objects are in fact disposed to look red under standard conditions, and that these are the objects that are generally seen as red. These premisses yield the conclusion that the experience of red is generally veridical, since it represents an object as having a disposition that it probably has—namely, a disposition to look red under standard conditions.

The first premiss of this argument corresponds to a biconditional of the following form:

(iii) *Red* [i.e., the property that objects are seen as having when they look red] = def a disposition to appear red under standard conditions

The right side of biconditional (iii) can be interpreted in two different ways, however; and so there are two different versions of the associated argument.

Two Versions of Content-Dispositionalism

The first version of the argument interprets the phrase 'a disposition to look red' on the assumption that the embedded phrase 'to look red' has its usual semantic structure. The entire phrase is therefore taken to mean 'a disposition to give the visual appearance of being red'.[6] The second version interprets the phrase on the assumption that 'to look red' has a somewhat unusual structure. The predicate following 'look' is interpreted as expressing, not a property that a thing is disposed to give the appearance of having, but rather an intrinsic property of the visual appearance that it is disposed to give. The phrase 'a disposition to look red' is therefore taken to mean something like 'a disposition to cause reddish visual appearances'.[7]

Under these two interpretations, (iii) assigns two different contents to colour experience. Under one interpretation, the property that things are seen as having when they look red is defined as a disposition to give the visual appearance of

---

[6] See McDowell 1985, Wiggins 1987, and Evans 1980 (see pp. 94–100, esp. n. 30).

Wiggins and McDowell favour a similar strategy for vindicating our perceptions of other qualities such as the comic and perhaps even the good. See McDowell 1987.

[7] Peacocke 1984.

being red; under the other, the property that things are seen as having is defined as a disposition to cause reddish visual appearances. In either case, the content of colour experience is claimed to be true, on the grounds that objects seen as red do have the appropriate disposition.

We regard both versions of the argument as faulty. In the next section, we shall raise an objection that militates against both versions equally. In subsequent sections, we shall consider each version in its own right.

A General Problem in Content-dispositionalism

Both versions of the present argument are to be faulted, in our opinion, for misdescribing the experience of colour. In assigning colour experience a dispositionalist content, they get the content of that experience wrong.

When one enters a dark room and switches on a light, the colours of surrounding objects look as if they have been revealed, not as if they have been activated. That is, the dispelling of darkness looks like the drawing of a curtain from the colours of objects no less than from the objects themselves. If colours looked like dispositions, however, then they would seem to *come on* when illuminated, just as a lamp comes on when its switch is flipped. Turning on the light would seem, simultaneously, like turning on the colours; or perhaps it would seem like waking up the colours, just as it is seen to startle the cat. Conversely, when the light was extinguished, the colours would not look as if they were being concealed or shrouded in the ensuing darkness: rather, they would look as if they were becoming dormant, like the cat returning to sleep. But colours do not look like that; or not, at least, to us.

More seriously, both versions of (iii) also have trouble describing the way in which colours figure in particular experiences, such as after-images. The colours that one sees when experiencing an after-image are precisely the qualities that one sees as belonging to external objects. When red spots float before one's eyes, one sees the same colour quality that fire-hydrants and maraschino cherries normally appear to have.[8] The problem is that dispositionalist accounts of colour experience must analyse the appearance of colour in after-images as the appearance of a disposition to look red under standard conditions; and after-images simply cannot appear to have such a dispositional property.

This problem would not arise if after-images were full-blown illusions. That is, if seeing an after-image consisted in seeming to see a material object suspended in physical space, then that object, though in fact illusory, could still appear to have the same colour quality as any other material object. But after-images are not seen as material objects, any more than, say, a ringing in one's ears is

---

[8] Perhaps the best argument for this claim is that no one who can identify the colours of external objects needs to be taught how to identify the colours of after-images. Once a person can recognize fire hydrants and maraschino cherries as red, he can identify the colour of the spots that float before his eyes after the flash-bulb has fired. He does not need to be taught a second sense of 'red' for the purpose of describing the latter experience.

heard as a real noise. The items involved in these experiences are not perceived as existing independently of being perceived. On the one hand, the after-image is seen as located before one's eyes, rather than in one's mind, where visual memories are seen; and the ringing is likewise heard as located in one's outer ear, rather than in the inner auditorium of verbal thought and musical memory. But on the other hand, one does not perceive these items as actually existing in the locations to which they are subjectively referred. The ringing is heard as overlaying a silence in one's ears, where there is audibly nothing to hear; and similarly, the after-image is seen as overlaying the thin air before one's eyes, where there is visibly nothing to see. The ringing is thus perceived as a figment or projection of one's ears, the image as a figment or projection of one's eyes: both, in short, are perceived as existing only in so far as one is perceiving them.

Thus, the possibility of a red after-image requires that one see something as simultaneously a figment of one's eyes and red. But how could something that looked like a figment of one's eyes also appear disposed to look a particular way under standard conditions? Because an after-image is seen as the sort of thing that exists only in so far as one is seeing it, it cannot be seen as the sort of thing that others could see nor, indeed, as the sort of thing that one could see again oneself, in the requisite sense. In seeing an after-image as a figment of one's eyes, one sees it as the sort of thing that will cease to exist when no longer seen and that will not be numerically identical to any future after-images, however similar they may be. One does not see it, in other words, as a persisting item that could be reintroduced into anyone's visual experience; and so one cannot see it as having a disposition to present this or any appearance either to others or to oneself on other occasions.

The foregoing, phenomenological problems are common to both versions of the dispositionalist argument currently under consideration. Each version of the argument also has peculiar problems of its own, which we shall now consider in turn. We begin with the first version, which understands a disposition to look red as a disposition to give the visual appearance of having the property red.

Problems in the First Version of Content-dispositionalism

The problem with this version has to do with the property expressed by the word 'red' in the phrase 'a disposition to appear red under standard conditions' — the phrase constituting the right side of biconditional (iii). Keep in mind that the entire phrase has itself been offered as expressing the property that objects are seen as having when they look red. When things are seen as red, according to the present argument, what they are seen as having is a disposition to appear red under standard conditions. But does the word 'red' here express the same property that the entire phrase purports to express?

Suppose that the answer to our question is no. In that case, what biconditional (iii) says is that the property that things are seen as having when they look red is a disposition to give the appearance of having some *other* property called red. This other property must naturally be a colour, since the property red could hardly be seen as a disposition to appear as having some property that was not a colour. For the sake of clarity, let us call this other property red*.

Now, in order for objects to have the property red that they appear to have, under the present assumption, they must actually be disposed to give the appearance, under standard conditions, of having the property red*; and in order to have that disposition, they must actually give the appearance of having the property red* under standard conditions. Thus, if the property that things are seen as having when they look red is a disposition to appear red*, then the experience of seeing them as red is veridical, as the dispositionalist wishes to prove, only if they also appear red*. And the question then arises whether red* is a property that things ever do or can actually have. The dispositionalist's argument does not show that the appearance of having red* is ever veridical, since that property is admitted to be different from the disposition whose existence the dispositionalist cites in vindicating the appearance of red. The consequence is that there must be colour experiences that the dispositionalist has failed to vindicate.

Suppose, then, that the dispositionalist answers yes to our question. That is, suppose he says that 'red' expresses the same property on the right side of (iii) as it does on the left. In that case, the dispositionalist's account of colour experience is circular, since in attempting to say what property things appear to have when they look red, he invokes the very property that is at issue.

The dispositionalist may refuse to be troubled by this circularity, however.[9] He may point out that a circular account of a property can still be true, and indeed informative, despite its circularity. For instance, to define courage as a disposition to act courageously is to give a circular definition, a definition that cannot convey the concept of courage to anyone who does not already have it. Even so, courage *is* a disposition to act courageously, and this definition may reveal something important about the property—namely that it is a behavioural disposition. The dispositionalist about colour claims that the circularity in his explication of red is similar.

We grant that circularity alone does not necessarily undermine a definitional equivalence. Yet the circularity in biconditional (iii) is significantly different from that in our circular definition of courage. Our definition of courage invokes courage in an ordinary extensional context, whereas the right side of (iii) invokes red in an intentional context expressing the content of a visual experience, an experience that happens to be the very one whose content (iii) purports to explicate. The result is that the visual experience of seeing something as red can satisfy (iii) only if it, too, is circular, and hence only if it is just as uninformative as (iii). Not only does (iii) fail to tell us which colour red is, then; it also precludes visual experience from telling us which colour an object has. The former failure may be harmless, but the latter is not.

[9] See McGinn 1983, pp. 6–8; McDowell 1985, n. 6; Wiggins 1987, p. 189; and Smith 1986.

Let us illustrate the difference between an unproblematic circular definition and a problematic one by means of an analogy. Suppose that you ask someone who Sam is and are told, 'Sam is the father of Sam's children'. This answer does not tell you who Sam is if you do not already know. But it does tell you something about Sam—namely, that he has children—and, more importantly, it places Sam in a relation to himself that a person can indeed occupy. In order for Sam to satisfy this assertion, he need only be the father of his own children. Now suppose, alternatively, that your question receives the answer 'Sam is the father of Sam's father'. This response also identifies Sam by reference to Sam; but it has a more serious defect. Its defect is that it asserts of Sam that he stands to himself in a relation that is impossible for a person to occupy.

These two circular identifications of Sam are analogous to the two circular definitions that we are considering. The definition of courage as a disposition to act courageously is uninformative, but it places courage in a relation to itself that a disposition can occupy. In order to satisfy this definition, courage must simply be the disposition to perform actions that tend to be performed by someone with that very disposition. By contrast, the dispositionalist about colour not only invokes the content of colour experience in explicating that content; he places that content in a relation to itself that is impossible for it to occupy. For his explication says that the content of the visual experience of red must contain, as a proper part, the content of the visual experience of red. To see something as red, according to (iii), is to have an experience whose content is that the thing is disposed to produce visual experiences *with the content that it is red*. The experiential content that something is red is thus embedded within itself, and this is a reflexive relation that no determinate content can occupy. Consequently, (iii) requires that the visual experience of red have an indeterminate content that fails to represent its object as having any particular colour.

Under the terms of (iii), an experience can represent its object as red only by representing it as disposed to produce visual experiences that represent it as red. The problem here is that the experiences that the object is thus represented as disposed to produce must themselves be represented as experiences that represent the object as red, rather than some other colour—lest the object be represented as disposed to appear something other than red. Yet these experiences can be represented as representing the object as red only if they are represented as representing it as disposed to produce experiences that represent it as red. And here the circle gets vicious. In order for an object to appear red rather than blue, it must appear disposed to appear red, rather than disposed to appear blue; and in order to appear disposed to appear red, rather than disposed to appear blue, it must appear disposed to appear disposed to appear red, rather than disposed to appear disposed to appear blue; and so on. Until this regress reaches an end, the object's appearance will not amount to the appearance of one colour rather than another. Unfortunately, the regress never reaches an end.

One might attempt to staunch the regress simply by invoking the relevant colour by name. 'To appear red', one might say, 'is to appear disposed to appear red—and that's the end of the matter.' 'Of course,' one might continue, 'if you don't already know what red is, then you haven't understood what I've said. But that doesn't impugn the truth of my assertion, nor its informativeness, since you have learned at least that the property things appear to have in appearing red is a disposition to produce appearances.'

This reply cannot succeed. Staunching the regress with the word 'red' can work, but only if the word is not understood in the sense defined in biconditional (iii). We readily agree that red things do appear disposed to look red, and that they appear so without requiring the viewer to run an endless gamut of visual appearances. But what they appear disposed to do is to give the appearance of being red in a non-dispositional sense—the appearance of having a non-dispositional redness. And the way they appear disposed to give that appearance is usually just by giving it—that is, by looking non-dispositionally red.[10] Similarly, objects can appear disposed to look square just by looking square, but only because they look square intrinsically and categorically.

As we have seen, however, the dispositionalist cannot admit an intrinsic and categorical sense of the word 'red' into his formulation. For then he would have to acknowledge that objects appear disposed to look red, and do look red, in a non-dispositional sense. And he would then have acknowledged that an object's being disposed to look red does not guarantee that it is as it looks, in respect to colour, since the redness that it is thereby disposed to give the appearance of having is a different property from the disposition that it admittedly has. The dispositionalist must therefore say that although an object looks disposed to look red just by looking red, this looking red does not involve looking anything except disposed to look red. *In short, the object must look disposed to look a particular way without there being any particular way that it looks, or looks disposed to look, other than so disposed.* And that is why the vicious regress gets started.

Note, once again, that the problem created by the regress is not that we are unable to learn what red is from the statement that red is a disposition to look red. The problem is that, under the terms of that statement, the subject of visual experience cannot see what colour an object has. For he cannot see the particular colour of an object except by seeing the particular way the object tends to appear; and he cannot see the way it tends to appear except by seeing the way it tends to appear as tending to appear; and so on, ad infinitum. To be sure, a person can see all of these things if he can just see the object as having a colour, to begin with; but under the terms of dispositionalism, he cannot begin to see the object as having a colour except by seeing these dispositions; and so he can never begin to see it as having a colour at all.[11]

---

[10] See McDowell 1985, p. 112: 'What would one expect it to be like to experience something's being such as to look red, if not to experience the thing in question (in the right circumstances) as looking, precisely, red?'

[11] When McDowell discusses dispositionalism about the comic, in his 1985, he tries to make the circularity of the theory into a virtue, by arguing that it blocks a projectivist account of humour.

The Second Version of Content-dispositionalism

The only way to save dispositionalism from its fatal circularity is to ensure that the disposition with which a colour property is identified is not a disposition to give the appearance of having that very property. Christopher Peacocke has attempted to modify dispositionalism in just this way.

According to Peacocke, the property that an object is seen as having when it looks red should be identified as a disposition, not to appear red, but rather to appear in a portion of the visual field having an intrinsic property that Peacocke calls red'. Let us call these portions of the visual field *red' patches*. We can then say that looking red, according to Peacocke, is looking disposed to be represented in red' patches under standard conditions—an appearance that can be accomplished by being represented in a red' patch under recognizably standard conditions, of course, but also in other ways as well, such as by being represented in an orange' patch when illuminated by a yellow-looking light. The upshot, in any case, is that objects often are as they look when they look red, because they both look and are just this: disposed to be represented in red' patches under standard conditions.

Peacocke's qualified dispositionalism eliminates circular experiential contents because it says that appearing to have a colour property is appearing disposed to present appearances characterized, not in terms of that very property, but rather in terms of a different quality, a 'primed' colour. Peacocke can also account for the role of red in the experience of seeing a red after-image, because he can say that the experience consists in a red' patch represented, in the content of one's experience, as a figment of one's eyes.

Peacocke's qualified dispositionalism differs from pure dispositionalism in that it introduces a visual field modified by qualities that—to judge by their names, at least—constitute a species of colour. Peacocke thus abandons a significant feature of the theories that we have examined thus far. Those theories assume that visual experience involves colour only to the extent of representing it. They analyse an experience of red as an experience with the content that something is red—an experience that refers to redness. Because the role of colour in experience is restricted by these theories to that of an element in the intentional content of experience, we shall call the theories intentionalist.

Peacocke's theory is not intentionalist, because it says that visual experience involves colour (that is, primed colour) as a property inhering in the visual field, and not just as a property represented in the content of that experience. We have two points to make about Peacocke's anti-intentionalism. We shall first argue that Peacocke is right to abandon intentionalism and to introduce

He says, 'The suggestion is that there is no self-contained prior fact of our subjective lives that could enter into a projective account of the relevant way of thinking'—that is, no independently specifiable subjective response that we can be described as projecting onto the world (p. 6). We would argue that the same problem afflicts, not just a projectivist account of the comical, but our very perceptions of things as comical, as McDowell interprets those perceptions.

colours as intrinsic properties of the visual field. But we shall then argue that, having introduced such properties, Peacocke is wrong to remain a dispositionalist about the colours that visual experience attributes to external objects. Peacocke's modification of dispositionalism is unstable, we believe, in that it ultimately undermines dispositionalism altogether.

The Case Against Intentionalism

Peacocke has argued elsewhere, and on independent grounds, for the need to speak about a sensory field modified by intrinsic sensational qualities.[12] We should like to add some arguments of our own.

Our first argument rests on the possibility, noted above, of seeing an after-image without illusion. Consider such an experience, in which an after-image appears to you *as* an after-image—say, as a red spot obscuring the face of a person who has just taken your photograph. Since you suffer no illusion about the nature of this spot, you do not see it as something actually existing in front of the photographer's face. In what sense, then, do you see it as occupying that location at all? The answer is that you see it as merely appearing in that location: you see it as a spot that appears in front of the photographer's face without actually being there. Now, in order for you to see the spot as appearing somewhere, it must certainly appear there. Yet it must appear there without appearing actually to be there, since you are not under the illusion that the spot actually occupies the space in question. The after-image must therefore be described as *appearing in* a location without *appearing to be in* that location; and this description is not within the capacity of any intentionalist theory. An intentionalist theory will analyse the visual appearance of location as the attribution of location to something, in the intentional content of your visual experience. But the intentional content of your visual experience is that there is nothing at all between you and the photographer.

The only way to describe the after-image as appearing in front of the photographer without appearing to be in front of the photographer is to talk about the location that it occupies in your visual field. In your visual field, we say, the after-image overlays the image of the photographer's face, but nothing is thereby represented as actually being over the photographer's face. The after-image is thus like a coffee-stain on a picture, a feature that occupies a location on the picture without representing anything as occupying any location. Similarly, an adequate description of the after-image requires reference to two kinds of location—location as an intrinsic property of features in the visual field, and location as represented by the resulting visual experience.

One might think that this argument cannot be applied to the after-image's colour, since you may see the after-image not only as appearing red but also as actually *being* red. But then intentionalism will have trouble explaining what

---

[12] Peacocke 1983, ch. 1. Other arguments are provided by Sydney Shoemaker in his 1990.

exactly your experience represents as being red, given that the experience is veridical. Your experience cannot represent some external object as being red, on pain of being illusory. And if it represents an image as being red, then its truth will entail that colour can enter into visual experience as an intrinsic property of images, which is precisely what intentionalism denies. Hence there would seem to be nothing that the experience can veridically represent as being red, according to intentionalism. And if the experience represented something as merely appearing red, then our foregoing argument would once again apply. For how could you have a veridical experience that something appeared red unless something so appeared? And if something did so appear, it would have to appear *to be* red, according to intentionalism, which would be an illusion in the present case, unless images can be red.[13]

There are other, more familiar cases that refute intentionalism in a similar way. These, too, are cases in which something is seen without being represented in the content of experience as intentionalism would require. If you press the side of one eyeball, you can see this line of type twice without seeing the page as bearing two identical lines of type. Indeed, you cannot even force the resulting experience into representing the existence of two lines, even if you try. Similarly, you can see nearby objects double by focusing on distant objects behind them, and yet you cannot get yourself to see the number of nearby objects as doubling. And by unfocusing your eyes, you can see objects blurrily without being able to see them as being blurry. None of these experiences can be adequately described solely in terms of their intentional content. Their description requires reference to areas of colour in a visual field, areas that split in two or become blurry without anything's being represented to you as doing so.

The Case Against Peacocke's Dispositionalism

We therefore endorse Peacocke's decision to posit a visual field with intrinsic sensational qualities. What we question, however, is his insistence that the colours of external objects are still seen as dispositions. We believe that once one posits a visual field bearing properties such as red', one is eventually forced to conclude that objects presented in red' areas of that field are seen as red' rather than as possessing some other, dispositional quality.

The reason is that visual experience does not ordinarily distinguish between qualities of a 'field' representing objects and qualities of the objects represented. Visual experience is ordinarily naïvely realistic, in the sense that the qualities presented in it are represented as qualities of the external world. According to

---

[13] Intentionalism cannot characterize the experience in question as being similar to, or representing itself as being similar to, the experience you have when you see redness as attaching to a material object. Such an experience would have a different content from the one you are now having, and so it would not be like your present experience in any respect that the intentionalist can identify. Of course, once we abandon intentionalism, we can say that your present experience and the experience of seeing a red material object are alike in their intrinsic qualities. But such qualities are denied by intentionalism.

Peacocke, however, the aspects of visual experience in which external objects are represented have qualities—and, indeed, colour qualities—that are never attributed by that experience to the objects themselves. Peacocke thus gets the phenomenology of visual experience wrong.

Try to imagine what visual experience would be like if it conformed to Peacocke's model. The visual field would have the sensational qualities red', blue', green', and so on, and would represent various external objects; but it would not represent those qualities as belonging to those objects. Where, then, would the qualities appear to reside? What would they appear to be qualities of? They would have to float free, as if detached from the objects being represented, so as not to appear as qualities of those objects. Or perhaps they would seem to lie on top of the objects, overlaying the objects' own colours—which would be seen, remember, as different, dispositional qualities. The result, in any case, would be that visual experience was not naïvely realistic, but quite the reverse. A veil of colours—like Locke's veil of ideas—would seem to stand before or lie upon the scene being viewed. But one does not continually see this veil of colours; and so visual experience must not conform to Peacocke's model.

The failure of Peacocke's model to fit the experience of colour can be seen most clearly, perhaps, in the fact that the model is a perfect fit for the experience of pain. When one pricks one's finger on a pin, pain appears in one's tactual 'field', but it is not perceived as a quality of the pin. Rather, the pin is perceived as having a disposition—namely, the disposition to cause pain, and hence to be presented in areas of the tactual field bearing the quality currently being felt. The ordinary way of describing the experience would be to say that by having an experience of pain one perceives the pin as disposed to cause pain. But this description can easily be transposed into Peacocke's notation, in which it would say that one perceives the pin as painful by perceiving it in a painful' patch.

Peacocke's theory is thus ideally suited to describing the experience of pain. Yet the experience of pain is notoriously different from the experience of colour. Indeed, the difference between pain experience and colour experience has always been accepted as an uncontroversial datum for the discussion of secondary qualities. The difference is precisely that pain is never felt as a quality of its apparent cause, whereas colour usually is: the pain caused by the pin is felt as being in the finger, whereas the pin's silvery colour is seen as being in the pin. Hence Peacocke's model, which fits pain experience so well, cannot simultaneously fit colour experience. When applied to colour, that model would suggest that the experience of seeing a rose contains both the flower's redness and the visual field's red'ness, just as the experience of being pricked by a pin contains both the pin's painfulness and the finger's pain.

One might respond that our objection to Peacocke is undermined by an example that we previously deployed against intentionalism. For we have already argued that seeing something blurrily involves a blurriness that is not attributed to what is seen. Have we not already admitted, then, that visual experience contains qualities that it does not attribute to objects, and hence that it is not always naïve?

We have indeed admitted that visual experience is not always naïve, but that admission is consistent with the claim that visual experience is naïve most of the time, or in most respects. Seeing blurrily is, after all, unusual, in that it involves seeing, as it were, 'through' a blurry image to a visibly sharp-edged object. It is an experience in which the visual field becomes more salient than usual, precisely because its blurriness is not referred to the objects seen. Peacocke's theory does manage to improve on intentionalism by explaining how one can blurrily see an object as being sharp-edged. But Peacocke goes too far, by analysing all visual experience on the model of this unusual case. He says that every perception of colour has this dual structure, in which the colours that are attributed to objects are seen through colour qualities that are not attributed to them. According to Peacocke, then, the redness of external objects is always seen through a haze of red'ness, just as the sharp edges of an object are sometimes seen through a blur.

THE PROJECTIVIST ACCOUNT

We have argued, first, that visual experience cannot be adequately described without reference to intrinsic sensational qualities of a visual field; and second, that intrinsic colour properties of the visual field are the properties that objects are seen as having when they look coloured. We have thus arrived at the traditional projectivist account of colour experience. The projection posited by this account has the result that the intentional content of visual experience represents external objects as possessing colour qualities that belong, in fact, only to regions of the visual field. By 'gilding or staining all natural objects with the colours borrowed from internal sentiment', as Hume puts it, the mind 'raises in a manner a new creation'.[14]

Talk of a visual field and its intrinsic qualities may seem to involve a commitment to the existence of mental particulars. But we regard the projectivist view of colour experience as potentially neutral on the metaphysics of mind. The visual field may or may not supervene on neural structures; it may or may not be describable by means of adverbs modifying mental verbs rather than by substantives denoting mental items. All we claim is that, no matter how the metaphysical underpinnings of sense experience are ultimately arranged, they must support reference to colours as qualities of a visual field that are represented as inhering in external objects.

---

[14] Hume 1975, Appendix 1. Of course, this passage is literally about the projection of value, not colour. But surely, Hume chose colour as his metaphor for value, in this context, because he regarded projectivism about colour as an intuitively natural view.

Pros and Cons

The projectivist account of colour experience is, in our opinion, the one that occurs naturally to anyone who learns the rudimentary facts about light and vision. It seemed obvious to Galileo, as it did to Newton and Locke as well.[15]

The Principle of Charity as Applied to Visual Experience

Given the intuitive appeal that the projectivist account holds for anyone who knows about the nature of light and vision, the question arises why some philosophers go to such lengths in defence of alternative accounts. The reason, as we have suggested, is that these philosophers are moved by a perceived requirement of charity in the interpretation of representational content. External objects do not actually have the colour qualities that projectivism interprets visual experience as attributing to them. The projectivist account thus interprets visual experience as having a content that would be systematically erroneous. And it therefore strikes some as violating a basic principle of interpretation.

In our opinion, however, applying a principle of charity in this way would be questionable, for two reasons. First, a principle of charity applies primarily to a language, or other representational system, *taken as a whole*; and so, when rightly understood, such a principle is perfectly consistent with the possibility that large regions of the language should rest on widespread and systematic error. Second, what a principle of charity recommends is, not that we should avoid attributing widespread error at all costs, but that we should avoid attributing inexplicable error. And the error that a Galilean view of colour entails is not inexplicable; it can be explained precisely as an error committed through projection—that is, through the misrepresentation of qualities that inhere in the visual field as inhering in the objects that are therein represented.

We therefore think that the usual motives for resisting projectivism are misguided, on quite general grounds. Nevertheless, some philosophers have criticized projectivism for being uncharitable to visual experience in rather specific ways; and we think that these more specific charges deserve to be answered. We devote the remainder of this section to three of these criticisms.

Colours as *Visibilia*

One argument in this vein comes from the dispositionalists. They contend that failing to see colours as dispositions to look coloured would entail failing to see them as essentially connected with vision, as *visibilia*.[16] But nothing can be

---

[15] Newton 1979, Book I, part i; Locke 1975, Book II, ch. viii. Jonathan Bennett has interpreted Locke as a dispositionalist about colour (1971, ch. iv). But the textual evidence is overwhelming that Locke believed colour experience to be guilty of an error, and a projectivist error, at that. Locke was a dispositionalist, in our opinion, only about the properties of objects that actually cause colour experience, not about the properties that such experience represents objects as having.

[16] See McDowell 1985, pp. 113–15.

seen as a colour without being seen as essentially connected with vision, the dispositionalists continue, and so colours cannot possibly be misrepresented in visual experience.

This version of the argument from charity relies on the assumption that the only way to see colours as essentially connected with vision is to see them as dispositions to cause visual perceptions. We reply that colours can be seen as essentially connected with vision without being seen as dispositions at all. In particular, they can be seen as essentially connected with vision if they are seen as the qualities directly presented in visual experience, arrayed on the visual field. The experience of seeing red is unmistakably an experience of a quality that could not be experienced other than visually. Consequently, red is seen as essentially visual without being seen as a disposition to cause visual perceptions.

A Berkeleyan Objection

Another version of the argument from charity begins with the premiss that qualities of the visual field cannot be imagined except as being seen, and hence that they cannot be imagined as intrinsic and categorical qualities of material objects—qualities belonging to the objects in themselves, whether they are seen or not. This premiss is taken to imply that visual experience cannot possibly commit the error of representing colour *qualia* to be intrinsic and categorical qualities of objects, as projectivism charges, simply because it cannot represent the unimaginable.[17]

Our reply to this argument is that its premiss is false. The colour qualities that modify the visual field can indeed be imagined as unseen. Of course, one cannot imagine a colour as unseen while instantiated in the visual field itself, since to imagine a quality as in the visual field is to imagine that it is seen. But one can imagine a colour as instantiated elsewhere without being seen—by imagining, for example, an ordinary red-rubber ball, whose surface is red not only on the visible, near side but also on the unseen, far side.

What exponents of the present objection are pointing out, of course, is that one cannot imagine the unseen side of the ball as red by means of a mental image whose features include a red area corresponding to that side of the ball. Here they may be correct.[18] To form an image containing a coloured area corresponding to the unseen side of the ball would be to imagine seeing it, and hence not to imagine it as unseen, after all. But one's imagination is not confined to representing things by means of corresponding features in one's mental image.

---

[17] See Evans 1980, pp. 99–100. Berkeley carried this argument farther, by claiming that unperceived qualities, being unimaginable, were also inconceivable and hence impossible. Berkeley's willingness to equate imagination with conception was due to his theory of ideas, which equated concepts with mental pictures.

[18] We grant this point for the sake of argument; but we think that it, too, underestimates the representational powers of the imagination. For surely one can form a mental image that contains a 'cut-away' view, showing how the far side of the ball looks while implying that it is, in reality, unseen.

If it were, then one would be unable to imagine any object as being both opaque and three-dimensional; one would be reduced to imagining the world as a maze of backless façades, all artfully turned in one's direction. In actuality, one imagines the world as comprising objects in the round, whose unseen sides are represented in one's image indirectly and, so to speak, by implication. One can therefore imagine unseen colours, despite limitations on how one's imagination can represent them.

Visual experience has the same representational capacity, despite similar limitations. That is, although one cannot visually catch colours in the act of being unseen, one nevertheless sees the world as containing unseen colours—on the far sides of objects, in areas obscured by shadow, and so on. Just as one sees one's fellow human beings as having hair at the back, skin up their sleeves, and eyeballs even when they blink, so one sees them as possessing these unseen features in their usual colours. Thus, one has no trouble seeing colours as intrinsic and categorical properties that exist even when unseen.

Can Experience Commit Category Errors?

A third version of the argument from charity alleges that according to projectivism, visual experience commits not just a mistake but a *category* mistake, by representing external, material objects as having properties that can occur only within the mental realm.[19] Such a mistake is thought too gross for visual experience to commit.

It is not clear whether it is a necessary or merely contingent fact that external objects do not possess the sorts of property we understand colours to be; hence, it is not clear whether the mistake projectivism attributes to visual experience is categorial or merely systematic. But even if it were a category mistake, why should this necessarily be considered a difficulty for projectivism?

The assumption underlying the objection is that it is somehow extremely difficult to see how experience could commit a category mistake. But as the following remark of Wittgenstein suggests, just the opposite seems true.

Let us imagine the following: The surfaces of the things around us (stones, plants, etc.) have patches and regions which produce pain in our skin when we touch them. (Perhaps through the chemical composition of these surfaces. But we need not know that.) In this case we should speak of pain-patches just as at present we speak of red patches.[20]

In the normal experience of pain, pain is not perceived as a quality of its cause. As Wittgenstein remarks, however, this seems to be thanks only to the fact that the normal causes of pain constitute such a heterogeneous class. Were pain to be caused solely, say, by certain specific patches on the surfaces of plants, we

---

[19] See Shoemaker 1990, p. 10.

[20] *Philosophical Investigations*, section 312. We do not necessarily claim that the use to which we should like to put this passage coincides with Wittgenstein's.

might well experience pain as being in the plant, much as we now experience its colour. Far from being unimaginable, then, it would seem that nothing but a purely contingent fact about our experience of pain stands between us and a category mistake just like the one that projectivism portrays us as committing about colour.

INTERPRETING COLOUR DISCOURSE

Thus far we have discussed colour concepts as they are exercised in the representational content of colour experience. Let us turn, somewhat more briefly, to the content of ordinary discourse about colour.

We assume that ordinary discourse about colour reports the contents of visual experience. The most plausible hypothesis about what someone means when he calls something red, in an everyday context, is that he is reporting what his eyes tell him. And according to our account, what his eyes tell him is that the thing has a particular visual quality, a quality that does not actually inhere in external objects but is a quality of his visual field. We therefore conclude that when someone calls something red, in an everyday context, he is asserting a falsehood. Indeed, our account of colour experience, when joined with the plausible hypothesis that colour discourse reports the contents of colour experience, yields the consequence that all statements attributing colours to external objects are false.

One would be justified in wondering how we can accept this consequence, for two related reasons. First, we will clearly want to retain a distinction between 'correct' and 'incorrect' colour judgements, distinguishing between the judgement that a fire-hydrant is blue and the judgement that it is red. And it seems a serious question what point we error theorists could see in such a distinction. Second, it seems perfectly obvious that colour discourse will continue to play an indispensable role in our everyday cognitive transactions. Yet how are we error theorists to explain this indispensability, consistently with our claim that the discourse in question is systematically false? We shall begin with the second question.

The Point of Colour-talk

Consider one of the many harmless falsehoods that we tolerate in everyday discourse: the statement that the sun rises. When someone says that the sun rises, his remark has the same content as the visual experience that one has when watching the horizon at an appropriately early hour. That is, the sun actually looks like it is moving, and that the sun moves in this manner is what most people mean when talking about sunrise. So interpreted, of course, talk about sunrise is systematically false. When someone says that the sun rises, he is wrong; and he usually knows that he is wrong, but he says it anyway. Why?

When one understands why talk about sunrise is false, one also understands that its falsity makes no difference in everyday life. We do not mean that nothing in everyday life would, in fact, be different if the sun revolved around the earth, as it seems to. No doubt, the tides and the phases of the moon and various other phenomena would be other than they actually are. But those differences are not missed by the ordinary person, who does not know and has no reason to consider precisely how the tides and phases of the moon are generated. Consequently, someone who has a normal background of beliefs will find no evidence in everyday life to controvert his belief that the sun revolves around the earth. That belief will not mislead him about any of the phenomena he normally encounters; and it will in fact give him correct guidance about many such phenomena. His judgements about the time of day, the weather, the best placement of crops, the location of glare and of shadows at noon, will all be correct despite being derived from premises about a stationary earth and a revolving sun. Indeed, he is likely to derive more true conclusions from his belief in a revolving sun than he would from a belief in a rotating earth, for the simple reason that the consequences for earthlings of the former state of affairs are easier to visualize than those of the latter, even though those consequences would be the same, for everyday purposes. Talking about horizon-fall rather than sunrise would thus be downright misleading, even though it would be more truthful. Only an undue fascination with the truth could lead someone to reform ordinary discourse about the sun.

Talk about colours is just like talk about sunrise in these respects. That is, life goes on as if objects are coloured in the way that they appear to be. Experience refutes few if any of the conclusions derived from beliefs about objects' colours; and many true conclusions are derived from such beliefs. Most of those true conclusions, of course, are about how objects will look to various people under various circumstances. And these conclusions are extremely useful in everyday life, since one's ability to communicate with others and with one's future selves about the external world depends on the ability to describe how various parts of that world appear. The point is that such conclusions are more easily and more reliably drawn from the familiar false picture of colours than they would be—by the ordinary person, at least—from the true picture of wavelengths and spectral-reflectance curves. Why, then, should one replace such a useful false picture with a true but misleading one?

Correct vs. Incorrect Colour-talk

The case of colour differs from that of sunrise in one important respect. The sun never seems to do anything but move in a regular arc across the heavens, whereas objects often seem to have different colours in different circumstances. The ordinary speaker therefore finds himself drawing a distinction between the colours that objects really have and the colours that they only seem to have on some occasions. How can we countenance this distinction between real and illusory colours, given that our theory brands all colours as illusory?[21]

---

[21] We should point out that a similar question will confront those who adopt a dispositionalist interpretation of colour discourse. For according to dispositionalism, the colours of objects are their

The answer is that classifying an object by the colour that it appears to have under so-called standard conditions is the most reliable and most informative way of classifying it, for the purposes of drawing useful conclusions about how the object will appear under conditions of any kind. Obviously, classifying an object by how it appears in the dark is not at all informative, since all objects appear equally black in the dark, even though they appear to have different colours in the light. Hence one can extrapolate an object's appearance in the dark from its appearance in the light, but not vice versa. The same is true—though to a lesser degree, of course—for other non-standard conditions. For instance, distance tends to lend a similar appearance to objects that look different at close range; coloured light tends to lend a similar appearance to objects that look different in daylight; and so on. The common-sense calculus of colour addition and subtraction therefore enables one to infer an object's appearance under non-standard conditions from its appearance under standard conditions, but not its appearance under standard conditions from that under non-standard conditions. That is why one set of conditions, and the accompanying colour-illusion, are privileged in everyday life.

There are notable exceptions to our claim about the varying informativeness of various colour appearances. But these exceptions actually support our explanation of why particular colour-illusions are privileged in ordinary discourse, because consideration of them leads the ordinary speaker to reconsider the distinction between true and illusory colour.

Some pairs of objects that appear to have the same colour in daylight—say, green—can appear to have different colours under incandescent lighting, where one may appear green and the other brown.[22] In these cases, how an object appears in daylight is not an indication of how it will appear under other less standard conditions.

Yet in these cases, one begins to wonder whether the object has a 'true' or standard colour at all. If an object's apparent colour does not vary, from one set of conditions to the next, in the same way as the apparent colour of objects that share its apparent colour in daylight, then one is tempted to say that the object does not have any one colour at all. Consider the object that looks green in daylight but brown in incandescent light, where most other objects that look

dispositions to present the appearance of colour; and objects are disposed to present the appearance of different colours under different circumstances. Corresponding to every colour that an object ever appears or would appear to have, there is a disposition of the object to give that appearance under the circumstances then prevailing. Now, dispositionalism denominates only one of these innumerable dispositions as the object's real colour, and it does so by defining the object's colour to be that disposition which is manifested under conditions specified as standard. But surely, dispositionalism should have to justify its selection of dispositions—or, what amounts to the same thing, its selection of standard conditions. For if colour is nothing but a disposition to produce colour appearances, one wants to know why a particular disposition to produce colour appearances should be privileged over other such dispositions. And this is, in effect, the same question as why one colour-illusion should be privileged over other colour-illusions, given the assumption that all colours are illusory.

²² This phenomenon is called metamerism. See Hardin 1988, pp. 28, 45 ff.

green in daylight still look green. Is the object really green? really brown? Does it have any single 'real' colour at all?[23] Here intuitions diverge and ultimately give out. The reason, we think, is precisely that the common-sense notion of an object's real colour presupposes that it is the one apparent colour from which all its other apparent colours can be extrapolated, by fairly familiar rules of colour mixing. When that assumption is threatened, so is the notion of real colour.[24]

[23] People who spend much time considering these cases have been known to give up the notion of true colour entirely. We once asked a scientist who performs research on colour vision why people think that most opaque objects have a real colour. His answer was, 'They do? How odd.'

[24] We have benefited from discussing the material in this paper with: David Hills, Mark Johnston, Sydney Shoemaker, Larry Sklar, and participants in a seminar that we taught at the University of Michigan in the fall of 1987. Our research has been supported by Rackham Faculty Fellowships from the University of Michigan.

14 *Physicalist Theories of Color*

With J. David Velleman.

THE PROBLEM OF COLOR REALISM

The dispute between realists about color and anti-realists is actually a dispute about the nature of color properties. The disputants do not disagree over what material objects are like. Rather, they disagree over whether any of the uncontroversial facts about material objects—their powers to cause visual experiences, their dispositions to reflect incident light, their atomic makeup, and so on—amount to their having colors. The disagreement is thus about which properties colors are and, in particular, whether colors are any of the properties in a particular set that is acknowledged on both sides to exhaust the properties of material objects.

In a previous paper we discussed at length one attempt to identify colors with particular properties of material objects—namely, with their dispositions to cause visual experiences.[1] Here we shall discuss a different and perhaps more influential version of realism, which says that the colors of material objects are microphysical properties of their surfaces.[2] We shall call this theory physicalism about color (physicalism, for short). In order to evaluate this theory, however, we shall first have to clarify some methodological issues. Our hope is that we can bring some further clarity to the question of color realism, whether or not we succeed in our critique of the physicalists' answer.

Metaphysics and Semantics

To say that the question of color realism is really about the nature of color properties is not yet to define the question sufficiently. One is tempted to ask, Which are the properties whose nature is at issue?

---

[1] Boghossian and Velleman 1989 (this volume, Chapter 13).
[2] Our earlier paper contained a brief discussion of this theory, pp. 82–3 (this volume, pp. 294–5). The present paper can be regarded as expanding on that passage.

Of course, the latter question may seem like an invitation to beg the former. For in order to say which properties are at issue in the debate about the nature of colors, one would have to say which properties colors are—which would seem to require settling the debate before defining it. How, indeed, can one ever debate the nature of a property? Until one knows which property is at issue, the debate cannot get started; but as soon as one knows which property is at issue, it would seem, the debate is over.

Well, not quite. One can pick out a property by means of a contingent fact about it. And one can thereby specify the property whose nature is to be debated without preempting the debate. Such indirect specifications are what motivate questions about the nature of properties. One knows or suspects that there is a property playing a particular role, say, or occupying a particular relation, and one wants to know which property it is, given that playing the role or occupying the relation isn't the property in question.

The role in which colors command attention, of course, is their role as the properties attributed to objects by a particular aspect of visual experience. They are the properties that objects appear to have when they look colored. What philosophers want to know is whether the properties that objects thus appear to have are among the ones that they are generally agreed to have in reality.

Yet if the question is whether some agreed-upon set of properties includes the ones that objects appear to have in looking colored, then it is partly a question about the content of visual appearances. When philosophers ask whether colors are real, they are asking whether any of the properties acknowledged to be real are the ones attributed to an object by the experience of its looking colored; and so they are asking, in part, which properties are represented in that experience—which is a question of its content.

What is Looking Colored?

The foregoing attempt to define which properties are at issue in the question of color realism may seem viciously circular. For we identified colors as the properties that things appear to have when they look colored; and how can this description help to pick out the relevant properties? It specifies the properties in terms of their being represented in a particular kind of experience, but then it seems to specify the relevant kind of experience in terms of its representing those properties. Which properties objects appear to have in looking colored depends on what counts as looking colored, which would seem to depend, in turn, on which properties colors are—which is precisely what was to be defined.

This problem is not insuperable, however. The phrase "looks colored" and its determinate cousins—"looks red," "looks blue," and so forth—have a referential as well as an attributive use. That is, one learns to associate these phrases directly with visual experiences that are introspectively recognizable as similar in kind to paradigm instances. Paradigm cases of looking red fix a reference for the phrase "looks red," which then refers to all introspectively similar experiences. We can therefore speak of something's looking red and rely on the reader to know which kind of visual experience we mean, without our having to specify which property red is.[3] There is no circularity, then, in identifying red as the property attributed to objects by their looking red and, more generally, in identifying colors as the properties attributed to objects by their looking colored.[4]

Color Experience vs. Color Discourse

One might think that the references we have stipulated here are simply the references that color terms have anyway, in ordinary discourse. Surely, words like "red" and "blue" are sensory terms, designed to report what is seen. One may therefore feel entitled to presuppose that the term "red," as used in ordinary discourse, already denotes the property that things appear to have when they look red.

Yet the validity of this presupposition may depend on the answer to the question of color realism. For whether the ordinary term "red" always expresses the property that things appear to have in looking red may depend on whether

[3] These remarks are intended to apply exclusively to expressions of the form "looks colored." Expressions of the form "seeing something as colored," "appearing to be colored," and so forth, will be interpreted compositionally.

Note that the problem discussed in this passage doesn't preclude "looks red" from *meaning* "visually appears to be red," in the sense of contributing that content to the statements in which it is used. If the kind of experience denoted by "looks red" is the kind that represents its object as red, then the phrase may indeed be used to introduce the content "visually appears to be red." The problem discussed here merely restricts the way in which the phrase may acquire its reference to that kind of experience. (See note 17, below.)

[4] Here a further complication arises. We assume in the text that there is a single property represented by all or most instances of looking red. There will certainly be such a property if the way in which experiences qualify as instances of something's looking red is by representing the same property as the paradigm instance. In that case, the paradigm of something's looking red will define a kind of experience whose instances attribute the same property to their objects, and so all instances of looking red will represent the same property. The name "red" can then be fixed by the phrase "the property attributed to an object by its looking red."

But what if kinds of visual appearance are individuated differently? In that case, the kind of appearance defined by a paradigm case of something's looking red may include appearances representing different properties; and so there may be no property represented in most instances of looking red. Our attempt to attach the name "red" to the property attributed to an object by its looking red will consequently fail, since there will be no single property predominantly satisfying that description.

Physicalists who regard this outcome as a live possibility sometimes think that the reference of "red" cannot be fixed to a single property; and so they make a definition out of the description that we have treated as a reference-fixer. That is, they treat "red" as synonymous with the phrase "the property attributed to an object by its looking red," and they expect the term, so defined, to denote different properties in different circumstances (see Jackson and Pargetter 1987).

These philosophers may find our usage strange, as we do theirs. But our linguistic differences with them will not prevent us from engaging them in argument. For they believe that red is a microphysical property in some circumstances, in the sense that a microphysical property is the one attributed to an object, in those circumstances, by its looking red. And we shall argue that an object's looking red never represents it as having a microphysical property, under any circumstances at all. Our arguments will therefore address their view, though not necessarily in their terms.

For a related problem, see the following note.

that appearance is veridical or illusory. Suppose that an error theory of color experience is correct, in that the property that things appear to have when they look red is a property that they do not (and perhaps could not) have. In that case, the meaning of "red" in ordinary discourse will be subject to conflicting pressures. The term may still be used to express the property that objects are seen as having when they look red. Yet statements calling objects red in that sense will be systematically false, even if such statements tend to be made, and to garner assent, in reference to objects that have some physical property in common. In the interest of saying what's true, rather than what merely appears true, speakers may then be inclined to shade the meaning of "red" toward denoting whatever property is distinctive of red-looking objects.[5] The pressure towards speaking the truth will thus conflict with the pressure towards reporting the testimony of vision. How the meaning of "red" will fare under these conflicting pressures is hard to predict; it may even break apart, yielding two senses of the term, one to express the content of color experience and another to denote the property tracked by color attributions.

We are not here proposing or defending such an account of color language. We are merely pointing it out as a possibility and suggesting that this possibility shouldn't be excluded at the outset of inquiry about color. To assume that color terms denote the properties represented in color experience is to assume that terms used to attribute those properties to objects wouldn't come under pressure from the systematic falsity of such attributions—something that may or may not turn out to be the case but shouldn't be assumed at the outset. One should begin as an agnostic about whether color terms ordinarily denote the properties that are represented in color experience. If they are to be used in a debate about those properties, their reference to them must be explicitly stipulated.

---

[5] Some may contend that if there is a physical property that's distinctive of red-looking objects, then it will inevitably be the property that's attributed to objects by their looking red. But this contention simply assumes that the content of color experience is determined in a way that's conducive to the truth of physicalism about color—which should not be assumed from the outset. We shall consider at length whether the content of color experience is determined in this way. At the moment we are merely pointing out that until one has ascertained how colors are visually represented, one must allow for the possibility that their visual representation may have a content that is less useful for people to put into words than other facts correlated with color perception. One must therefore allow for the possibility that the content of color talk may diverge from that of color experience.

Some may argue that even if color experiences somehow represented properties other than external properties correlated with them, they would *also* represent those external properties, by virtue of the correlation. In that case, color experiences would attribute two different properties to their objects, and our identification of colors as the properties attributed to objects by color experiences would be ambiguous. (We owe this suggestion to Sydney Shoemaker.)

What is being imagined here—if it is indeed imaginable—is that visual experiences representing one property would be correlated with another property and would thereby come to indicate it, much as a Cretan's saying "It's raining" may come to indicate sunshine. If visual experiences representing one property could thus come to indicate another, the former property would still be identifiable as the one that they represented *in the first instance* (just as rain would be identifiable as what the Cretan was reporting in the first instance). Our identification of colors as the properties attributed to objects by their looking colored could therefore be easily disambiguated.

VERSIONS OF PHYSICALISM

If physicalism is to settle the debate over color realism, it must be formulated as a thesis about the properties at issue in that debate. When the physicalist says that colors are microphysical properties, he must mean that microphysical properties are the ones attributed to objects by their looking colored. Otherwise, his claim will not succeed in attaching the uncontroversial reality of microphysical properties to the properties whose reality is in question—that is, the properties represented in color experience. Physicalism must therefore be, in part, a thesis about which properties color experience represents.

The Naive Objection

When the physicalist thesis is so interpreted, however, it tends to elicit the following, naive objection. The microphysical properties of an object are invisible and hence cannot be what is represented when the object looks colored. One can tell an object's color just by looking at it, but one cannot tell anything about its molecular structure—nor, indeed, that it has such a structure—without the aid of instruments or experimentation. How can colors, which are visible, be microphysical properties, which are not?

Physicalists regard this objection as obviously mistaken, although different physicalists regard it as committing different mistakes. A particular physicalist's response to the objection will be conditioned by his brand of physicalism, on the one hand, and his conception of visual representation, on the other. We therefore turn our attention, in the next two sections, to these potential differences among proponents of physicalism.

Colors vs. Ways of Being Colored

The claim that red is a microphysical property can express either of two very different theses. On the one hand, the claim may state a strict identity between properties. In that case, it means that having a particular microphysical configuration is one and the same property as being red. On the other hand, the claim may mean that having this microphysical configuration is a way of being red and, in particular, the way in which things are red in actuality. In that case, the relation drawn between these properties is not identity. Rather, red is envisioned as a higher-order property—the property of having some (lower-order) property satisfying particular conditions—and the microphysical configuration is envisioned as a lower-order property satisfying those conditions, and hence as a realization or embodiment of red.

The difference between these two views is analogous to that between type-physicalism and functionalist materialism in the philosophy of mind. Physicalism says that pain is one and the same state as a configuration of excited neurons.

Functionalist materialism says that pain is the higher-order state of occupying some state that plays a particular role, that this role is played in humans by a configuration of excited neurons, and hence that having excited neurons is the way in which humans have pain. Both views can be expressed by the claim that pain is a neural state, but this claim asserts a strict identity only when expressing the former view.

We shall distinguish between the corresponding views of color by referring to them as the *physical identity* view and the *physical realization* view, or *identity-physicalism* and *realization-physicalism*.[6] To repeat, only identity-physicalism says that red is one and the same property as a microphysical configuration; realization-physicalism says that the microphysical configuration is merely a way of being red.

Adherents of both identity-physicalism and realization-physicalism will dismiss the naive objection mooted above, but they will dismiss it on different grounds. A realization-physicalist can say that the naive objection confuses color properties with the properties that embody them. The ability to see which color an object instantiates is perfectly compatible, in his view, with an inability to see the particular way in which it instantiates that color. For in his view, seeing that an object is red consists in seeing that it has some property satisfying particular conditions; and seeing that an object has *some* such property need not entail seeing *which* such property it has. The invisibility of microphysical properties therefore doesn't preclude them from realizing or embodying colors.

This refutation of the naive objection is not available to the identity-physicalist, of course, since he doesn't draw any distinction between colors and their realizations. The identity-physicalist can still fend off the objection, however, by claiming that it misconstrues the use to which he puts the phrase "microphysical properties." The objection construes this phrase, he says, as articulating a mode of presentation under which colors are represented in visual experience—as expressing what colors are *seen as*—whereas the phrase is actually intended only to identify the nature of color properties. The physicalist points out that although one never sees anything as a layer of molecules—never sees anything under the characterization "layer of molecules"—one nevertheless sees things that are, in fact, layers of molecules, since that's precisely what the visible surfaces of objects are. Similarly, the physicalist argues, seeing nothing under the mode of presentation "microphysical property" doesn't prevent one from seeing things that *are* microphysical properties. And that colors *are* such properties is all that any physicalist means to say.

---

[6] Note that in our terminology, identity-physicalism entails that colors have their microphysical natures necessarily. For in our terminology, the thesis "red = microphysical property x" is an identity statement whose arguments are rigid designators of properties.

As we explained in note 4, some physicalists treat "red" as synonymous with a non-rigid property description. These physicalists can therefore treat the thesis "red = microphysical property x" as a contingent truth.

The Propositional Content of Visual Experience

Thus, the suggestion that physicalism requires colors to be seen under microphysical modes of presentation will be rejected by physicalists of all stripes. Some physicalists will go further, however, by denying that colors are seen under any modes of presentation at all. Whether a physicalist makes this further denial depends on his views about the propositional content of color experience.

On the one hand, a physicalist may take a Fregean view of the visual representation of color. According to that view, the experience of seeing something as red has that content by virtue of the subject's relation to a proposition containing a concept, characterization, or (as we have put it) mode of presentation that is uniquely satisfied by instances of red. The property itself is not an element of the propositional content, as the Fregean conceives it; rather, it is represented by an element of the content, namely, a characterization.

On the other hand, a physicalist might take a completely different view of how color is visually represented, a view that we shall call Russellian. According to that view, the experience of seeing something as red has that content by virtue of the subject's relation to a proposition containing the property red—the property itself, not a conception, characterization, or presentation of it. A Russellian believes that the property is introduced into the content of experience by something that directly refers to it. This item may be an introspectible, qualitative feature of visual experience, for example, or a word of mentalese tokened in some visual-experience "box." Whatever it is, it must be capable of referring to the property red directly—say, by virtue of a correlation or causal relation with it[7]—rather than by specifying it descriptively, in the sense of having a meaning uniquely satisfied by red objects.[8]

A strict Russellian may believe that the mental symbol for red has no descriptive meaning at all—just a reference. A more liberal Russellian may believe that

---

[7] For correlational theories of reference, see Dretske 1981 and Stampe 1977. We have reservations of a general nature about the prospects for correlational semantics, but we shall suspend these reservations for present purposes. A discussion of this issue can be found in Boghossian 1989b and 1991 (this volume, Chapters 1 and 3 respectively).

[8] For a Russellian view of how colors are visually represented, see Armstrong in Armstrong and Malcolm 1984, p. 172: "A perception of something green will involve a green-sensitive element, that is to say, something which, in a normal environment, is characteristically brought into existence by green things, and which in turn permits the perceiver, if he should so desire, to discriminate by his behaviour the objects from things which are not green."

See also Jackson and Pargetter 1987, pp. 129–30:

What is it for an experience to be the presentation of a property? How must experience E be related to property P, or an instance of P, for E to be the presentation of P, or, equivalently, for E to represent that P? One thing ... is immediately clear. A necessary condition is that there be a causal connection. Sensations of heat are the way heat, that is, molecular kinetic energy, presents itself to us. And this is, in part, a matter of kinetic energy *causing* sensations of heat. We say 'in part', because, for instance, the causation must be in the 'right way'. ... For present purposes, however, the causal part of the story is enough. We can work with the rough schema: redness is the property of objects which causes objects to look red. ...

it has a meaning, but that its meaning is not sufficient to specify the property red or to determine a complete proposition about redness, and hence that the content of seeing something as red must still be completed by the property itself, introduced via direct reference. The difference between these two variants of Russellianism is analogous to that between two variants of the familiar causal theory about natural-kind terms. On the one hand, the word "gold" can be viewed as a name that has no descriptive meaning over and above its reference to gold (although this reference may have been fixed, of course, with the help of a description). On the other hand, "gold" can be viewed as having a descriptive meaning such as "a kind of matter," which is not sufficient to specify a particular kind of matter and must therefore be supplemented by a causally mediated relation of reference to gold. According to the latter view, "gold" and "silver" share the meaning "a kind of matter" but refer to different kinds of matter; and their contributions to the content of sentences must include not only their shared meaning but also their distinct referents. According to the corresponding view about the visual representation of color, there are mental symbols for red and orange that may contribute a shared meaning to the content of visual experiences—say, "a surface property"—while introducing different properties as their referents.

A proponent of this liberal Russellianism will acknowledge that visual experience contains some characterization of colors, but his stricter colleague will not, since the strict Russellian believes that red is introduced into visual content by an item possessing no descriptive meaning at all. The strict Russellian will therefore deny that colors are seen under any modes of presentation. And he will consequently think of the naive objection to physicalism as doubly mistaken—not only in suggesting that he uses the phrase "microphysical property" to articulate such modes of presentation but also in suggesting that he acknowledges their existence.

Further Distinctions

The foregoing responses to the naive objection are cogent, as far as they go; but in our opinion, they don't go far enough. The physicalists have described a way in which microphysically constituted colors *aren't* represented in visual experience—namely, under microphysical characterizations—but they haven't yet told us how else such colors *are* represented. Similarly, the realization-physicalist has described what color properties are not—namely, microphysical properties—but he hasn't yet told us what colors are instead. The realization-physicalist therefore owes us an account of the higher-order properties that are identical with colors, in his view; and all of the physicalists owe us an account of how the properties with which they identify colors can be the ones represented in visual experience.

Once again, different physicalists are likely to respond differently. The distinction between Fregeanism and Russellianism and the distinction between the physical identity view and the physical realization view define a four-fold partition of physicalist theories. And within each cell of the partition, further variation is possible. For example, some physicalists believe that the experience of seeing something red normally has a distinctive, introspectible quality in addition to its representational content—a visual "feel," if you will—and that what the experience represents cannot be understood independently of how it feels. Others believe that a visual experience doesn't have intrinsic qualities, or that such qualities are in any case incidental to its content. Different physicalists are also motivated by different intuitions about how physically constituted colors are best identified and hence about how they are likely to be picked out in visual experience. Some identify colors as those physical properties which are common to various classes of objects; they consequently treat the perception of colors as the recognition of physical similarities and differences.[9] Others identify colors as those physical properties which cause particular visual effects, and consequently treat color perception as the recognition, via those effects, of their physical causes.[10]

These disagreements might be thought to require further subdivision of physicalist territory, into eight or even sixteen regions instead of four. But we begin to wonder, at this point, whether all of the resulting regions would be occupied by theories that were even remotely plausible. We shall therefore proceed less abstractly, by developing the latter intuitions about how to identify physically constituted colors. Each of these intuitions could in principle lead to eight different theories, as it is combined with Fregeanism or Russellianism, with identity theory or realization theory, and with credence or skepticism about qualia. As we have suggested, however, not all of the resulting permutations are viable. What's more, the lines of thought departing from these intuitions ultimately tend to converge. We shall therefore attempt to formulate only those accounts of color experience which are both plausible and distinct.

The First Intuition: Similarity Classes

One way of picking out an object as red is by saying that its surface shares a property with the surfaces of ripe tomatoes, British phone booths, McIntosh apples, and so on. Perhaps, then, an object can be visually represented as colored by being represented as sharing a property with certain other objects.

But do references to phone booths and tomatoes crop up in the visual representation of objects as red? Surely, people can see things as red without even having the concept of a tomato or a phone booth. Of course, this particular problem could be circumvented if each person's visual experience were conceived as characterizing red objects in terms of paradigms familiar to that person. But the resulting conception of visual experience would still be wrong, for two reasons.

[9] See Smart 1975 and Armstrong 1987.
[10] See Jackson and Pargetter 1987. This view also appears in Shoemaker 1990.

First, the experience of seeing one thing as red makes no explicit allusion to other instances of the color, familiar or not. No matter how conversant one is with tomatoes, and no matter how centrally tomatoes may have figured in one's acquisition of color concepts, seeing a red fire engine doesn't appear to be an experience about tomatoes. Second, visual experience never represents objects as having their colors necessarily or trivially, whereas it would represent tomatoes (or some other objects) as necessarily and trivially red if it represented things as red by characterizing them as sharing a property with tomatoes (or with those other objects).[11]

The moral of these observations is not that an object's color isn't visually represented as a property shared with other objects; the moral is simply that if it is so represented, the other objects aren't specified individually. The possibility remains that the experience of an object as red represents it as sharing a property with objects in a set that includes tomatoes but which is specified without reference to them or to any other individual members.

Yet how can the appropriate set of objects be specified in the content of visual experience, if not in terms of its members? To suggest that it be specified in terms of a property characteristic of those members would defeat the point of the current intuition. The point of the intuition is that a color can be represented in terms of a set of objects precisely because it's the only property common to all members of the set. Specifying the set in terms of the property characteristic of its members would therefore require an antecedent capacity to represent the color—which would render specification of the set superfluous.

A Humean Proposal

Nevertheless, the intuition that an object's color is seen as a property shared with other objects can be preserved, with the help of a proposal dating back to Hume's *Treatise*.[12] Imagine that the experience of seeing an object as red has the indexical character "It's one of *that* kind," wherein the reference of "that kind" is determined by the subject's disposition, at the prompting of the experience, to group the object together with other objects. If the latter objects do constitute a kind, by virtue of possessing some common property, then the experience will have as its content that the former object belongs to that kind and hence that it possesses the characteristic property—a property that could easily be microphysical or realized microphysically.

This account of color experience is of the liberal Russellian variety, since it suggests that visual content characterizes its object as belonging to a kind,

---

[11] The only way to circumvent this problem would be to suppose that the redness of everything but tomatoes is seen as a surface similarity to tomatoes, whereas the redness of tomatoes is seen as a similarity to fire engines. Yet this supposition would imply that the redness of tomatoes looks different from that of other objects—which is false.

[12] Hume 1978, I.i.vii. This proposal may also be what Armstrong has in mind in some parts of his 1968, chapter 12.

but that the kind in question must be specified by direct reference rather than by a more specific characterization. Direct reference is mediated in this case by a correlation between potential classificatory behavior of a subject, on the one hand, and a microphysically constituted kind of object, on the other. As we have seen, the proposal has no Fregean version, because it requires specification of a kind, and no such specification can be found in the introspectible content of color experience.

An Information-Theoretic Proposal

Here is an alternative way of preserving the first intuition. Imagine that a particular mental symbol is regularly tokened in response to visual encounters with objects of a particular kind, whose members belong to it by virtue of possessing some characteristic property. The symbol may then qualify as indicating—and thus, in a sense, as referring to—the kind with which it is correlated.[13] And tokenings of the symbol may consequently introduce its referent into the content of visual experiences, in such a way that objects are represented as members of the kind to which the symbol refers. Such an experience will naturally be described, on the one hand, as registering the similarity of its object to other members of the kind and, on the other, as attributing to its object the property characteristic of the kind. In a sense, then, the object will be seen as having a property by being visually associated with other objects that have it. A microphysical or microphysically realized property may thus be attributed to an object by way of the object's visually detected similarity to other objects.[14]

Introducing Qualia

Now suppose that the mental correlate of a color category were not some item of a subliminal mentalese but, rather, an introspectible sensation or quale. To begin with, this supposition could simply be appended to the foregoing Russellian account. The visual sensation associated with the appearance of a particular object could then be treated like a numeral in a paint-by-numbers scene, assigning the object to a kind, and hence attributing to it an associated property,

---

[13] A full correlational theory would identify the referent of a mental item not with its actual causes or correlates but, rather, with the causes or correlates that it would have under counterfactual ideal circumstances. Different theories propose different sets of ideal circumstances, but these differences needn't concern us here. We shall gloss over these issues by saying simply that under such a theory, a mental item refers to its normal or predominant cause.

[14] This account of how colors are visually represented follows the strict Russellian line, in that it credits the mental symbol for a color with no meaning beyond a correlationally determined reference. There is some room here for liberalization. The mental symbol for red may have a very general sense, such as "a kind of object," and the visual representation of something as red may therefore characterize it, literally, as of a kind. Which kind is being represented, however, will still be determined by the symbol's reference, since this account, like the preceding one, offers no resources for a descriptive characterization of the kind.

without characterizing the kind or property in any way. Which kind or property a particular sensation denoted would be fixed, as before, by causation or correlation.[15]

Once the mental correlate of a color category is imagined as accessible to introspection, however, the resources for a Fregean theory become available. The content of a visual experience can then be imagined to invoke the accompanying sensation and hence to characterize its object under the description "having the property that is this sensation's normal or predominant cause."

Such an account of how colors are represented can be adopted by proponents of both identity- and realization-physicalism. An identity-physicalist can say that red is the property referred to within the proposed characterization—the property that tends to cause the accompanying sensation. A realization-physicalist can say that red is the higher-order property expressed by the entire characterization—the property of having a property that tends to cause the sensation. On the first reading, colors may turn out to be identical with microphysical properties; on the second, they may turn out to have microphysical realizations.

The Second Intuition: Causes of Visual Effects

At this point our development of the first intuition, that colors can be identified in terms of similarity classes, has brought us around to the second intuition, that colors can be identified in terms of their visual effects. Indeed, we have already canvassed the only plausible theories derivable from the latter intuition—namely, theories according to which colors are visually represented by, or by reference to, visual sensations that they cause.

These theories can be paraphrased as saying that colors are visually represented as the properties that normally cause objects to look colored. But such a paraphrase will make sense only if looking colored is understood to consist in giving a visual appearance that's accompanied by particular visual sensations, rather than in being visually represented as having colors. For if colors were

---

[15] An identity-theoretic version of this account would say that color sensations denote microphysical properties. A realization-theoretic version would say that they denote higher-order properties that have microphysical realizations.

We do not wish to rule out either of these possibilities entirely. However, one realization-theoretic version of the current proposal can be excluded in advance. This version would be the Russellian counterpart of a Fregean theory that we shall introduce below. The Fregean theory says that visual experience characterizes each color as the higher-order property of having some property that tends to cause a particular color sensation. The Russellian counterpart of this theory would say that each color sensation is appropriately correlated with, and hence refers to, the higher-order property of having a property that tends to cause it.

The problem with the latter theory is that it would utterly trivialize the correlational semantics on which Russellianism depends. Almost every property is correlated with the higher-order property of there being a property that tends to cause it. A semantics that allowed such a correlation to ground a relation of reference would be unable to draw a distinction between what has a reference and what doesn't.

represented as the properties that normally cause objects to be represented as having colors, the content of color experience would be viciously circular.

Now, some philosophers have denied that this circularity would be vicious. One philosopher has even claimed that it would be a virtue, in that it would account for the notorious indefinability of colors. Colors are indefinable, he says, precisely because their definitions are unavoidably circular.[16]

We think, however, that the proposed circular definition would imply that the content of color experience is vacuous. When one describes an object as having properties that would cause it to be visually represented as red, one is describing it in terms of the experiences that it is equipped to cause, and one is describing those experiences in terms of their content—namely, as experiences of seeing the thing as red. The content of one's description therefore includes, as a proper part, the content of the experiences that the thing is described as equipped to cause; and the content of one's whole description depends on that component. For this reason, the description cannot express the content of the experiences in question. If the content of seeing something as red were that the thing was equipped to cause experiences of seeing it as red, then the content of seeing something as red would include and depend upon the content of experiences of seeing it as red. The content of seeing something as red would thus include and depend upon itself; it would characterize the thing, in effect, as having a property that would cause experiences containing this very characterization; and hence it would fail to attribute any particular property to the object. Circularity in the content of color experience would render that content vacuous.[17]

Thus, the content of visually representing something as colored cannot be that the thing has whatever normally causes objects to be visually represented as colored. As we have seen, however, the content in question can still be that the thing has whatever normally causes objects to look colored, in the sense that it causes their visual appearances to be accompanied by a color sensation.

Outline of the Argument

We have now developed various proposals for ways in which visual experience might represent microphysically constituted color properties. We began with the

---

[16] McDowell 1985.

[17] We develop this argument at length in our 1989, pp. 88–91 (this volume, Chapter 13, pp. 299–302).

Note that the circularity at issue here is significantly different from the circularity at issue in our earlier discussion of the expression "looks red." There we were concerned with a circularity that could result from the structure of this expression. Identifying red in terms of things' looking red will be circular, we argued, if "looks red" gets its reference by logical composition, in a way that depends on the reference of "red." Here we are concerned with a circularity in the content of a visual representation, irrespective of which symbols bear that content or how they are structured. We argue that if the content of representing something as red is that the thing has the property that causes objects to be represented as red, then that content will be embedded in itself. The former circularity can easily be resolved, since "looks red" can be restructured as a unitary expression referring directly to a kind of experience. The latter circularity cannot be resolved by any restructuring of symbols. (See note 3.)

Humean proposal that colors are directly denoted by the subject's classificatory dispositions. We then introduced an information-theoretic proposal, which says that colors are directly denoted by mental correlates, whether they be items of mentalese or introspectible qualia. We concluded with a Fregean variant of the latter possibility, to the effect that colors are characterized descriptively as the properties that normally cause color sensations.

Despite the diversity of these proposals, we think that they are uniformly unsuccessful in showing that visual experience might represent microphysical or microphysically realized colors. Each of them fails to satisfy one of two fundamental requirements for an adequate theory of color vision.

First, we shall argue, a theory of color must respect the epistemology of color experience: it must be compatible with one's knowing what one knows about color properties on the basis of seeing them. The epistemological problem for physicalism is not that the microphysical nature of colors cannot be known on sight; it is rather that other things about colors are known on sight but could not be known in this way if physicalism were true.

Second, we shall argue that a theory of color must respect the phenomenology of color experience: it must be compatible with what it's like to see the world as colored. Mere reflection on what it's like to see colors does not reveal whether the properties being seen are microphysical, but it does yield various constraints on any theory of what those properties are. In particular, such reflection reveals that color experience is naive, in that it purports to acquaint us directly with properties of external objects. In our opinion, no physicalist theory can meet this phenomenological constraint while meeting those imposed by the epistemology of color as well. We consider these constraints in turn, beginning with the epistemological.

EPISTEMOLOGICAL CONSTRAINTS

What do you know about colors, not as a student of physics or physiology, but simply in your capacity as a subject of visual experience? We think that you know, for example, that red and orange are properties; that they are different properties, though of the same kind—different determinants of the same determinable; that they are not as different from one another as they are from blue; and that they cannot simultaneously be instantiated in exactly the same place. Finally, you know that red and orange are properties that things visually appear to have, and you know when things appear to have them.

All but the last two items of knowledge are necessary propositions. Red and orange—that is, the properties that things appear to have in looking red and in looking orange—not only are distinct, similar determinates of the same determinable but are essentially so. A property that wasn't a determinate of the same determinable as red, or wasn't distinct from red, or wasn't similar to red—such a property simply wouldn't be orange. And vice versa.

What's more, mere reflection on color experience provides all the support that might ever be needed for all of the knowledge cited above. That is, you need only reflect on the experiences of seeing things as red and as orange in order to know that they are two distinct, incompatible, but rather similar determinates of a single determinable property; you need only reflect on particular experiences in order to tell which of these properties they represent; and there are no possible circumstances under which more evidence would be needed. We wish to remain neutral on the explanation for this phenomenon. The knowledge in question may be delivered in its entirety by introspection on the contents of the relevant experiences. Alternatively, it may require the recognition of relations among the contents of these experiences, so long as the relations are such as can be recognized a priori. It may even require empirical support, so long as the support required is no more than what's provided by the experiences themselves. All we claim is that the experiences of seeing red and orange provide whatever is necessary for this rudimentary knowledge about those properties.

Consider the consequences of denying that your knowledge about colors has this status. If the experiences of seeing red and orange didn't provide all of the support required for the knowledge that they're distinct but similar determinates of the same determinable, then your knowledge of these matters would be host-age to future empirical discoveries. You would have to consider the possibility of obtaining evidence that red and orange are in fact the same property or, con-versely, that they aren't similar at all. And given how the references of "red" and "orange" are fixed, evidence that red and orange are the same property, for example, would amount to evidence that the property that objects appear to have in looking red is the same as the property that they appear to have in looking orange.

Does visual experience leave room for the hypothesis that things appear to have the same property in looking red as they do in looking orange? We think not. Nor does it leave room for the hypothesis that red and orange are less alike than red and blue, or that something seemingly seen as red on a particular occasion is being represented as having a property other than red. Your knowledge on these matters is such that nothing would count as evidence against it.

Meeting the Epistemological Constraints

Yet would such knowledge be possible if physicalism were true? We believe that the answer may be yes in the case of Fregean realization-physicalism, but that in the case of all other versions of physicalism—that is, Russellian theories and identity theories—the answer is no.

What sets the latter theories apart from Fregean realization-physicalism is their implication that visual experiences like yours represent colors only as a matter of contingent fact. Under the terms of these theories, an experience internally indistinguishable from your experience of seeing something as red might fail to represent its object as having that color. The reason is that red is represented by your experience, according to these theories, only by virtue of facts incidental to the internal features of the experience.

Which facts these are depends on the physicalist's conception of visual representation. Under the terms of Russellianism, they are the causal or correlational facts by virtue of which some mental item, or some behavioral disposition, introduces the microphysically constituted property red into the contents of experiences. Twin-earth examples, in the style of Putnam,[18] will readily demonstrate that the same mental item or the same classificatory behavior might have been correlated with objects of a different kind, sharing a different property—in which case, internally similar experiences would not have represented the property that, according to physicalism, is red.

Under the terms of Fregeanism, the facts in virtue of which visual experience represents a microphysical property are the facts in virtue of which instances of that property uniquely satisfy the characterization by which things are visually represented as red. And these facts, too, are bound to be contingent if red is identical with a microphysical property, for reasons illuminated by the naive objection discussed above. Although the naive objection cannot defeat physicalism, it does force the Fregean identity-physicalist to concede that the characterization by which things are visually represented as red does not represent what it is to be red. For as an identity-physicalist, he believes that to be red is to have a particular microphysical property, and yet the objection forces him to concede that things aren't seen under microphysical characterizations. The Fregean identity-physicalist must therefore believe that things are seen as red by means of a contingent characterization—a characterization that is, in fact, uniquely satisfied by instances of the property red, but not because it represents what redness is. And twin-earth examples will once again demonstrate that such a characterization might not have been uniquely satisfied by instances of red or might have been uniquely satisfied by instances of another property. Just as a mental symbol might have tracked a different property, so the visual characterization "whatever causes this feeling" might have been satisfied by a different property; and in either case, your visual experiences wouldn't have represented red, under the terms of the corresponding theory.

Thus, Fregean identity-physicalism is like Russellian physicalism in implying that your experience of something's looking red might have been exactly as it is, in all respects internal to you, while failing to represent anything as red. And this consequence has the corollary that there are circumstances under which you couldn't tell, by mere reflection on the experience of something's looking red, whether it is being represented as having the property red.

The physicalist may object, at this point, that something's being contingent doesn't entail its being a posteriori. He will argue, more specifically, that the reference of "red" has been fixed for you by a description alluding to your visual

---

[18] Putnam 1975a; see also Burge 1979.

experiences: red is, by stipulation, whatever property is attributed to objects by their looking red. That red is the property that something appears to have in looking red is therefore knowable a priori, even though it is contingent, just like the length of the standard meter-bar in Paris.[19]

This response misses the epistemological point. The term "red" has been stipulated as denoting the property attributed to objects by their looking red; but the phrase "looks red" has been stipulated as denoting experiences introspectively similar to some paradigm experience. The problem is that under the terms of the theories now in question, there is no introspectively recognizable kind of experience for which you can always tell by introspection whether the same property is represented in all or most experiences of that kind. These theories therefore imply, to begin with, that, for all you know by reflection on visual experience, the attempt to fix the referent of "red" as the property attributed to objects by their looking red may have failed, since there may be no property that predominantly satisfies that description. They imply furthermore that, even if there is a property represented by most instances of things' looking red, you cannot necessarily tell by reflection when a particular experience is representing that property.

This problem can best be illustrated by imaginary cases of context-switching.[20] Suppose that your environment were to change in such a way that your mental designator for red was correlated with, or your visual characterization of red was satisfied by, a new and different property that replaced the current property red wherever it occurred. At first the content of your visual experiences might remain the same, with the result that you saw objects as having a property that they no longer had. But gradually your visual designators or characterizations would come to denote the new property rather than the old. Tomatoes would therefore appear to have a new and different color property—appear to have it, that is, in the only sense in which a Russellian or an identity-theorist can conceive of them as appearing to have any color at all. Yet in all respects internal to you, your experiences would remain unchanged, and so you would

---

[19] See Kripke 1972, pp. 54 ff.

Of course, those who define "red" as synonymous with "the property attributed to an object by its looking red" will think that it is not only necessary but analytic that red is the property something appears to have when it looks red. They will therefore claim that their view is compatible with your ability to tell that something appears to be red, since things necessarily appear to be red whenever they look red, and a thing's looking red is (by stipulation) an introspectively recognizable kind of experience.

True enough. But what these philosophers describe as the ability to tell that something appears to be red is less than meets the ear. It's the ability to tell that whatever property the thing appears to have is to be called red on this occasion. It's not the ability to tell when something appears to have that property.

Our claim that you can tell when something appears to be red means that there is a property, red, such that you can tell when something appears to have it. And this claim cannot be accommodated by these linguistic maneuvers.

[20] Context-switching and its relevance to self-knowledge is discussed at greater length in Boghossian 1989a (this volume, Chapter 6).

be unable to tell by reflection that you were no longer seeing tomatoes as having the color property that you had previously seen them as having.

Russellianism and identity-physicalism therefore entail that without investigation into the physical causes and correlates of your visual experiences, you cannot necessarily know whether tomatoes appear today to have a different color property from the one that they once appeared to have. You might know that whatever property they appear to have is likely to be the current holder of the title "red," if any property is. But you may not be able to tell when things have appeared to have that property in the past; and you may not be able to tell in the future when things appear to have it. Hence there remains a significant sense in which you don't necessarily know when things appear to be red.[21]

Indeed, these theories entail that you cannot always tell without investigation whether objects appear to have any color properties at all. For just as experiences internally indistinguishable from yours might represent different properties, so too they might simply fail to represent properties. Such a failure would occur if the characterizations applied to objects in visual experience were not satisfied, or if the corresponding mental designators were not systematically correlated with visual stimulation from objects of any particular kind.

Consider the Russellian theories, which say that visual experience represents objects as colored by means of symbols or behavioral dispositions that designate microphysically constituted kinds. Reflection on such an experience wouldn't necessarily reveal whether the symbols being tokened, or the behavior being prompted, were correlated with objects sharing a common property and constituting a genuine kind. For all one could tell from having the experience, the objects associated with the symbol or behavior might be utterly miscellaneous, and so these purported designators might not indicate membership in a kind or possession of a property. Hence one would be unable to tell, when things looked red, whether there was a property that they thereby appeared to have. And if one didn't know whether things appeared to have a property in looking red, one wouldn't know whether there was such a property as red at all.

The same problem attends the Fregean theory, in all but its realization-theoretic form. According to Fregean identity-physicalism, as we have developed it, visual experience represents red by characterizing it as the property that normally causes a particular sensation. Yet reflection on a visual representation of this form would not necessarily reveal whether there was a property that

---

[21] This problem is especially acute for the Humean proposal, according to which objects are represented as colored by being characterized as "one of *those*," where the reference of "those" is determined by the subject's classificatory dispositions. Not only would one be unable to tell by introspection whether the property characteristic of a particular set of objects was the same as it was previously; one would also be unable to tell whether an object was being assigned to the same set of objects as it was previously. In order to tell whether the set to which tomatoes were visually assigned today was the same as the one to which they were assigned yesterday, one would have to investigate precisely which other objects one was disposed to include in that set on each occasion. Mere introspection would therefore fall even further short of revealing whether tomatoes appear to have the same color that they once appeared to have.

normally caused the sensation, and so it wouldn't reveal whether the associated characterization succeeded in denoting a property.

Of course, the possibility of there being no colors represented in visual experience is only the most bizarre of many possibilities that introspection could not rule out if the present theories were true. A less bizarre possibility is that visual experience might represent only two color properties—one when things look either red, orange, or yellow, and another when they look either green, blue, or violet. The correlational or causal facts could certainly be arranged in such a way as to give these experiences one of only two contents, under the terms of Russellian or identity-theoretic physicalism. These theories therefore imply that one cannot always tell without investigation whether red and orange are different colors, the same color, or no color at all.

Some Defenses and Replies

Now, physicalists sometimes admit that visual experience, as they conceive it, is compatible with the possibility that there are no colors.[22] We wonder, however, whether the full import of this concession is generally appreciated. The statement that there may be no colors sounds as if it should gladden the heart of an anti-realist, but it is in fact different from, and perhaps even incompatible with, the views that many anti-realists hold. What these anti-realists believe is that colors are properties that visual experience attributes to objects even though no objects instantiate them. What proponents of the present theories must concede, however, is that there may be no properties attributed to objects by their looking colored, and hence that there may be no such properties as colors, not even uninstantiated ones. They must allow that color experience not only may attribute properties to objects that don't have them, as the anti-realists claim, but may actually fail to attribute properties to objects at all, by failing to express any properties. If this possibility were realized, color experience would lack the representational competence required to be false, strictly speaking, whereas the falsity of color experience is what anti-realism is usually about. And in our opinion, the fact that color experience can at least be false is evident on the face of it.

A physicalist might respond that the designators and characterizations involved in color experience can be assumed to indicate some properties, since something or other is bound to be responsible for one's visual sensations, as specified in the characterizations, and something or other is bound to be correlated with the designators. But the liberal criteria of visual representation that would enable one to assume that some properties or other were being represented would simultaneously undermine one's claim to other items of knowledge about those properties.[23] For if one's experiences of things as red and as orange represented

---

[22] See, for example, Armstrong 1968, p. 289.

[23] Such liberal criteria are also unlikely to yield a plausible theory of representation. But as we said in note 7, we are ignoring such general problems in correlational semantics.

whatever properties in heaven or earth were correlated with two different designators, or responsible for two different sensations, then one would be even less
able to tell by reflection whether those properties belonged to the same determinable, or required extension for their instantiation, or bore greater similarity
to one another than to some third property. For all one could tell from seeing
colors in the way imagined here, red might be an electrical charge, orange a
degree of acidity, and blue a texture.

A physicalist might respond that if the similarities and differences among colors were conceived as relative to an observer, then they would indeed be revealed
by reflection on visual experience.[24] Let the imperfect similarity between red
and orange consist in the fact that they have distinct but similar effects on normal human observers, and any normal human observer will be able to detect
their relation on sight.

The problem with this suggestion is that it can account only for our knowledge
of contingent similarities and differences. Red and orange, as conceived by the
physicalist, are properties that happen to have distinct but similar effects on
human observers, but they might have had effects that were not distinct or
were even less similar. Hence the similarity relation that would be accessible by
reflection on visual experience, according to physicalism, is a relation that red
and orange might not have had. In reality, however, reflection on the experiences
of seeing red and orange tells us that if two properties didn't stand in precisely
this relation, they wouldn't be the properties we're seeing.[25]

Smart's Analogy

Now, the epistemology of color similarities and differences has received considerable attention from some physicalists who are aware that their theories appear
unable to account for it. Because these physicalists subscribe to Russellian or
identity-theoretic versions of physicalism, they are committed to the proposition
that visual experience doesn't characterize objects in terms that would reveal
wherein their color properties consist. The problem is that if visual experience
doesn't reveal wherein colors consist, it cannot reveal wherein they are essentially alike or different. In order for visual experience to represent how being red
is essentially similar or dissimilar to being orange, it would have to represent
what it is to be red or to be orange—which it doesn't do, under the terms of
the theories in question. These theories therefore seem unable to explain why
the similarities and differences among colors can be known on sight.

Physicalists have attempted to meet this challenge by disputing its premise—
namely, that visual experience would have to represent the nature of color properties in order to reveal their similarities and differences. They insist upon "the

---

[24] We owe this suggestion to Sydney Shoemaker.

[25] Here, as elsewhere, a physicalist may reply that our sense of having introspective knowledge
can be explained away. We shall consider this objection below.

possibility of being able to report that one thing is like another, without being able to state the respect in which it is like."[26]

J. J. C. Smart once offered an analogy to illustrate this possibility. He wrote:

If we think cybernetically about the nervous system we can envisage it as being able to respond to certain likenesses ... without being able to do more. It would be easier to build a machine which would tell us, say on a punched tape, whether or not ... objects were similar, than it would be to build a machine which would report wherein the similarities consisted.

David Armstrong quotes this passage in application to color similarities and concludes, "No epistemological problem, then."[27]

What Armstrong seems to be suggesting is that one detects the bare fact that red and orange are similar by means of a sensory mechanism that responds to their similarity and produces an awareness of it in one's mind. This similarity-detecting component of the visual sensorium is what corresponds, in Armstrong's view, to the similarity-detecting machine described by Smart.[28] Unfortunately, such a detector, though perfectly conceivable, would not yield the right sort of knowledge about color similarities. For if the similarities among colors were detected by sight, then one's knowledge of them would be defeasible, by evidence of an optical illusion or malfunction. The experience of seeing things as red and as orange would reveal that these colors looked similar, and hence that they were similar if one's eyes could be trusted; but one would have to acknowledge the possibility that their apparent similarity might be an illusion, and that they might not be similar, after all.

In reality, of course, the similarity between red and orange is known beyond question and could not turn out to be an illusion. One needs to have seen red and orange in order to know that they're similar, of course, but only because one needs to have seen them in order to know which properties they are. Once acquainted with them, one doesn't depend on visual evidence for one's knowledge of their similarity, since nothing would count as counter-vailing evidence.

Armstrong's Analogy

Armstrong has suggested that one's ability to perceive color similarities without perceiving their bases is analogous to the ability to perceive family resemblances:

How can we be aware of the resemblance and the incompatibility of the colour-shades, yet be unaware of, and have to infer, the nature of the colour-properties

---

[26] These words are from J. J. C. Smart's "Sensations and Brain Processes." They are quoted in application to color by Armstrong 1987, p. 12.

[27] Quoted in Armstrong 1987, pp. 12–13.

[28] See Armstrong 1978, p. 127: "[W]hy should not the colour-properties act on our mind (or, rather, why should not states of affairs involving these properties act on our mind), producing awareness of resemblance and incompatibility, but not producing awareness of those features of the properties from which the resemblance and incompatibility flow?"

from which these features flow? The answer, I take it, is in principle the same ... as for the cases where resemblance of particulars such as faces is observed but the respect of resemblance cannot be made out. Despite the fact that the respect in which the faces resemble one another is not identified, it can still act upon our mind, producing in us an awareness of resemblance.[29]

Now, if we follow Armstrong's instructions to interpret this analogy as comparing the perceived similarity of color properties to the perceived similarity of particular faces, then it does nothing to overcome our stated objection. Although one can often see that two faces are alike, one remains aware that the appearance of likeness may be illusory, and hence that the faces may turn out not to be alike, after all, whereas the appearance of similarity between red and orange is not subject to empirical refutation.

Yet Armstrong's analogy is open to a slightly different interpretation, which might seem to suggest a case in which knowledge of bare resemblance need not be defeasible, either. Let the similarity between colors be compared not to that between particular faces but, rather, to that between the contours that the faces appear to have, which are properties rather than particulars.[30] When the perception of family resemblance is thus interpreted as the perception of similarity between complex shapes, it no longer seems exposed to the risk of illusion. The faces may not have the shapes that they appear to have, of course, but the similarity between those shapes remains unmistakable, even though one may not be able to articulate the respects in which they're alike. Why, then, can't the similarity between perceived colors be equally unmistakable and yet equally unanalyzable?

The problem with this version of Armstrong's analogy is that one's ignorance of the respects in which perceived shapes are alike is not analogous to the ignorance that one would have of color similarities if Russellian or identity-theoretic physicalism were true. Although one cannot say what's common to the contours that two faces appear to have, one sees those contours under modes of presentation that represent their nature, since shapes are spatial properties and are visually characterized in spatial terms.[31] Information about the aspects in which shapes are similar is therefore included in the introspectible content of their visual appearance. One may just be unable to isolate that information or extract it or put it into words. Under the terms of Russellianism or identity-physicalism, however, one's inability to tell what colors have in common isn't due to the difficulty of processing information contained in their visual characterization;

---

[29] Armstrong 1978, p. 127. See also his 1968, pp. 275–6.

[30] Armstrong himself sometimes suggests that shapes rather than individuals are the relevant analogue. See Armstrong and Malcolm 1984, pp. 178–9.

[31] One might well have reservations about whether the spatial terms in which shapes are visually characterized fully capture their spatial nature. But such reservations tend to undermine Armstrong's claim that similarities of shape are evident on sight. In assuming that shapes are visually represented in terms that reveal their nature, we are simply taking Armstrong's view of the matter.

it's due to the absence of that information, since colors aren't characterized in terms that represent their nature.

The difference between these cases is like that between purely referential concepts, which have no sense, and concepts whose sense is difficult to explicate. If one has the concept of gold without being able to say what gold is, the reason may be that having the concept consists in nothing more than standing in the right causal relation to the appropriate objects. But if one has the concept of compassion without being able to say what compassion is, the reason is probably that one's concept has a *de dicto* content that one cannot immediately explicate. Thus, reflection on one's concepts of compassion and pity may not reveal how compassion and pity are alike, any more than reflection on concepts will reveal the relation between gold and silver—but not for the same reason. In the case of gold and silver, the reason will be that one's concepts simply don't reflect the basis of similarity; in the case of compassion and pity, it will be that a relation reflected in one's concepts isn't easy to articulate.

This difference is manifested by differences in one's authority about proposed accounts of the relevant objects or similarities. If someone proposes an account of what gold is, or how it is like silver, one cannot confirm his account simply by consulting one's concepts. But if someone proposes an account of what compassion is, or how it is like pity, reflection on one's concepts may indeed suffice to reveal whether he's right, even if it wouldn't have enabled one to formulate the account on one's own.

To judge by this test, the visual representation of shape is like a concept that's difficult to explicate, since one can indeed confirm an account of the resemblance between two faces by reflecting on how they look. There is thus good reason to believe that one's knowledge of family resemblance depends on visual information of a sort that is not contained in the appearance of colors, as understood by Russellian or identity-theoretic physicalism. One does see the respects in which two faces are alike, although one may be unable to isolate or describe them, whereas the versions of physicalism under discussion imply that the respects of similarity between colors are utterly invisible. Hence one's ability to be certain about family resemblances is no indication that one could be equally certain about color resemblances if these versions of physicalism were true.

Explaining the Epistemological Intuitions Away

We believe that the foregoing epistemological objections rule out any theory that portrays visual experience as representing colors contingently—that is, without characterizations that denote them necessarily. They thereby rule out Russellian versions of physicalism and Fregean identity-physicalism as well.

Although such theories cannot respect ordinary intuitions about the epistemology of color, some of them can attempt to explain those intuitions away. In particular, any physicalist who acknowledges the existence of distinctive color sensations, or qualia, can argue that we have mistaken introspective knowledge about those sensations for knowledge about the color properties that they help to represent. What the ordinary observer knows by reflection, this physicalist may claim, is not that there are distinct but similar properties that red-looking and orange-looking objects appear to have but, rather, that there are distinct but similar sensations that accompany these appearances. According to this response, we have displaced—indeed, projected—these items of knowledge from their true objects, which are color qualia, onto color properties.

But can the physicalist extend this explanation to our most fundamental knowledge claim, that color experience can be known on reflection to represent properties? He can try. For he can say that we have mistaken the introspectible presence of color qualia in visual experience for an introspectible *re*presentation of color properties. Because reflection on visual experience does reveal that things look colored in the sense that their visual appearances are accompanied by color sensations, the physicalist may argue, we have mistaken it as revealing that they look colored in the sense of being represented as having color properties.

But why would we commit this mistake in the case of color, when we have no tendency to commit it in the cases of other, equally vivid sensations? One isn't tempted to think that sensations of pain, for example, attribute any properties to the objects that cause them. Reflection on the experience of being pricked by a pin doesn't yield the conviction that the pin is being represented as having a pain-property. Why, then, should reflection on an experience accompanied by a color sensation yield the conviction that its object is being represented as colored?

Here again the physicalist may think that he has an explanation. For as Wittgenstein pointed out, sensations of pain, unlike sensations of red, are not regularly received from particular objects or surfaces; if they were, "we should speak of pain-patches just as at present we speak of red patches."[32] Perhaps, then, we believe that visual experience attributes color properties to objects because we've observed the regularity with which color sensations are associated with the perception of particular surfaces. According to this explanation, the knowledge that we have claimed to possess on the basis of mere reflection is in fact derived from observed patterns and correlations within visual experience.[33]

Unfortunately, the patterns and correlations cited here would provide no grounds whatsoever for believing that visual experience attributes color properties to objects in the ways required by Russellian or identity-theoretic physicalism. From the fact that particular objects are individually associated in visual experience with a particular sensation, no conclusion can be drawn about whether the sensation has any normal or predominant cause, and hence about

---

[32] *Philosophical Investigations*, p. 312.
[33] This suggestion, too, is due to Sydney Shoemaker.

whether there is an external property that it can help to represent. Various objects regularly occasion sensations of red, but those objects are so various that they may not have any surface properties in common, for all one can tell from visual experience. Hence their observed association with one and the same quale provides no grounds for thinking that the quale has any informational potential.

What's more, the association of color sensations with particular objects is no more regular or reliable than that of pain with particular kinds of events. After all, pain serves its monitory function only because young children can learn that it regularly accompanies bumps, scrapes, punctures, encounters with extreme heat or cold, and so forth. Having obvious external correlates is essential to the evolutionary purpose of pain. If what led us to view a sensation as the representation of something external were its observed correlation with various external stimuli, we would have no more occasion to take this view of color than of pain.

Thus, the point of Wittgenstein's remark about pain patches cannot be that pain appears to have no representational content because it has no apparent external correlates. What, then, is the point? Surely, it's that sensations like pain (and color) involve qualities that we can easily think of as located in the external world, but that this thought is blocked, in the case of pain, by there being no particular places where it seems to be located. The external correlates of pain aren't places, and so pain isn't subject to the sort of displacement that the mind practices on other sensations.

Thus, what the association of sensations with particular surfaces produces, and what Wittgenstein was suggesting that it would produce even in the case of pain, is a tendency to perceive the sensations as located on those surfaces—an inducement, in short, to the projective error. But the result of this error is precisely that the qualia themselves, rather than microphysical properties, are attributed to objects in visual experience. Thus, if the patterns cited by the physicalist have their most likely result, they result in the falsity of physicalism as an account of the properties that visual experience represents.

The physicalist explanation of our basic epistemological intuition is therefore unstable. The physicalist wishes to claim that visual experience does not project sensations onto external objects, as their perceived properties, but that reflection on visual experience does project our knowledge about sensations onto objects, as knowledge about their perceived properties. What is cited as accounting for the latter projection doesn't really account for it, however, and would in fact account for the former projection instead.

FREGEAN, REALIZATION-THEORETIC THEORIES

Russellian and identity-theoretic versions of physicalism fail to cope with the epistemology of color because they must portray visual experience as representing color without a characterization that denotes it necessarily. Such visual representations would denote properties only contingently, and would therefore fail to provide the appropriate introspective knowledge of the properties denoted.

This problem does not affect Fregean, realization-theoretic theories. A realization-physicalist can concede, in response to the naive objection, that red objects aren't visually characterized in microphysical terms, and yet hold a version of Fregeanism according to which they are characterized in terms that express what it is to be red; for he doesn't believe that to be red is to have a microphysical property. His theory of visual representation may then enable him to account for the epistemology of color experience. For if visual experience represented red by means of a characterization that represented what it is to be red, then introspection on the content of such an experience would leave no doubt whether there was such a property, introspection on experiences containing the same characterization would leave no doubt whether they represented the same property, and introspection on experiences containing characterizations of various colors would reveal the relations of similarity among them—all because the introspectible content of each experience would reveal what it is to have the property therein represented.

We therefore turn to a consideration of Fregean, realization-theoretic versions of physicalism. One such theory was already introduced, in our initial survey of physicalist theories. Before returning to that theory, however, we shall briefly introduce a new proposal, which is motivated by epistemological arguments of the sort considered above. This proposal has little intuitive appeal of its own; indeed, it would hardly have been intelligible before our epistemological arguments against the other proposals had been aired. As a response to those arguments, however, it has some apparent plausibility.

A New Proposal

The new proposal is an attempt to kill two birds with one stone.[34] It purports to explain at a stroke how colors are visually represented and how their similarities

---

[34] The following remarks of Armstrong's sound like the theory developed in this section:

The vital point to grasp here, I think, is that, with an exception or two to be noticed, our *concepts* of the individual secondary qualities are quite empty. Consider the colour red. The concept of red does not yield any necessary connection between redness and the surface of ripe Jonathan apples or any other sort of object. It does not yield any necessary connection between redness and any sort of discriminatory behaviour, or capacity for discriminatory behaviour, in us or in other creatures. It does not yield any necessary connection between redness and the way that the presence of redness is detected (eyes, etc.) in us or in other creatures. Finally, and most importantly, it does not yield any necessary connection between red objects and any sort of perceptual experience, such as looking red to normal perceivers in normal viewing conditions.

There may be a conceptual connection between redness and extendedness. ... There is certainly a conceptual connection between redness and the other colours: the complex resemblances and differences that the colours have to each other. But these conceptual connections do not enable us to break out of the circle of the colours.   (Armstrong 1987, p. 11)

However, the rest of Armstrong's work makes clear that he does not subscribe to the theory developed here. In his 1978, he attributes such a theory to R. W. Church (pp. 108–11).

and differences are known. The explanation is that colors are visually characterized precisely as those properties which bear the appropriate similarities and
differences to one another.

How could all of the similarities and differences among colors be included
in their visual characterization? Here is how.

Let a *pigmentation* be any property of extended things that stands with its co-
determinates in relations of similarity and difference representable by a spheroid
space in which distance around the circumference, distance from the ends, and
distance from the interior correspond to differences in three different respects (to
be called, for our purposes, hue, lightness, and saturation). Then let coordinates
be defined so that any determinate pigmentation can be labelled by three numbers
specifying its longitude, latitude, and depth in the property space. The description
"pigmentation *xyz*" will then have as its condition of satisfaction the presence
of a determinate whose relation to its co-determinates corresponds to position
xyz in a property space of this structure.

Now suppose that visual experience characterized surfaces as having pigmentations, specified by their coordinates in pigmentation-space.[35] Under the
terms of Fregeanism, such experiences would represent the surfaces as having some appropriately related determinates of some appropriately structured
determinable. Under the terms of realization-physicalism, colors would be the
second-order properties expressed by such characterizations—that is, the properties of having appropriately related determinates of an appropriately structured
determinable.

We believe that this version of the proposal can account for all of the
knowledge claimed in our epistemological intuitions. Reflection on the visual
characterization of objects as having pigmentations *xyz* and *qrs* would yield the
appropriate knowledge about the higher-order properties that the objects were
thereby seen as having. That is, it would reveal that the experience represented its objects as having genuine, co-determinate properties, properties identical
to those represented by internally similar experiences and differing from one
another in degrees proportionate to $x - q, y - r$, and $z - s$. One would therefore
know when one was seeing things as red or orange, and one would be able to
tell their similarities and differences.

Unfortunately, this remedy for earlier epistemological problems only creates
new ones. Once all of the requisite information has been encoded into the
proposed visual characterization of colors, the resulting proposal—in any version—credits the subject of that experience with too much knowledge rather than
too little. For it implies that the characterization of any one color encompasses
that color's relations to all of the others, by locating it in a fully conceived color

---

[35] The use of numerical coordinates is not essential to this conception of color experience. Visual
experience can be conceived as locating colors in the property space directly, without the use of
coordinates; or it can be conceived as locating them in a network of similarity relations, without
the use of any spatial analogy at all.

space. If color experience conformed to this proposal, the difference between red and orange would not only be evident from the experiences of seeing red and orange; it would be evident from the experience of seeing red alone, since that experience, by representing red as located in a property space of a particular shape, would already intimate the locations of co-determinate properties. The characterization of something as having a property located at longitude x, latitude y, and depth z in a space of co-determinate properties would already suggest the location of properties to the north or south, properties to the east or west, and properties above or below. Yet the experience of seeing something as red does not by itself reveal that the property now in view has a yellower neighbor (orange) and a bluer neighbor (violet), nor that it has more or less bright and more or less saturated neighbors, either. The current proposal has the unfortunate consequence that to see one color is, in a sense, to see them all.[36] The current proposal thus continues to get the epistemology of color wrong.

The Initial Fregean, Realization-Theoretic Proposal

We therefore return to the initial candidate for a Fregean, realization-theoretic version of physicalism. This was the theory that objects are visually characterized as having properties that normally cause color sensations, and that colors are the higher-order properties expressed by these characterizations.[37]

The content that this theory assigns to visual experience, say, of red would be introspectively recognizable as representing a genuine property; for even if there is no property that's predominantly responsible for sensations of red, the property

---

[36] A proponent of this theory may reply that the complete conception of color space may be acquired gradually, as the subject of visual experience encounters new colors. But this reply isn't to the point, because our objection is not especially about the acquisition of color concepts. What refutes the present theory of color representation is not just that someone who has never seen orange cannot derive the concept of it from seeing red. It's also that someone who has seen both red and orange still does not have experiences of either color that, by themselves, would ground knowledge about the other.

What's more, the most plausible account of how a naive subject might discover color space is not compatible with the proposal under consideration. For according to the proposal, either one already sees colors in terms of their locations in a space of co-determinates—in which case the appearance of one color already alludes to the others—or one doesn't yet see colors in terms of their locations in color space—in which case, their appearances furnish no grounds for drawing the similarities and differences constitutive of such a space. One colored surface will appear to differ from another along three dimensions, according to the proposal, only if each surface is already seen under characterizations specifying three coordinates for its pigmentation. Hence the proposal doesn't allow for the possibility of *discovering* the dimensions of color space *on the basis of* what is seen in color experience. If one doesn't already see colors under characterizations locating them in such a space, then one sees nothing on the basis of which locations could be assigned to them.

[37] Whether one regards realization-physicalism as equivalent to dispositionalism will depend on one's views on the relation between dispositions and their bases. For a dispositionalist theory of color that may be equivalent to realization-physicalism, see Peacocke 1984.

of having such a property is undoubtedly genuine. Furthermore, any internally similar experience would be introspectively recognizable as representing the same (higher-order) property, by virtue of containing the same characterization. And color properties, so defined, would stand in relations of similarity and difference generated by similarities and differences among the associated sensations. If one visual sensation differed from another in various respects, then the properties of being equipped to cause those sensations would differ isomorphically, by differing as to the sensations caused. Reflection on how it feels to see things as red and as orange would therefore be sufficient to reveal similarities and differences among those colors.

This Fregean, realization-theoretic version of physicalism can therefore account for our knowledge of colors. Unfortunately, it does so at the expense of misrepresenting the *phenomenology* of color experience.

The present theory implies that the content of visual experience alludes to color qualia as properties distinct from the perceived colors of objects.[38] In order for one to see an object as having the property that causes visual experiences with a particular feel, one's experience would have to represent that feel as well as the property causing it. And one's experience would then lack the naiveté characteristic of vision.

Visual experience is naive in the sense that it doesn't distinguish between the perceived properties of objects and the properties of perceptions. Whereas the experience of pain, for example, distinguishes between an external cause (a pin's sharpness) and its sensory effect (a finger's pain), visual experience does not distinguish between color as it is in the object and as it feels to the eye: one feels sharp points as causing pains but one doesn't see colored surfaces as causing visual feels. The normal experience of seeing an object as red no more alludes to a sensation as distinct from the object's redness than it does to tomatoes or fire engines.

Thus, the only version of physicalism that gets the epistemology of color experience right gets the phenomenology wrong. In our opinion, any version of physicalism that acknowledges color *qualia* will commit the same phenomenological error, since it will imply that visual experience always has introspectible color qualities over and above the color properties that it attributes to objects. But this general thesis need not be defended here, since the only version of the second proposal that has survived our epistemological arguments is the Fregean, realization-theoretic version, which portrays visual experience not only as having introspectible qualities but also as alluding to them in its representational content. This version of the proposal implies that visual experience not only involves color sensations but is also about those sensations, in addition to color properties—which is clearly mistaken.

---

[38] The following argument is developed more fully in Boghossian and Velleman 1989, pp. 94–6.

CONCLUSION

We do not pretend to have proved that any physicalist theory of color must be inadequate, since we have not canvassed every possible theory. We think of our arguments as posing a challenge to any aspiring physicalist. We challenge the physicalist to explain how the physical properties that constitute colors, in his view, are represented in visual experience, and to explain it in a way that meets reasonable epistemological and phenomenological constraints.

One might think that the constraints that we have applied cannot be met by any theory of color, and hence that they must be unreasonable. The solution to the problems we have raised, one might conclude, is not to reject physicalism but rather to relax our epistemological and phenomenological constraints. In our view, however, there is a theory that satisfies these constraints, and it is one of the oldest and most familiar. It is the theory that colors are qualitative properties of visual experiences that are mistakenly projected onto material objects. A defense of that theory must be deferred, however, to another occasion.[39]

[39] For comments on earlier drafts of this paper, we are grateful to David Armstrong, C. L. Hardin, David Hills, Sydney Shoemaker, and Steve Yablo.

Part IV: Suggestions for Further Reading

Bigelow, J; J. Collins and R. Pargetter. (1990) 'Colouring in the World', *Mind* 99 (394): 279–88.

Byrne, A. (2001) 'Do Colours Look Like Dispositions? Reply to Langsam and Others', *Philosophical Quarterly* 51 (203): 238–45.

—— (2003) 'Color and Similarity', *Philosophy and Phenomenological Research* 66: 641–65.

—— and D. Hilbert. (2003) 'Color Realism and Color Science', *Behavioral and Brain Sciences* 26: 3–21.

—— —— (1997) 'Colors and Reflectances'. In *Readings on Color, Volume I: The Philosophy of Color*, edited by A. Byrne and D. R. Hilbert. Cambridge, MA: MIT Press.

Johnston, M. (1992) 'How to Speak of the Colors', *Philosophical Studies* 68 (3): 221–63.

Langsam, H. 'Why Colours *Do* Look Like Dispositions', *Philosophical Quarterly* 50 (198): 68–75.

McGinn, C. (1996) 'Another Look at Color', *Journal of Philosophy* 93 (11): 537–53.

Pautz, A. (2006) 'Can the Physicalist Explain Colour Structure in Terms of Colour Experience?', *Australasian Journal of Philosophy* 84 (4): 535–64.

Pautz, A. (2008) 'Color: Philosophical Issues'. In *Oxford Companion to Consciousness*, edited by T. Bayne, A. Cleeremans, and P. Wilken, Oxford: OUP.

Tye, M. (2000) *Consciousness, Color and Content*. Cambridge, MA: MIT Press.

Watkins, M. (1997) 'What Our Colour Experiences Don't Teach Us: A Reply to Boghossian and Velleman', *Dialogue: Canadian Philosophical Review* 36 (4): 783–6.

Bibliography

Alston, W. (1986) 'Epistemic Circularity', *Philosophy and Phenomenological Research* 47: 1–30.

Armstrong, D. (1968) *A Materialist Theory of the Mind*. London: Routledge & Kegan Paul.

_____(1978) *A Theory of Universals: Volume 2*. Cambridge: Cambridge University Press.

_____(1987) 'Smart and the Secondary Qualities'. In *Metaphysics and Morality: Essays in Honour of J. J. C. Smart*, eds. P. Pettit, R. Sylvan and J. Norman. Oxford: Basil Blackwell.

_____ and N. Malcolm (1984) *Consciousness and Causality: A Debate on the Nature of Mind*. Oxford: Basil Blackwell.

Ayer, A. J. (1952) *Language, Truth and Logic*. New York: Dover Publications.

Baker, L. R. (1988) 'Cognitive Suicide'. In *Contents of Thought*, eds. R. H. Grimm and D. D. Merrill. Tucson: University of Arizona Press, 1–18.

Baker, G. and P. Hacker. (1984) 'On Misunderstanding Wittgenstein: Kripke's Private Language Argument', *Synthese* 58 (3): 407–50.

Bennett, J. (1971) *Locke, Berkeley, Hume: Central Themes*. Oxford: Clarendon Press.

Blackburn, S. (1984a) *Spreading the Word*. Oxford: Oxford University Press.

_____(1984b) 'The Individual Strikes Back', *Synthese* 58 (3): 281–301.

Block, N. (1986) 'Advertisement for a Semantics for Psychology', *Midwest Studies in Philosophy* 10: 615–78.

Boghossian, P. (1986) *Essays on Meaning and Belief*. Princeton PhD Dissertation.

_____(1988) 'The Problem of Meaning in Wittgenstein'. Unpublished manuscript.

_____(1989a) 'Content and Self-Knowledge', *Philosophical Topics* 17 (1): 5–26.

_____(1989b) 'The Rule-Following Considerations', *Mind* 98: 507–49.

_____(1990) 'The Status of Content', *Philosophical Review* 99 (2): 157–84.

_____(1991) 'Naturalizing Content'. In *Meaning in Mind: Essays on the Work of Jerry Fodor*, ed. B. Loewer. Oxford: Basil Blackwell, 65–86.

_____(1992a) 'Externalism and Inference', *Philosophical Issues* 2: 11–28.

_____(1992b) 'Reply to Schiffer', *Philosophical Issues* 2: 39–42.

_____(1994a) 'Inferential Role Semantics and the Analytic/Synthetic Distinction', *Philosophical Studies* 73: 109–22.

_____(1994b) 'The Transparency of Mental Content', *Philosophical Perspectives* 8: 33–50.

_____(1996) 'Analyticity Reconsidered', *Noûs* 30: 360–91.

_____(1997) 'Analyticity'. In *A Companion to the Philosophy of Language*, eds. B. Hale and C. Wright. Cambridge, MA: Blackwell, 331–68.

Boghossian, P. (2000) 'Knowledge of Logic'. In *New Essays on the A Priori*, eds. P. Boghossian and C. Peacocke. Oxford: Oxford University Press, 229–54.

_____ (2001a) 'How Are Objective Epistemic Reasons Possible?', *Philosophical Studies* 106 (1): 1–40.

_____ (2001b) 'Inference and Insight', *Philosophy and Phenomenological Research* 63: 633–40.

_____ (2003a) 'Blind Reasoning', *Proceedings of the Aristotelian Society*, Suppl. Vol. 77: 225–48.

_____ (2003b) 'Epistemic Analyticity: A Defense', *Grazer Philosophische Studien* 66: 15–35.

_____ (2003c) 'The Normativity of Content', *Philosophical Issues* 13: 31–45.

_____ (2005a) 'Is Meaning Normative?' In *Philosophy–Science–Scientific Philosophy: Fifth International Congress of the Society for Analytical Philosophy*, eds. C. Nimtz and A. Beckermann, 205–18.

_____ (2005b) 'Meaning, Rules and Intention', *Philosophical Studies* 124 (2): 185–97.

_____ (2008) 'Epistemic Rules', forthcoming in *Journal of Philosophy*.

_____ (Forthcoming) *Rules and Intentionality in Nature*.

_____ and J. D. Velleman (1989) 'Colour as a Secondary Quality', *Mind* 98: 81–103.

Bonjour, L. (1985) *The Structure of Empirical Knowledge*. Cambridge: Harvard University Press.

_____ (1998) *In Defense of Pure Reason*. Cambridge: Cambridge University Press.

Brandom, R. (1984) 'Reference Explained Away', *Journal of Philosophy* 81 (9): 469–92.

_____ (1988) 'Pragmatism, Phenomenalism and Truth Talk', *Midwest Studies in Philosophy* 12: 75–93.

_____ (1998) *Making it Explicit*. Cambridge, MA: Harvard University Press.

_____ (2000) *The Articulation of Reasons*. Cambridge, MA: Harvard University Press.

Brueckner, A. (1986) 'Brains in a Vat', *Journal of Philosophy* 83 (3): 148–67.

_____ (1992) 'What an Anti-Individualist Knows A Priori', *Analysis* 52: 111–18.

Burge, T. (1979) 'Individualism and the Mental', *Midwest Studies in Philosophy* 4: 73–121.

_____ (1982) 'Other Bodies'. In *Thought and Content*, ed. A. Woodfield. New York: Oxford University Press.

_____ (1986) 'Cartesian Error and the Objectivity of Perception'. In *Subject, Thought and Context*, eds. J. McDowell and P. Pettit. Oxford: Clarendon Press, 117–36.

_____ (1988) 'Individualism and Self-Knowledge', *Journal of Philosophy* 85 (11): 649–63.

_____ (1993) 'Content Preservation', *Philosophical Review* 102 (4): 457–88.

Burtt, E. A. (1954) *The Metaphysical Foundations of Modern Science*. Garden City, NY: Doubleday.

Carroll, L. (1895) 'What the Tortoise Said to Achilles', *Mind* 4: 278–80.

Chisholm, R. M. and W. Sellars (1972) 'The Chisholm-Sellars Correspondence on Intentionality'. In *Intentionality, Mind and Langauge*, ed. A. Marras. Urbana: University of Illinois Press.

Churchland, P. (1981) 'Eliminative Materialism and the Propositional Attitudes', *Journal of Philosophy* 78 (2): 67–90.

_____ (1984) *Matter and Consciousness*. Cambridge: MIT Press.

Coffa, A. (1991) *The Semantic Tradition*. Cambridge: Cambridge University Press.

Creath, R. (1992) 'Carnap's Conventionalism', *Synthese* 93: 141–65.

Dancy, J. (2006) *Ethics Without Principles*. Oxford: Oxford University Press.

Davidson, D. (1980a) 'Actions, Reasons and Causes'. In *Essays on Actions and Events*. Oxford: Oxford University Press, 3–19.

_____ (1980b) 'Mental Events'. In *Essays on Actions and Events*. Oxford: Oxford University Press, 207–25.

_____ (1987) 'Knowing One's Own Mind', *Proceedings of the American Philosophical Association* 60 (3): 441–58.

Davies, M. (1997) 'Externalism, Architecturalism, and Epistemic Warrant'. In *Knowing Our Own Minds*, eds. C. Wright, B. Smith and C. MacDonald. Oxford: Oxford University Press, 321–63.

Dennett, D. (1971) 'Intentional Systems', *Journal of Philosophy* 68: 87–106.

_____ (1978) *Brainstorms: Philosophical Essays on Mind and Psychology*. Cambridge, MA: MIT Press.

_____ (1987) *The Intentional Stance*. Cambridge, MA: MIT Press.

Devitt, M. (1995) *Coming to our Senses*. New York: Cambridge University Press.

Dretske, F. (1981) *Knowledge and the Flow of Information*. Cambridge: MIT Press.

Dummett, M. (1973) *Frege: Philosophy of Language*. New York: Harper and Row.

_____ (1978) *Truth and Other Enigmas*. Cambridge, MA: Harvard University Press.

_____ (1991) *The Logical Basis of Metaphysics*. Cambridge, MA: Harvard University Press.

Evans, G. (1980) 'Things Without the Mind—A Commentary Upon Chapter Two of Strawson's "Individuals"'. In *Philosophical Subjects: Essays Presented to P. F. Strawson*, ed. Zak van Straaten. Oxford: Clarendon Press, 76–116.

Field, H. (1977) 'Logic, Meaning and Conceptual Role', *Journal of Philosophy* 74 (7): 379–409.

_____ (1986) 'The Deflationary Conception of Truth'. In *Fact, Science and Morality: Essays on A. J. Ayer's "Language, Truth and Logic"*, eds. G. MacDonald and C. Wright. Oxford: Basil Blackwell, 55–117.

_____ (2000) 'Apriority as an Evaluative Notion'. In *New Essays on the A Priori*, eds. P. Boghossian and C. Peacocke. Oxford: Oxford University Press, 117–49.

Fodor, J. (1981) 'Methodological Solipsism Considered as a Research Strategy in Cognitive Psychology'. In *Representations*. Cambridge, MA: MIT Press, 225–53.

_____ (1984) *Psychosemantics*. Unpublished manuscript.

_____ (1987) *Psychosemantics*. Cambridge, MA: MIT Press.

_____ (1989) 'Making Mind Matter More', *Philosophical Topics* 17 (1): 59–79.

_____ (1990) *A Theory of Content and Other Essays*. Cambridge, MA: MIT Press.

_____ (1994) *The Elm and the Expert*. Cambridge, MA: MIT Press.

_____ and E. Lepore (1991a) *Holism: A Shopper's Guide*. Oxford: Blackwell.

_____ and E. Lepore (1991b) 'Why Meaning (Probably) Isn't Conceptual Role', *Mind and Language* 6 (4): 328–43.

Frege, G. (1950) *The Foundations of Arithmetic*, trans. J. L. Austin. Oxford: Blackwell.

_____ (1966) 'Sense and Reference'. In *Translations from the Philosophical Writings of Gottlob Frege*, eds. P. Geach and M. Black. Oxford: Blackwell.

Galilei, G. (1842) *Opere Complete di G.G.*, vol. iv. Firenze.

Gibbard, A. (1990) *Wise Choice, Apt Feelings*. Cambridge, MA: Harvard University Press.

——(2003a) *Thinking How to Live*. Cambridge, MA: Harvard University Press.

——(2003b) 'Thoughts and Norms', *Philosophical Issues* 13 (1): 83–98.

Glüer, K. (2003) 'Analyticity and Implicit Definition', *Grazier Philosophische Studien* 66: 37–60.

Goldfarb, W. (1985) 'Kripke on Wittgenstein on Rules', *Journal of Philosophy* 82: 471–88.

Grice, H. P. (1957) 'Meaning', *Philosophical Review* 66: 377–88.

——and P. F. Strawson (1956) 'In Defense of a Dogma', *Philosophical Review* 65: 141–58.

Grover, D. L., J. L. Camp and N. D. Belnap (1975) 'A Prosentential Theory of Truth', *Philosophical Studies* 27 (2): 73–125.

Hale, B. (1986) *Abstract Objects*. Oxford: Blackwell.

Hardin, C. L. (1988) *Color for Philosophers: Unweaving the Rainbow*. Indianapolis: Hackett.

Harman, G. (1967) 'Quine on Meaning and Existence I', *Review of Metaphysics* 21: 124–51.

——(1973) *Thought*. Princeton, NJ: Princeton University Press.

——(1994) 'Doubts About Conceptual Analysis'. In *Philosophy in Mind: The Place of Philosophy in the Study of Mind*, eds. M. Michael, and J. O'Leary-Hawthorne. Dordrecht: Kluwer, 43–8.

——(1996) 'Analyticity Regained?' *Noûs* 303: 392–400.

——(2003) 'The Future of the A Priori'. In *Philosophy in America at the Turn of the Century*, APA Cent. Suppl. to *Journal of Philosophical Research*. Charlottesville: Philosophy Documentation Center, 23–34.

Heil, J. (1988) 'Privileged Access', *Mind* 42: 238–51.

Horwich P. (1998) *Meaning*. Oxford: Clarendon Press.

——(2000) 'Stipulation, Meaning and Apriority'. In *New Essays on the A Priori*, eds. P. Boghossian and C. Peacocke. Oxford: Oxford University Press, 150–69.

Hume, D. (1975) *Enquiry Concerning the Principles of Morals*, ed. L. A. Selby-Bigge. Oxford: Oxford University Press.

——(1978) *A Treatise of Human Nature*, ed. L. A. Selby-Bigge. Oxford: Clarendon Press.

Jackson, F. and R. Pargetter (1987) 'An Objectivist's Guide to Subjectivism About Colour', *Revue Internationale de Philosophie* 160: 127–41.

James, W. (1978) 'Pragmatism'. In *The Meaning of Truth*. Cambridge, MA: Harvard University Press.

Kim, J. (1984) 'Concepts of Supervenience', *Philosophy and Phenomenological Research* 45 (2): 153–76.

Kripke, S. (1972) 'Naming and Necessity'. Oxford: Blackwell.

——(1982) *Wittgenstein on Rules and Private Language*. Cambridge: Harvard University Press.

——(1988) 'A Puzzle About Belief'. In *Propositions and Attitudes*, eds. N. Salmon and S. Soames. Oxford: Oxford University Press, 102–48.

Kyburg, H. (1965) 'Comments on Salmon's "Inductive Evidence" ', *American Philosophical Quarterly* 2: 274–6.

Lehrer, K. (1990) *The Theory of Knowledge*. Cambridge, MA: Harvard University Press.

Lepore, E. and B. Loewer (1986) 'Solipsistic Semantics', *Midwest Studies in Philosophy* 10: 595–614.

_____ _____ (1987) 'Mind Matters', *Journal of Philosophy* 84 (11): 630–42.

Loar, B. (1988) 'Social Content and Psychological Content'. In *Contents of Thought*, eds. R. H. Grimm and D. D. Merrill. Tucson: University of Arizona Press, 99–110.

Locke, J. (1975) *An Essay Concerning Human Understanding*, ed. P. H. Nidditch. Oxford: Clarendon Press.

Lycan, W. (1991) 'Definition in a Quinean World'. In *Definitions and Definability: Philosophical Perspectives*, eds. J. Fetzer, D. Shatz, and G. Schlesinger. Dordrecht: Kluwer, 111–31.

Lyons, W. (1986) *The Disappearance of Introspection*. Cambridge, MA: MIT Press.

Mackie, J. (1977) *Ethics: Inventing Right and Wrong*. London: Penguin.

Margolis, E. and S. Laurence (2001) 'Boghossian on Analyticity', *Analysis* 61: 293–302.

McDowell, J. (1984) 'Wittgenstein on Following a Rule', *Synthese* 58: 325–64.

_____ (1985) 'Values and Secondary Qualities'. In *Morality and Objectivity; a Tribute to J. L. Mackie*, ed. T. Honderich. London: Routledge & Kegan Paul, 110–29.

_____ (1987) 'Projection and Truth in Ethics', 1987 Lindley Lecture. University of Kansas.

McGinn, C. (1983) *The Subjective View*. Oxford: Clarendon Press.

_____ (1984) *Wittgenstein on Meaning*. Oxford: Basil Blackwell.

McLaughlin, B. (1989) 'Type Epiphenomenalism, Type Dualism, and the Causal Priority of the Physical. *Philosophical Perspectives* 3: 109–35.

McKinsey, M. (1991) 'Anti-Individualism and Prividged Access', *Analysis* 51: 9–51.

Mellor, D. H. (1978) 'Conscious Belief', *Proceedings of the Aristotelian Society* 78: 88–101.

Millikan, R. (1987) *Language, Thought and Other Biological Categories*. Cambridge, MA: MIT Press.

_____ (1993) 'White Queen Psychology; or, The Last Myth of the Given'. In *White Queen Psychology and Other Essays for Alice*. Cambridge, MA: MIT Press, 279–363.

Nagel, T. (1996) *The Last Word*. Oxford: Oxford University Press.

Newton, I. (1979) *Opticks*. New York: Dover Publications.

O'Connor, D. J. and B. Carr (1982) *Introduction to the Theory of Knowledge*. Minneapolis: University of Minnesota Press.

Owens, J. (1990) 'Cognitive Access and Semantic Puzzles'. In *Propositional Attitudes: The Role of Content in Logic, Language and Mind*, eds. C. A. Anderson and J. Owens. Stanford: CSLI, 147–73.

Papineau, D. (1987) *Reality and Representation*. Oxford: Basil Blackwell.

Pautz, A. (Forthcoming) *Color Eliminativism*.

Peacocke, C. (1981) 'Rule-Following: The Nature of Wittgenstein's Arguments'. In *Wittgenstein: To Follow a Rule*, eds. S. H. Holtzman and C. M. Leich. London: Routledge & Kegan Paul.

Peacocke, C. (1983) *Sense and Content: Experience, Thought, and their Relations.* Oxford: Clarendon Press.

_____ (1984) 'Colour Concepts and Colour Experience', *Synthese* 58: 365–82.

_____ (1992a) *A Study of Concepts.* Cambridge: MIT Press.

_____ (1992b) 'Sense and Justification', *Mind* 101: 793–816.

_____ (1993a) 'How Are A Priori Truths Possible?', *European Journal of Philosophy* 1: 175–99.

_____ (1993b) 'Proof and Truth'. In *Reality, Representation and Projection*, eds. J. Haldane and C. Wright. New York: Oxford University Press, 163–90.

_____ (2000) 'Explaining the A Priori: The Programme of Moderate Rationalism'. In *New Essays on the A Priori*, eds. P. Boghossian and C. Peacocke. Oxford: Oxford University Press, 255–85.

_____ (2004) *The Realm of Reason.* Oxford: Oxford University Press.

Pettit, P. (2002) *Rules, Reasons and Norms.* Oxford: Oxford University Press.

Pollock, J. and J. Cruz. (1999) *Contemporary Theories of Knowledge.* Oxford: Rowman and Littefield.

Prior, A. (1960) 'The Runabout Inference Ticket', *Analysis* 21: 38–9.

Pryor, J. (2000) 'The Skeptic and the Dogmatist', *Noûs* 34: 517–49.

Putnam, H. (1975a) 'The Meaning of "Meaning"'. In *Mind, Language and Reality: Philosophical Papers Volume 2.* Cambridge: Cambridge University Press, 215–71.

_____ (1975b) 'The Refutation of Conventionalism'. In *Mind, Language and Reality: Philosophical Papers Volume 2.* New York: Cambridge University Press, 153–91.

Quine, W. V. (1953) 'Two Dogmas of Empiricism'. In *From a Logical Point of View.* Cambridge, MA: Harvard University Press, 20–46.

_____ (1960) *Word and Object.* Cambridge, MA: MIT Press.

_____ (1975) 'Reply to Hellman'. In *The Philosophy of WVO Quine*, eds. L. Hahn and P. Schilpp. La Salle: Open Court.

_____ (1976a) 'Carnap and Logical Truth'. In *The Ways of Paradox and Other Essays: Revised and Enlarged Edition.* Cambridge, MA: Harvard University Press, 107–32.

_____ (1976b) 'Truth by Convention'. In *The Ways of Paradox and Other Essays: Revised and Enlarged Edition.* Cambridge, MA: Harvard University Press, 77–106.

_____ (1986) *The Philosophy of Logic.* Cambridge, MA: Harvard University Press.

Rorty, R. (1982) *Consequences of Pragmatism.* Minneapolis: University of Minnesota Press.

_____ (1986) 'Pragmatism, Davidson and Truth'. In *Truth and Interpretation: Perspectives on the Philosophy of Donald Davidson*, ed. E. LePore. Oxford: Basil Blackwell.

Rosen, G. (2007) 'The Case Against Epistemic Relativism: Reflections on Chapter 6 of "Fear of Knowledge"', *Episteme*: 10–29.

Ryle, G. (1949) *The Concept of Mind.* London: Hutchinson.

Salmon, N. (1993) 'Analyticity and Apriority', *Philosophical Perspectives* 7: 125–33.

Schiffer, S. (1972) *Meaning.* Oxford: Clarendon Press.

_____ (1987) *Remnants of Meaning.* Cambridge, MA: MIT Press.

_____ (1992) 'Boghossian on Externalism and Inference', *Philosophical Issues* 2: 29–37.

Searle, J. (1983) *Intentionality*. Cambridge: Cambridge University Press.

Sellars, W. (1963) 'Empiricism and the Philosophy of Mind'. In *Science, Perception and Reality*. London: Routledge & Kegan Paul.

Shoemaker, S. (1990) 'Qualities and Qualia: What's in the Mind?' *Philosophy and Phenomenological Research* 50: 109–31.

Smart, J. J. C. (1975) 'On Some Criticism of a Physicalist Theory of Colour'. In *Philosophical Aspects of the Mind-Body Problem*, ed. Chung-yin-Chen. Honolulu: University of Hawaii.

Smith, M. (1986) 'Peacocke on Red and Red''', *Synthèse* 68: 559–76.

Soames, S. (1998) 'Skepticism About Meaning: Indeterminacy, Normativity and the Rule Following Paradox', *Canadian Journal of Philosophy*, Suppl. Vol. 23: 211–49.

Stalnaker, R. (1984) *Inquiry*. Cambridge, MA: MIT Press.

Stampe, D. (1977) 'Towards a Causal Theory of Linguistic Representation', *Midwest Studies in Philosophy* 2: 81–102.

Stich, S. (1983) *From Folk-Psychology to Cognitive Science: The Case Against Belief*. Cambridge, MA: MIT Press.

Strawson, P. (1964) 'Truth'. In *Truth*, eds. G. Pitcher. Englewood Cliffs: Prentice Hall.

Strawson, P. (1971) *Logico-Linguistic Papers*. London: Methuen.

Tennant, N. (1989) 'Against Kripke's Sceptic'. Abstract in *Journal of Symbolic Logic* 54: 685.

Van Cleve, J. (1979) 'Foundationalism, Epistemic Principles, and the Cartesian Circle', *Philosophical Review* 88: 55–91.

Van Cleve, J. (1984) 'Reliability, Justification and the Problem of Induction', *Midwest Studies in Philosophy* 10: 555–68.

Wedgwood, R. (2002) 'Internalism Explained', *Philosophy and Phenomenological Research* 65 (2): 349–69.

Wiggins, D. (1987) 'A Sensible Subjectivism?'. In *Needs, Values, Truth*, pp. 185–214. Oxford: Basil Blackwell.

Williamson, T. (2003) 'Understanding and Inference', *Proceedings of the Aristotelian Society*, Suppl. Vol. 77: 249–93.

Wittgenstein, L. (1953) *Philosophical Investigations*, trans. G. E. M. Anscome. Oxford: Basil Blackwell.

_____ (1956) *Remarks on the Foundations of Mathematics*, trans. G. E. M. Anscome Oxford: Basil Blackwell.

Woodfield, A. (1982) *Thought and Object*. Oxford: Clarendon Press.

Woodward, J. and T. Horgan (1985) 'Folk Psychology is Here to Stay', *Philosophical Review* 94 (2): 197–226.

Wright, C. (1980) *Wittgenstein on the Foundations of Mathematics*. Cambridge, MA: Harvard University Press.

_____ (1984a) 'Inventing Logical Necessity'. In *Language, Mind and Logic*, ed. J. Butterfield. Cambridge: Cambridge University Press, 187–209.

_____ (1984b) 'Kripke's Account of the Argument Against Private Language', *Journal of Philosophy* 81: 759–77.

_____ (1986) 'Does *Philosophical Investigations* I. 258–60 Suggest a Cogent Argument Against Private Language?'. In *Subject, Thought and Context*, eds. P. Pettit and J. McDowell. Oxford: Clarendon Press, 209–66.

Wright, C. (1989) 'Wittgenstein's Rule-Following Considerations and the Central Project of Theoretical Linguistics'. In *Reflections on Chomsky*, ed. A. George. Oxford: Basil Blackwell, 233–64.

____(1993) 'Anti-Realism: The Contemporary Debate—Whither now?'. In *Reality, Representation and Projection*, eds. J. Haldane and C. Wright. New York: Oxford University Press pp. 63–84.

____(2001) 'On Basic Logical Knowledge; Reflections on Paul Boghossian's "How Are Objective Epistemic Reasons Possible?"', *Philosophical Studies* 106 (1): 41–85.

____(2003) *Rails to Infinity*. Cambridge, MA: Harvard University Press.

____(Forthcoming) 'Wittgenstein on Rule Following: Five Themes'.

____Manuscript. On the Acquisition of Warrant by Inference: Moore, McKinsey, McDowell.

Yablo, S. (1992a) 'Mental Causation'. *Philosophical Review* 101: 245—280.

____(1992b) 'Review of Alan Sidelle's "Necessity, Essence, and Individuation: A Defense of Conventionalism",' *Philosophical Review* 101 (4): 878—881.

Index

Access Internalism 270, 277
after-image 298−9, 303−4
agreement 23, 35−6, 44
Alston 254, 256
analyticity
    analytic theory of the a priori 198,
        204, 210−12, 219, 222, 226−7, 279
    analytic theory of necessity 195, 200
    Carnap-analyticity 203
    epistemic concept of 198, 201, 222−4,
        225−9
    Frege-analyticity 201−9
    metaphysical concept of 198−201, 225
    see also error theory; non-factualism
anti-individualism about content 146−8
anti-realism
    about color 315, 333
    about logic 212−13
anti-reductionism 28, 41−5, 48−50, 111,
    125−6, 134
a priori knowledge, see analyticity;
    knowledge
Aqua 281−4
Armstrong 335−6
assertability condition 20−4
asymmetric dependence 76−80, 91−2
Ayer 27, 53−4, 57, 68

bad company 244−5, 254, 261−2
begging the question 244−5, 260
Blackburn 19, 34
blameless
    blameless reasoning 278−80, 282, 285
    epistemically blameless 250−1, 270,
        276−7
blind reasoning 276−80, 285; see also
    rule-following, blind

Block 32
boche 280−1, 286−7
Bonjour 231−2, 259−60, 269−72
Brandom 280
Burge 146, 151, 155−8, 164, 167, 176,
    172, 223, 241

Carnap 212−13, 216, 283
Carnap-analyticity 203
Carnap sentence 287
Carroll 128, 255−6, 260, 273, 275
causal theory 74−6, 81−4, 87, 90−1,
    321−2, 330; see also dispositional
    theory of; information theory
Churchland 59−60, 67
charity, principle of 293−5, 308−10
Coffa 210−11, 214
color, see anti-realism; dispositional
    theory of; error theory; knowledge;
    physicalism about color; realism
communitarianism 23−4, 35−7, 44
compatibilism 177, 181, 184
compositionality 182, 185−6
concept
    atomic 179−87
    defective 282−5
    possession conditions 242, 280, 282−5
conceptual role semantics 29, 32,
    218−24, 261−3
content, see anti-individualism;
    anti-reductionism; causal theory;
    conceptual role semantics; dispositional
    theory of; error theory; externalism;
    functionalism; holism; indeterminacy;
    informational theory; instrumentalism;
    irrealism; judgement-dependence;
    naturalism; non-factualism;

content, (*cont.*)
  normativity; quietism; realism;
  reductionism; teleological theory
conventionalism 212–13, 215–16, 264
correctness condition 15–19, 32–6, 44,
  100, 124

Davidson 151, 161–2
de dicto 104, 166–7, 169–70, 172, 175,
  337
de re 104, 166–72
default reasonable belief 240–2
defective concept 282–5
deflationism, *see* reference; truth
Dennett 59
Descartes 140–1
disjunction problem 74, 76
dispositional theory of
  color concepts 295–307
  meaning, content or
    rule-following 10–16, 28–41, 92,
    95–8, 130–3, 218, 258–60
disquotation 54–6; *see also* reference;
  truth
Dry Earth 185–7
Dummett 159, 210, 263–4, 280

entitlement 222–6, 228, 232–3, 244–5,
  258, 260–3, 279–82
epistemic principles 236–9, 246–8,
  250–4
epistemic responsibility 142, 259–60,
  270, 285, 287
error theory 24, 51–3, 58
  about analyticity 205, 207–9
  about color 293–6, 308–11
  about meaning or content 24–5, 28,
    63–5
expressivism 53–4
  about justification 247, 251–3
extension 31–7, 74–5, 81–8, 96,
  178–80, 183–7
externalism
  about content 159–66, 172, 175,
    177–87
  about justification 142–3, 256–60,
    268–9, 276–7

Flash-Grasping 211–12
flurg 282, 284–5
Fodor 30, 71–81, 89–94, 167, 219–21
functionalism
  about attitudes 104–5
  about content 42, 125, 149

Galileo 293, 308
General Conservatism 278
Gibbard 99–100, 251
Glüer 230–2
Grice 11–12, 42

Harman 199–200, 221, 277–8
holism
  about belief formation 40, 89
  about meaning or content 208–9, 220
Hume 149, 307, 324, 328

ideal conditions 30–4, 45–6, 131, 236
implicit definition 203, 210, 212, 220,
  229–33
Implicit Definition 212–19, 222
indeterminacy
  of meaning or content 195–8, 207,
    220–2
  of translation 196–7
inference 127–34, 171–2, 267, 8; *see
  also* meaning-constituting inference
  or rule
  inferential justification of logic 243–6,
    260–2
  inferential self-knowledge 140–4
  transfer of warrant 254–8, 260–2,
    267–71, 273–8
informational theory 29, 73, 82–7, 106,
  325; *see also* causal theory;
  dispositional theory of
instrumentalism 53, 58
intentionalism 303–7
Intention View 121–8
Intentional View 121, 128–30, 33
internalism about justification 142–5,
  258, 259, 270–6; *see also* Access
  Internalism; Simple Inferential
  Internalism
internalization 118–19, 124, 129, 133

introspection 41–2, 145–6, 161–2, 166–9, 235–6, 338–40, 342–3
intuition 198, 211, 239–40
Intuition 211
irrealism 51–2
  about meaning or content 24–8, 48, 58–70

judgement-dependence 45–7
justification, *see* expressivism; externalism; inference; internalism; non-factualism; realism; relativism about justification;

knowledge
  a priori 197–8, 209–12, 222–4, 226–8
  of color 295, 328–33
  of epistemic principles 237–46, 265
  of logic 209–12, 222–4, 254–8; *see also* inference
  of meaning 162–5, 202, 222, 226, 230
  self-knowledge 139–58, 161–2, 177, 182–4
Kripke 9–23, 29–34, 41–6, 59, 82, 95–7, 102–3, 110–12, 118–26, 130–4, 162, 174, 214

language of thought 13–16, 123–5, 140, 161, 163–6
Laurence 227
Lepore 219, 220–1
Loar 163
Lycan 195–6

McDowell 43–4
McGinn 12–15, 29
Margolis 227
meaning, *see* anti-individualism; anti-reductionism; causal theory; conceptual role semantics; dispositional theory of; error theory; externalism; functionalism; holism; indeterminacy; informational theory; instrumentalism; irrealism; judgement-dependence; naturalism; non-factualism;

normativity; quietism; realism; reductionism; teleological theory
Meaning Assumption 123–6, 132
meaning-attributing sentence 21–3, 24–5
meaning-constituting inference or rule 212, 217–18, 220–3, 232–3, 258–60, 263, 278–85
meaning-determining 12, 33, 37, 75–9
Meaning-Entitlement Connection 280
memory 157–8, 164–5, 171
mental causation 49
meter stick 214, 216
Millian content 162, 166–70, 172–5

Nagel 264
natural kind term 82–5, 87–8, 92, 179–80, 182–5, 185, 322
naturalism 28, 38–41, 71–3, 76–7, 79–82, 88–91, 95–6, 106–7, 121–3.
necessity 72–3; *see also* analyticity
non-factualism 53–8
  about analyticity 205–7
  about justification 251–3
  about logic 212–15
  about meaning or content 19–20, 24–8, 48, 58–9, 63–5, 69
normativity
  epistemic norm 101, 111–14, 249–53
  hypothetical 97, 99, 102
  normative proposition 111–15
  of belief 99–103
  of meaning or content 11, 13–6, 31–4, 95–107

optimality conditions 35, 38–40, 96
order-of-determination 45

pain 141, 306, 310, 338–9, 343
Peacocke 242, 255, 281, 303–7
phenomenology 328, 343
physicalism about color 294–5, 315, 319–23, 326, 328–34
  identity-physicalism 320, 326, 330, 332, 336
  realization-physicalism 320, 326, 340–3
pigmentation 341

possession conditions, *see* concept
Prior 245, 261, 280
private language 44; *see also* solitary
    language
projectivism 25–6, 307–10
Putnam 82, 146, 179–80

qualia 309, 325, 328, 338–9
quietism 44
Quine 61, 195–209, 213, 216–21, 228,
    232, 264, 277
Quine–Duheim 208

realism
    about color 315–17, 319
    about justification 253
    about logic 212–13
    about meaning or content 48, 71, 102,
        195–6, 224, 228
reductionism 28–30, 34–5, 48, 62,
    71
reference
    deflationism about 57–8, 68–70
    robust concept of 57–8, 63–4, 68–9
relativism about justification 213, 235,
    247–53, 263 ·
reliabilism 143, 257–9, 269–70, 277
representation, visual 321–3, 330, 332–3
    Fregean 321–3, 326, 328–32, 339–43
    Russellian 321–6, 329–37
rule
    as an imperative 111–14
    as a normative proposition, *see*
        normativity
    epistemic 109–15, 119, 122, 235–6
rule following 9–10, 18–19, 43–4, 48,
    97, 121–34, 218
    picture of rational belief 109–10,
        114–19
    blind 129–30, 276–80, 285; *see also*
        blind reasoning
    see also dispositional theory of;
        Intention View; Intentional View;
        internalization
rule-circular 243–7, 254–5, 260–3; *see
    also* bad company; begging the
    question

Ryle 141–2

sceptical conclusion 13, 18, 22, 24, 28,
    43
sceptical solution 19–25, 28
Schiffer 67
self-verifying judgment 152, 155–8
Sellars 11–12, 103
semantic assent 27, 55–6; *see also*
    reference; truth
Shoemaker 293
Simple Inferential Externalism 268–9,
    276–7
Simple Inferential Internalism 270,
    273–7
Smart 334–5
solitary language 20–4; *see also* private
    language
standard conditions 295–300, 303,
    312–13
Stich 61
straight solution 21–2
Strawson 54
supervenience 71–3
synonymy 201–4, 206–9, 226–30; *see
    also* analyticity

teleological theory 75–6, 90
tonk 245–6, 261–2, 280–2
transmission of warrant, *see* inference
transparency 159–66, 170–5, 202
truth
    deflationism about 27, 54–8, 63–4,
        66–70
    robust concept of 27–8, 57–8, 63–5,
        68–70
Twin Earth 147–8, 157, 160, 163–5,
    178–85, 330

verificationism 81, 86–7, 209, 237

Williamson 287–8
Wittgenstein 9–10, 21–3, 32, 35, 43–8,
    59, 110–11, 126–30, 203, 211–14,
    310, 338–9
Wright 17–18, 26, 35, 45, 67, 116, 120,
    254, 258–9, 275